MW00712714

THE RIGHT PLACE

An ANECDOTAL HISTORY
of the COLLEGE *of*
HOTEL ADMINISTRATION
UNIVERSITY *of* NEVADA LAS VEGAS

❧

As recounted to and compiled by
JEROME J. VALLEN, PH.D.
DEAN EMERITUS
and FLORENCE L. VALLEN,
HONORARY MEMBER,
HOTEL ALUMNI

Book design by Edward Horcharik
and Matthew Williams

CIP Data Available

A Stephens Media Group Company
Post Office Box 1600
Las Vegas, NV 89125-1600
www.stephenspress.com
Printed in Hong Kong

Table of Contents

Acknowledgments

In his short story, *Three Hours Between Planes*, F. Scott Fitzgerald's character muses about "the hopeless impossibility of reconciling what different people remember about the same event." The insightfulness of Fitzgerald's observation came home to us during our very first interview. Even as we wondered at the apparent discrepancies of well-intended witnesses, we ourselves were unable to reconcile differences about events in which we had participated two or three decades earlier. Comments from former university president Donald Moyer:

> There are a lot of things going on that presidents don't know anything about

and hotel faculty member, Frank Borsenik:

> My universe was much smaller than the dean's

help explain the inconsistencies. The authors, at an organizational level between the two, were at a third level of cognition.

This record would not have come to pass without the participation and cooperation of individuals who were, and still are, friends and supporters of UNLV's College of Hotel Administration. They are identified throughout the text and in the list below.

Our appreciation also goes to Dean Stuart Mann who vigorously supported the idea of a history; to Annette Kannenberg who carefully coordinated the internal mechanics; to Meghan Theriault Moore who transcribed the initial interviews so accurately; and to Cynthia Fuller who finished the task. Sherri Theriault helped to find old records. So did Registrar Jeff Halverson who dug through 40-year-old files to provide the statistics we needed. Joyce McNeill, a long-time staffer at the Nevada Resort Association, helped in her usual friendly manner. Cleanup was left to our editor, Jeff Burbank.

Special note is extended to Robert (Bob) Smith, who not only came to Las Vegas to be interviewed, but also brought files dating back to 1966. (Smith arrived on campus in 1961 as one of a dozen new hires that boosted the faculty to 36 persons.)

Thanks also to The Lied Library's Special Collections Room with its very special staff under the supervision of Peter Michel, which helped locate appropriate university records for our inspection.

Finding the unpublished manuscript of Gabriel R. Vogliotti during a dinner conversation with Bill Thompson, College of Business and Economics, was an especially serendipitous joy. We so appreciate the loan of his material.

We also recognize Dr. John R. Goodwin whose initial publication about the origins of the hotel program, *Diamond in the Desert*, was published in 1992. Goodwin's work is a careful review of the legalities and events that shaped UNLV and the hotel program. This more personal accounting, from those who lived the experience, offers a different perspective.

The history is a composite of conversations with persons who knew of, participated in, observed, or gave of themselves to enable the college to achieve its worldwide reputation. Naming them here and identifying their associations at the time of their involvement is our way of acknowledging those efforts and saying thanks, not only for the interview, but for the years of association and support.

Placing the interviewee's comments in perspective will be enhanced if the reader returns periodically to the listing and identification.

Some interviews were completed by mail, some by e-mail, and some by telephone, but most of the meetings were face-to-face. Unless specifically punctuated, none of the attributed materials is a direct quote. Paraphrasing like this permits errors to creep into facts. If so, they are of the authors' doings either because we misinterpreted the comments or because we edited with too heavy a hand. There's great temptation to put one's own spin on the interview especially when the contributor recounts situations diametrically opposite to the authors' recall. After all, there is " . . . the hopeless impossibility of reconciling what different people remember about the same event." We apologize to both the contributors and the readers for any inconsistencies that remain.

The body of the text represents the authors' research and recall. Instances when the authors are cited are printed as if there had been an interview. Several persons are named even though they were not interviewed. Their words are recall that the authors had from informal discussions. On that list are Mrs. William Carlson, Malcolm Graham, Herb Wells, Mike Mavros and Bill Sears among others.

A note on format: Paragraphs are used within the interviews to indicate a time shift. The material in the second paragraph was taken from the same interview but did not necessarily follow the comments of the preceding paragraph. Bracketed explanations have been inserted to clarify interviewee's references because some readers may be less familiar with events of long ago. Complete names of the interviewees are given but once at the start of each chapter. The Browns (father and son) and the Vallens (husband and wife) are exceptions because there are two with the same name.

Jerry and Flossie Vallen,
Las Vegas

With appreciation, we acknowledge the contributions of the following 43 interviewees:

Contributors	Position at the Time of Their Involvement
Jim Abbey*	Faculty member, College of Hotel Administration
Sari Phillips Aizley	Spouse of Boyce Phillips, the hotel program's first faculty member
Phil Arce*	Hotel Manager, Sahara Hotel and adjunct faculty member
Donald Baepler	Vice President and President, UNLV; and Chancellor UN System
Richard Basile	Faculty member, College of Hotel Administration
Joan Reynolds Beitz	Administrative Assistant, College of Hotel Administration
Tom Bell	Regent and legal counsel for Hughes Nevada (telephone interview)
Frank Borsenik*	Faculty member, College of Hotel Administration
Gary Brown	Student and alumnus, 1973 (mail interview)
Richard Brown	Donor and parent of alumnus Gary Brown (telephone interview)
Joe Buckley	Director Industrial Relations, Summa Hotels (telephone interview)
Kaye Chon	Graduate student and faculty member, College of Hotel Administration
Tola Chin	Donor, patron and local restauranteur.
Jerry Crawford	Dean of Faculty, Southern Regional Division, University of Nevada
Leslie Cummings	Faculty member, College of Hotel Administration
Joe Delaney	Columnist and adjunct faculty member, College of Hotel Administration
Joe Digles	Nevada Resort Association associate (telephone interview)

Contributors	Position at the Time of Their Involvement
Ralph Durgin	UNLVino coordinator for Southern Wine & Spirits of Nevada
Brock Dixon	President and Vice President, UNLV (mail interviewed)
Ken Edwards	Student and alumnus, 1981 (e-mail interview)
Sig Front	Vice President of Sales, Sahara Hotel (telephone interview)
Jerry Goll	Faculty member, College of Hotel Administration
George Hardbeck	Dean, UNLV College of Business and Economics
Van Heffner	Executive, Nevada Hotel & Motel Association (telephone interview)
J. Kell Houssels	Owner, Tropicana Hotel and President, Nevada Resort Association
Al Izzolo	Faculty member, College of Hotel Administration
Ken Kaufman	Student and alumnus, 1971 (e-mail interview)
Claude Lambertz	Faculty member, College of Hotel Administration
Leo Lewis	Financial Officer, Binion's Horseshoe Club and adjunct professor
Dwight Marshall*	Director, General & Technical Institute; Dean of Continuing Education
Rik Medlik	Visiting faculty member from England (interviewed by mail)
Toshio Mohri	Head of the Tokyo, YMCA (e-mail interview)
Patrick Moreo	Alumnus, 1969; faculty member, College of Hotel Administration
Donald Moyer*	Chancellor (President), Nevada Southern University
Reuben Neumann	Faculty member, College of Business and Economics
David Patterson	Student and alumnus, 1981 (e-mail interview)
Ann Rittal, nee Seidl	Student and alumnus, 1981 (e-mail interview)
Larry Ruvo	Senior Managing Director, Southern Wine & Spirits of Nevada
Dunnovan Sapienza*	Faculty member, College of Hotel Administration (mail interview)
Robert Smith	Dean of the College of Science, Mathematics and Engineering
Alan Stutts	Faculty member, College of Hotel Administration
Frank Watts	Chief Financial Officer, Riviera Hotel
Michael Unger*	Student and alumnus, 1971

* Joining in their respective interviews were Colleen Abbey, Dorothy Arce, Ann Borsenik, Mary Ann Marshall, Jewel Moyer, Carol Sapienza, and Roberta Unger.

Dedicated to the scores of persons named herein and to the many others whose contributions have fallen victim to poor memory or to the constraints of time.

I have said many times and seriously feel that the College of Hotel Administration turned out to be one of the best things that ever happened to UNLV.

I always used the hotel college as a feature of the university. . . . And, in fact, it has turned out to be one of the few programs that UNLV is known for nationally and internationally. That's a fact today, 30 years later.

Donald H. Baepler, May 24, 2000,
Vice President and President, UNLV;
Chancellor, University of Nevada System

PART 1

Blueprint For A Hotel College

C H A P T E R   1

The Beginnings

No one event accounted for the origin of the College of Hotel Administration or for the success that it experienced. The temper of the times, the changes that were working on the city, the individuals who stepped forward in leadership roles, the generosity of the donors, the willingness of the hoteliers, the hard work of the staff, the support of the administrators, the adventurous nature of the student body, and the quality of the initial faculty produced a scenario that swelled into a full narrative. The tale begins as the developing university finds a changing and supportive community.

THE SETTING

Las Vegas began the 21st Century as a major metropolitan area with nearly 1.25 million residents, about 70% of Nevada's population. Just the reverse of the 1940's, '50s and '60s when Reno and Carson City were the centers of political, economic and educational activity. Even as late as the 1950 census, Reno was larger than Las Vegas by some 7,500 persons.

> The North always had the edge because they teamed up with the Cow Counties and just laid it on the South.   JOE DIGLES, NEVADA RESORT ASSOCIATION

At the other end of the state was Las Vegas, the frontier town. That frontier image—reality, in fact—was shaped by the city's very rapid growth, starting with the construction of Hoover Dam (1930s) and the legalization of gaming. Tourism, which required an ever-expanding workforce to staff the new high-rise hotels, became the driving force after World War II. Growth at Nellis Air Force Base, heavy industry at the Henderson complex and atomic testing at the Nevada Proving Grounds at Frenchman's Flat (the Nevada Test Site, 70 miles north) contributed to the population swell. And with population came political clout.

The 1950 census added additional southern legislators to the state's biennial sessions. Among them was a strong educational advocate, a former principal and superintendent of schools, Assemblywoman Maude Frazier. A second assemblywoman, Flora Dungan, was elected in 1964. Both made significant contributions to education in Southern Nevada, evidenced by the two campus buildings named for them. Dungan was one of several plaintiffs to sue Governor Grant Sawyer in federal court for reapportionment of the legislature based on the one-man, one-vote decisions of the U.S. Supreme Court (1962 and 1964). The northen cow counties lost some of their stranglehold on the legislature paving the way for better representation of Clark County and more money for the campus.

> The northern legislators were just wetting their pants to get something [for themselves] before the 1970 census changed the redistricting. Up to that point, we [the campus] had nothing to work with. We saw dramatic increases in the budget with the 1970 redistricting.   ROBERT SMITH, DEAN OF SCIENCE, MATHEMATICS AND ENGINEERING

> Las Vegas grew from 15,000 persons in 1940 to 125,000 in 1970.

> There was a big influx of people between 1959 and 1963. The population jumped about 50,000 persons in three or four years.   PHIL ARCE, SAHARA HOTEL MANAGER

> In the seven years between my first visit and the time I moved here in 1966, there had been an unbelievable growth in the city.   DWIGHT MARSHALL, DEAN OF CONTINUING EDUCATION

This population growth dictated the direction taken by the total community, but specifically transformed Nevada Southern University into UNLV. But that was still some time ahead.

> The Board of Regents was stacked in favor of UNR in those days. The 1969 legislature gave us our first appropriation independent of Reno.   DONALD BAEPLER, UNLV PRESIDENT AND UNS CHANCELLOR

> We got 45 new positions the first year of reapportionment.   JERRY CRAWFORD, DEAN OF FACULTY

During this period the hotel program was planned (1965–1966) and implemented (1966–1967). By the time its first director was in place, so was the campus.

The Location

Despite its name, the University of Nevada Las Vegas is not in Las Vegas. Most of Southern Nevada's population, including UNLV and the Strip hotels that gave birth to the hotel program, are in the unincorporated County of Clark, not in the City of Las Vegas. That was not by accident. Las Vegas, the city, had once eyed annexing the Strip and its tax base. But Lieutenant Governor Cliff Jones, a later donor to the hotel program, blocked the move at the state level. Technicalities aside, UNLV'ers and most other residents of the Valley consider themselves to be Las Vegans.

The Campus. The site for the new campus was a desert full of tumbleweed and snakes far from the center of activity but close to the noise of the airport. Too close, some worried, which held up building construction at first. Not even the wisest planner could have anticipated the central location that the university now enjoys or the probability that the campus would outgrow the vast desert space that was its original home. For the College of Hotel Administration, whose students needed access to the hotel-casinos, the setting proved to be ideal. Besides, the campus location wasn't chosen—it was given.

With Maude Frazier's urging, the legislature voted $200,000 for the first campus building, but not for the land. Moreover, there was a sunset clause: Failure to acquire the land by June 30, 1956 or raise an additional $100,000 meant the appropriation bill would expire. Political clout still laid with northern legislators. One wonders whether they hoped to strangle the struggling initiative. If so, they must have been surprised by the positive response—the first of many positive responses to come from the local community. The Nevada Southern Campus Fund Committee of some 750 contributors raised the $35,000 needed to buy the 20 acres and the additional $100,000 to meet the legislative mandate. John Goodwin, a hotel faculty member, saw it as a seminal event:

> "... countless thousands can give thanks to the far-sighted vision of a handful of men who formed an organization designed to benefit the university in the future. . . . that effort could have been turned toward private gain. . . . But that is not the way it happened." [*Diamond in the Desert.*[1]]

Moe Dalitz, a reputed former bootlegger, racketeer and legitimate Las Vegas entrepreneur, paid for the first building's furnishings. But it was not precedent setting. Many years later a reconstituted campus refused Dalitz' second gift worth many, many times more.

> Barbara [Schick, of the Schick razor family] brought Moe [Dalitz] to visit me. He offered a donation to the College of Business provided no one would object to taking his money. I was unable to get that pledge from the entire faculty and the gift was lost.   GEORGE HARD-BECK, DEAN OF BUSINESS AND ECONOMICS

The land was purchased from a California real estate dealer and his wife, Howard and Estelle Wilbourn, who then donated an additional 60 acres. Estelle Willbourn was originally a Las Vegas resident, having attended high school here; her mother an early pioneer. The achievement and the momentum toward a new campus was dimmed slightly when it was learned later that the Wilbourns had but recently purchased the land from the federal government for about $100.

Maude Frazier Hall opened on Maryland Parkway in 1957 and one year later the legislature voted funds for building number two, Grant Hall, which opened in 1959. Archie Grant, Chairman of the Board of Regents, was the honoree this time. Eight years after it opened, Grant Hall became the hotel program's first home. At that time, hotel, business, art, education, music, and some administrators were squeezed into that small building.

You've got to realize that 4505 Maryland Parkway [the campus address] was way out in the country [in 1961]. I could drive from Sahara Avenue [along Maryland Parkway] and not pass a structure between there and campus. Part of Maryland Parkway was dirt road. A diagonal road ran off of Flamingo to the science building. I parked there rather than at Frazier Hall. A huge sand dune full of rattlesnakes anchored the area between the two buildings. One just didn't walk that way.

There was a species of opium poppy that grew north of the EPA buildings. There was no consideration for endangered species when the chemistry building was erected; it was the end of the poppy legend.   SMITH

[Maryland Parkway] was a two-lane, dirt road between campus and San Francisco Boulevard, now called Sahara Avenue. The only building between the two was Sunrise Hospital.   CRAWFORD

We drove around and found the Broadway [Department Store] the day we arrived [1967]. It was on Maryland Parkway and a half-a-mile away, it seemed, was Sears [Department Store]. And that was it; they were working on Penny's, and there wasn't anything between.   SARI PHILLIPS AIZLEY, SPOUSE OF THE COLLEGE'S FIRST FACULTY MEMBER

Everything was downtown including all the department stores. The positive side: It was possible to drive to Macayo Vegas on Charlestown, eat and get back to campus within the lunch hour.   JOAN REYNOLDS BEITZ, ADMINISTRATIVE ASSISTANT

One would go down Maryland Parkway until the big dip. I remember hitting that thing for the first time. I went off like this and came down like that. It was a dirt road and they just paved over it. After all, there was nothing out there.   ARCE

My first impression was that there seemed to be an awful lot of sand in front of Maude Frazier Hall.   MARSHALL

My first encounter was when I was invited to speak. I had a tough time finding it after I left the Sahara [hotel].   SIG FRONT, VICE PRESIDENT, SAHARA HOTEL

Land has always been at issue for the UNLV campus. The danger of the university becoming landlocked was apparent from the beginning, and became more real with each passing year. As early as 1970, Paul Aizley penned a foresighted memo to the 1970 Ad Hoc Committee on the Developing University. He advocated moving the campus even then, a scant 13 years after the first building was erected, and giving the existing campus to the just-emerging community college.

> Don Moyer [University President] put a lot of stress on acquiring more land. He used to talk about 20,000 students, which was beyond our imagination in those days, and his fear that we would be landlocked. And here we were in Frazier [on Maryland Parkway] looking [west] at desert all the way to Paradise Road. There was almost nothing between Tropicana and Flamingo [south/north along Maryland Parkway.]   MARSHALL

The Nevada University Land Foundation was established 10 years after the Nevada Southern Campus Fund. Both were successful responses by the community to the needs of higher education. They were two among many such efforts including some that targeted the hotel college specifically. A nonprofit corporation was formed in 1967 to acquire real estate for the future expansion of the campus. Through donations, about 270 additional acres were added to the Wilbourne's original acreage (20 purchased plus 60 donated) rounding the campus to approximately 350 acres.

> "[Parry Thomas and Jerome Mack] discovered that UNLV owned only 55 acres. The bankers knew that land prices around the university would skyrocket if UNLV waited to purchase land until the state appropriated funds. . . . So the two bankers formed the Nevada University Land Foundation, then personally guaranteed loans to it. The foundation used the money to acquire 300 acres and resell it to the university at cost whenever the college [university] had money to buy it." [*The First 100.*[2]]

> Thomas and Mack were very influential and they started talking [circa 1965–1966] about how we were going to get the land reserved because we were going to need a lot of buildings and space, and other people were buying it. And they said, We've got the money. We'll buy it for you and hold it, and as you get your state appropriations, you can get it. We'll reserve it for you. A tremendous idea!
>
>   They even acquired land as far [west] as the Continental Hotel [Flamingo and Paradise Roads], but the first thing I knew, they had sold it. I expect they made a profit, but they always had the university at heart.   DONALD MOYER, PRESIDENT, NEVADA SOUTHERN UNIVERSITY

> I remember sitting with Parry and Don [Baepler] and Herman [Westfall, UNLV's financial officer] forming the Nevada Southern Land Foundation. The guys went out and bought all the acreage and put it in trust.   CRAWFORD

> Parry Thomas and Jerry Mack stand out in my mind as the two most important persons in the life and growth of the UNLV campus.   PAT GOODALL, PRESIDENT, UNLV

Being a land foundation donor was one of the most prestigious things a person could do. There was great emphasis given to acquiring land and great prestige for those who gave it.

The land foundation was extremely forward-looking and viewed as an incredible idea by those who knew about it.   MARSHALL

Parry Thomas and Jerry Mack were the University's main supporters.   ARCE

Las Vegas, The City.   In an article about Strip resort developer and operator, Steve Wynn, *The Wall Street Journal* noted that Las Vegas is "the largest American city born in the 20th Century."[3] The city was started around the railroad as were so many other towns across the country. In the words of one author, Las Vegas was only a ranch and an abandoned church mission in 1900; it was only a village on the railroad in 1905. Official city status came in 1911 when the state legislature passed an enabling act. Because of its water wells—the Las Vegas Valley is a major aquifer, the town became a primary watering stop for coal-fired, steam locomotives crossing the desert. The site was named Las Vegas—Spanish for The Meadows—in the early 19th Century because the output from Big Spring, Middle Spring and Little Spring produced waist-high grass in the middle of the desert. A host of service industries including hotels and bars sprang up on Fremont Street near the train terminal, today's site of the Union Plaza Hotel. They materialized because the railroad encouraged development of the area.

There wasn't very much here until 1905 when the railroad wanted a community to service trains because we had this water. So they gave away the plots on Fremont Street at $5 an acre.

Transportation wasn't sophisticated. We were so remote that nobody bothered us. We didn't even have [enforcement of] prohibition [1920–1933]. That's why they had the Hollywood premiers here.   JOE DELANEY, COLUMNIST AND PART-TIME FACULTY MEMBER

Historically, hotels have always located along the travelers' way. The khans of the Middle East and the tabernas of Rome were built to service foot and animal traffic. Colonial inns followed stage lines inland as the country moved westward. Hotels appeared by the wharves to service river steamers, and then railroad stations and airports took their turns at sparking hotel development. Las Vegas was no different, except it added gaming to the mix.

Nothing much happened [in the early 20th Century] except we had gambling. And in 1931, Phil Tobin [Humboldt County Assemblyman] introduced an Enabling Act. [Legalized gaming was signed into law on March 19, 1931.] They tacked on another important provision: the six-week divorce.   DELANEY

In keeping with that transportation dependency, the first hotel-casinos to be built outside of Fremont Street's railroad area were along the main highway, the automobile route between Las Vegas and Los Angeles, the "Old Los Angeles Highway." The El Rancho was first, 1941.

"Big Jim [Cashman] said, 'What we really need here [in Las Vegas] is a big resort.' . . . Cashman . . . suggested a tract at what is today Maryland and Sahara [then San Francisco Boulevard]. . . . 'I don't want to build there,' [Tommy] Hull said. 'I want to build on the road going into town.'

. . . The Las Vegas Strip started with Hull . . . for the Strip corridor took shape from his resort [the El Rancho at San Francisco and the Strip] south [a few feet south of the line separating the city from the county]." [*The First 100.* [4]]

These early ranch-style properties built low-rise rooms—63 at the El Rancho—to hold casino players. Swamp coolers, evaporative systems using water, worked relatively well in the hot, dry climate of the southwestern desert. But growth in the city really took off after World War II. Automobiles and gasoline were available again and roads were being built by the Eisenhower Administration. Mechanical air conditioning, which was perfected during the war, made the city more attractive in the summer. December, 1946 marked the next era of growth with the opening of Bugsy Siegal's Flamingo Hotel.

In 1946, I said to my New York attorney that I would really like to live in Las Vegas. He said, Joe, it's a freak; it'll be a ghost town. DELANEY

We did all our interviewing [for a faculty position] over the telephone. I flew in from the green countryside of Michigan State to take the job sight unseen in August, 1973. I looked at the desert and said, Oh no, what have I done. This is terrible; I'll never last. JIM ABBEY, HOTEL FACULTY MEMBER

Gradually, the high-rise hotels appeared. The Bermuda pink and green-trimmed Desert Inn (the DI), the fifth and largest of the Strip hotels (229 rooms, 380 employees and a child-care center), was just three stories when it opened on April 24, 1950. It was the tallest property on the Strip. The DI enjoyed a colorful history from its very beginning. Included among its owners were Wilbur Clark, a California card-room businessman; Moe Dalitz, a mob-linked businessman; Howard Hughes, an eccentric businessman; Kirk Kerkorian, a no nonsense businessman; and Steve Wynn, a public-relations businessman.

There were several real high-rise hotels on the Strip by the time the hotel program started. Among them were the Dunes, the Sands, the Sahara and Caesars Palace. Caesars opened on August 5, 1966 preceding the hotel program's first term by just a few weeks. The move to high-rise hotels started on the Strip with the 11-floor Riviera (April 29, 1955) and downtown with the Fremont (May, 1956).

The first real high rise was the Riviera. That was the one that started the high rises. I can still hear the jingle: 'There's a new, new high in the Las Vegas' sky; it's the Hotel Riviera.' J. KELL HOUSSELS, JR., HOTELIER AND ELECTED PRESIDENT OF THE NEVADA RESORT ASSOCIATION

One of the Riviera's executives, J. Dee Goodman, took a leadership role in founding the university program.

I knew J. D. Goodman. He was a lawyer and accountant and a very good man. He was like Leo [Lewis]. Leo is an accountant primarily, but Leo thinks like a hotelman. I could see J.D. being the one who would come out and roll up his sleeves.   DELANEY

Jess was a very popular guy, a chamber-of-commerce type.   DIGLES

Robbins Cahill was very complimentary in his oral history about both Houssels and Goodman. He points out further that neither was "a gaming man as such." High-rise buildings and nongambling executives were not the only changes coming to the gaming business. It took a whole new environment to accommodate a college-level hotel program.

Sidney Korshak, a Chicago attorney, was important in the film business. Hollywood was his primary connection, but he was very close to the development of the Riviera. He was really the brains behind it because the original Riviera was Chicago [-conceived, -funded and -controlled]. Sidney's brother, Marshall, was an Illinois state senator. They made a formidable team.   DELANEY

Korshak was the lawyer for both the Riviera [which was Goodman's base of operations] and the Sands.   HOUSSELS

Korshak was hired by the [Nevada Resort] Association to help in labor negotiations. At the same time, he was the teamsters' lawyer!   FRANK WATTS, RIVIERA FINANCIAL OFFICER

Korshak was on retainer with the Resort Association. He was also the mouthpiece for a lot of guys [a euphemism for the mob] out of Chicago.   DIGLES

By the mid-1960s, casino-hotels were concentrated in two locations. The downtown properties clustered by the original railroad station and the Strip properties catered to auto/air traffic. That distinction jelled with the formation of the Nevada Resort Association (NRA) as a group of Strip properties only. It was the NRA that was to fund the hotel program. Gabe Vogliotti, NRA executive:

"In the autumn of 1961 the owners of Nevada gambling . . . were caught in a deep fear. They were at war with Congress, were loathed by the FBI and were called hoods by the nation's press. . . . That year they organized. They put aside their rivalries, their inter-casino feuds, and formed the Nevada Resort Association. They choose [the first] director [Joe Wells, manager and part owner of the Thunderbird] . . . and then . . . they choose a second . . . , me."[5]

Robbins (Bob) Cahill, who followed Vogliotti at the NRA, had a different recall. In his oral history, Cahill identifies former city manager, George Allium, as the first NRA executive.

Downtown wasn't involved in the Resort Association. It was several years before the downtown properties came in.   HOUSSELS

Most observers believe that the Resort Association started with the Strip properties, but in Gabe Vogliotti's (second NRA executive) personal notes he mentions that the Fremont Hotel (a downtown property) was represented at one of the meetings. Offsetting that single reference are several newspaper articles listing the membership as "composed of nine Las Vegas Strip hotels," or "created by the Nevada Resort Association, an organization of Strip hotels."

Buck Blaine, who ran the Golden Nugget [an important downtown property subsequently acquired by Steve Wynn], was a hardcore anti. He was real anti-strip. If he said it's Monday, you knew it had to be Friday.   DIGLES

The [Nevada Resort] Association wasn't well organized until the mid '60s. That was the first time we actually had meetings and minutes. [Previously] we'd just sit around and take instructions from the powers that be. Mr. [Big] from the Sands would come in every now and again and give the orders that everyone was supposed to salute. He was from Chicago [another euphemism for the mob].   HOUSSELS

"Basically the [Nevada Resort] Association was Moe Dalitz's idea."
     "No question it was politically oriented to control campaign donations." [Cahill.[6]]

"In organizing the owners had no hope of softening a nation's anger, none of softening Congress and certainly none of changing the contempt of what seemed [to be] all of the nation's press. But with an association, they could meet. They could set up a war fund. . . . There was [state gaming] law to be written. While they already had strong political control . . . , [it] was sloppy, disorganized, amateurish. No one was running things. There were governors to elect, legislatures to steer." [Vogliotti.[7]]

[Beldon] Katleman at the El Rancho was on the outs with the boys so he would send me to the union meetings or any other sessions. [Katleman, who was very mercurial and on the outs with everyone, bought the hotel from Tommy Hull.] It didn't take long to see that those meetings didn't mean much because the boys [another euphemism for the mob] from the Middle West came here the night before and at the Desert Inn or at the Sands everything was already settled.   WATTS

"In keeping with the Nevada way, [there was] an unremitting, no-nonsense steady hit on the owners for everything, for political costs, for taxes, charities, jobs for infinite free-loading. . . . ". [Vogliotti.[8]]

Everyone, bands, schools, charities, was "on" the hotels to give, to support this and to support that, so the association was formed in part because of that [need to funnel and control charitable giving]. The idea was to center it all on Gabe [Vogliotti, paid NRA executive] and let us run our businesses. If they made a commitment, it would keep people off their back because there was an out.

It was never written that way, but it's what one owner told me.

It was my understanding that the hotel school was part of that whole story. An allocation of resources. My view may be half-cocked, but that's my firm impression.   JOE DIGLES, NEVADA RESORT ASSOCIATION

The very same motive that drove the industry to fund the college in 1966 might have been present still in 1986 when the college's Hospitality Research and Development Center was established and the industry signed up for classes:

The Center had a special advantage with the gaming industry. They wanted to legitimize themselves, and they felt that education was a way to do it.   ALAN STUTTS, HOTEL FACULTY MEMBER

THE ENVIRONMENT

A we-can-do-anything attitude permeated the culture of the community. It flourished because of the frontier nature, the youth and the tight physical location that was the city. The cognition was evident: It was sensed and was apparent in both the emerging campus and the bustling community. That culture created an environment that made possible the launch and ultimate success of the hotel program.

The city was beginning to become aware. Why don't we have a symphony or ballet? Why don't we have this or that? And the best way of doing those things in the community is with a university.   DELANEY

There was another group that wanted to get more diversification for the community. To get that, one needs a recognizable, accredited university. A great deal was going on in Vegas; there was a transition from the old guard to the corporations. The town was growing.   PHIL ARCE, SAHARA HOTEL MANAGER

It was a young man's place; it was very exciting. In 1965, which was my third year on campus, there were 45 faculty, 550 full-time students, four buildings and no grass.

Dean Irwin, Reno's Dean of Arts and Sciences looked down on me from the head of the table like I was an underling scrub, a butch-haired kid. There were many jokes about that up there. Moyer [chancellor of the Las Vegas campus] named a 29-year old [Crawford] as dean of faculty! Moyer was proud of that and used it as part of his image: A young dean for a young school.   JERRY CRAWFORD, DEAN OF FACULTY

"[The university] was pregnant with opportunity. If you were willing to do something, people would see [make sure] that you were able to do it." [Goodwin, quoting Moreo.[9]]

When I came, I was told, Fertilize the ground and the desert will grow.   VAN HEFFNER, EXECU-
TIVE, NEVADA HOTEL & MOTEL ASSOCIATION

We were busy; busy building the place. It was a stimulating atmosphere to be in. The place
was small enough so if you wanted to do something you did it. But it was up to you to get it
funded and find a way to pay for it.   MARSHALL

There were certain academic activities that were not dependent upon our budget: Dwight
Marshall and his infamous operations [for example].   BAEPLER

The early thinking was that a few guys in the casino controlled everything. Everything went
through the casino [including the foot traffic]. You wanted the bathroom, you went though
the casino; you wanted to eat, you went through the casino to the restaurant; you wanted
to check in. . . .   DELANEY

The City's Environment

Serious consideration for a hotel program coincided with the resort industry's change
from a gambling-based business to a gaming-based (entertainment) one. That began
statewide, but especially in Las Vegas, in the 1950s. The evolution was rapid as full-
service resorts with guest rooms replaced the gaming-only clubs.

"Prior to 1945 [World War II era], casino gaming was conducted in the backrooms
of saloons, out of sight and without public attention. Gaming was not directly
taxed by the state, nor were state government services dependent on gaming-
derived tax revenues.
  After World War II , the widespread use of marketing innovations radically
changed the basic nature of gaming." [*Nevada Gaming License Guide.* [10]]

Publicity was the best of those marketing innovations. PR men like Harvey Diederich and Al Freeman helped to bring Las Vegas to the world's attention.

"It was Al Freeman who engineered what is perhaps the most famous Las Vegas
publicity shot—the 'floating' crap game. That picture, taken July 1, 1953 depicts
a group of gamblers in swimsuits standing waist deep in the hotel pool around a
crap table. It wasn't a prop, but a real crap table that Freeman had removed from
the casino." [*The First 100.* [11]]

Although the city's economy was tourism-casino based, Las Vegas was about
more than tourism. It was flexing muscle in other directions as well.

Las Vegas was three communities then [1965]. There was the old, downtown Las Vegas: folks
who had come in 1950 [and earlier] when the railroad first came thorough. Good solid folk.
Then there was the technical community associated with the test site. They tended to live on
the west. The old-timers were downtown. Paradise Valley was home to the resort community.

> The idea of a university was foreign to many of them. They were high school graduates, not formally educated. Their [children's] attitude was: why should I [go to college]; you [college grads] make one-third of what my dad makes in the pit.   SMITH

Smith, who hadn't resided in Las Vegas for two decades before his interview, overlooked another neighborhood: the black community on the so-called Westside, although northwest would probably be as accurate a description. Racism was a sad reality that faced the city for many years. Black residents were here as early as the 1920s. Employment opportunities started with the railroads and spread to the hotel-casinos. War industry brought increasing numbers, who found poor and restrictive housing as well as open discrimination. The issue was explosive because no blacks, neither locals nor visitors, were permitted in the hotel-casinos except as back-of-the house employees. The situation was somewhat resolved by the time the hotel college was up and running in the late 1960s. A later chapter of this history recounts how discrimination had an unexpected connection to the hotel program.

Another trauma facing the state's major industry was the Kefauver hearings in 1950–51. Tennessee's Senator Estes Kefauver, who had presidential aspirations, focused Senate hearings on gaming and organized crime. The committee's report gave a black eye to Nevada's regulatory machinery and put a scare into the professional community.

> Del Webb [a construction company] took a part interest in the Sahara when the original partners were unable to pay [for the building]. Those were the years [1950s] when the [federal] government wanted to shut gaming down. [The industry took the matter very seriously.] When the pit bosses had their breaks, they would always end up in my office. Some already had plane tickets out of town.   ARCE

> I don't know how Ginny [secretary to the NRA] kept them [NRA minutes], but I had a clear sense that I'd better keep those things as brief and sparse as possible. The idea was to say as little as possible because there was a lot of federal heat on the gaming industry in those days. Bill Campbell [NRA labor consultant and, later, its executive officer] was so secretive that he even forgot his own name.   DIGLES

Using the self-inspection that followed the negative publicity of the Kefauver hearings, Governor Grant Sawyer persuaded the 1959 legislature to act. Separate agencies, the Nevada Gaming Control Board and the Nevada Gaming Commission, were created and charged with enforcing the gaming laws. Before then, gaming control had been under the jurisdiction of the Nevada Tax Commission. The Secretary— the real executive—to the part-time Tax Commission was Robbins Cahill, who later played an important role in the development of the hotel program. Under Cahill's watch, gaming oversight became a state function, dislodged from the control of the counties.

The move by Sawyer and the legislature was de facto recognition that gaming taxes were now a major source of state revenues and that the future of the state and its citizenry was economically dependent on the industry. The State's next major moves came in 1967 and 1969 when the Corporate Gaming Acts opened casino ownership to public corporations. Many believe that the Howard Hughes empire was behind the change.

> "Before 1967, public companies were effectively precluded from owning a Nevada casino because the law required full investigation and licensing of every shareholder."
>
> ". . . The full licensing policy previously employed would have seriously restricted Nevada's access to sources of capital." [*Nevada Gaming License Guide.* [12]]

It is an open question whether the hotel program would have been funded in 1966 if widely held public corporations had been in place. Individual owners, small partnerships and privately held corporations were the model that funded the college.

> The casinos started off originally as partnerships. The individual had to be licensed, a corporation could not get a license. So it was a bit of hocus-pocus. The individual would get the license and lease it back to the corporation. But it wasn't a public corporation.   J.K. HOUSSELS, PRESIDENT OF THE NEVADA RESORT ASSOCIATION

Giving money to the hotel program or to the University as a whole was, and continues to be, more a personal decision than corporate policy. In their histories of the university, both John Goodwin and Pat Goodall agree with the authors' position on that score:

> "Corporate ownership would wait for a few more years and Vallen feels that if corporate ownership had been the watchword in 1966, the hotel school may never have been developed at all." [Goodall.[13]]

As corporate ownership became the standard, the character and function of the Nevada Resort Association, the parent of the College of Hotel Administration, began to change. There was probably just a brief window when the program could have been funded.

> The NRA was becoming more and more a political arm and less and less a force in the community.   DELANEY

> The town was growing. More and more hotels were being built, and there was a need for professionals in the hotel industry.
>
> A different cast of characters emerged. These were "hired hands" [professional manager as opposed to owner/managers]; damn good professionals. When we [owners who were managing our own properties] started we weren't near that good, and we weren't hired hands!

The professional appeared at the Resort Association [as well]. What really made the Resort Association work were professionals like Gabe Vogliotti and Robbins Cahill. What really got the Resort Association going was Robbins Cahill.   HOUSSELS

Essentially I see it just as Ike [Houssels] describes. Ike was involved with the board [of the NRA] or what they later called the executive board.   DIGLES

For the college, jobs for students were the plus side of the new corporate structure. The old gaming crowd was somewhat suspicious of college types

It is typical of a corporation to look to the universities for resources.   TOM BELL, ATTORNEY TO THE HUGHES CORPORATION

I arrived in Vegas in '62, which was the start of a transitional period from the old guard to a modern manager. And when I came, I mean it wasn't unheard of, pit bosses were packing guns!   PHIL ARCE, SAHARA HOTEL MANAGER

When the owners began to build larger hotels, they needed hotel people [managers]. Then these hotel people began to have a little more control, a little more say. The owners looked at us for a lot of things they didn't want to do, or couldn't do. Once they began to depend on us, they listened more.   FRANK WATTS, RIVIERA FINANCIAL OFFICER

As we went corporate, [the city] began to import university graduates. [The old style of hotel managers] were reformed tough guys from elsewhere. They were a different element. Give them [Jimmy] Durante or Phil Harris [Hollywood stars, 1940–60] and 150 people in the showroom and you can have Wayne Newton with 900 [persons]. The 150 who went to see Durante had no credit limit in the cage.

The introduction of entertainment came in the late 1940s and '50s especially at Wilbur Clark's Desert Inn, with Sinatra, and Edgar Bergen and Charlie McCarthy [a ventriloquist and his dummy]. The El Rancho had Sophie Tucker, Harry Richmond and Milton Berle. Production shows came in the mid-1950s when Mo Dalitz brought them to the stardust. Minsky came to the Dunes with pasties and started the battle of the boobies.   JOE DELANEY, COLUMNIST AND PART-TIME FACULTY MEMBER

Of course, there was much to be said about the "old days," where a handshake, or a verbal understanding underpinned the business of the city. The environment was still like that when the first hotel faculty arrived.

In my mind, from day one, Las Vegas has been far and above any other place because everyone pulled together. Everyone cooperated!   FRONT

Jake [Jacob] Kozloff called Jimmy Durante and said Jimmy what are you doing the last two week of July? Jimmy said, I'm not booked. How would you like to come to the Frontier for two weeks? You got a deal. They didn't even discuss money; it was that loose.   DELANEY

Wally Budge was the manager of the motel that we camped in as we searched for our initial housing. When he learned of our mission and our intent to become residents, he began to help and remained a strong supporter for years thereafter.   JERRY VALLEN

Shortly after our arrival, I took ill. The whole town responded with casseroles and baby sitting, just as it would have done in the small, university/agricultural community that we left.   FLOSSIE VALLEN

Downtown owners would lend each other large amounts of money on a handshake.   LEO LEWIS, BINION'S FINANCIAL OFFICER AND PART-TIME FACULTY MEMBER

"I [Gabe Vogliotti] mentioned [the matter of all NRA funds on my signature only] to Moe [Dalitz]. I wonder if I should be put under a bond. 'Ridiculous,' he said, 'any man who has to have a bond they [the casino owners] don't want.'" [Vogliotti.[14]]

Even the University's business was done informally.

Vegas faculty had to fly Bonanza Air in order to attend meetings in Reno. That's one way we came to know the state's important people. I got to know [Lieutenant Governor] Harry Reid when he needed a ride from the airport, so I took him to Henderson. On another trip, I struck up a conversation with Floyd Lamb and he asked what we needed. About two weeks later a bill went through the legislature giving us the authority to purchase locally rather than through Reno.   ROBERT SMITH, DEAN OF SCIENCE

I was behind Harry Reid checking in at the L.A. airport. One agent said to the other, here's a package going to Batista [a restauranteur] in Las Vegas. I'll take it to him said the lieutenant governor. After he left with the package they asked each other who was that guy? They were nonplused at my declaration of his rank. Everyone in line expressed amazement at his youth [Reid was just 31] until I explained that only three of us lived in the state: the governor, the lieutenant governor and I.   JERRY VALLEN

The Campus Environment

The University of Nevada Reno was Nevada's land-grant school. As such it had educational responsibility for the entire state. Engineering, mining, sciences, all the traditional university courses were being offered there long before the Vegas campus was functioning. Moreover, junior colleges were the academic frontier of the 1950-1970 decades. It followed that the initial planning for the southern campus involved some serious discussions about establishing it as a junior college. Maude Frazer actually introduced such a bill and saw it enacted into law in 1951. By the vagaries of fate, the Nevada Attorney General's office decided it was unconstitutional. [*Cornerstone Ceremony.*[15]] Although UNLV's status as an emerging university was cast, there was nothing to prevent a university from offering junior-college credits.

Fred Anderson [chair of the Board of Regents] wanted UNLV, I should say NSU [Nevada Southern University], to be a junior college. They had to fight him tooth and nail on that. I was hired [1966] to be the director of something curiously called the General and Technical Institute; in essence, associate-degree programs. One or two already existed, the nursing program particularly. I added radiation health, x-ray technology, and nuclear medicine. I gave them 13 associate degree programs, including law enforcement, office administration, electronics technology and others.

Almost no one that I can recall held any brief for an associate degree program in hotel, although there might have been one advocate [for creating hotel as a junior-college program]. There was some brief talk about that, but I wasn't familiar with such programs and didn't have an opinion.   DWIGHT MARSHALL, DEAN OF CONTINUING EDUCATION

There were a number of discussions [about making hotel a junior college program], but it was a misunderstanding because we were not training for service jobs like bartender or food server.   DON BAEPLER, UNLV PRESIDENT

Since there was to be no junior college, Reno initially serviced Las Vegas with extension courses only. Constituent pressure on both the legislature and the Board of Regents forced Reno to dispatch the first, full-time faculty member, James R. Dickinson, in 1951. The issue was sharpened further ten years later:

We were a threat to Reno from day one, and the first breakthrough on that came in 1961–62, the year I came. Reno created a committee to take a state-wide look at population dynamics. There was a famous report that by 1970 there might be 1,000 to 2,000 students on the southern campus. At that time, we had about 500.   SMITH

Using the facilities of the public schools and some part-time teachers, Dickinson began offering "regular" classes. Dickinson, the titular head, was a very young man. He was a junior member of the English Department at Reno; an instructor without rank who hadn't even as yet finished his own graduate degree.

Jim Dickinson and [Registrar] Muriel Parks had a little office at the Las Vegas High School under a stairway.   JERRY CRAWFORD, DEAN OF FACULTY

The faculty was in a common room separated from Dickinson by only a curtain. One could hear his every word. The classroom we used was in a nearby Baptist Church.   MALCOLM GRAHAM, MATHEMATICS FACULTY MEMBER

We had classes [from the Educational Institute of the American Hotel & Motel Association] at the high school, and the university had the use of the auditorium and a couple of rooms at the back.   WATTS

It wasn't until 1954 that the Board of Regents held its first meeting in Las Vegas and shortly thereafter upgraded Dickinson to Director of the Southern Regional Division (of Reno).

"In 1954 the program was expanded to offer a full freshman curriculum. Beginning with the fall semester 1955 course offerings were further expanded to include as wide a selection of both freshman and sophomore courses as possible. . . ." [Hulse.[16]]

Dickinson held that post until 1957 when President Charles Armstrong retitled the position to Dean and appointed William D. Carlson, formerly Reno's Dean of Men, to the job.

> Actually, Carlson had driven around Jim Dickinson.   CRAWFORD

Dickinson didn't like administration and after six years on the job, three years with a title, was content to become Director of Humanities and Fine Arts. From that position he later made major contributions to the campus. Working with Don Moyer and Jerry Crawford they raised funds to build the performing arts center.

> I was with Jim Dickinson the day he died [at age 47] of a heart attack.   CRAWFORD

Carlson, like Dickinson, originated on the Reno campus. Although both were very decent men, their Reno linkages doomed them. It accounted for most of the hostility that newly arriving faculty—the Young Turks—felt toward them.

> Those two [Dickinson and Carlson] were martyrs. If there was a saint in education, it was Carlson. He never really had a title of any kind and he had to go around begging for money. And he had to deal with people like Maud Frazer and all the high brows from Nevada who had a Reno agenda. Carlson did a lot of the legwork [for UNLV] and got very little credit for it.
> JOE DIGLES, NEVADA RESORT ASSOCIATION

Even Carlson was seen to be Reno's representative despite the impression sometimes left by President Armstrong that there was little value from Carlson's services. [Hulse [17]]

> Carlson didn't pay much attention to [President, then; Chancellor, now] Armstrong because he knew that Armstrong was a lackey of northern interests. Carlson realized that he had to build from the South, so he didn't pay much attention to the North; he knew he would get screwed from them anyway.
>   Bill was an independent and a hard-working individual. He set his own priorities and didn't listen to Armstrong.   DIGLES

Carlson held the post for seven years during a period of rapid change, turmoil and many new hires. During his tenure, the Las Vegas faculty created (July 24, 1963) the first organizational plan for the Southern Regional Division (SRD) of the University of Nevada. Eighteen months later, Dallas Norton, elected secretary of the now newly named Nevada Southern University (NSU), penned a letter to the Chairman of the Board of Regents, Archie Grant. The faculty had voted and were requesting another name change, this time to the University of Nevada Las Vegas (UNLV).

Calling the campus UNLV signaled parity with the north. The tempo was accelerating. The first brochure published by the campus was titled, *Facts About Nevada Southern* with a sub-identification, *Your Southern Regional Division of the University of Nevada Fall and Spring Semester 1956–1957.*

> We [Crawford and Moyer] started putting the community and students on committees. That just wasn't done before; it was run [exclusively] by Carlson.   CRAWFORD

Both Dickinson and Carlson returned to faculty after leaving their administrative slots. That seemed to set a precedent because several of the later presidents retained faculty status when their administrative assignments were over. Chancellor—that was now the new title—Donald C. Moyer (1965–1968), Carlson's immediate successor, was one of those who left. But not before he completed the launch of the hotel program.

Pressure from Nevadans advocating more educational services was not the only force for change. The Regents were well aware that an ever increasing share of state revenues was coming from Clark County. Equally disturbing was the small number of students from southern Nevada coming to the Reno campus. For one, the percentage of local, high-school graduates going on to further education was low even then, and this was especially true of the number entering the Nevada system.

> There was a different type of mentality then. If you wanted to be educated—and not everyone did—you had to go to Reno. The university here was known [among the local populace] as Tumbleweed Tech.   ARCE

> People tolerated NSU as a struggling little place. We didn't run with the movers and shakers on the Strip. There was very little formal interaction.
>   General education, broad education, didn't count that much [to the casino operators]. In fact, the few approaches that we made were rebuffed for the most part.   MARSHALL

> A good part of the city in the '60s had no idea that UNLV existed!   SMITH

> We came in 1967. I really hadn't heard much about the university when I worked for Girl's Parole, which was in the old part of town. If it hadn't been for Charlie Levinson [hotel faculty member and friend of Joan's husband, Pick] I probably wouldn't have thought of working there.   REYNOLDS BEITZ

> The family moved here from California and I planned to major in mining, but found out that was Reno. Since the family had owned restaurants, I registered in hotel the same year the program began.   MIKE UNGER, '71 STUDENT

Competition was another issue that the Regents faced. Many schools in Utah and California were closer to Las Vegas than was Reno. Moreover, without any effort by

Reno to make its presence known, these other schools had better name recognition for the newly arriving populace than did Nevada's university, nearly 500 miles away. And there was still another factor:

> Everyone went three-and-one-half years here, and didn't go to Reno to finish their degrees [as was the original plan], so we had a city full of fledgling possible graduates.   CRAWFORD

> "Students who would otherwise be unable to begin work toward a degree are now assured of obtaining their freshman year—and in most cases their sophomore year as well—while they remain at home."[NSU Brochure, *Facts About Nevada Southern*. [18]]

The educational needs and wants of the new city were quite different than those of a traditional university. This was as true of the young faculty who were being recruited as it was of the nontraditional students who were attending. Crawford, Dean of Faculty, wasn't yet 30 and most of his colleagues were around the same age.

Special students, those not officially matriculated, made up a large portion of the student body. Many attended night classes. For them, Reno's admission standards and academic requirements did not seem appropriate. Yet faculty in the Southern Regional Division were part of the northern staff and were required to abide by system-wide standards. Admissions, curriculum, academic probation, faculty promotions and so on had to conform to Reno's catalog and code. Las Vegas faculty members reported to and were accountable to their Reno counterparts. It didn't work smoothly, and animosity grew so long as Dickinson and Carlson—both seen to be agents of the north—were in place.

> In my third year, 1965, I was elected chairman of the senate and also president of the AAUP [American Association of University Professors—an academic union]. I liked Carlson and he liked me, but there were some pretty clear concerns. In that year, a committee was formed. We saw the inevitability of a two-sister campus and so did the Regents.   CRAWFORD

> There was a Young Turks rebellion. We were not happy with the administration. [President] Armstrong came down from Reno and invited people to come in and talk. There may not have been a connection but a few months later word came down from Reno that Matt Graham would not be reappointed as chairman of math and science. Carlson, who was dean, had a bad temper, which I witnessed on occasion. He resigned in reaction to Armstrong's decision. That's how we got the new position of chancellor.   SMITH

Carlson then reversed himself, deciding to stand for the chancellor's appointment. Titles were transposed then. The "president" (Charles Armstrong) administered the entire system from Reno; the "chancellor" (to be Don Moyer) was the campus chief. In his capacity as head of the senate, Crawford—who wasn't Dean of Faculty yet—was appointed chair of the search committee. Tensions were high.

Carlson was the incumbent. There was no way we were going to keep Bill off of the final card, and we were smart enough not to try. Besides, the committee had become public domain. We recruited two strong, national candidates: Miller and Moyer. On the first ballot, committee members Chuck Sheldon and I prevailed with Reuben Neumann to halt the election of Ed Miller. Miller was a lovely man and since everything you wanted had to go through Reno the faculty there knew him and hired him as their president [chancellor]. [We felt] Moyer had the advantage. He was coming as a president of a small, growing southwestern university, Eastern New Mexico. It was a very explosive meeting with the vote 3-2. When the vote came for Moyer, Floyd Scritchfield [Education] threw a pop bottle at the three of us.   SMITH

I made some fiscal comments while on that search committee [Crawford, Neumann, Scritchfield, Chuck Sheldon, Herb Wells] and someone from the arts said you're nothing but a damn cash register.   REUBEN NEUMANN, BUSINESS FACULTY MEMBER

Carlson's withdrawal from the race cleared the way for the appointment of Don Moyer in 1965. Author James Hulse, *The University of Nevada: A Centennial History*, said that:

> "Moyer was a dynamic promoter, willing to run risks and to fight battles for the sake of advancing his campus even if this meant embarrassment to the president and the Board of Regents.[19]

Moyer's efforts to identify Las Vegas as a separate entity created tension at the upper echelons of the university system even as it rallied the local faculty. It took a person of this temperament and courage to loosen the bonds from Reno and to set in place the machinery that made possible the founding of the hotel program.

Reno had a heavy thumb on what was going on down here.   NEUMANN

> "Moyer's troubles and Armstrong's problems were opposite sides of the same coin. They were both men in the middle, between southern Nevada's demands for more autonomy and larger programs and the official regent's policy of slow, gradual growth for Nevada Southern." [Hulse.[20]]

During the late 1960s. Don Moyer was in a duel with the North. The duel had to do with academic independence and with autonomy from the North. The autonomy might have been granted, but the Board of Regents was controlled by the northern regents. As chair, Dr. Fred Anderson had an extremely strong hand in running university affairs.

The issue then was of north-south autonomy. We wanted to be completely free of UNR in every respect. And with the regents being dominated by northerners, it was a tough, tough row to hoe. I believe that's what got Moyer in the end.

[Later,] Don Baepler told me to stop those people in Reno from running extension courses in our backyard. Don Moyer and Jerry Crawford believed that their extension courses were taking revenues out of southern Nevada. That really galled them. I promptly started an extension or continuing education function.   MARSHALL

It [Reno's political and educational loss of power] was inevitable; what form it would take was another matter. [Therefore,] it was essential [to establish the hotel program] correctly and with some style.   DIGLES

Appointing a vice chancellor was one of Moyer's first acts. He made that title "Dean of Faculty" because "Vice Chancellor" sounded too exalted for what was still the Southern Regional Division of the University of Nevada . . .

. . . Although it was clear that we were going to get autonomy.   CRAWFORD

So, a new Dean of Faculty was recruited from New York.

He had wonderful credentials! That's when all of us starry-eyed kids were talking about the Harvard-of-the-West and that sort of nonsense.   SMITH

Within six weeks, everyone realized that the choice had been a mistake, more like a disaster. The new dean had a drinking problem; he stopped coming to work; he began romancing one of the staff members; he gambled heavily; and several paternity suits—one from a student—haunted him from former jobs.

I asked the committee members, did you guys take him out to a dining room in a casino? Take him there and watch his eyes. Walk him by the machines, by good-looking women. Offer him martinis, entice him. Did you do that with this candidate? No, they didn't. Moyer notified the new dean by registered mail that he must appear in the office on a given Monday or be terminated for breach of contract. My gosh! he doesn't show!
     So Moyer convened what-were-called the department heads. They included Richard Burns, Paul Harris, Ralph Roske and others. After hearing the news, they looked around: Which one was going to be picked as the replacement? Now the title was to be "Dean of Faculty Pro Tem."   CRAWFORD

Because this job was Dean of Faculty, Moyer wanted someone close to the faculty. He picked Jerry Crawford, who was chair of the faculty senate as well as president of the local chapter of the American Association of University Professors (AAUP).

At that time Jerry was chairman of the faculty senate. I was vice-chair, so when Jerry moved up, I moved to chairman.   SMITH

(There's a footnote to the story: Later the same week, the ousted dean came to Jerry Crawford, the very individual who had taken his job. The ex-dean was seeking support and representation on his appeal for improper discharge. After all,

Crawford was still AAUP president and this, so the claimant maintained, was AAUP business!)

These 1965 events reflected the atmosphere on campus, the looseness of the structures and the need to get things moving. It was the perfect environment for a nontraditional academic program like hotel administration, of which only a handful existed nationwide in 1965.

There was a great spirit of excitement and cooperation! It was a stimulating place to be.
MARSHALL

This was the time of SRUD, Students to Remove Upstate Domination. One year, a state-wide bond ballot that was designed to give NSU more buildings was defeated. Students built a little village out of campaign posters next to Frazier and Grant Halls. An outhouse was built at the entry to the campus. This did not go over big with the Regents.   SMITH

The ongoing battle between the North and the South and the impact of changing demographics brought excitement and stimulation to both the community and the campus. The stage was set—a perfect environment for Crawford, a dramatist—for the professional community to father the hotel program and the campus to nourish it.

ENDNOTES FOR CHAPTER 1

1. John R. Goodwin, *Diamond in the Desert: The University of Nevada Las Vegas and its William F. Harrah College of Hotel Administration* (Las Vegas: Sundance Publishing, 1992), p. 58.
2. A. D. Hopkins and K. J. Evans, ed., "E. Parry Thomas." *The First 100, Portraits of the Men and Women Who Shaped Las Vegas* (Las Vegas: Huntington Press, 1999), p. 158.
3. Andres Martinez, "Manager's Journal: Wynn's Loss is Wall Street's Win," *The Wall Street Journal*, February 28, 2000, p. A40.
4. Hopkins and Evans. "Thomas Hull, Creator of the Strip." *The First 100*, p. 90.
5. Gabe Vogliotti, Unpublished manuscript, pp. 1-1 and 2-3; from the personal collection of Bill Thompson.
6. Robbins Cahill, "Reflections of Work in State Politics, Government, Taxation, Gaming Control, Clark County Administration and the Nevada Resort Association." *Oral History Project* (Reno: University of Nevada, Reno, Library), v.6, pp. 1,350, 1293.
7. Vogliotti, Unpublished manuscript, p. 1-7.
8. Vogliotti, Unpublished manuscript, p. 2-1.
9. John R. Goodwin. "Dr. Patrick J. Moreo, His Reflections as a Hotel Student." *UNLV Hotel Alumni Association Newsletter*, College of Hotel Administration, Summer, 1988, vol. 12, No. 2, p. 4.
10. Lionel Sawyer & Collins, Jerome J. Vallen, ed., *Nevada Gaming License Guide* (Las Vegas: Lionel Sawyer & Collins, 1988), p. 9.
11. Hopkins and Evans. "Harvey Diederich." *The First 100*, p. 121.
12. Lionel Sawyer & Collins, p. 14.
13. Goodall, Leonard. From manuscript page 73 of a work in progress documenting UNLV's history at the turn of the millennium, quoting John Goodwin, *Diamond in the Desert*, p. 171.
14. Vogliotti, Unpublished manuscript, p. 2-5.
15. *Cornerstone Ceremony for the First Building, Nevada Southern Campus, University of Nevada, Las Vegas, Nevada.* (Las Vegas: The Grand Lodge Free and Accepted Masons, Sunday, March 17, 1957.) From the collection of Judi Watts, Hotel El Rancho Vegas.

16. James W. Hulse, *The University of Nevada: A Centennial History* (Reno: University of Nevada Press, 1974), p. 66.

17. Hulse, *The University of Nevada*, p. 66.

18. *Facts About Nevada Southern*, first brochure printed for the Southern Regional Division, 1956–57.

19. Hulse, *The University of Nevada*, p. 66.

20. Hulse, *The University of Nevada*, p. 67.

CHAPTER 2

The Vision

Two developments carried the hotel program from vision to reality. The Las Vegas hotel industry was coming of age and The Southern Regional Division of the University of Nevada was becoming the University of Nevada Las Vegas. Las Vegas—exciting and unique, constantly reinventing itself—was throbbing in the 1960s. Hotel-casinos drove the economy then, as they do now. A free-wheeling atmosphere permeated both the city and the university as each considered, tested and rejected many ideas before selecting the few that promised success.

> [Don] Moyer was a mover. Just do it. Boom! Don was famous for floating battleships. If we send 40 ships across this town and 15 get there, those are the 15 that are going to do something.   JERRY CRAWFORD, DEAN OF FACULTY

> Talk about experimenting: Jay Sarno required guests entering his new Circus Circus Casino to pay an admission to get in!   JERRY VALLEN

Somehow, the two communities focused on the one idea that was a win/win for both, hotel education. The decision wasn't instantaneous; it gained credence over time. As early entrepreneurs shifted away from daily operations to oversee an increasingly complex environment of capital growth and regulation, the need for better trained executives grew more apparent. Managers, not gamblers, were the key to the transition from gaming capital to resort destination.

[The program's creation] was a combination of things. We couldn't hold on to good people. There were a number of hotels and casinos that went belly up. So it wasn't any one organization [behind the effort]. The accountants were talking about it; some of the bosses were concerned; there was a big influx of people. It was part of the growing up of the town.   PHIL ARCE, SAHARA HOTEL MANAGER

We were always looking for new ideas. I can't tell you just where it [the idea for the hotel program] originated but there was no question we were going to go after it. We discussed it with the local committee of the Board of Regents. Among them were Archie Grant and Juanita White. [Two campus buildings bear their names.]   DONALD MOYER, PRESIDENT, NEVADA SOUTHERN UNIVERSITY

We weren't lucky, we were needed. The old guys knew it even before the corporate types came in with their slide rules. There was a small hard core of casino types but they weren't growing new ones. I'm glad the industry responded as well as it did.   JOE DELANEY, COLUMNIST AND PART-TIME FACULTY MEMBER

Both the hotel industry and the campus were experimenting with new ideas. Caesars Palace, considered to be the first extensively themed hotel-casino, opened in 1966, the same year that the Nevada Resort Association and Southern Nevada University entered into their educational partnership.

When Jay Sarno gave the faculty and students a tour of the soon-to-be-opened Circus Circus Hotel [1968], we commented on the very narrow aisles around the experimental game arcade. Sarno's answer focused on his belief that people want to feel as if the place is busy and that they are, therefore, in on what was going on. Crowding them accomplished that.   JERRY VALLEN

The hotel program flourished from the start. Despite continuing tension throughout the university system and ongoing competition for funding within the campus, hotel developed without mortal enemies.

On the contrary, people were accommodating. There was absolutely no discrimination against hotel students. In fact, if anything, the campus saw us as something different.   PAT MOREO, '69 STUDENT AND HOTEL FACULTY MEMBER

The fact that the program never received its fair share of the budget may have helped. No one ever accused hotel of sucking up funds. Perhaps the idea was too new. The launch of later programs put strains on the system. According to the *Las Vegas Review-Journal*:

"It's a typical pattern, straight out of Politics 101. Gain support for a new program [referring to the new dental school] by offering soothing assurances it won't burden taxpayers—and when that proves false (it always does), who cares?

The program's already been approved and lawmakers will never pull the plug." [*Review-Journal.* [1]]

The total reserve at the beginning of the 1968 fiscal year—I came in the summer of 1968— was approximately $1,000.

It was ludicrous to contemplate adding football [which was done that year], the most expensive sport a university can have, when we couldn't buy paper clips.

Hotel was not a program that was readily accepted by the academicians, but it did not demand our resources, so they permitted it to exist. In that context it was a relief to know it was funded by the Nevada Resort Association.   DONALD BAEPLER, UNLV PRESIDENT AND UNS CHANCELLOR

Although some faculty members in other departments were less enthusiastic than others, none undermined the program. On the contrary, almost everyone offered help and remained supportive for years thereafter.

No, I don't think there was too much objection. It [hotel] is a little way out [of the academic stream] so there was always someone who might be a little stiff, but we had no trouble getting it born. We had money behind it and it was a natural for the this locale.   MOYER

Hotel seemed to be a good idea: Relevant for Las Vegas. It was timely too, the town was booming in 1965, '66 and '67.   DWIGHT MARSHALL, DEAN OF CONTINUING EDUCATION

It's the same as anything else. Some welcomed it and others didn't.   ARCE

Faculty concerns were more about curriculum content [specifically food science], which would have been faculty senate business, than about form and faculty credentials.   ROBERT SMITH, DEAN OF SCIENCE, MATHEMATICS AND ENGINEERING

Training people for the hospitality industry was not a commonly accepted concept at universities. Most of us had come from institutions where these subjects had never been thought of.   BAEPLER

THE PARTICIPANTS
Reno's Non-Role
UNR, University of Nevada Reno, was minutely involved with every aspect of the Vegas campus. Even the initial checks that the Resort Association gave to fund the hotel program ran through the machinery of the Reno campus and were acknowledged by Charles Armstrong, President of the University of Nevada System. It was a bitter and contentious relationship in every respect.

The southern campus was unable to get air conditioning in its autos because Reno had none [weather didn't require it] and the business officer there could not be convinced otherwise. One July, when the business officer came down [to Vegas] to do business, Bill Carlson had an auto left for him at the airport. Carlson's instructions were to leave the car in the sun three hours early with the windows rolled up.   MRS. MARIAN CARLSON

Reno insisted on meeting every candidate. Anything we wanted here had to go through the deans up there. I was one of eight. It was 7-1 every time.

When I was Dean [of Faculty], I had to carry promotions up to Reno. I made an argument for our first full professor, Floyd Scritchfield. They said it was more theater [drama is Crawford's field] then substance, but they gave him the promotion.   CRAWFORD

Jerry Crawford [a playwright] would have to go up and do Oscar-winning performances with the deans to get promotion and tenure through.   SMITH

Given this North-South rivalry, one would think that the parent campus would have bid for the new hotel program with its extra, special funding. After all, the hotel-casinos in the North were more established at that time than those in Las Vegas. Moreover, Robert Weems, Jr., who was Dean of the College of Business at Reno, was very active in the American Hotel Institute, later renamed the Educational Institute (EI) of the American Hotel & Motel Association (AH&MA).

Bob [Weems] was unassailable on the Reno campus. He was an institution, almost like Charlie [Armstrong, President of the University System]. He had a stranglehold on the college.   MARSHALL

There is little doubt that the North in the person of Bob Weems could have made some loud noises about the location of the hotel program as it did a short time later with the medical school gift of $200,000 from Howard Hughes.

One big wave in my era was when Howard Hughes was trying to get his first [gaming] license and the northern legislators were trying to get the medical school [located in Reno] before [the reapportionment of] the 1970 census.   SMITH

Weems did not make waves; on the contrary, he offered support and help to the newly appointed director, Jerry Vallen. Both men knew each other slightly from their activities with the Educational Institute: Weems was a trustee and Vallen an author. Reno, including Bob Weems, simply didn't want such a program.

At the Puerto Rico meeting of the America Hotel & Motel Association [1960], I discussed the hotel program with Bob Weems, who answered me, Yes, we're interested, but first things first. Meaning there were more important things [for the southern campus] than trying to start a hotel school.   FRANK WATTS, RIVIERA FINANCIAL OFFICER

Reno was 20 times as traditional as UNLV. They have always been hoity-toity, looking down their noses. Reno aspires to the leagues of research universities without the population and resource base to do the job. Any program that was not hard-core academic had a tough time. SMITH

Reno faculty never saw themselves as an urban university. As a state school, they saw themselves tied to agriculture and mining.

I never felt an attitude up there that they were connected with [urban] Reno at all. Not like our connection to Vegas.   CRAWFORD

The northern people really didn't care about it because in those days they didn't think in terms of hotels. So a school of hotel administration meant very little to them.   JOE DIGLES, NEVADA RESORT ASSOCIATION

Dwight Marshall, who worked as personnel manager for Harrah's in Reno during the early 1960s, adds another perspective:

Because I worked 8 to 5 and then came back at night, I got to know Bill [Harrah] pretty well because he tended to stay in the office late at night . . . and he liked to sit and talk.

The industry [in Reno] was not ready for academics to encroach upon its operations. Corporate structure had not yet taken over. You still had men like Fitzgerald, Boyd, Harrah, and Primm. There was no incentive for private owners to educate their people. They wanted technical skills. Attitude didn't count then, nor did general education. Although that wasn't the case at Harrah's

There was absolutely no incentive for Weems [to seek a hotel program] and little chance that the owners up and down Virginia Street [Reno's main avenue] would support one. MARSHALL

Reno had limited hotels at that time. In fact, they weren't too active. We tried to get our [accounting] association active up there and didn't have much success. Most of the power, most of the demand was from down here.   WATTS

[The Reno campus wasn't interested] because the school never identified with the city. Someone in the city would have had to tell the campus, Yes, we have hotels. I don't think they had the vision.   SMITH

[In 1994] the head of Reno's nutrition program came to talk to us [Professors Cummings, McCool and Stefanelli] about cooperation because she thought their program was too clinical. That was something that Audrey [McCool] and I had complained about for years. We are both RDs [registered dieticians, and Ph.D.s] and we knew [that to be so]. This proposal [to give Reno students a UNLV class using technology] was just amazing; you know UNR and UNLV never speak!   LESLIE CUMMINGS, HOTEL FACULTY MEMBER

For whatever reasons—including the probability that the southern campus had matured enough to simply ignore Reno—Reno never was involved in the original hotel program. However, several years later, seeing its success, Weems considered starting one.

> I distinctly remember discouraging him because I wanted hotel to be a prerogative of UNLV. We argued and I told him I would take it to the regents. Reno had used that argument whenever we wanted to start a new program—you don't need nursing, Reno has it. You don't need that program, Reno has it. I remember jealously guarding our one program [hotel], and I would go to war to make certain that they did not duplicate the only program that was unique to us.   BAEPLER

So much for academic Reno; administrative Reno was another matter. The university's hierarchy was still anchored in the North, so the formalities of permissions and money flows were channeled there through Charles Armstrong, President of the University of Nevada System.

> The northern campus was definitely not involved [with the program's development]. The [Resort Association's] contact was always down here, but maybe they [the university's chain of command] had to go through Reno.   J. KELL HOUSSELS, JR., HOTELIER AND ELECTED PRESIDENT OF THE NEVADA RESORT ASSOCIATION

> They always screwed the South. Everyone, even some Johnny-come-latelys within the Resort Association quickly realized that. It was understood that to hell with those guys [in the North] so far as the hotel school idea. So the NRA would not have approached anyone in Reno.   DIGLES

The Major Academic Players

There were several key members on hotel's first team. Along with Chancellor Donald Moyer were the Chair of the Division of Business, Rex Johnson, and the Chair of the Accounting Department, Richard Strahlem. Identifying the team's ramrod from historical data and interviews is difficult. It was probably Richard (Dick) Strahlem. Everyone worked hard contributing in different ways. There was a good deal of synergy among the three, even though two of them had serious differences.

> I remember Strahlem as a very active player. I think it makes sense [attributing the push for the program] to Dick; he was a real player. Much more energetic than Rex [who was ill and about 25 years older than Dick]. Dick was also in the faculty senate. He was sort of an ambassador for the business school.   SMITH

> I remember him as a uniquely, almost self-appointed, sophisticated man. He saw himself as a man of more visions than many of his colleagues. And I do remember him coming to see me about this [the hotel program]. Strahlem jumps out of memory as a key supporter.   JERRY CRAWFORD, DEAN OF FACULTY

> Dick tended to be a rather serious, almost dour, person, but he would tell it like it was! He was a good sounding board for me. He was solid, but had a negative personality.   DONALD BAEPLER, UNLV PRESIDENT

I do remember Strahlem coming into a lot of the conversations because he was usually up to something.   DONALD MOYER, PRESIDENT, NEVADA SOUTHERN UNIVERSITY

Attributing the development of the hotel program to Dick Strahlem is an interesting personal call because Strahlem was the one person with whom the new director, Jerry Vallen, did not get along. The problem started during their first interview, grew during the second interview and probably had its base in the fact that Strahlem wanted the director's job for himself, although he never officially applied for it.

Oh, yes, I remember Dick very well. I think he really wanted to be head [of the hotel program].   JOE DIGLES, NEVADA RESORT ASSOCIATION

Wanting to be head of the new hotel program was actually second best, he really wanted to be the business division head, Rex's job. So the two of them were also at loggerheads.

Strahlem and Johnson didn't get along at all; sometimes they didn't even speak to one another. That animosity was very evident on the day that my appointment was finalized during my second visit. Four hours before I boarded the plane to return to New York, Johnson told me that Strahlem had purchased an expensive National Cash Register (NCR) accounting machine for the accounting department using hotel funds. I canceled the order—although I wasn't officially on the job until several months later—much to the satisfaction of Johnson and to the distress of the business officer, Herman Westfall. Westfall had to cancel a long-standing purchase order with NCR. No hard feelings: Years later when NCR was trying to adapt its electro-magnetic machine to the approaching electronic era, it hired the hotel faculty as consultants.   JERRY VALLEN

Like so many other stories, there is a postscript to this one. Herman Westfall does not recall the incident. Neither do Neumann, Crawford nor Moyer, but then the latter two may have been too high in the organization. Only after researching library files, does the possibility of Johnson's artifice emerge. Strahlem's memo recommends the acquisition of the NCR and reports that Jess Goodman of the Riviera Hotel was interested in making a gift. It was just this time, 1967, that the Vegas hotels began experimenting with the earliest commercial computers. Several years later, the Riviera gifted some computer accessories when it invested in second generation equipment.

While Strahlem didn't get along well with colleagues, he was much better cooperating and collaborating with the administrators over him. And we were aware of that.
   Johnson didn't like Dick's arrogance and aloofness, and sense of stated superiority, which Dick had no qualms about letting him [Johnson] know.   CRAWFORD

Strahlem and Johnson were at odds. Strahlem was kind of a department head—if there was such a thing. [The 1966–67 catalog lists Strahlem as departmental chair.] Strahlem wrote a scathing letter to Johnson chastising him for bypassing Strahlem for my promotion, which he [Strahlem] would not have recommended.   REUBEN NEUMANN, BUSINESS FACULTY MEMBER

Dick Strahlem had a manner about him. He looked out of the corner of his eye at you and sneered. It was just a personal quirk, but he always struck me as a character out of *Treasure Island*. SMITH

Strahlem was just very ambitious and I'm sure he felt that it [the hotel program] was his baby. NEUMANN

Strahlem and Bill Carlson had pieces of land right in the middle of the campus, and there was a lot of gossip and scandal about it, which didn't help their relationships with people. ANONYMOUS

Most people underestimated Dick Strahlem.   GEORGE HARDBECK, DEAN OF BUSINESS AND ECONOMICS

Strahlem's character and hard work, which cannot be minimized, was certainly one driving force behind hotel's conception and launch. Overseeing that was Rex Johnson in his role of what would be called today Dean of Business. Making it all possible with his foresight and bravery, which can be seen most clearly in retrospect, was Donald Moyer. In support of this first team were Jerry Crawford, Dean of Faculty; and Robert Smith, an influential faculty member, Chairman of the Senate and later Dean of Science, Mathematics and Engineering.

Although Don Moyer doesn't recall much about his leadership in achieving the hotel program, other interviewees point to him as the expediter of everything that was happening on campus in those days. And there was plenty going on!

One day Don and I were talking about the city. He said this was going to be an urban university. I don't think anyone recognized that. Early on hotel was only a light in the eyes of a few visionaries and the business people, but far down in the pecking order. That is, until Don Moyer got here.

The real gestation of it came from all of us, led by Moyer.   CRAWFORD

Everyone wants to take credit [for starting the hotel program] and I understand that. I can't tell you exactly [the first time the idea was approached] but I know that we said, If with all these hotels, this place is going to be the entertainment capital of the world, then we have to get in on the business—gaming, everything.   MOYER

I said to Don, we have the best theater facilities in the world here. They're a natural laboratory for theater students. I'll take you over to the Tropicana Hotel and show you staging that came right out of the Italian Renaissance. And it was in those types of conversations that the idea for a hotel program was sparked.   CRAWFORD

We couldn't have done it without Moyer.   LEO LEWIS, BINION'S FINANCIAL OFFICER AND PART-TIME FACULTY MEMBER

In part, the idea of a hotel program—like many other of Moyer's projects—arose from a need to define the direction of the Las Vegas campus vis-a-vis the mother campus at Reno.

> Don Moyer had ideas! I think the basic strategy was let's get a lot of new programs on the books and then go to the legislature and say, look what we're trying to do, and you don't give us the money. It took the whole of the 1970's to recover [financially] from that. Hotel was one of those new programs. He saw what was unique in Las Vegas and tied into it.
>
> This was years before UNLV finally caught on to the fact that there was money in town if the community was served.   ROBERT SMITH, DEAN OF SCIENCE, MATHEMATICS AND ENGINEERING

One Possible Scenario

Dick Strahlem pioneered the idea of off-campus employment. He and several other faculty members worked regular, second jobs in the resort industry during the mid-1960s. The practice continued for many years.

> Yes, I know Strahlem was working part time. It was not unreasonable for people to moonlight some.   REUBEN NEUMANN, BUSINESS FACULTY MEMBER

> We had more trouble with that [off-campus work]. One man was dealing, another had a full-time [stage] career with the Stardust. And we couldn't get that stopped.   JERRY CRAWFORD , DEAN OF FACULTY

Strahlem worked in the accounting department at the Sands Hotel. This gave him a conduit to the professional community, especially to the accountants who were growing in importance. Gaming control places heavy burdens on the accounting profession because it requires self-audits by the hotels. That responsibility fell to the accountants.

> The Gaming Board and the Commission would often come to us [the accountants] and ask, What would you do? We would tell them and they would write the rule or regulation.   FRANK WATTS, RIVIERA FINANCIAL OFFICER

> Indeed, I witnessed that during the late 1960s and early 1970s at many monthly meetings of the accountants when the issues were discussed and recommendations were forwarded.   JERRY VALLEN

More than any one else on campus, Strahlem had access to one of the important segments of the resort industry.

> Those of us who belonged to the Hotel Accountants Association were probably more interested in the school than anyone else in the hotel industry. Because at that time a good many of the other executives were casino people, who came from the Middle West and East [career gamblers] and belonged to a different group than we accountants did.

Whenever we had [citywide] meetings, one of the Cleveland guys would call me and say, Frank are you coming? You gonna bring the percentages? You gonna do this . . . ? So they began to realize that they needed help; that they didn't have the backgrounds.

Our hotel manager was Dick Chappell. Nice Guy! Came to the Riviera from Bugsy at the Flamingo. Well dressed, could remember names, shake hands and treated everyone nicely. But when we had anything come from the state or the county, he would say, Frank, take care of it. WATTS

Strahlem had access to the accountants and the accountants were a conduit to management. Through these channels, Strahlem may have been the one to spark the idea for a hotel program.

I think he [Strahlem] was the one we would talk to. He would come to the hotel accountants' meetings, so we knew him, and we [the accountants] had a good relationship with him, and we didn't know too many people out there [on campus]. And he had the same interests as we. He was a kind of go-between. WATTS

Strahlem's boss at the Sands was Jim West, who was the first president of the Nevada Hotel Accountants Association. Later, West lost a leg and after being out of work for some time joined Frank Watts at the Riviera. Frank and his wife had helped to nurse Jim West.

In 1957 a group of 15 of us met at the Flamingo and formed the Nevada Hotel Accountants Association. WATTS

The group would later become a chapter of the Association of Hotel/Motel Accountants, later renamed the International Association of Hospitality Accountants and still later the Hospitality Financial and Technology Professionals. It would prove to be an active participant in the development of regulated gaming in the state and an advocate for the hotel program. The first of many scholarships to come originated with the hotel accountants.

Jim West was Mr. Cut-the-nut! He was the ax, but he was very good. Jim West had a reputation for being a real professional in the business.

Yes, very definitely, I can see Jim involved in getting the hotel program started. Somehow the message got across that we needed people and they needed to be trained. That would break the ice at the top to gain active support for the hotel program. J. K. HOUSSELS, JR., HOTELIER AND ELECTED PRESIDENT OF THE NEVADA RESORT ASSOCIATION

Strahlem and West were buddies. NEUMANN

Jim West was at the [accountant's] meeting—if he wasn't actually president then—and he said, Listen, I got a guy working for me who teaches at the university. He would be a major help to us. So I said, If he's that good, he's chairman of the committee. He wasn't even there [at the meeting]. At the first meeting when he [Strahlem] was there, he said, Don't you guys worry, I'll guide you through. I think he went to Moyer.   LEWIS

Still, no one has offered an explanation of why Rex Johnson would have appointed Strahlem—if, in fact, it was Johnson's doing—as the first acting head of the program-to-be. They suffered one another and that was widely known.

Strahlem and Johnson were enemies, very much so.   NEUMANN

Recognizing Strahlem's strategic position with the hotel industry, Johnson, Strahlem's campus boss, who was a very ethical man, probably set aside his own negative feelings toward Strahlem for the benefit of the new hotel program.

Rex retired from George Washington University so there was a culture shock when he got here. There was one hell of a difference between the East and Las Vegas. Determined to stay, he bought his house for cash.   NEUMANN

Speculation all, but it raises another issue. How was it that Johnson, a traditional business dean, would support a hotel program, which is an anathema to most college business faculties? Support it he did, both in the early stages of development and during the two years that he remained in the job before a new business dean, William (Tom) White, was recruited.

Rex was not at all reluctant. He was trying to do the job.   SMITH

An Intriguing Alternative. Rex Johnson's predecessor as head of the business program was Maurice de Young (1959–1965). He had come to Nevada from Haiti where he had been, by coincidence, a hotelier. Some say he advocated bringing hotel management to the campus. De Young may have been the catalyst for the hotel program although there is no archival evidence to support the idea.

Frank Watts recalls a luncheon meeting years before 1965 during which a hotel program was explored with university representatives, but he cannot remember who attended. Watts does recall that one educator at the luncheon had degrees from Arkansas. Since Herb Derfelt (division of education) often told Jerry Vallen that he, Derfelt, first explored the idea, perhaps it was Derfelt. Derfelt was the only one on that early campus with a degree from Arkansas! Moreover, he had assumed some administrative functions including the summer school program.

When de Young left, Rex Johnson, who was already on the marketing staff, was chosen over Strahlem to head the business program.

Strahlem felt that he should be dean or head honcho. He felt that he should have the job because it was his nature to call the shots. That was part of Strahlem. I don't recall who made the decision that Rex Johnson would be it [head of business], but it made sense because Johnson had a Ph.D. and he had [educational] administrative experience. On paper, Johnson was a much better candidate.   NEUMANN

Degrees were getting to be important at this time. Rex Johnson had the terminal degree, which Strahlem lacked.   HERB WELLS, SCIENCE, MATHEMATICS AND ENGINEERING FACULTY MEMBER

Rex had the right personality and respect and wisdom that was needed in Business. Another kind of leader might have made it more difficult [to get the hotel program started].   CRAWFORD

The Major Industry Players

After the preliminary initiatives, leadership shifted from Dick Strahlem working with Jim West and the accountants to Rex Johnson and Don Moyer meeting with hotel executives like Jess Goodman of the Riviera and Bob Cannon from the Tropicana.

Jess Goodman was strong for the school!   LEWIS

Everyone had a great deal of respect for Jess, and there's no doubt that he was pro-university.   HOUSSELS

Jess was president of the Riviera. He was also an outgoing fellow who didn't mind talking about things.   WATTS

It was no small coincidence that Jess Goodman was originally an accountant and, in fact had been president of the local chapter.

Oh, I know Jess was one of the founders of the hotel accountants, he helped start the national association in the New York chapter.   LEWIS

Clearly, the local accountants had a good deal of influence in fusing the hotel program and the hotel industry. Like the campus, industry persons at several levels worked toward the one goal. The university hierarchy started with faculty members and built upward to Department Chair, Dick Strahlem. The next level was the Chairman of the Division of Business Administration, Rex Johnson. At the top were Chancellor Don Moyer and President Charles Armstrong. Chief supporters on the Board of Regents were local members Archie Grant and Juanita White.

 Hoteliers had a similar ladder: from middle executives such as Jim West, Leo Lewis and Frank Watts to persons like Tropicana manager Bob Cannon and Riviera President Jess Dee Goodman. At the top of the pyramid was the industry's trade group, the Nevada Resort Association (NRA). The NRA had elected officers, presidents such as J. Kell (Ike) Houssels, Jr. and paid executive directors, particularly two of the earliest ones, Gabe Vogliotti and Robbins (Bob) Cahill. Both men were staunch friends and reliable supporters of the hotel program. Both men, but especially Cahill, were well respected and strong advocates of hotel education.

The guys that really wanted it got the word out. Goodman, West and Cannon—not necessarily the owners—were the ones doing the real work.

What really got the NRA started was Robbins Cahill. He was a hell of a man.   HOUSSELS

Later, Bill Campbell, who was the NRA's labor executive, was another big booster.

Bill Campbell handled the negotiations for all of the labor contracts. I think he was the school's biggest supporter. He really believed in it! Bill Campbell was very instrumental in the school's launch and as I got close to him, he asked if I would participate and help, and I did.   ARCE

There was tremendous enthusiasm for the school from everyone on the Strip, with boosters like Al Benedict.   TOM BELL, ATTORNEY TO THE HUGHES CORPORATION

IT STARTS TO COME TOGETHER

What was said about public corporations in the previous chapter—the hotel gift would probably not have come if the hotels had been public corporations—might be said now about the campus administration. One interviewee suggested that if more traditional academics other than Moyer, whose discipline was education, and Crawford, whose discipline was theater, had been in place, the program might never have come to reality.

I had never heard of a hotel discipline, so it took some education, which happened quickly, and I credit Vallen with that. Scientists [Baepler is an ornithologist] are pragmatic so I never fought against applied areas, not even Marshall's programs.   BAEPLER

The campus was academically immature. If it had been more mature, launching the hotel program would have been more difficult organizationally.   SMITH

The school was started at the right time in the right place with the right people. A couple of years later, it might not have worked.   DICK BASILE, HOTEL FACULTY MEMBER

Although some individual hoteliers took a positive, leadership role, others—like their counterparts on campus—were quietly critical. Fortunately, there were no major objections from either camp.

We had a lot of discussion about it. There were a number of persons who didn't think we needed a hotel school, and there was another group [of hoteliers] who felt very strongly that we did.

Those who thought we did not need one started changing. When the first allotment of money was called for, it was pretty much unanimous.   ARCE

I recall some of the meetings because I was taking notes then. Alex Shoofey [who took 33 staffers from the Sahara with him when he became President at the Flamingo] was a real naysayer, bitching about the control and the money.   DIGLES

I don't remember any objections about starting a program. Once it began to emerge, there was a lot of resistance among traditional academics, partly because non-credentialed faculty were coming in.   SMITH

It is a hazy recollection, but it seems to me that the business faculty were passive, but somewhat negative. I do recall some concerns about this "abstract" college depriving them of funds and their much sought after accreditation.   MARSHALL

The greatest reluctance, I recall, came from the business faculty.   CRAWFORD

The business program had its own image problems, which more than likely contributed to its reticence in embracing the hotel program.

You know at that time we also had an area in business of office administration, which was typing, shorthand and that sort of thing. The Fine Arts faculty viewed the teaching of typing, shorthand, food preparation, whatever, as a trade school. It was obvious that they looked down on us. No question about that.

Initially, the division of business was behind it until such time as it looked too heavy on food prep and too little on management. There was some concern it was going to be more of a trade school training kitchen help.   NEUMANN

Most faculty went along with the leadership. That would be expected in industry, but it was also true on the campus because faculty governance was not strongly in place as yet.

There was some skepticism within the ranks, but there was enough input from the top down. It's going to work, end of story.   ARCE

In the Moyer administration, things came down from the top.   SMITH

At that time there wasn't much done by committee. It was a completely different situation then, it was more what the captain said.   NEUMANN

A series of meetings took place within the campus community and between the campus and the resort association.

We went to the Association, rather than to the individual hoteliers.

It was a very small town and ideas spread rapidly.   CRAWFORD

The files contain a handwritten memo from Don Moyer to himself itemizing what he hoped to do with the hotel program. It included the use of the new Student Union building, which was later named the Moyer Student Union.

Moyer made an appearance or two at the Resort Association. He certainly didn't come with his hat in his hand though; He enjoyed a good relationship.   HOUSSELS

I remember picking up Rex [Johnson, Division of Business] and going to Association meetings several times to make the case. Vogliotti and Houssels were there with some others.

We went to them [the Resort Association] and they were hot for the idea; said they
would give us money to get started. So there was no question that we would get it done.

Houssels was at the Tropicana then, and we used to meet him there [as well].   DON
MOYER, PRESIDENT OF NSU

Correspondence from Gabe Vogliotti suggests that the idea for a hotel program
lay in waiting for several years. Frank Watts' interview supports that idea.

In 1959, Dean Carlson met for luncheon at the Riviera with Jess Goodman and me to discuss
the possibility of starting a hotel program.

And I know it was in 1960 when I discussed the matter with Weems in Puerto Rico.

The University people didn't show too much excitement; it seems we had to keep the
ball rolling.   FRANK WATTS, RIVIERA FINANCIAL OFFICER

Frank Watts, who was the CFO of the Riviera, was one of the individuals who was very much
in favor of the hotel program.   PHIL ARCE, SAHARA HOTEL MANAGER

The difficulty [in getting the program launched] was the executive board [of the NRA]
which couldn't make up its mind. They couldn't come to grips with it because they hadn't
sought out enough advice. I don't think Gabe [Vogliotti, NRA executive officer] pressed it
that much; he wasn't much of a follow-through guy. Not much of an expediter; not much of
a sprinter.   JOE DIGLES, NEVADA RESORT ASSOCIATION

"Gabe was an idea man. He had these ideas, but they were a little bit in the clouds."
[Cahill.[2]]

On December 27, 1967, Gabe Vogliotti wrote to Al Freeman, the publicity director
of the Sands Hotel and a well respected figure of the resort community[3], that the idea
of a hotel program has been broached "a number of times before." Vogliotti wrote that
Moyer and Johnson began proposing it to individual owners in the summer of 1965.

Gabe always wanted to go for lunch—he loved to go for lunch—when I was Editor-in-Chief
of the *Review-Journal*. He was new at the Association, where there was only Gabe and a
secretary. Gabe mentioned the idea [of a hotel program] several times. Not to try it on for
size, more like rambling.

As I recall, Harvey Diederich also may have mentioned it, saying if they were going to do
it, it had better be done first class.

It basically meant nothing except there was always talk about doing something, but it
was always pretty vague.   DIGLES

Vogliotti's letter may have been a response to an inquiry from Freeman asking for
information about the NRA assessment being levied on the Sands. At the time it was
written, the program had been operating for almost a year. In fact, Vogliotti refers

Freeman to Vallen, who was already hired, for certain issues. The letter contains this observation: "The idea came at a junction that owners thought particularly timely as a way of helping the image."

> It probably was tossed around for a time. They had to get outside support. There was no external push [from the professional community] as there was [later] with the attorneys for the law school. I don't think it blossomed overnight.
>
> No, I didn't see it as a public relations gimmick by the Resort Association. Not in my opinion, although I guess it was [a] positive [thing]. Public relations was not the reason, although it always plays a part. When the Resort Association woke up to the need for more professionals, and that they were really going to get something out of it, they were very much in favor of supporting it. [but . . .]
>
> . . . I don't think the idea [for a hotel program] stemmed from the hotel industry. And there is certainly no basis [for your question] that the NRA had to prod the university.
>
> Both sides were laid back, but boy, it's become the Cornell of the West!   J. K. HOUSSELS, JR., HOTELIER AND ELECTED PRESIDENT OF THE NEVADA RESORT ASSOCIATION

> Well, I don't remember them [university people] coming to us; we went to them.   WATTS

> The NRA probably got interested because things were changing. Maryland Parkway was being paved south from San Francisco Avenue [now Sahara Avenue]. Frazier Hall was up on the campus. Things were good! We had a political voice of our own down here. Funding was coming from the state. There would be growth.   DIGLES

A Second, Probable Scenario

The date mentioned in Vogliotti's letter, the summer of 1965, seems to be as good as any as the origin for the final push. Vogliott wrote that the idea for a hotel program was never formally proposed to the NRA before 1965. But there is ample evidence that the idea smoldered for some time before then. According to Vogliotti's letter, Moyer and Johnson "began proposing the idea to individual owners" in the summer of 1965. Moyer acted quickly because he didn't arrive on campus until July of that year.

On May 28, 1965, prior to Moyer's arrival, Rex Johnson wrote to A. A. McCollum at the Sahara Hotel. Johnson asked for $60,000 to launch the program. Johnson's choice of McCollum at this early stage is intriguing because:

> A. A. McCollum was not one of the [industry's] main players.   JOE DELANEY, COLUMNIST AND PART-TIME FACULTY MEMBER

Delaney's observation about McCollum's worth is at odds with Cahill, who not only gives McCollum high marks, but ascribes much of the project's success to him:

> "A. A. McCollum . . . came up with the idea of supporting the hotel school. He was one of the original supporters and probably the most enthusiastic."

"The mainsprings [for the hotel program] were McCollum, Allard Roen, Jess Goodman and Ike Houssels.

"I'm not sure, but I believe Johnson came to McCollum with the idea of it." [Cahill. [4]]

Johnson's letter is intriguing because McCollum is addressed as "Mr." That suggests that either Johnson scarcely knew McCollum or that it was awkward to address him as "A. A." No reference to McCollum contains a first name, all list him as A.A. Moreover, Johnson's very brief letter gives no hint of any earlier discussions, nor does it ease into this astonishing dollar request by citing previous understandings. All this speculation may be off base because Johnson was an old-school gentlemen who might have written "Mr." out of courtesy. Evidence of some previous understanding is the promptness of McCollum's reply. Ten days later, on June 7, 1965, McCollum answers, " . . . let's talk, inasmuch as I have some variations to it that could be of interest to you." McCollum's words, "to it," do support Vogliotti's comments that there had been previous contacts with the owners.

The meeting took place on June 9 at 2:00 p.m. after which Johnson scribbled notes on the bottom of the letter:

"Met with McCollum and after full and lengthy discussion, he agreed with my recommendation that financial assistance to the tune of several thousand dollars per year would be needed. He agreed that such a move would not only be to the credit of the hotels but would provide for better personnel."

Johnson wrote that he called Vogliotti, who promised to hold a meeting to get financial support "at least for the first year." Johnson's notes indicate that "several preliminary discussions were held during June [1965] with McCollum, Vogliotti, Houssels and Goodman." During which "I was able to obtain agreement that the Resort Association would support the new program to the tune of several thousand dollars over a few years." Johnson notes that Don Moyer immediately approved this initial effort when he became Chancellor on July 1.

Additional meetings were held with individual NRA members culminating in an informal gathering at the Association's headquarters. McCollum, as NRA president, then announced the $277,000 grant, starting with $15,000 for 1965–1966 and $45,000 for 1966–1967.

I remember that there was a general consensus [on campus] that this was a logical location for such a school. I think someone came up with $40,000 or something like that as seed money.   REUBEN NEUMANN, BUSINESS FACULTY MEMBER

I recall meeting several times [with the NRA] and getting $65,000 as the first gift.   DONALD MOYER, PRESIDENT OF NEVADA SOUTHERN UNIVERSITY

A different set of letters throws light on Johnson's view of his own role in the hotel program. On January 12, 1967, a year after the program began, Johnson sent a memo to

Crawford, the Dean of Faculty, asserting with no uncertainty that the hotel program was Johnson's. "It's mine," he wrote! What lead up to that declaration is not known. But the interchange took place about the same time that Crawford asked Johnson to remain on hotel's advisory board. That was necessary because an announcement had been made that Tom White was to succeed Rex Johnson in six months as the new director of the business school. A few days later (January 16, 1967), Crawford wrote to Chancellor Moyer that the Nevada Resort Association was complaining about Johnson "thinking that the hotel program was his."

The Pace Quickens

On December 20, 1965, just seven months after Johnson's letter to McCollum, Moyer and Johnson met with the NRA. The final budget was discussed along with the need for an advisory committee.

> The budget request came from the university. We certainly didn't sit around and debate it; that's for sure.   J.K HOUSSELS, JR,, HOTELIER AND ELECTED PRESIDENT OF THE NEVADA RESORT ASSOCIATION

Houssels' certainty about the budget is supported by Vogliotti's letter to Freeman.

> "The budget for five successive years was prepared by the university and tailored to a rising curve of activity. Advice on staffing levels, curriculum and budgeting was obtained from Dr. Meek, professor emeritus of the Hotel School at Cornell University, considered the best in the nation. Dr. Meek was retained as consultant on the project."

On December 29, 1965, just nine days later, Moyer wrote to Dr. Charles Armstrong, president of the University of Nevada. He requested that Armstrong and the Board of Regents approve in principle the start of the hotel program for the fall of 1966. The letter also asked that Gabe Vogliotti, executive officer of the NRA, be permitted to attend the meeting when the issue came before the Board. Obviously, the NRA was now fully committed. So, too, was the university because one month later on January 15, 1966, the Board of Regents passed Resolution #66-5 (see Exhibit 2-1) accepting the agreement between what was now Nevada Southern University and the Nevada Resort Association. The agreement came only months after the young institution was renamed Nevada Southern University (NSU).

> Moyer and I brought about the name change in 1965.   JERRY CRAWFORD, DEAN OF FACULTY

Copies of the Regents' action were sent: to Houssels, NRA's elected president; to Jack Donnelly, general counsel and executive vice president of the Desert Inn; to J. Dee Goodman president of the Riviera; to Vogliotti; to Allard Roen, manager of the Desert Inn and Moe Dalitz's representative; and to Howard "Bud" James. Bud James was the executive vice president of Del E. Webb's Sahara Nevada Corporation (the Sahara Hotel's

Resolution No. 66-5

WHEREAS, the Nevada Resort Association of Las Vegas has agreed to join with Nevada Southern University in the initiation and support of a four-year Hotel Administration program to begin this fall of 1966;

WHEREAS, the Nevada Resort Association has proposed to underwrite the development of this program over a 4½ year period, pledging funding support of $15,000 for planning and the director's salary through September 1, 1966, $45,000 in support for the academic year $1966–67, $53,000 for 67–68, $71,000 for 68–69 and $93,000 for 69–70;

WHEREAS, the Nevada Resort Association has agreed to participate in advising the programs with one-half of the membership of an Advisory Committee to the program.

NOW THEREFORE BE IT RESOLVED, by the Board of Regents of the University of Nevada, that it accept the above mentioned pledges from the Nevada Resort Association this 15th day of January, 1966, and express its sincere and profound gratitude to the membership of the Nevada Resort Association for their generous assistance in the initiation and development of this Hotel Administration program and pledges its good faith in the fulfillment of the purposes of this agreement.

EXHIBIT 2-1. The resolution adopted by the Board of Regents of the University of Nevada acknowledging the gift of the Nevada Resort Association and pledging mutual support for the goals of the partnership.

parent company) which also owned the Mint in downtown Las Vegas. James wrote back on behalf of the NRA acknowledging the acceptance by the Board of Regents.

> Later, Bud James became the President and Chief Operating Officer of Boston-based Sheraton Hotels. He told me that his first meeting with the board of directors was a shock. James showed up in Las Vegas style clothing. Everyone else was in dark blue suits. Since James and I were of a size, he promised to give me his wardrobe. Guess he forgot the address.   JERRY VALLEN

> Yes, that's what happened to Bud. We were wearing green suits and purple outfits. Pretty snazzy.   ARCE

Another copy of the Regent's action went to Hacienda Hotel owner, Judy Bayley, whose later donation to the campus, supplemented by a gift from singer Wayne Newton, built the Judy Bayley theater.

> I don't know if it was Wayne's influence that got the $65,000—I think it was $65,000—to name the building after her.
> I think Wing Fong [Las Vegas businessman and spouse of Regent Lilly Fong] helped get the Bayley/Newton money, that's probably when he [Wing] got involved with the campus.   JERRY CRAWFORD, DEAN OF FACULTY

Later, Wing and his wife, Lilly, then a member of the Board of Regents, helped get the gift from Tom Beam for the hotel/business building.   JERRY VALLEN

We went through fund-raising campaigns, and Wing Fong was one of our primary guys.   MOYER

Vogliotti did appear at the Regent's meeting according to the newspaper reports the day following the meeting. He pledged to launch a department of hotel management with $277,000 from the 10 strip hotels that comprised the NRA. (See Exhibit 2-2.)

That $277,00 was big, huge dollars! Far more than a college budget.   SMITH

At that time we thought it was a very large gift.   CRAWFORD

[The amount that each hotel gave] was not a serious bite.   ARCE

"There was simply no concern with costs [in running the NRA, and] no one worried about costs when . . . they voted $300,000 to fund a hotel school." [Vogliott.[5]]

The grant was made without conditions. Funding was pledged for four years of operations after which the university would assume the budget. Fred Anderson, chairman of the Board of Regents, was quoted:

"The university, particularly Nevada Southern, has been looking forward to this for many years, but we just haven't been able to fund it." [*Review-Journal.* [6]]

Anderson's words, "for many years," support previous assumptions about the program's long incubation and give credence to Frank Watt's recollection that he, Jess Goodman and Herb Derfelt met over lunch to discuss the idea as early as 1959!

The *Review-Journal* reported Vogliotti's pledge to help fund a building like Statler Hall at Cornell University and to raise endowments for scholarships. The article pointed out the hotel industry's desperate need for management talent and its search for that talent among eastern universities.

Dr. H. B. Meek, executive director of the Council on Hotel, Restaurant and Institutional Education (CHRIE) is mentioned in the story as consultant to the project. Although similarities between the proposed program and Cornell's, including the building and the curriculum, are cited, the newspaper story fails to identify Meek as the retired, first dean of the Cornell program [*Las Vegas Sun.* [7]] Likely, the omission is intentional: As a private consultant, Meek could not ethically evoke the Cornell name. Parenthetically, only Phil Arce among all the interviewees remembers meeting Meek or receiving his report, and even he isn't certain. Bob Smith and Jerry Crawford have only faint recall. Still, no written report has been found at either the University or at the Resort Association. Perhaps, it was all done verbally in person or by telephone. Nowhere in Cahill's extensive oral history of the college's founding does he mention H. B. Meek.

Hotel Management Budget

1965–6 (2/66–7/66)

Director	$ 7,500
Secretary	2,500
Printing and Publicity	2,500
Division Chairman	2,500
	$ 15,000

1966–7

Director	$ 15,000
Associate Professor (Psychology)	10,000
Equipment	9,000
Secretary	5,500
Printing and Publicity	2,500
Division Chairman	3,000
	$ 45,000

1967–8

Director	$ 17,000
Associate Professor	11,000
Associate Professor (Data Processing)	11,000
Secretary	5,500
Printing and Publicity	4,500
Division Chairman	4,000
	$ 53,000

1968–9

Director	$ 19,000
Associate Professor	12,000
Associate Professor	12,000
Associate Professor (Foods)	12,000
Secretary	6,000
Printing and Publicity	5,500
Division Chairman	4,500
	$ 71,000

1969–70

Director	$ 19,500
Associate Professor	12,500
Associate Professor	12,500
Associate Professor	12,500
Associate Professor (Engineering)	15,000
Associate Professor (Gaming)	15,000
Secretary	6,000
	$ 93,000

EXHIBIT 2-2. The budget that the university submitted and the Nevada Resort Association adopted as part of the partnership agreement entered into on January 15, 1966.

Gabe [Vogliotti] would throw little things out on the water to see what fish would bite, and be very vague about things.

I'd bet my last dollar that Meek was one of Gabe's straw men, someone that Gabe liked to set up and quote. He sent them checks, but no one ever saw them. Now I don't know that Meek was that type, but I am not surprised that almost no one remembers him because I sure don't; I never saw him.

Gabe liked to associate himself with people like that, with a school like Cornell. But he kept them out of town. Then he would come up with characters out of the blue.   DIGLES

Digles' comments are consistent with a report authored by the College in preparing for an accreditation visit some ten years later.

"Some of the early planning was carried out by Dr. H. B. Meek, who apparently acted as a consultant to the hotel people with whom he was acquainted. This preceded the establishment of the program and no written report was ever made available." [*A Report to the Academic Vice-President*.[8]]

No, Meek didn't have anything to do with my son, Gary's, interest in UNLV. [Even though I was a strong Cornell booster,] I didn't know about Meek's [UNLV] connection until much later. We visited during a NRA [National Restaurant Association] Golden Plate Award dinner and I spent quite a bit of time chatting with Prof Meek.

   Now there are many to whom I tell the story because people are not aware that Meek found Vallen.   RICHARD BROWN, DONOR INTERMEDIARY AND FATHER OF ALUMNUS, GARY

The NRA grant rated an editorial in the *Review-Journal*, which noted that it was the first major gift to Nevada Southern University and suggested other gifts be given to the struggling institution. (That wasn't entirely accurate. The Southern Nevada Campus Fund was initiated in 1956, but technically there was no NSU at the time.) The editorial extolled the action and predicted that graduates would be "equipped to handle problems ranging from financial records to broken doorknobs." The decision to consult "top men in this specialized field of learning to pound out a practical course of study" referred again to Meek and his influence on the planning.

Just three weeks later, in a February 8, 1966 letter, Moyer implemented one provision of the resolution. He appointed the first advisory committee for the hotel program. Rex Johnson was named chairman. Other campus members were Jerry Crawford and Robert Smith with Don Moyer acting *ex officio*.

Jerry [Crawford] and I were on it. Rex Johnson was the person Don [Moyer] asked to get the whole thing started. That's the earliest record I have of my participation.   SMITH

Representing the NRA were its president, J. Kell Houssels, Jr. and its vice president, A.A. McCollum. NRA members Jack Donnelly and Allard Roen were appointed as alternate secretaries; J. Dee Goodman as treasurer. Vogliotti was also on the board.

The advisory committee decided that its first order of business was to find a director for the hotel program; and its second, to retain Meek as a consultant. Here, the word "retain" in the committee's minutes must mean "to keep," rather than "to hire." Meek appears to have been in place at the time the gift was announced, three weeks prior to the committee's formation.

On March 30, 1966 the first check for $15,000 was received by the university. It was part of a five-year budget (see Exhibit 2-2) submitted by the university. The first year was designated for planning and for the director's salary. As good budgets should do, it highlighted the program's direction by identifying the faculty hires.

Of the $15,000, $7,500 was earmarked for the director, Rex Johnson, and $2,500 for the Division Chairman, Richard Strahlem. Both drew these additional salaries as compensation for the extra workloads they carried. Although a request for $2,500 for Rex Johnson was recorded on March 8, 1966, it is unclear whether he or Strahlem drew those amounts.

Strahlem drew a stipend, some extra money for doing that [working on the hotel program].
NEUMANN

Vogliotti's letter to Freeman stated that, "the first year's budget was used almost entirely . . . for travel to study other hotel schools and to interview candidates. . . . " Cahill echoed Vogliotti's statement in his oral history, "Most of the $15,000 went for interviews."

Reno was still the seat of the university, so the initial check, dated March 30, 1966 was acknowledged in a letter to the NRA by Neil Humphrey, Vice President of Finance. Later, Humphrey became acting president of the university system, and in that role he accepted a check for the hotel program's fiscal year 1967–68.

Hotel's terminology (program, department, division, school, college) has never laid easily on anyone's tongue. In his letter of acknowledgment, dated January 5, 1968, Humphrey referred to the program as "the hotel school." Despite numerous restructuring, the appellation of "hotel school" was never formally assigned to the program.

The After Role of the NRA.   Contrary to the assumptions that many outsiders held, the Nevada Resort Association never involved itself in campus issues. The NRA did so only in 1966 and 1967 when its members reviewed resumes submitted by candidates for the first directorship. It also held interviews with those candidates selected by the university. And there was, of course, the initial advisory committee established with the gift. Aside from those exceptions, The Nevada Resort Association held to a hands-off attitude. That was best demonstrated by its failure to even comment on the hotel program's widespread use and cooperation with non-contributing properties, many of which weren't even Association members.

The Resort Association stepped back after it gave the money—very much so. If anyone had anything to say, it would go through Vogliotti or later Cahill.

Except they wanted a good school; good students! The NRA had its own problems. Didn't want to take on someone else's; no more political problems.   HOUSSELS

I don't think anyone [in the hotel-casino business] had enough knowledge to express views. There were very few people back then who had college educations. [J. Dee Goodman was an attorney.]   FRANK WATTS, RIVIERA HOTEL

I felt it was critical for the continued success of hotel to be established as a separate college when the campus was reorganized in 1971. However, in keeping with its ongoing policy, the NRA declined my request for support during the debate on campus reorganization.   JERRY VALLEN

My understanding was let the university handle it.   JOE DIGLES, NEVADA RESORT ASSOCIATION

Money talks. You may create us, but you do not own or control us. Some donors don't like that, but the Resort Association didn't want to run the thing!   CRAWFORD

Since only the Strip properties initially belonged to the NRA, the assessment of the $277,000 was divided among member hotels: Caesars Palace, Dunes, Desert Inn, Frontier, Hacienda, Riviera, Sahara, Stardust, Thunderbird, and Tropicana hotels. [Cahill letter.[9]] Missing was the Aladdin, which had reopened in 1966 as the Tally Ho.

Downtown wasn't really involved in the Resort Association until after we had been going for two or three years.   HOUSSELS

The downtown people and the Strip guys didn't get along.   DIGLES

At that time, the Resort Association and the Casino Center Association were segregated, but some guys were in both. Binion's Horseshoe Club was such a member.
So [Benny] Binion was throwing money into the pot as well as allowing me the time [to participate in the planning and to teach].   LEWIS

Binion didn't have any crossover that I knew of. Guys like Ike Houssels' family had a piece of the Showboat, the Cortez, and the Trop[icana]; so they had cross interests. I never heard that Benny had anything on the Strip.   DIGLES

Members who subsequently joined the NRA contributed or declined to participate on an individual basis. As a small property, the Hacienda paid only a one-half share, although the Thunderbird, which paid a full share, had only a few rooms more.

Judy Bailey always pleaded poor mouse. She always said we're way the hell out here. Of course, that was why the Hacienda was called Hay Seed Heaven.   DIGLES

There were a whole bunch of different ways of figuring out who paid what [for all NRA assessments]. There was one formula for dues, another for special assessments. None of them was cast in iron. They were changed. Generally speaking, though, it was based on the number of games.   HOUSSELS

There was a similar allocation when the hotels contributed to the Catholic church on the Strip. We all contributed a certain amount to save people the trek over to St Anne's.   WATTS

"The budget was elastic, the treasury to have whatever it had to have. They set up assessments, agreeing that the Stardust, which was the world's biggest casino, should pay most, and that the T-Bird [Thunderbird], the enduring cripple of the Strip, pay least." [Vogliotti.[10]]

"Ten members supported the hotel school."
"Supported it by a separate assessment. The Riviera paid up even after it dropped out of the NRA." [Cahill.[11]]

The Contribution of the Business Program. A great deal of careful work was done by Richard Strahlem to prepare the University. During 1966, Strahlem traveled to other campuses and spoke to other hotel administrators and faculty members. He was looking both for ideas and for candidates.

> Don [Moyer] asked who are the other great hotel programs: Michigan State, Cornell? He said they are all schools, ours will be a college. This will be a solid academic program, not a trade school. We'll be delivering high management. Along the way, we may train a chef or two because my brothers [Crawford's] were both chefs. CRAWFORD

During this trip, Strahlem visited Cornell. Perhaps then is when Howard B. Meek entered as a consultant. Even Meek's close Cornell associate, Assistant Dean Paul Gaurnier, has no recall of his mentor's participation. Yet Meek is not only mentioned in the newspaper reports, it was he who solicited Vallen's application for the directorship.

Strahlem returned from the tour with some strong and accurate opinions. Three stand out: (1) Faculty in this discipline were few and far between; (2) There was a complete lack of textbooks; and (3) The program should include an internship. Despite Strahlem's energy, progress was paced, if not just slow.

> **Question:** Did Rex Johnson aggressively follow up on recruitment?
> **Smith:** Rex? I wouldn't say aggressively.

In August of 1966, Strahlem wrote a memorandum to the faculty explaining that Johnson's illness accounted for the suspended faculty meetings and, by inference, the delay in the program's development. In a follow-up letter, September 6, 1966, to the faculty he reported on his trip and his suggestions on faculty staffing and qualifications. By October, a four-year hotel curriculum proposal had been submitted including details on the internship. Unclear was how much input, if any, Meek had.

> My recollection is that Meek did come and did write a report. I don't have a vivid memory of it, but he may have given an oral report to Don and me. CRAWFORD

> Strahlem had no doubt or hesitation. So at the second meeting [of Strahlem, Lewis and Arce], he brought the Cornell four-year program and the Michigan State four-year program. And he said, Leo, get out your pad. Then we went down the classes, like a Chinese menu: One from column A and one from column B. When he finished, we had a degree program. LEWIS

The campus' 1965–67 Biennial Activities Report, released on October 3, 1966, noted that the hotel program had started with support from the Nevada Resort Association. It named Richard Strahlem as the acting head, the one responsible for recruiting a director. Interestingly, this report stated that the course would lead to a Bachelor's degree in Hotel Administration, not to a degree in business even though hotel was part of the business program.

So from tentative beginnings—perhaps as early as 1959 when Rivera hotel executives J. D. Goodman and Frank Watts lunched with Dean William D. Carlson, or when Gabriel Vogliotti speculated over lunch with Joe Digles—the hotel program materialized in 1966, with a BHA degree, no less. Finding a director and classroom faculty was the next hurdle even as planning began for the first classes.

ENDNOTES FOR CHAPTER 2

1. "Hat in hand already," *Las Vegas Review-Journal*, April 12, 2000, p. 8B.

2. Robbins Cahill, "Reflections of Work in State Politics, Government, Taxation, Gaming Control, Clark County Administration and the Nevada Resort Association." *Oral History Project* (Reno: University of Nevada, Reno, Library,) v. 6, p. 1,317.

3. Al Freeman was a well known publicist whose floating crap game was probably the most famous public relations stunt ever in a city of superlatives.

4. Robbins Cahill, *Oral History Project*, pp. 1,353, 1,354.

5. Gabe Vogliotti, Unpublished manuscript, p.1-19; from the personal collection of Bill Thompson.

6. *Las Vegas Review-Journal*, Sunday, January 16, 1966, pp. 1, 2.

7. *Las Vegas Sun*, January 16, 1966, p. 9.

8. "The Program in Perspective," *A Report to the Academic Vice-President from the College of Hotel Administration*, Spring, 1975, p. 1.

9. Letter from Robbins Cahill, executive office of the Nevada Resort Association to the NRA membership, June 6, 1972.

10. Vogliotti, Unpublished manuscript, p. 2-1.

11. Cahill, *Oral History Project*, pp. 1,353, 1,354.

PART 2

The Early Years

C H A P T E R   3

Start-Up

With money-raising concerns behind it, the university prepared to implement the two directives ordered by the joint professional/academic committee: Retain Meek and find a program head. Actually, the two charges were intertwined because Meek knew more hotel faculty members than anyone else in the United States. He was the first dean of Cornell's School of Hotel Administration. Now, as its emeritus dean, Meek was still housed on that New York State campus, which was the leading source of new faculty members.

> I was only the third student to pursue a doctoral degree at Cornell's School of Hotel Administration [late 1950s]. I recall having coffee with the other two men at the height of the Cold War. One of them joked that our specie would be eradicated if the Russians dropped a bomb at that moment. JERRY VALLEN

Even more important to the search, Meek was by then the part-time executive director of an association of hotel and food faculty, known as CHRIE, The Council on Hotel, Restaurant and Institutional Education. ("International" was added later.) Meek threw a wide academic net and his selection as consultant, which resulted either from Dick Strahlem's visit to Cornell or Gabe Vogliotti's access to special talent, was an excellent choice.

The new committee intended to put the program's director on staff immediately so that classes could begin as soon as the fall of 1966. Finding the right person by that date, which was still about 8 months away—Moyer appointed the committee in the first week of February, 1966—seemed an attainable goal.

> Moyer said that we didn't know what we were talking about, we've got to get the right person.
>
> I was looking for a man with his feet on the ground, a practical man who could select a vision and develop it. I wanted a pragmatic man who could work with a dream, but was not a dreamer. Don also wanted someone with vision. Don operated on charm and energy; I operated on theatrics and energy. Our man had to have energy, not low-keyed like Strahlem or Johnson, putting their walking handicaps aside. We wanted movers and shakers because we had a lot of battles to win, a war to fight.   JERRY CRAWFORD, DEAN OF FACULTY

THE SEARCHES

Certainly, prior to Strahlem's exploratory trip and his subsequent report on the shortage of faculty in October, 1966 (see Exhibit 3-1), it was reasonable for both the faculty and the administration to believe there would be no problem filling the post of director. After all, the campus—new as it was—had already attracted some very capable people in other disciplines.

Search for the Director

> We set up enrollment for February of '66. We had an official school with students beginning to enroll.
>
> So I said to Dick Strahlem, We have to have teachers, instructors, a director, whatever. No problem, he said. It's very easy; we'll put an ad in a teacher's journal. They all read the same paper and they'll respond.   LEO LEWIS, BINION'S FINANCIAL OFFICER AND PART-TIME FACULTY MEMBER

Strahlem's reference to the *Chronicle of Higher Education* explains the lack of applicants. The *Chronicle* was not widely read by hotel faculty. In truth, there weren't many hotel faculty members to read it. Furthermore, Las Vegas' reputation was a major stumbling block, which Cahill laments in his oral history:

> "Time after time we would get: 'I'll have to go back and think this over.'"[1]

Invariably when the spouse was consulted, the answer was "no." Similar responses were to come from faculty applicants over the next 25 years. Cahill suggested :

> "It should be set up as a school to train hotel executives, don't put it [gaming] into any of the required curriculum."[2]

> We didn't have many applicants because it was too rare an animal and was not tested. Not only a new university, but a new city and a new program. Cornell and Michigan State thought we were a little presumptuous.   CRAWFORD

Strahlem Report on Trip to Denver, Michigan State and Oklahoma State

At Denver U. (hotel enrollment: approximately 230) I talked with Director Ralph Wilson and with 2 of their 2½ faculty members in the hotel school and I examined their library and foods lab as well as other physical facilities.

Only Wilson has a doctorate in their hotel school (which is attached to the College of Business Administration, although housed in a separate building). Maintaining a faculty, or even people with only a Master's degree, is a major problem at Denver's school, largely solved by hiring their own graduates after they have obtained a Master's degree elsewhere.

Denver has its own hotel administration library housed in a single basement room of their ancient building. Books and periodicals specifically related to the hospitality industry might fill one wall of shelves; the remainder of the library consists of publications in Business Administration or Home Economics.

Denver's food lab is a stainless steel kitchen about 20' × 20', for which the equipment was largely donated by various manufacturers. It sparkles in contrast to the generally shabby condition of the school's remaining facilities; and I gained the impression that it was for display more than for use.

Denver has no program for nor requirement that its students acquire practical work experience although some do get jobs at the Brown-Palace and other Denver hotels and in on-campus housing, the director of which is a part-time instructor (in foods courses).

In my opinion, when we get our full four-year program launched, we shall then have a better hotel school than has Denver.

At Michigan State (hotel enrollment approximately 480) I talked to Dr. Henry Barbour, Director, (Cornell graduate) and one faculty member (undergraduate work in Agricultural Engineering) of the School of Hotel Administration, as well as to Mrs. Helen Weiss, Director, Operational Training Division of the Educational Institute of the American Hotel and Motel Association.

The hotel school is attached to and housed in the College of Business Administration, while the Educational Institute is housed in the Kellogg Center for Continuing Education—a kind of special Union Building for the University's extension division, with hotel rooms and various eating facilities included.

Director Barbour and I discussed the general shortage of publications and faculty in the hotel field, finding no good explanation for the former and concluding that teachers were in short supply because by the time they acquired the practical experience desirable for teaching they were too well paid to return to the campus.

Asked why there appears to be a considerable emphasis upon food courses in hotel curricula, Doctor Barbour thought it is probable because more has been written in that area. He said, however, that he is not convinced that actual practice (he termed it "finger dexterity") in food preparation is essential in a hotel administration program, pointing out that in Europe such training is left entirely to trade or vocational schools. He also volunteered that when he arrived at Michigan State he abolished the chemistry requirement then in effect.

M.S.U. supplied me with bibliography, course descriptions, lists of required texts, various course outlines and a multi-page description of their "professional experience" program, which should be of great value to us. The latter program provides for 800 hours of practical work experience (for no credit) which each hotel student must acquire before enrolling for the final quarter of his senior year. Some may acquire that experience at the Kellogg Center, which is operated by the hotel administration students.

I discussed with Mrs. Weiss the contents of the various Educational Institute courses (including a couple of new ones) and concluded that we can probably build several of our courses around Institute materials, although they are used for the most part, at the college level, by junior colleges. She supplied me with outlines of all the Institute courses.

At Oklahoma State I found that Director John McAllister and his one-woman faculty (both M.S.) were vacationing; but from the secretary, I learned that:

1. OSU is attached to Home Economics and is housed within.
2. Its Hotel Administration program is somewhat more modest than that which we propose.
3. The school's "library" fills two bookcases in the Director's office plus numerous periodicals spread about tables in an adjoining room.
4. Students' "practical" experience is obtained in Home Economics labs and in campus facilities.

CONCLUSIONS

On the basis of my trip (which largely confirmed impressions gained from prior study and observations) I would conclude:

1. That text materials and library backup are amazingly scarce. We shall be obliged to employ substantial amounts of materials from periodicals in many of our courses.
   a. Practically astonishing is the fact that, after 44 years of operation, practically no writing has emerged from Cornell (which prompts me to suspect that Michigan State is the leading school in hotel administration).
2. That faculty members are similarly scarce and, as a result, over-priced. Probably a majority have Home Economics backgrounds (perhaps the real reason for a preponderance of foods courses)—not necessarily the best foundation for teaching in hotel administration. It appears that we might well consider some plan for affording some of our Business Administration teachers some practical work experience and converting them into Hotel Administration teachers. Certainly it is going to [be] unrealistic to attempt to secure teachers with doctorates for the hotel program—probably for several years to come.
3. That our approach (the "European plan") in emphasizing administration, with minimal provision for skilled courses, is the modern approach—one which, in my opinion, can vault NSU hotel administration program into the top three in the nation in four years, if all concerned are devoted to achieving that goal.

RECOMMENDATIONS DERIVING FROM CAMPUS VISITATIONS

1. That we adopt Michigan State's 800-hour practical experience program (description herewith) or some refinement thereof.
2. That we hire a foods teacher as early as possible, followed by other H.A. graduates who might teach a combination of subjects in areas other than foods. Some courses will doubtless have to be taught by part-time people.
3. That we publish by mid-December, a brochure (in color) containing "sales" material, a four-year curriculum, and pictures of the campus and of the 10 hotels that were, in affect, founders of NSU's administrative program. Said brochure to be useful in advertising the program and in attracting both students and faculty.
   a. Also needed: pictures of the same hotels for hanging in the Hotel Administration

office (both in recognizing the hotel's contributions to the program and to glamorize it for the students).

4. That we contact local people in the industry to talk about the area to be covered in meetings 10 to 20 in the HA 101 Course Outline (herewith). All suggestions in this regard will be gratefully received by the Acting Director.

5. That any of the sponsoring hotels that may see it as a possible employee-moral booster adopt a policy (publicized) of paying all or part of the tuition for employees who enroll in H.A. courses and receive satisfactory grades. (Such a policy is already pursued by E.G.&G., Pan-Am, Titanium, and other local enterprises.)

6. That we accept the NCR 2000 offered by Mr. Goodman and consider acquiring some other sophisticated accounting machine (NCR or other) for use in the Front Office Operations, Hotel Accounting and Hotel Accounting Machines course

EXHIBIT 3-1. Strahlem's report on his information-seeking trips reflects sharp insight into the discipline. The only minor error is his acceptance of Henry Barbour's inference that Henry held a terminal degree.

Despite the lack of applicants, several very good resumes were received. First among them was that of Herbert Witzky from New Jersey. The authors knew Herb well because they were living in the East at that time. Witzky, one of the industry's early authors, was writing about hotel management at a time when most other texts were about foodservice. Management not food was to be the focus of the Nevada program. Herb Witzky looked good! Unfortunately, he had just begun the healing process from a terrible, terrible auto accident that left him in a full-body brace and in serious pain. The authors knew that; perhaps those in Las Vegas did not.

Witzky furnished detailed course outlines and a personal biography. His first interview took place on May 24, 1966. That was more than three months before the new fall term. Tight, but there was just enough time to get a program director seated. Nevertheless, a second interview, and what was likely to be the hiring interview, was not scheduled until September 17, 1966. Witzky never came. Just days before his scheduled arrival, he declined the second interview in a letter to the committee citing personal reasons, including the health of both his and his wife's parents, "even though we have already purchased and picked up our tickets."

The search committee was also fortunate to have initial interest from Kemper Merriam, who had a fine reputation at the University of Hawaii. No archival details are available except a strongly worded letter (April 5, 1966) from him to the committee. He bowed out of consideration because, "I did not take the time and energy to venture to Las Vegas to put on a 'hard sell'—I expected to receive one!"

In April of 1966, we had communication with Kemper Merriam. They were out trying to find someone to run the thing. He was in Hawaii and wasn't about to come back to the desert.   ROBERT SMITH, DEAN OF SCIENCE, MATHEMATICS AND ENGINEERING

Another well known applicant may have been Michigan State's Ed Kazarian. The only record of his application is a receipt for reimbursement of expenses at the Desert Inn. He probably came for an interview. Frank Borsenik was another applicant from Michigan State. At that time, Michigan State's hotel program was entering a difficult stage of leadership that lasted for more than a decade.

> Don Greenaway was in charge of the [Michigan] program, but it was reorganized and Don left. [Then] the university split off pieces of the program and Earl Thompson took over. He left, too, after years of turmoil. There was no one for a while then Henry Barbour came. I took over briefly when Henry left. [Neither Greenaway nor Barbour had terminal degrees and undoubtedly that caused some of the turmoil for Michigan State, a long established program.]
> FRANK BORSENIK, HOTEL FACULTY MEMBER

UNLV benefitted immensely from Michigan's problems. Several of its top faculty eventually transferred to Nevada. Dick Acosta and Jim Abbey (both Michigan grad students) were the first to come. Lendal Kotschevar, who had retired, came several times as a visiting professor. Don Greenaway considered a position. Borsenik was fifth in the sequence, moving some half-dozen years after coming for an interview and a look-about and after consulting with Kotschevar, who had been on Borsenik's doctoral committee. He was followed by Michigan State faculty members John Stefanelli and Donald Bell. Each came in a staggered pattern as UNLV's program matured. Borsenik's knowledge of the UNLV program predated all the others including even Vallen's because Dick Strahlem visited with him at East Lansing during Dick's 1966 tour of hotel programs.

> I remember that Strahlem gave me a gold-plated lighter from the Sands. We got along quite well, which was very unusual. We talked about the direction the university might go. Later, he wrote and asked me if I wanted to be a candidate. I had just witnessed three program heads go through divorces, and I asked myself whether this was a pattern.   BORSENIK

In a memo dated September 26, 1966, Jerry Crawford suggested that Rex Johnson obtain Borsenik's personal papers.

"Candidate Dr. Frank D. Borsenik of the Michigan State University Hotel School appears to be an excellent man indeed. I suggest that we obtain a complete set of recommendations and consider an interview as soon as possible."[3]

Borsenik's and Kazarian's papers, and even Witzky's second interview, were dated during the fall of 1966. So the window of opportunity had been lost. The 1966 fall term was underway, and there were no candidates on the horizon. A whole new batch had to be solicited, Jerry Vallen among them.

> At the spring, 1966 Chicago Restaurant Show, Meek told me about the opening in Las Vegas. At that time, I was chairman of a junior-college program in upstate New York and was just

beginning to write my doctoral dissertation at Cornell, where Meek was housed after his retirement as dean. I had just returned to work after taking off one and one-half years for residence on the Cornell campus. My priorities precluded investigating anything further despite Meek's great enthusiasm. Indeed, Meek was more than exuberant, he was proselytizing. JERRY VALLEN

Jerry brought a group of students to the November, 1966 New York Hotel Show [held about six months after the Chicago show]. I came along each year as a chaperone. The Show falls on our anniversary date, so that was the second reason. We spoke to Meek and he asked why Jerry hadn't acted on the Las Vegas opening. He stressed the missed opportunity. It was the first I'd heard about it.   FLOSSIE VALLEN

On Meek's urging, I submitted paperwork to Las Vegas. At the 1966 annual CHRIE meeting [Christmas time in those years], I met in Chicago with Crawford and Strahlem, representing the search committee. Strahlem was selling hard, boasting about his sun tan and contrasting it with the cold Christmas weather in Chicago and Canton, New York, our current residence. (I later learned that he used a sunlamp!) By Spring of 1967, I had taken the offer and was waiting to report to Las Vegas during the approaching summer.   JERRY VALLEN

Meek met us at the spring 1967 Chicago Restaurant Show, where we were sporting the NSU identification badges. He looked askance! Don't tell me you've taken that job, he exploded. How can you raise children there? He knew we had four.   FLOSSIE VALLEN

The Hiring

For his first interview, at the CHRIE meeting in Chicago (December, 1966), Vallen met with Strahlem and Crawford. Although Vallen expressed strong interest in the post, he also stipulated his desire to hire his own faculty.

The meeting in Chicago was a very good session. I remember calling back and being presumptuous enough to tell Don [Moyer], we've got the man.   CRAWFORD

A few weeks later (January 5, 1967), Dick Strahlem penned a very pessimistic memorandum to Dean Crawford and the search committee (see Exhibit 3.2). The hiring delay that Strahlem deplored in the memo came from Vallen's expressed preference for doing his own hiring and for waiting until the turn of the academic year.

In February, 1967, the candidate and his spouse traveled to Las Vegas, the first either one had been beyond the center of the country. They left home in a ranging snow storm for the drive to the nearest airport in Watertown, New York, about 70 miles south. Las Vegas was a startling contrast to the below-zero temperature of northern New York. Tulips were in bloom, the sky was blue and the temperature was in the high 60s. More important than the view of the garden was the view of the future.

As arranged beforehand, a university auto was left for us by the curb at the airport. We retrieved the car keys from the airline clerk. I know that sounds unimaginable today. But Rex

In light of the apparent decision to defer hiring H.A. teachers until a new H.A. director is found, I feel obliged to record here my observations of the availability of such teachers.

[He then enumerates his recruiting efforts including his program appearance at the recently held CHRIE meeting in Chicago.]

The yield from all of that publicity has been 13 applicants, which includes no one with a doctorate:

With Master's Degree	6
With Master's Degree pending, 1967	1
With Bachelor's Degree	3
With Bachelor's Degree pending, 1967	1
With no degree	2
	13

Teaching experience, 4-year school	4
Graduate assistant, 4-year school	1
Teaching experience, 2-year school	4
Other teaching experience	1
No teaching experience	3
	13

The foregoing is a rather sorry picture and may suggest why I recommended hiring Robert B. Harris whom we just turned down.

From my observations and discussions at Chicago it is apparent that (1) most teachers are foods—rather than management oriented (the convention program was similarly oriented) and (2) they do not think in terms of doctorates (the Master's Degree doesn't even interest them, except as a "union card").

[The memorandum then lists and describes four of the 13 candidates as possible faculty hires. Vallen is not among them.]

There is no assurance, of course, that any of the applicants will accept an offer; and *I believe that we are in very real danger of having no faculty for September.* We could get through another year without a director but failure to hire teachers would, it seems to me, be a disaster to our fledgling program.

EXHIBIT 3-2. Undated memorandum (Summer, 1966) from Richard Strahlem to the Search Committee regarding faculty hiring issues.

Johnson and his wife, Edith, were also there to greet us. After following their car around, we parked our car in the public school across Tropicana from the campus [later, the temporary home of the law school] and joined them for a tour of the city.   JERRY VALLEN

The Interview. The Vallens were housed at the Tropicana Hotel, which was owned by the Houssels family. At that time, J. K. (Ike) Houssels, Jr. was president of the Nevada Resort Association.

Our baggage was lost. All we had was rumpled, winter clothing. During the night we called the airport several times. No luck. Bleary eyed, we tripped over our suitcase in the lobby on the way to breakfast the next morning. We have been searching for this! we told the captain. His reply, We never awaken anyone in Las Vegas before 10:00 a.m. Thus, our introduction to Vegas.   FLOSSIE VALLEN

During the next few days, the couple was busy exploring the city and meeting the academic and professional communities. Flossie Vallen concentrated on schools and housing. Jerry Vallen made the interview rounds. One of the interviews was held with the NRA board.

My recollection is that the [NRA] meeting was engineered by Moyer.

The resort Association was critical. We could have done it if they didn't like Vallen, but it would have been difficult.   CRAWFORD

The professional community had some say [about naming the director]; we were the ones coming up with the money.   PHIL ARCE, SAHARA HOTEL MANAGER

"The advisory committee met a number of times to interview applicants for the Director's position and finally agreed to the selection of the present director, Dr. Jerome Vallen." [Vogliotti's letter to Al Freeman.[4]]

All over the country, educators were complaining about the difficulty of getting the ear of industry people. And here I was sitting in just such a meeting. It seemed as if the whole city was behind it. When I threw out what was to me a brazen idea, internships in their hotels, it was greeted with enthusiasm!   JERRY VALLEN

Oh yes, that's [internships] exactly what we wanted!   J. KELL HOUSSELS, JR., HOTELIER AND ELECTED PRESIDENT OF THE NEVADA RESORT ASSOCIATION

We looked at other schools and asked what do they not have that we do? Hotels sitting in a row. The first thing I remember being discussed was the apprenticeship program. [Strahlem's idea, see Exhibit 3-1.]   CRAWFORD

That meeting settled two issues. One, I would take the job if offered; two, Strahlem was not my friend. I had just published my first book, *The Art and Science of Innkeeping*. Throughout the session Strahlem bemoaned the lack of texts in the field and belittled my work as less than senior-college level although he knew it had been written for use by the AH&MA's Educational Institute as a correspondence course. Dick had just been to Michigan State where the EI was housed, saw the courses and even recommended adopting them at NSU [see Exhibit 3-1, paragraph 12] even though they weren't senior-college level. Part of the issue could have been his own text proposal, which he was trying to get subsidized using the NRA money.   JERRY VALLEN

A visit to Las Vegas would have been incomplete without a run at the slots. After we returned from a night out with the Johnsons, we hit a small jackpot. What to do with all the nickels? I filled my long white evening gloves—that was the dress in those days—and we used the coins to tip the chambermaid and the waitress. Who knew about converting coins to bills?   FLOSSIE VALLEN

Obviously, everyone needed to get to know each other because it was going to be a very close relationship. Several members of the committee hosted the applicant and his wife each night, Mr. and Mrs. (Ruth) Vogliotti among them.

I am very allergic to dogs. The Vogliottis picked us up in their car. Immediately, I began to sneeze and cough. I didn't realize the cause until we arrived at their home for a pre-dinner drink. They had two huge dogs which they transported in the back seat of the car. It was agony until we arrived for dinner. Allergies cleared up and I was fine until the ride back to the hotel. Not an auspicious beginning. Gabe kept saying what's wrong with you? What's wrong with you? and looking at me strangely! Persons who love dogs like he did don't understand, so I said nothing.   JERRY VALLEN

[That's a story I hadn't heard], but Vogliotti wasn't making the decision.   DONALD MOYER, PRESIDENT, NEVADA SOUTHERN UNIVERSITY

"Three years after [Vogliotti became director of the NRA], the Association would get the idea to fund a hotel school with the University of Nevada. . . . We set it up, voted $300,000 to get it started, and then began the search for a director. . . . We offered the job to six different academes (none of any great academic standing) and were snubbed by five. We saw the disdain of men who refused to touch anything funded by gangsters. One dean told us frankly that it would take big, big money to persuade any scholar to come here and become the laughing stock of American universities. The man who finally took the job was a youngster, so new to scholarship that he had little stature to lose." [Vogliotti.[5]]

The six academes referred to by Vogliotti must have been Frank Borsenik; Ed Kazarian; Kemper Merriman; Jerry Vallen; Herb Witzky and—just a wild, wild guess—Howard Meek! who was but recently retired from Cornell.

I made a recommendation to Strahlem: Cornell is the oldest program, why don't you consider someone from Cornell. He nodded and said that sounded pretty good.   BORSENIK

What Role Was Food to Play? The new director was not to be a shoo-in, not by any means. The business faculty were very concerned about what they viewed to be his tilt toward foods. Moreover, there was a great deal of ambivalence about the whole topic of food in a college of business. A *Business Week* article, dated February 27, 1965, which was found in Witzky's file, must have influenced the NSU search committee. In reporting Witzky's 1964 appointment to head New York University's restaurant program, the story highlighted three items. There were no foods labs; internships were planned; and industry demand for graduates was heavy.

Despite being down on foods, Strahlem's memo of January 5, 1967 recommended two food faculty among his list of four possible hires. Robert Smith believes Strahlem was chair of the search committee. But a copy of Crawford's memo regarding Borsenik's tentative interest was sent to Smith, not Strahlem, which supports Vallen's belief that Smith was the chair. Moreover, in a letter dated October 10, 1967 (after the director was hired), Chancellor Moyer thanks Dr. Smith "for outstanding assistance to this program in the past."

There was back and forth between the business school and the rest of the campus about whether there should be a hotel program and especially whether it should have a food emphasis and whether Vallen should be hired.

I had a peculiar perspective on the whole issue because my brother-in-law was the protegee of Louis Szathmary [a famous, but mercurial restauranteur, who monitored education from his Chicago restaurant, *The Bakery*. Much later, Louie joined the UNLV faculty part time].   ROBERT SMITH, DEAN OF SCIENCE, MATHEMATICS AND ENGINEERING

There were conversations and faculty meetings about whether or not hotel should be part of business. It was decided with the heavy emphasis on food, it would be better to have hotel as a separate entity. That was all tied to accreditation [which took another 25 years to happen]. REUBEN NEUMANN, BUSINESS FACULTY MEMBER

I know there was some discussions whether hotel should be part of business. But the Resort Association was going to fund the school and whatever the university wanted would have to be done through the Association.   ARCE

We led the way on campus organization. Not many of them [hoteliers] would have understood the difference between a college and a school, but I think we explained it as part of the package.   CRAWFORD

Vallen had entered Cornell from the family's restaurant business. However, since his undergraduate years, he had worked almost exclusively in hotels: in Massachusetts as a bellman; in New Jersey as a night manager/auditor; in Pennsylvania as a desk clerk and a bar manager; in Florida as an assistant manager; in New Hampshire as a hotel accountant and assistant manager; and in New York as a general manager. All of which were itemized on the resume. His post-graduation food experience had been limited to running the Cornell alumni facility, *The Big Red Barn,* part time during his doctoral residency. Food wasn't his thing. Yet one of the search committee members must have felt otherwise, writing:

His [Vallen's] background is vocational and sub-college (Cornell will not accept his school's [Ag and Tech Junior College as part of the State University of New York] credits) and he is mentally foods-oriented. . . . In short, he talks management, but thinks foods.   UNKNOWN SEARCH COMMITTEE MEMBER

There were two issues raised about Vallen. He was biased for foods—you know, can a theater man be a provost, and he lacked the terminal degree [Vallen was ABD, all but dissertation]. In those days, this place was built by people with masters and half doctorates. CRAWFORD

My perceived bias toward foods is curious. It was only with the greatest pressure from the faculty that I agreed to include a food lab when we planned the new building a decade later. A food facility was not my first choice.   JERRY VALLEN

Vallen's advise has come back to me many times. Be careful of how deeply involved educational programs go into restaurants and kitchens.   PAT MOREO, '69 STUDENT AND HOTEL FACULTY MEMBER

I wasn't in the food area much, but I remember Jerry dragging his feet about [building] the kitchen. He never wanted to have it.   JIM ABBEY, HOTEL FACULTY MEMBER

Can't have a world-class hotel without a world-class kitchen. From the beginning that was both clear and a concern with us. That's why Smith was crucial, his chemistry background keeps coming to mind.   CRAWFORD

I recall a lot of talk about a food lab, but nothing specific. I know it was a big issue. We talked about it in the sciences. Whether there would be a scientific component that might develop [within the hotel program]. And that's where some of the traditional academic fear [that hotel would teach science] was generated. Foods labs were another issue as well. Facilities were a huge issue in the '60s because we didn't want to be kept down by the northern legislators. We didn't want food facilities to replace other building priorities.   SMITH

The food/no food debate was especially curious in light of Acting Director Strahlem's recommendation that the first hire be a foods faculty member (see Exhibit 3-1, Recommendation Number 2). The issue was, of course, a reflection of one's orientation. Some ten years later, in a December 16, 1976 letter, the restaurant chain Village Inn Pancakes withdrew from recruiting because the college "lacked food courses," which it didn't! Food instruction in a food lab was apparently not a negative issue for Don Moyer. During Vallen's first week on campus, Moyer invited him to tour the new Student Union Building. On the second floor in a still unfinished area behind the ballroom, he pointed out his planned location for the kitchen, with assurances that he would raise the money to equip it. That was not to be because Moyer was gone within the year. After he left, the building was named the Moyer Student Union.

It was during this tour that Don Moyer told me to plan for 1,000 students. I looked at him as if he were mad! At the time, we had a handful. [Enrollment eventually exceeded 2,000.]
JERRY VALLEN

The Search Culminates.   There's an apocryphal tale about how Mother Nature intervened on behalf of Jerry Vallen.

I had a terrible habit of putting things on the roof of our VW Beetle. Anytime I did that, I was bound to drive out from under it. One windy night I carried out a large file of dossiers, which I tossed on the top of the car and ran back to the office for something I had forgotten. I was about half way home when I realized what I had done. I returned and started searching up and down Harmon Avenue. Vallen's file was found with tire tracks all over it.
SMITH

Jerry Vallen: I had always believed that you said mine was the only paper retrieved and that's how I got the job.
Smith: Well it's a good story, but I don't think any of the elements are true.
Crawford: I don't believe it, but it is a delightful story.

Several days after the campus visit, Jerry Crawford telephoned Jerry Vallen in New York to offer the job extending a fair amount of time to consider the offer. No need, positive professional and personal decisions had been made beforehand in case there was an offer.

We lived in a very small town, which was wonderful when the family was young. We knew we had to move on because other families had seen their children leave the town and not return. There were no opportunities for young people in a small, agricultural town. Our oldest was entering junior high school.   FLOSSIE VALLEN

The post was accepted immediately with the several conditions that had been discussed during the interviews.

Conditions are the sort of things that focus the issue.   SMITH

There were to be no faculty hires unless made by Vallen.

That had a mixed review. Moyer and I agreed that if we were in his shoes, we wouldn't have it any other way, so everyone backed off.   CRAWFORD

Further, the position as director of the hotel program was to report to the provost even though hotel was a program within business. Moving expenses were to supplement the $17,000 per year salary, which was a $4,000 (30%) increase over the $13,100 Vallen was earning in New York. Apparently, the search committee found the conditions acceptable.

Knowing the way Don Moyer and Jerry Crawford worked I would be surprised if the conditions ever came back to the [search] committee. Usually things were brought to the faculty senate after the fact.
We didn't do things then the way we do now. If you spotted a good candidate, go out and hire him.   SMITH

At their home in upper New York State, the Vallens received a gracious welcoming letter dated April 5, 1967 from Charles Armstrong, president of the University of Nevada System. The search for the director was concluded. Now the program needed two faculty members.

The Faculty Search
From his base in Canton, New York, Vallen began his search in March of 1967 for two new faculty members. East Coast schools (in Massachusetts, New York, New

Hampshire, New Jersey and Pennsylvania) were the heart of hotel education in those days. So that's where the search began. Ads in the CHRIE publication drew the most response, but the new director also had the grapevine to help. The original applicant file from Nevada—the list from which Strahlem had picked his nominees—contained some good candidates as well. They were added to the pool.

Although the original planners had budgeted for psychology and data processing posts (see Exhibit 2-2) the new director felt otherwise. His search followed Strahlem's first recommendation, a foods position, which probably caused some heavy sighing in Nevada, and then one position in rooms management. One was back of the house and one was front of the house.

Strahlem's memo of January 5 listed seven food persons among the 13 applicants, but only half had master's degrees. One of whom Vallen knew well and rejected. A few additional leads, most without graduate degrees, also trickled in. George Bussell, who was on Strahlem's list as one of his 4 possible hires, proved to be the most aggressive. He was teaching at the University of New Hampshire and volunteered to drive from Durham, New Hampshire to Canton, New York. On a Spring day in 1967 the two sat and talked about what could be done. Without the facilities of the NSU campus, the traditional hospitality offered to interviewees was unavailable. It didn't matter, Bussell really wanted the job! His intense interest was a major attribute since the tenure of the program was a serious unknown. It was that uncertainty, the negative reputation of the destination and the distant western location that had dissuaded other faculty applicants and probably accounted for the difficulty of the director's search.

> "Because of early difficulties in reaching agreement on a director, the school was launched by an interim director, Professor Richard Strahlem." [Vogliotti's letter to Al Freeman.[6]]

The Bussell deal was closed a few weeks later with the formal contract coming from Las Vegas. The first hire was on board and due to report on August 1, 1967.

The search for the second faculty position was equally comfortable. This time the selection was not from the original list but from the recruiting that the new director had developed. After some correspondence and telephone calls, the focus was on Boyce W. Phillips. Phillips, like Vallen, was on one of the junior college campuses of the State University of New York (SUNY). Vallen was at SUNY Canton and Phillips at SUNY Morrisville. Canton was north of Syracuse, New York by 125 miles and Morrisville was 50 miles east. To avoid the city traffic of a hotel meeting the two agreed to meet at the Syracuse Airport. They talked there for several hours during which time a typical spring snow storm of the "North Country" raged outside. That day, Mother Nature contributed to Phillips' resolve to go west. Like the Bussell interview, the conditions were sparse—there was no frequent-flier lounge at the Syracuse Airport in those days—so there was no cost to NSU for either interview.

We were ready for new experiences. I was afraid that I would never get further west of the Mississippi, and I was just ready to go to something new. [Boyce had traveled, he served in the Pacific in World War II.]   SARI PHILLIPS AIZLEY, SPOUSE OF B. W. PHILLIPS

As was arranged with Bussell, Phillips also reported on August 1, 1967. Putting the two on payroll one month early was possible because of the Resort Association's budget. It helped assure a smooth beginning with the regular faculty. The director was in place a month earlier, on July 1, 1967.

Friends and relatives of all three candidates were disbelieving.

All I heard about was the sin. Everyone said, what are you going to do there; there's only gambling and prostitution.

I know everyone got the endless, But nobody lives there. Are you going to live in a hotel-casino?   PHILLIPS AIZLEY

I transferred to UNLV in 1978 from a small Catholic college in the Midwest. My friends said I was going from church city to sin city.   ANN RITTAL, '81 STUDENT

People called on the telephone and asked if the streets were paved and if there were hitching posts for the horses.   PHIL ARCE, SAHARA HOTEL MANAGER

Jerry's boss in New York said it's only a dirt road leading to Los Angeles. And, of course, Meek couldn't believe we were going to raise children there.   FLOSSIE VALLEN

My father said it was better to make a big splash in a small pond than a small splash in a big pond.   JERRY VALLEN

The negative connotation of Las Vegas was obvious to people in the East. You had to justify your intelligence for coming. But as you saw the people and the potential, the future looked great. No question about that. Where else was there such a laboratory facility nearby?   DICK BASILE, HOTEL FACULTY MEMBER

Despite the negative slings, the three families proceeded west by automobile.

Having endured 14 years of New York snow, cold and rain from October to May, I hoped to allay the children's uncertainty about moving by stressing the weather in Las Vegas, where it never rained. We drove into town in one of those torrential downpours that make up our summer monsoon season.   JERRY VALLEN

Housing was everyone's first priority. The university very generously had brought the new candidate and his wife back several months earlier for a second familiarization trip. Two events highlighted that visit. The Moyers gave a wonderful reception for the couple in their home.

I remember receptions at Moyer's home very vividly. I think there was a lot that went on personally between Moyer and people because they did a lot of entertaining at their home. SMITH

and the Resort Association gave a welcoming luncheon for them at the Dunes Country Club.

Bill Campbell formed the committee that arranged the luncheon at the Dunes Country Club. ARCE

We were late for the Dunes luncheon because we were house shopping and overshot the Dunes freeway exit. I thought we were headed to Los Angeles. FLOSSIE VALLEN

I gave an introductory talk at the Dunes luncheon outlining what I saw as the issues facing the school. Unknown to me, because I have only recently seen all the planning materials, my ideas and those of UNLV and the NRA were the same. The speech was well received, except for one item. Afterwards, someone whispered to me, it's Ne-vad-da not Ne-vaw-da. Foiled again by the eastern accent. JERRY VALLEN

I probably said something about Ne-vad-da and Ne-vaw-da so you wouldn't embarrass yourself, and then I thought well he sure is going to hear from others to set him straight. JOE DIGLES, NEVADA RESORT ASSOCIATION

Boyce had gone out to see what Las Vegas was all about. He called and said that I was going to hate the place. It's 150° in the shade and every house is surrounded by a concrete wall that looks like a prison. So I said, Ok when do we leave.

It was actually 126° the day we arrived in a car that was not air conditioned! The children were hot and ill. To make matters worse, the motel's air conditioning stopped working that night. We filled the tub with ice water and soaked in it and then lay on the bed until the wet evaporated.

And I had thought if we moved to Las Vegas, we would have a big property with horses. I do have a nice porcelain horse. PHILLIPS AIZLEY

The success of the undertaking was very uncertain so we decided to rent rather than to buy. Problem was, no landlord wanted four children! We gave $400 to a friend of a friend of a friend to find us accommodations. She was a fat, homely woman. It was a scam. We didn't get our money back until Jerry said she was an ugly person, meaning her demeanor. She took it to mean her physique. Gave us the money and threw us out. FLOSSIE VALLEN

The timing was fortunate because home real estate was in a slump. Layoffs at the Test Site had emptied the town. The Vallens bought in an area where the bank, Frontier Fidelity, was selling repossessed houses from an office on the street. No mortgage payments for the first several months. Still, it was a bit frightening to sell a $22,500 house in upper New York State and to pay $32,500 six months later. Francisco Park, east of Eastern Avenue between Desert Inn Road and Sahara Avenue, was the in-place for new arrivals. Later, Charlie Levinson and his family settled there.

> One realtor persisted in showing us 'the best house in town' because it was across the street from the home of Betty Grable, the actress. As it was, we bought across from one of the Ink Spots and down the street from the boxer, Sonny Liston. Several hotels maintained houses for their stars on Ottawa Drive behind the Boulevard Mall. Remember, it was small town then.   FLOSSIE VALLEN

> About 5,000 people had left town and the relatively new houses in Parkdale had been renovated by Frontier Fidelity. The bank gave us a six month rental and then the option to buy. We didn't like the area so we moved even though the price was only $18,500 for a three bedroom, two bath home.   PHILLIPS AIZLEY

> We bought our house in 1968, and it didn't cost much. Back then things weren't too good in this town.   FRANK WATTS, RIVIERA FINANCIAL OFFICER

> We had been in town but a short time when my parents visited from the East. The entire east frontage on Maryland Parkway south of Harmon was up for sale. My dad wanted to put up the down payment and leave me to carry the loan. What would we want with that desert I asked, and dissuaded him from buying it.   JERRY VALLEN

You could walk into the bank, say First Western on Sahara, and they would walk you into the closet. Here are the house keys, take your pick.   ARCE

> Indeed, that happened to me. Bill Capri, the owner of the Lucerne Motel where we stayed upon arrival, took me to lunch at a small deli hidden in a drug store in the Commercial Mall. Then we walked to the bank next door and he introduced me to the person selling houses. Take your pick.   JERRY VALLEN

MEANWHILE, BACK ON THE CAMPUS

The Immediate Need

The delay in filling the director's job and the decision to postpone faculty hires caused some consternation with those line managers who "had to meet the payroll." Two questions hung in the air: Who was going to teach? And to whom were they going to teach?

> Jack Binion said do anything you have to do to help. So I started taking telephone calls at the Horseshoe. Every call was almost identical. You're starting a new school? Yes we are. Do you have extensive library facilities? Well, not at the moment, but we are going to have them. Do you have graduate programs? Well, not at the moment, but we are going to have them. Who is starting the school? The Nevada Resort Association. Is that casinos? Well, it is a hotel organization and some of the hotels have casinos. And then they asked: What's Binion's Horseshoe? Is that a casino? Well we have a casino in the hotel! Some student even sent letters and resumes and then enrolled.   LEWIS

There was a definite effort to recruit students from within the campus, the community and from outside.   ARCE

The new director was also concerned about students, but his concern came a year later. He used the six months between the job offer (February, 1967) and the reporting date (July, 1967) to recruit from his own and other junior colleges. None of the senior college programs such as those at Cornell, Penn State, Michigan State, Massachusetts or Washington State had the space or inclination to accept junior-college transfers. Vallen knew this from his own experience as a junior-college advisor. That was the market to be targeted!

I remember that in those days there were not many four-year programs that would take transfer students. If they did, you would lose the credit.   MOREO

Finding faculty for the first year was even more pressing than finding students. The program's launch date, the fall term 1966—a year before Moreo's class came— was fast approaching. The new director had not yet been chosen so responsibility was still with Johnson and Strahlem. Johnson had the responsibility, but Strahlem had to solve the problem.

Dick Strahlem, Phil Arce and I had another committee meeting. I said we have students but no teachers. No problem said Strahlem, we'll teach. The three of us will be the first teachers. But I don't know how to teach. Don't worry about it, it will be easy for you. I'll help you. And, Oh, Dick said, Ask the Binions if you can teach daytimes, which I did, but most of the classes were at night.

He said we'll make a lesson plan. Get your pad. Always Leo Lewis' pad. You make an outline, bring it to class and follow the outline. Nothing to it. But it wasn't that easy. The first class was an embarrassment. I put the pad on the desk and read the pad. In 35 minutes, I dismissed the 90 minute class.   LEWIS

We industry professionals came in believing that teaching was so easy. And then we taught everything we knew in three days. Say, this is hard work.

Now [with distance learning] you'd better be a good dancer. It's not possible [if the prepared lecture finishes early] to say, Its time to go. Students may be in 20 different places and they're waiting for the lecture.   ALAN STUTTS, HOTEL FACULTY MEMBER

I know that we all were supportive, and that all of a sudden the school was ready to open and we didn't have any faculty. It was: You know, we have a problem; you have to bail us out; you have to help us! So we said all right. It was a last-minute thing. We had classes, but no teachers.   ARCE

Ok, I'll do accounting. Phil [Arce] said he would do front office. So we each took classes. Strahlem might have taken some.   LEWIS

I couldn't believe the books that we were to use. I looked one over and said this goes back to the year of the flood! We needed to get some books in the place. Big difference between my first class and the second class a few years later when I had a text and was able to give assignments. But the students really wanted to know what was going on in my day-to-day activities.   ARCE

The books were terrible, except we had accounting texts.   LEO LEWIS, BINION'S FINANCIAL OFFICER AND PART-TIME FACULTY MEMBER

The text book issue was certainly not special to NSU. Few books were being published outside of the foods area. (See, for example, Strahlem's comments in paragraphs 3, 9 and 14 and his Conclusion 1 of Exhibit 3-1.)

Leo's class was next to mine so we took breaks at the same time. We would leave the doors open for ventilation. The only time I ever missed class is when my son, Joseph, was born.   PHIL ARCE, SAHARA HOTEL MANAGER

We had a hard time getting classrooms. There was no air conditioning and no heat. It was hot in September and cold in December.   LEWIS

The rooms in Grant Hall never cooled off. Did those air conditioners really work or were they just for show?   PAT MOREO, 69 STUDENT AND FACULTY MEMBER

Issues Separate from the Hotel Program

As recounted earlier, the rivalry between the Reno and Las Vegas campuses was ongoing. Within that perspective, the establishment of the hotel program was small potatoes. Shifting terminology from "Southern Regional Division" to "Nevada Southern University" was a step—but only the first step in a campaign of emancipation. Effecting that intermediate name change was surprisingly easy. It was put on the coattails of a proposal to grant the southern campus authority to issue baccalaureate degrees.

" . . . It was suggested to them [the Regents] that . . . the first degrees . . . be awarded in 1964. It was impressed upon them that this would be during the centennial of the State of Nevada, that the first graduating class would be designated as the 'Centennial Class' and when NSU celebrated its centennial graduating class, it would coincide with the State of Nevada's bicentennial. This description of historical significance . . . was sufficient to capture the imagination of the Regents. The proposal, [to change the name from the Southern Regional Division (of Reno) to Nevada Southern University] in a dubious position earlier, was enthusiastically accepted . . . " [Bill Carlson's papers.[7]]

Reno thought that if they gave us the Southern Rebel label they would be rid of us. After all, they were still "The" University of Nevada.   CRAWFORD

The change was realized in 1964, so the Resort Association's 1966 grant was to Nevada Southern University (see Exhibit 2-1). Interestingly, the Nevada Southern name was used (but in quotations) as early as 1957 when it appeared in the program of the cornerstone ceremony for the campus' first building. It was just the preliminary skirmish; the battle to establish autonomy involved more than merely changing names. NSU or no, Moyer was compelled as late as 1965 to write to President Armstrong for permission to pursue the NRA grant. Also at issue were major differences of budgets, buildings and faculty. Don Moyer had many irons in the fire at this time, but the hottest one was achieving a name change that carried administrative freedom with it. The change to "University of Nevada Las Vegas" would be a *fait accompli*, proof positive, of the final independence that had motivated and preoccupied the early life of the southern campus.

In the late '60s, there were issues over pay; there were issues over promotions from associates to full professors. We had a number of persons who met in front of the library and burned their contracts publicly.   DWIGHT MARSHALL, DEAN OF CONTINUING EDUCATION

"It was probably inevitable that he [Moyer] promoted his campus so energetically that he lost his rapport with fellow administrators in the north." [Hulse, *University of Nevada History.*[8]]

Don [Moyer] was just what we needed; he was the right man at the right time. But he was burning a lot of bridges. We were a three-year team, and we knew it. You ride white horses but take a lot of arrows because you alienate too many people.

Three years was all they gave him. But those were critical years. We turned this baby around; got the hotel school started; got those four things [the university's highlighted programs]; bought the first grass; put in the trees. . . . It was fun.   CRAWFORD

I believe Don Moyer put his job on the line to get the UNLV name. I believe that's what got Don in the end.   MARSHALL

Moyer may have laid the groundwork, but the final name change, from Nevada Southern University to the University of Nevada, Las Vegas, came a short time later.

I did not like the Nevada Southern name. Words like Southern and Eastern indicate the school's origin to be a normal school, a teacher's college. We didn't have that history. Even in the late 1960s it was evident that Las Vegas was going to be a well known place in the United States, and I wanted a name that would utilize Las Vegas. At first I was unaware that the Nevada Board of Regents was constitutionally separate from the legislature. It has all kinds of authority not given to other state boards. I brought up the issue of a name change at a board of regent's meeting asking for permission to pursue the matter at the next legislative session. First, I had planned to go back to campus and work it out with the faculty and student senates. I was asked what should the name be. I said University of Nevada, Las Vegas. Someone made a motion, seconded, and they changed the name! One regent said We can't just have a University of Nevada, Las Vegas; there has to be a University of Nevada, Reno. Without permitting Ed Miller, who was president at Reno, to speak—he sat there almost apoplectic—they changed that name to University of Nevada, Reno.   DON BAEPLER, UNLV PRESIDENT AND UNS CHANCELLOR

Moyer was gone by 1968 and the original support that Vallen had seen was now very uncertain. Crawford and Moyer were replaced by two new administrators, Chancellor Jay Zorn and Vice President Donald Baepler. Rex Johnson was replaced by Tom White.

Jerry Crawford announced his resignation as Dean of Faculty and we spent 1967–68 searching for a Vice President—that was the new title. We hired Don Baepler in May and by the time he arrived in July, 1968, Don Moyer had resigned. Baepler was now acting chancellor as well as vice president.   SMITH

Change of administrators or not, it was getting-down-to-business time for the hotel program. The hotel community was on board. The campus was anticipating the launch although there was trepidation among some faculty. The teaching staff was on hand. The curriculum was outlined. The budget was in place. And the students were eager. It was time to do something with all those assets.

"[Pat Moreo] came with the original term of students and recalls a spirit at the school that spawned a desire for the students to boast of the new College at every opportunity. He said that this "spark' has been kept alive through the years and has been passed on to new faculty." [Goodwin.[9]]

ENDNOTES FOR CHAPTER 3

1. Robbins Cahill, "Reflections of Work in State Politics, Government, Taxation, Gaming Control, Clark County Administration and the Nevada Resort Association," *Oral History Project* (Reno: University of Nevada, Reno, Library), v. 6, p. 1,358.

2. Cahill, p. 1,359.

3. Memorandum from Jerry Crawford to Rex Johnson, dated October 3, 1966.

4. Gabe Vogliotti's letter to Al Freeman, dated December 27, 1967.

5. Gabe Vogliotti, Unpublished manuscript, p. 1-9; from the personal collection of Bill Thompson.

6. Vogliotti's letter to Freeman.

7. John R. Goodwin, *Diamond in the Desert: The University of Nevada Las Vegas and its William F. Harrah College of Hotel Administration* (Las Vegas: Sundance Publishing, 1992), p. 108, quoting from a 1981 paper by William D. Carlson.

8. James W. Hulse, *The University of Nevada: A Centennial History* (Reno: University of Nevada Press, 1974), p. 66.

9. John Goodwin, "Dr. Patrick J. Moreo, His Reflections as a Hotel Student." *UNLV Hotel Alumni Association, College of Hotel Administration, Summer,* 1988, Vol 12, No. 2, p 4.

The First Years

THE INITIAL FOCUS

After the initial excitement waned and the early supporters stepped back, it was time to get to work.

> In the academic area there was suspicion because we had sold it as a college. The attitude [of the traditional academics] was we'll wait and see you prove it. Let's see whom they hire and what they do. No historian, sociologist or anthropologist who has written a book is going to say, well, wait a minute a book on hotel management . . . [equates to what?].
>
> Once the program began to prove itself academically, some of the early skepticism vanished quickly; I don't remember any harsh criticism.   JERRY CRAWFORD, DEAN OF FACULTY

> Hotel was grossly misunderstood. The general attitude of traditional academics was that hotel management was not a university program.
>
> No one could have predicted 30 years later that the service area would be the dominant economic force of the 21st century.   DONALD BAEPLER, UNLV PRESIDENT AND UNS CHANCELLOR

The new hotel director took office on July 1, 1967; a typical summer day in Las Vegas. Faculty were away and no students—certainly, no hotel students—were about during those first weeks. That was fine with the new director who, following the professional advice of his father (a restauranteur), had always employed great deliberation when taking on new hotel/restaurant jobs. Surveying the lay of the land, identifying the main actors and visualizing the tasks to be done were the first priorities. They would take time because spooking anyone with rash decisions would destroy long-range opportunities for short-range expediencies.

Getting to known the admissions officer, Dallas Norton, and the registrar, Muriel Parks, was a good starting place. So the invitation to serve on the admissions committee was quickly accepted. Few other faculty members wanted to serve and it was still not clear whether the hotel director was a faculty member who could serve on faculty committees or an administrator who could not. Admissions would prove to be a critical point for the hundreds of transfer students who were to form the foundation of the program's enrollment. The assignment lasted nearly ten years.

Reading the trade press was another good place to begin. Packing, moving and resettling had taken most of the summer of 1967, so it was now time to catch up on trade affairs. Other than telephone conversations with Gabe Vogliotti of the Resort Association, who was pressing for the start of the internships, and advice and guidance from Rex Johnson, everyone left the director alone.

> Now this is not gratuitous; it's the way I remember it. When Vallen was interviewed, there were not a lot of candidates. But he was by far the leading candidate. No holds barred. That feeling carried over: Let the guy do his thing; he knows how. Leave him alone.   DWIGHT MARSHALL, DEAN OF CONTINUING EDUCATION

Finding the support of an established secretary was a pleasant surprise. The first of several extremely able and personable college secretaries, Carol McCullough, was already in place. Both the secretary and the director shared one large office, which allowed for almost no privacy.

> One day soon after my arrival, Carol took a call from a friend and I could hear her asking what Carol was doing. The answer, with some disdain, I recall, was nothing; she was doing nothing. Which was true, since we had started out with nothing to do.   JERRY VALLEN

Some Early Decisions

The office was adequately staffed and equipped except for chairs. Looking at the very comfortable account balance, it was decided that a small, green sofa would fill the void and fit the budget. J. C. Penny was visited and the bill sent to the business office. There was a quick response from the business officer, Herman Westfall, and a clearly delivered lesson about purchasing procedures at Nevada Southern University.

> If you went in to see the dean, make sure you didn't stay too long; make sure that if you sat on the green sofa, you sat near the end, and make sure you knew exactly how much [money] you wanted.   PAT MOREO, '69 STUDENT AND FACULTY MEMBER

After reviewing the teaching schedule for the upcoming fall term, 1967, and comparing it to the richness of the teaching staff—three new faculty with only two dozen students, a decision was made about the part-time (adjunct) faculty. Phil Arce and Leo Lewis, who had carried the ball during the first school year, were excused. It created an incident that has been recalled over and over again, always with good humor.

> I had a P-99 contract [issued to part-time faculty] on my desk for the fall of 1967. One of the first things that Vallen did when he came to Nevada was call me and say, send your contract back, you won't have to teach. I said, Oh, you've broken my heart.   LEO LEWIS, BINION'S FINANCIAL OFFICER AND PART-TIME FACULTY MEMBER

> Well, I remember that you fired Leo.   JOE DELANEY, COLUMNIST AND PART-TIME FACULTY MEMBER

> Jerry fired him! That's the first thing Leo tells everyone.   FLOSSIE VALLEN

The first invitation to visit came from Frank Watts and Jim DeMaris at the Riviera Hotel. Watts had been instrumental in getting the professional community behind the idea of a hotel program. Along with the lunch, these new friends helped the naive director understand what was happening on the Las Vegas scene. The discussion included the role of the unions, the strength of the community's commitment and an invitation to attend meetings of the Hotel/Motel Accountants Association.

> After lunch, they taught me the horse racing game. It was an especially good lesson, since I walked away with a handful of quarters.   JERRY VALLEN

A second invitation, to attend the state's annual tourism conference, came in the fall, from the office of Governor Paul Laxalt. At dinner that night, the Vallen family discussed the unusual nature of a small state and the speed with which an invitation had come from the office of the governor.

> Just a few days later, our 6-year old met Governor Paul Laxalt at Ruby Thomas School where Laxalt was visiting. His teacher reported that our son spoke to the governor saying, I think you know my father.   FLOSSIE VALLEN

Changes Facing the New Program. Even as hotel was struggling to identify itself and to clarify its mission, its initial supporters were being replaced. Early on, Jess Goodman died.

> I was sitting in a rear pew at Jess' very full funeral. Two men plopped into a seat behind me and panted, catching their breath from what was obviously a hard run. One voice said, See governor, I told you we wouldn't get a seat if we didn't hurry. I sneaked a glance behind me to see Governor Laxalt. Wow, I had just moved from New York and was imagining Governor Rockefeller's entrance!
>
> Later that week, I was driving down the Strip where I saw Laxalt walking by himself. I stopped and offered a ride, which he declined.   JERRY VALLEN

Another major change took place at the Resort Association. Gabe Vogliotti was out. He explains why better than anyone else could:

"Like [Robert] Maheu [Howard Hughes' executive] I, too, read it [the circumstances and the manner of Vogliotti's own firing] in the papers. Like Maheu, I resented the way of it, but in my case I should not blame them: anyone with this much hauteur in him should have been fired sooner." [Vogliotti.[1]]

Robbins (Bob) Cahill, the new NRA director, proved to be a wonderful person and a major supporter of the hotel program. Cahill's distinguished career is traced in *The First 100, Portraits of the Men and Women Who Shaped Las Vegas*:

"In 1945 Cahill was appointed secretary to the Nevada Tax Commission. . . . [He] left state government to become Clark County manager. . . . Cahill returned to the gaming business as executive director of the Nevada Resort Association . . . [and later] as executive director of the Gaming Association of Northern Nevada."[*The First 100.* [2]]

Cahill immediately gave Vallen the nickname, "Tiger," which stuck during their positive and warm relationship until, in turn, Cahill left.

There was all sorts of turmoil: the civil rights movement; new ownerships; and the Howard Hughes issues [licensing, the medical school, monopoly of casino ownership]. Cahill, who had been called in previously as a consultant to give advice—like a professional gun slinger of the old days, came and replaced Gabe [Vogliotti] who was forced out. Gabe was still talking to the old timers, who were no longer making the decisions.   JOE DIGLES, NEVADA RESORT ASSOCIATION

Don Moyer had done what he could for UNLV and was replaced by Roman Jay Zorn. Donald Baepler replaced Jerry Crawford as dean of faculty (now the post had a vice president's title). To his surprise, Baepler also became president (chancellor) for a year before Zorn was recruited and appeared.

I came in the summer of 1968. Former president Don Moyer—he was called chancellor at that time—left the week before. I did not know we lacked a president until I arrived on campus. The first thing I discovered was that I was the acting president!   BAEPLER

Another surprise turnover was the resignation of William (Tom) White, as dean of business (a new title here also), after serving just a few years. White accepted a political appointment in Carson City and was replaced in 1971 by George Hardbeck, who served until 1985.

Tom White was a really nice guy but his ideas about what an economist can do will never agree with mine.   GEORGE HARDBECK , DEAN OF BUSINESS AND ECONOMICS

Meeting with the Unions. From meeting with Watts and DeMaris, Digles and Vogliotti and others, it was soon evident to the new director that the Culinary Union and the Teamsters Union were well established in Las Vegas, and that they represented a potential barrier to the implementation of the internships.

> Right, I remember we were worried about that from the beginning.   JERRY CRAWFORD, DEAN OF FACULTY

Resolving that issue was an early priority. With the blessing of Chancellor Moyer, a luncheon was scheduled with Al Bramlet of the Culinary Union, Local #226, and Richard (Dick) Thomas of the Teamsters Union, Local #881. (Ben Schmoutey replaced Bramlet after his disappearance on February 24, 1977. Bramlet's body was found in the desert some three week later.)

> Unions were strong, but they were also cooperative. Attitudes changed with the coming of the corporations. The old-line operators were still strong in the casino side and they fought the unions to keep their casinos union-free.   JOE DELANEY, COLUMNIST AND PART-TIME FACULTY

> Let's face it, there was a lot of trepidation then. Much of it unspoken, but it was there at all three levels: ownership, unions and employees. And these had to be smoothed out. It was easy for Bramlet because he didn't care an iota. Thomas had a better grasp on it and knew that the inevitable could be managed because some of the expertise of the [national office of the] Teamsters had rubbed off on him.   JOE DIGLES, NEVADA RESORT ASSOCIATION

> "The gamblers [Vogliotti's term for owners] were soon to face their worst crisis, a problem greater actually than the menace of the FBI, which was the threat of the unionization of dealers. Against this danger the owners formed up solid."
>
> "The owners formed the [Nevada Resort] association as much to deal with the scavenging local [union] as to deal with the national enemy." [Vogliotti.[3]]

Everyone met at the Desert Inn Country Club in those days, probably as a testament to the property's preeminence under Moe Dalitz, Jack Donnelly and company. The first gathering of the Advisory Committee (February 8, 1966) had been held there. The first graduating class luncheon was to be held there. So that's where the meeting of Vallen and Moyer, Bramlet and Thomas took place. The Tropicana Golf Club and still later the Las Vegas Country Club, where a semi-retired Moe Dalitz was something of a president emeritus, were the places "to be seen" for lunch.

> I came to the meeting with a bad mind set, having had some very unpleasant experiences with the family restaurants and the Philadelphia Culinary Union. Experiences there had actually become physical! The meeting was surprisingly cordial and productive.   JERRY VALLEN

After the union leaders heard the university's plan and expressed their own concerns, an agreement was struck over sandwiches. As was the practice of those days, the deal was sealed with a handshake.

> Things were changing. Before Bill Campbell [the NRA's labor executive] came, which was after I left, labor relations were done with a handshake. It was a good ole boy thing. It got to the point that you couldn't do that anymore.
>
> Roy Flippin was the nominal head of something that was given some funny name. He was the NRA's labor representative before Bill Campbell. Roy would deal with Al Bramlet and Dick Thomas and they would set up their sweetheart deals.
>
> [Similarly,] prior to corporate ownership, there was a different good ole boy syndrome [with the hotel and casino people], and things had to change there too.   DIGLES

It was agreed that interns would not be paid; that interns would not take permanent positions away from union members; and that any student who wanted full-time work would be encouraged to join the appropriate union. Nevada was then and still is a right-to-work state, but the hotels had agreed to a "hiring hall" clause. Cahill points out how inviolate was that clause:

> "The unions give lip service . . . to the hotel school and permit[ted] a student to intern . . . but they can't violate one basic principle that's always been a union principle, that he [the intern] can't do work that a union man can." [Cahill.[4]]

Some time elapsed before the union stewards in the hotels fully understood the agreement that had been reached at the Desert Inn. In the interim and for several years thereafter, the college furnished the union at the start of each term with lists of interns and their hotel assignments.

> There was some concern by the union stewards so far as student interns were concerned. I had one of the first interns at the Sahara when we encountered both unions. I said, Look, they're not replacing anyone. They're only here temporarily. We are not paying them, they are here merely to observe, and to work, and to get some knowledge. The unions were skeptical and feared we were replacing union members.   PHIL ARCE, SAHARA HOTEL MANAGER

Tensions eased once the stewards understood the arrangement and realized that the college would honor the limitations. Before long, interns began doing hands-on tasks without objections from the union representatives.

That 1967 meeting was the only formal one held. From that point on both parties adhered to the agreement and no substantial issues over the internships were ever raised by either side despite the college's later involvement in a major strike that rocked the city.

> I always told students to join the union and how to do it when the subject of work came up, which it did often because that was one major attraction of our location.   JERRY VALLEN

Both Bramlet and Thomas, but especially Thomas, participated in the labor seminars developed by Richard Basile, and both visited classrooms. Moreover, the Teamsters made annual scholarship gifts to the hotel program.

The Advisory Committee. The two union leaders served as ex officio members of the Hotel Advisory Committee, which was reconstituted for a brief period. Also ex officio were Cahill from the NRA (replacing Vogliotti) and Moyer, who remained through some of the 1967–68 school year. Voting membership was balanced between the community and the campus. From industry came: J. Kell Houssels, Jr. (Tropicana); Walter Fitzpatrick, (Desert Inn, replacing Allard Roen); J. Dee Goodman (Riviera); Howard P. James (Sahara, replacing A.A. McCollum); and Al Benedict (Stardust). From the campus came Jerry Crawford, Bob Smith, Jerry Vallen and Tom White (replacing Johnson). Other participating members of the NRA at this time were the: Aladdin; Castaways; Dunes; Flamingo; Frontier; Hacienda; International; Landmark; Sands; Silver Slipper; and Thunderbird. The Riviera was no longer a member.

> The Riviera wasn't a member of the Association during the first major [labor] strike, a 96-hour strike. The Riviera and Circus Circus, which had just opened, said we'll agree to any contract you guys sign.   JOE DIGLES, NEVADA RESORT ASSOCIATION

The special advisory committee remained active for only a short time. When the issues focused more on internal university problems than on NRA matters, the top executives bailed out and sent lower echelon staff. Then the hotel director decided to let the committee die quietly. The final meeting was February 20, 1968.

While the committee was active, an informal ten-year view, including student enrollment projections, was presented, and the faculty was introduced. On contract in addition to the director were the original hires, George Bussell and Boyce Phillips. Added to the faculty by the start of the second term in February, 1968 was Lothar Kreck, who had come sight unseen from an assignment overseas in India. The pool of hotel faculty was small and both Kreck and, later, Jack Rudd (from the Virgin Islands) were hired from overseas without interviews. Getting good teaching staff was difficult for the young program. Las Vegas was difficult to sell and the program was unproven.

From the start, part-time specialists from the community took on a major role. "On staff"—a special faculty identification that hotel created—were Lewis Kurtz, controller at Caesars Palace, and Jerry Snyder, a local attorney with Ross, Snyder and Goodman. Norman Jensen of the math faculty was teaching a course in mathematics of casino games.

The ten-year plan presented the college's objectives, its enrollment projections and faculty needs, scholarship expectations from the Resort Association and job placement forecasts. Plans for recruiting students, including a recruiting brochure, were also included.

The program's first recruiting publication, which had been prepared as part of Strahlem's earlier recommendations, had become dated by 1968–69. A new brochure entitled "New Modes New Moods and New Movements" was prepared with the aid of the campus publications officer, Marc Hughes. Sari Philips Aizley later joined Hughes' staff and helped with subsequent brochures. Featured on the cover page were the new, international tourist symbols that had just been adopted to service the increasing amount of world travel. At first, Joe Digles advised that there was too much copy. But then it was decided that potential readers would want as much information as possible. The campus was pictured with the student union, the dormitory, the social sciences building and the library. The brochure was one of the few university publications done in color and among the first to identify the campus with its new UNLV name. One paragraph read:

> "Education must keep in step. Hotel administration at the University of Nevada, Las Vegas has that cadence; it's paced to the changes that beckon the next generation. Unhampered by restraining traditions, a new university with an experienced faculty can structure a viable curriculum. That is what UNLV has done. From a joint effort of educators and practitioners has emerged a balanced course of study that promises the student an important place in both society and the hotel industry."

Paying for the brochure with "soft" money set a bad precedent. Fees from hotel's huge out-of-state enrollment contributed significantly to the campus' operating budget. Yet every subsequent brochure, which was used to recruit those very students, was paid for with hotel funds. So much for hotel being a special highlighted program.

REORGANIZATIONS
The Highlighted Programs

Even before the hotel program began, it was christened as a special discipline, one of four. The decision was taken by the entire university faculty in 1966 using a "Class A" (entire campus) vote that was reaffirmed in the 1971 reorganization.

> Somewhere [about 1966], Moyer and I sat down and said all this entrepreneurship is fine but how are we to sell it to the faculty, who are going to say hotel is some sort of technical school. We decided to put it to a Class A vote.
>
> In those days, if we wanted to get something done, we put it to a vote. I said we'll campaign for some select, some highlighted areas. We'll never build this place being all things to all people.
>
> So when we did the first four programs, we did them as a unit rather than ranking them. They're going to get high visibility, that meant national and international visibility. They were desert biology, fine arts, performing arts and hotel administration.
>
> The vote was fabulous. We got 90% voting for these four!
>
> And we were right. Performing arts are strong, so is desert ecology and, of course, hotel is the star.   JERRY CRAWFORD, DEAN OF FACULTY

Undoubtedly, hotel's inclusion in the Class A vote reflected the university's urban mission. The program linked the campus with the community's largest employer and its first major donor. Each of the selected programs was to be given high visibility and, by inference—at least in Crawford's and Vallen's eyes—enriched budgets. Those extra dollars never materialized for the hotel program, the hotel department or the hotel college.

No one was supposed to scream when the highlighted programs got a little extra treatment.

From [Chancellor] Jay Zorn on, it was tough [to get special funds]. They didn't have the mentality, the zeal for it. They were not part of the vision.   CRAWFORD

In 1978–79, hotel had over half of the out-of-state enrollment of the entire campus! Still, requests for travel funds to recruit out of state were denied.

Hotel was not departmentalized in 1979–80. Each faculty member was teaching 12 credits. There were 145 hotel graduates that year, comprising 20% of the graduating class. Needing extra administrative support—there was just the dean—we requested funds to have Boyce Phillips act as a department chair part time along with his teaching duties and be paid accordingly. Otherwise there was no administrative officer when the dean was off campus. Denied. So much for highlighted programs.   JERRY VALLEN

Hotel's identification as one of the elite programs of the campus was never challenged during the debates that preceded the numerous reorganizations of the university.

When one talks about reorganization, one must remember that we went through one reorganization after another in the late 1960s.

There was a system-wide reorganization that included the DRI [Desert Research Institute] and concurrently an internal campus reorganization. This went on for about a year and a half. So there was the reorganization of '65, '66 and '67. Subsequently, Don Moyer started pushing for new graduate programs, new colleges and whatnot. I think the hotel program emerged at that point.   ROBERT SMITH, DEAN OF SCIENCE, MATHEMATICS AND ENGINEERING

I remember in the early years that many individuals approached me claiming it was they who pushed through the hotel program.   JERRY VALLEN

They were right; they did: They voted for it!   CRAWFORD

I don't think anyone realized how big and how well known hotel was going to become. The whole university was small, but it turned out that the hotel school was the driver that brought the recognition.   ARCE

Yes, we had a plan. We would highlight theater; we would highlight music; we would highlight geology; we would highlight hotel. Only hotel has developed to where we hoped it would be. Theater is good, music is good, but hotel is premiere in the country.   BAEPLER

Hotel Machinations

Hotel's status was confusing from the start. The original plan called for the hotel "program" to be a unit within business. Business itself was a "division" because other terms, "school" and "college," were not yet in use.

> We weren't a school; we weren't a college we were called a division. That was the terminology before the new titles.
>
> The university had divisions before 1968 when they became colleges. [They actually became schools first: The 1967–68 catalog identified the hotel "program" in the "School of Business."]
>
> My recollection was that hotel was to start off as a program within business, and then become independent.   SMITH

The First Spin-off. Despite its affiliation with business, hotel reported not to the head of the business division but to the vice president of academic affairs. That was the new title given to Don Baepler, renamed from Jerry Crawford's post as dean of faculty. Provost is part of the current title. That reporting line was one of the terms agreed to by Crawford and Moyer during the employment discussion with the first hotel director. The arrangement didn't last long because Tom White replaced Rex Johnson. For one year, White retained the old director's title before it was changed to dean in 1968–69. White hoped to turn the business program from a small, obscure offering to one fully accredited by the American Assembly of Collegiate Schools of Business (AACSB). A difficult accomplishment so long as hotel's faculty lacked even one terminal degree among its four members (Bussell, Kreck, Phillips and Vallen).

> One of Tom White's concerns was that hotel would hinder accreditation. [He wasn't successful; accreditation took 25 years and several deans to accomplish.]
>
> Spinning off hotel had to do exclusively with viewing it as a drag on accreditation. I think he believed that the AACSB would look at it as a trade school. The spin-off took place about the same time that office administration [which was also in business] got shuffled off to the community college [1969].
>
> Losing FTE [full-time equivalents, a measure of student enrollment] money was certainly a consideration but that cost wasn't a determinant factor in the decision.   REUBEN NEUMANN, BUSINESS FACULTY MEMBER

> It [the reason Neumann advances] rings true to me. Tom was very good, I mean in a descriptive sense. He talked about it [accreditation] as did every other business dean I have ever known in an unaccredited business college.   SMITH

> They [business] were concerned about getting accredited by AACSB because we would be a millstone. And Vallen, in a wonderful low-keyed, theatrical way said, Well, okay, if we have to go.   PAT MOREO, '69 STUDENT AND FACULTY MEMBER

I don't think it [White's divestiture of hotel] related to accreditation. It was probably a ruse because there are hotel programs in business across the nation and those colleges are accredited.   BAEPLER

Two significant items were included in the 1968 meeting of the hotel advisory committee. One was a request to separate hotel from business. The other asked for better physical facilities. At least there was consistency. Both of these requests had been outlined two years earlier in Dick Strahlem's memorandum (see Exhibit 3-1). His recommendations were unknown to hotel's administration and faculty because they were still in the files of the business dean.

Vallen's October 30, 1968 memorandum to Dean White and to Vice President Baepler about separating hotel from business help set the wheels in motion. Two weeks later, Baepler placed the issue on the agenda of the Academic Council. On January 20, 1969, he wrote a letter to the Chair of the Faculty Senate, Roger Miller, suggesting the Faculty Senate's approval (see Exhibit 4-1).

I had forgotten the name Roger Miller [sociology] until you showed me that letter. Gosh, he was in the middle of everything in those days.   DONALD BAEPLER, UNLV PRESIDENT AND UNS CHANCELLOR

What Don Baepler says in the letter of January 20, 1969 is that the Academic Council, which was the Council of Deans, voted to recommend to the Faculty Senate that the HA program—rather than "division" it says "program"—be established as a separate college.   BOB SMITH, DEAN OF SCIENCE, MATHEMATICS AND ENGINEERING

The hotel program followed up with a letter to Miller asking to be placed on the agenda and offering the Senate a rationale for the move. It said in part that:

January 20, 1969

Dear Mr. Miller:

The Academic Council voted to recommend to the Faculty Senate that the Hotel Administration Program be established as a separate college at the University of Nevada, Las Vegas. Dr. White is in full agreement that this program should be separated from his college, and Mr. Vallen agrees that it would be to the advantage of the Hotel Administration people to be autonomous. I would be pleased to present my views on the topic to the Faculty Senate, and would suggest that you also ask Dean White and Mr. Vallen to present arguments for the change.

Sincerely,

Donald H. Baepler
Vice President for Academic Affairs

EXHIBIT 4-1. Memorandum that initiated hotel's separation from business.

"Professional colleges are the rule rather than the exception. Colleges of labor, architecture and law are by no means exceptional. Hotel programs are uncommon. It is this lack of hotel programs, not the absence of professional colleges that makes one think at first that academic precedent and tradition [for a hotel college] are missing. There is much to be said traditionally for the creation of a separate professional college."

Hotel was spun out of business in 1969, just 18 months after the first full-time faculty members appeared. But all of the issues were not resolved as indicated by the final two sentence of an accreditation statement prepared one year later.

"[The business college] had a strong, on-going program and a good faculty that afforded excellent incubation for the new hotel administration program. The reasons for making it an independent unit are somewhat obscure but it was accomplished with the approval of all concerned. One reason given was that the program would have 'greater visibility as an autonomous unit' and this would please the hotel industry. Apparently the administrative status of the [hotel] College is not finally determined. One evidence of this is that the chief administrative office has the title of Director instead of Dean."[5]

The program's director immediately moved to enlist the support of the Resort Association, asking it to lobby the move with the Regents. But the NRA maintained its hands-off stance.

When Vallen approached me in early 1969 [actually late 1968], I had been here only about six months. The issue was complex. First of all, hotel had a very small faculty [three plus the director]. [However,] we ran the institution with so many part-time and so few regular faculty members that almost none of the colleges had the right to be called a college. So the number of faculty was not a particular reason to veto the concept. The college of business had a traditional sense that this program was not the type it should sponsor; so they didn't fight to keep it.   BAEPLER

Unquestionably, hotel's enrollment, over 166 majors in the fall of 1968, which was 4.5% of total enrollment, weighed on the decision (see Exhibit 4-2). Hotel grew from a concept in 1966 to 225 students in the fall of 1969. Using projections prepared by Moyer and Zorn, the 1975 expected enrollment was 650, with 900 expected by 1979. Moyer's 1967 prediction of 1,000 seemed conservative a decade later. Hotel's out-of-state numbers amounted to an amazing 60% of the university's total although the program represented only 5% of total enrollment! Such growth indicated that a separate program could be easily sustained.

Growth in Hotel's FTE [full-time equivalents] was very helpful [in justifying the decision], and also the fact that it attracted out-of-state and foreign students. There were three varieties of out-of-staters: new residents who had not yet qualified; athletes; and hotel people.
BAEPLER

Enrollment Growth of Hotel Administration Program

	Hotel		Campus		Hotel's %	
Year	FTE	# of Students	FTE	# of Students	FTE	# of Students
1967	38.9	70	2,067	3,273	1.88	2.14
1968	85.4	166	2,946	3,651	2.90	4.55
1969	110.4	225	3,485	4,455	3.17	5.05
1970	132.1	277	4,090	5,340	3.23	5.19
1971	146.0	337	4,428	5,558	3.30	6.00
1972	168.3	304	4,178	5,658	4.03	5.19
1973	201.2	331	4,505	6,064	4.47	5.46
1974	272.0	372	4,936	6,676	5.51	5.57
1975	262.2	464	5,444	7,621	4.82	6.09
1976	313.3	542	5,380	7,801	5.82	6.95

EXHIBIT 4-2. Ten-year growth in the hotel program versus total campus enrollment. Values researched and computed by Registrar Jeff Halvorsen.

Hotels separation from business took place with very little fanfare within the university.

> Right after hotel and business separated, I said something to Tom White [Dean of Business] about the separation, I understand hotel isn't under business anymore. He responded, That's right, I don't have to be nice to you anymore either.   SARI PHILLIPS AIZLEY, SPOUSE OF THE COLLEGE'S FIRST FACULTY MEMBER

Coincidentally, the college was moved from the cramped quarters of Grant Hall to much newer facilities within Wright Hall, which housed the social sciences. Physical separation from business helped to emphasize the academic realignment.

Roger Miller's letter uses Nevada Southern University stationery, but the body of the letter references the institution's new name, the University of Nevada, Las Vegas. So the transition that cost Don Moyer his job was just beginning. Interestingly, the comma used after "Nevada" sent a bad signal to some, inferring that the University of Nevada (comma) Las Vegas was somehow subordinate to a University of Nevada Las Vegas without the comma.

> It was never an issue, talked about and quickly dropped. Write it as you wish.   BAEPLER

Baepler's letter to Miller references "Hotel Administration people." Hotel's identity continued to be a sensitive topic for some at the university. Even Neil Humphrey, who was acting president of the system, wasn't sure what hotel was. As Chapter 2 recounted, his letter of January 5, 1968 referred to hotel both as a program and as a school.

What the university saw as one of numerous reorganizations in its young life, the hotel faculty, indeed, the entire field of hotel education, saw as an impressive and far-reaching statement. It even warranted a note in a book about Las Vegas' coming of age. Zorn came to campus in March of 1969 just as the college's new status was finalized.

"The school [NSU] received another boost that June when newly appointed President Roman Zorn announced regent approval of the far west's first College of Hotel Administration." [*Resort City in the Sunbelt.* [6]]

Establishing the discipline as a separate college was so meaningful that the dean of the new college had announcements prepared as one does with the birth of a child. These were mailed in the Spring of 1969 after receiving official Regents' approval.

Among my memorabilia is a paper weight that Fred Swartz, Marketing Director of the Aladdin Hotel, made for me with the announcement shrunk and etched on wood.   JERRY VALLEN

Scores of announcements were mailed around the country and the unsolicited letters that came back reinforced the faculty's belief that this was, indeed, a major coup for hotel education.

When people ask me what was the most important thing that happened when you were in administration, I point out that when I was Acting President I was part of creating the first College of Hotel Administration in the United States and that was quite a distinction for UNLV.   BAEPLER

Excerpts from some of the numerous letters indicate how widespread and, perhaps, surprised were the college's colleagues, many of whom were not directly involved in education.

Congratulations on your establishment of the "College of Hotel Administration" and your appointment as Dean.
    Robert A. Beck, Dean, Cornell School of Hotel Administration

What good news, Jerry, to learn that the University of Nevada, Las Vegas has established a College of Hotel Administration and you are the Dean.
    Mike Daly, Redondo Beach, CA, Chamber of Commerce

My heartiest congratulations to you on the change and establishment of the College of Hotel Administration. The announcement speaks a great deal, not only for a forward looking Board of Regents, but also for a dedicated faculty and staff.
    Peter Dukas, Hotel Director, the Florida State University

Congratulations on the establishment of your College of Hotel Administration.
    Paul Handlery, President Handlery Hotels

Congratulations on your giant academic step to college status. It looks as though the action in Las Vegas isn't restricted to the hotels and casinos.
    Martin Judge, Editor, *Resort Magazine*

Congratulations, Jerry . . . on your appointment as Dean of the newly-founded College of Hotel Administration.
    Steve Laine, Cling Peach Advisory Board

Congratulations on the establishment of your program as a full college. It is only through such recognition that hospitality education can reach the status it deserves.
    R. W. Nestor, Chair, University of Minnesota

My sincere congratulations to you in your appointment as Dean of this new college and also to the Board of Regents for their vision and foresight in the establishment of this fine new program.
    Brother Herman Zaccarelli, Food Research Center for Catholic Institutions

The volume and the enthusiasm of the letters played an important role eighteen months later when still another reorganization, the Ad Hoc Committee on the Developing University, threatened the very existence of the just created "College."

The Ad Hoc Committee on the Developing University

The Regents approved the new status of hotel administration and simultaneously installed Roman Jay Zorn as the university's newest president. Third in the series of presidents (Moyer, and then Baepler, as acting president), Jay Zorn set his own priorities and goals.

"Zorn didn't use the shotgun approach of Moyer . . . he preferred instead to guide the University in the selection of a few areas of specialization. . . . 'We should now strengthen the programs we have rather than launching new ones without adequate funding,' Zorn said. This view characterized the first three years of his administration." [*The University of Nevada: A Centennial History.* [7]]

To accomplish his vision, Zorn created still another study committee in the fall of 1970, a year after his arrival.

Don [Baepler] went back to his regular position as Vice President, which takes us into the Zorn era when he set up the Ad Hoc Committee on the Developing University. And that was the next round of reorganization. SMITH

> Almost any administration looks at organizational charts and starts pushing little boxes around. One way to make administrative change is to reorganize, but also there were some fundamental problems with our basic organization. There was a need to merge the little colleges into the College of Arts and Sciences.   BAEPLER

The ad hoc committee, chaired by Paul Burns, worked diligently for nine months. It delivered its final report on March 11, 1971. Numerous topics were examined by the members from stacks of memorandums. Suggestions came from individuals, departments and colleges. Debate swirled about: the establishment of an "urban semester" and the subsequent creation of a 4-1-4 calendar; changes in the grading system to Pass/Fail; renumbering courses; the responsibilities of departmental chairs; the creation of a University College; handing off additional courses to the community college; and many others.

Although not oblivious to other issues, hotel was preoccupied by the potentially devastating reorganization. It submitted advisory documents as did other units of the campus. The first of these, dated October 16, 1970, was a position paper detailing hotel's organizational status. Hotel argued for the continuation of its independence, which it supported by attaching the congratulatory letters received 18 months earlier. The hotel faculty feared a public relations disaster if a reversal came so soon after the original announcement. Nevertheless, the position paper was couched in unemotional terms. It concluded: "A reversal of that position so soon after the action will have a detrimental effect of great magnitude. It will appear as if we failed and failed quickly."

> Jerry Crawford was hotel's liaison to the ad hoc committee. I recall with chagrin that I told Jerry, who had hired me, that I and all the faculty would leave if the action establishing us as a separate college was reversed. After all that publicity, how could we live with such a reversal?   JERRY VALLEN

> I remember saying to myself that I'm not going to pass on that remark. It was the passion of the moment and I respected it. Besides, I felt that we would talk you out of it if it came to that, but I also thought we would win the battle.   CRAWFORD

Hotel raised a second issue with the ad hoc committee. Dean Tom White had lobbied for hotel's separation in 1969, but a year later, was lobbying for its reentry into business! In advocating hotel's return, White cited his own intention of resigning and hence offered the idea as an unselfish motive:

> "The College of Business and Economics and the College of Hotel Administration might be combined usefully in a new College of Business. . . . Hotel Administration should become a School of Hotel Administration, headed by a director, who would . . . bear the rank of Associate Dean of the College.
>
> The [ad hoc] Committee should be advised also that I have tendered my resignation as Dean . . . these suggestions therefore, have no elements of personal interests. . . ."[8]

White had a different agenda, he was going to build a different type of ant hill. He had high aspirations and would have liked to become president here. He was a bright man and moved into state politics.   JERRY CRAWFORD, DEAN OF FACULTY

Tom White was pragmatic. If he saw that hotel was growing and prospering and attracting students, he would have wanted hotel back.   DON BAEPLER, UNLV PRESIDENT AND UNS CHANCELLOR

When Baepler asked me about it, I said it [hotel] should never have been spun off in the first place.   GEORGE HARDBECK, DEAN OF BUSINESS AND ECONOMICS

Although re-organization was the hotel faculty's major concern, it was just one item among many submitted to the ad hoc committee. One bizarre suggestion, certainly not of hotel's doing, recommended that UNLV built a large resort on campus with gaming and liquor licenses. "Properly handled it could be the first profit-making university in the country," read the suggestion. Of course, there was no provision to underwrite losses.

Failing that, it was suggested that the university take over and operate the never-yet-opened Landmark Hotel, which stood empty across from the Las Vegas Convention Center on Paradise Road. The Landmark eventually proved an economic disaster for its first owner, Howard Hughes, and an equal mistake for a subsequent buyer, Bill Morris.

I responded to these ideas as I did later when the dormitory's management was to be assigned to the college: When the college of health sciences handles student illnesses, and the department of accounting bills student tuition, then the college of hotel administration will run a hotel.   JERRY VALLEN

Hotel's second memorandum to the committee, February 5, 1971 discussed the organizational issues being floated. Some preliminary reports structured hotel as an independent college and some grouped it within a division of professional schools. None left the status quo untouched. One suggestion listed hotel as part of a College of Professional Studies, but identified it merely as "School of Hotel Administration." Every other head was identified as "Dean, School of Education," "Dean, School of Business," etc. Terminology, representing the academic community's ambiguity, continued to haunt the college/school/program/people.

The documentary evidence that I have suggests that in '70–'71 there was talk of recombining all the professional schools.   SMITH

Vallen had written to a number of colleagues soliciting comments about the likelihood of returning to non-college status. As was done with the original set of letters and the first memorandum, these new letters was attached to the second memorandum. Included among them were:

Hotel education, as you know, requires specialized courses considerably different from other disciplines. I hope for . . . the sake of the hotel program, they don't abolish your program and place you under a College of Professional Studies.

Douglas Keister, University of Denver

The news about the possibility of you College being merged into a group of other colleges under the rubric, College of Professional Studies, strikes me as most unfortunate.

Donald Lundberg, University of Massachusetts

There is no doubt in my mind that the autonomy of a Hotel College is the most desirable situation, as compared to offering a Hotel Program as one of several available within a College.

Richard Pew, University of New Hampshire

First of all, the most successful programs in hotel, . . . are those where the department or school has considerable autonomy to determine its own program.

Len Zendher, Florida State University

As a last resort, hotel's director proposed the creation of an umbrella college of recreation and leisure, which would include hotel, restaurant, sports, tourism and other emerging disciplines.

[The Committee] came up with some outrageous proposals in the first round of input, like the College of Culture and the College of Professional Studies.

In January, when a preliminary report came in, the whole thing was blown out of the water. Jay [Zorn] was inept in presenting things publicly and he made it sound as if it were a done deal. In about 15 minutes the whole thing blew up. Sheilagh Brooks from social science charged in one direction and others came from other directions. But I saw the whole thing as Don Baepler's way of getting rid of three inefficient deans.   ROBERT SMITH, DEAN OF SCIENCE, MATHEMATICS AND ENGINEERING

Then Vice President Donald Baepler was an important member of the committee.

It's awkward to reorganize and go from division heads, which tend to change and rotate and so are more equivalent to department chairs, to deans, who are not internally rotated. So some of the people who inherited the title of dean [in earlier reorganizations] were simply not able to keep up with the growth and development.   DONALD BAEPLER, UNLV PRESIDENT AND UNS CHANCELLOR

Working in hotel's favor was its identification among the four highlighted programs. The ad hoc committee's preliminary report of December 18, 1970 acknowledged the importance of these programs, which were put forth originally in 1966:

"UNLV [should] identify and develop preferentially certain fields which appear likely to achieve national prominence, due to their close relation . . . to the local community. In this category we suggest Hotel Administration [now listed first], Biology (desert and environmental studies), the Performing Arts (theater, music, dance) and Geology."

The committee's first stated priority was adequate funding for all programs! Identification of the highlighted programs was second. Riding that coattail, the college noted that financially, academically and geographically the college was in fact a highlighted program. It was organizational recognition that was lacking.

In the final report of March 11, 1971, the ad hoc committee recommended cooperation among the professional schools, but left them all intact. As Smith suspected, three small colleges were collapsed into one. It was an amazing turnaround from the preliminary report of only a month earlier, which had recommended a College of Professional Studies. Hotel was still on a separate budget and that might have had a some bearing on the decision.

> I cautioned Zorn that hotel needs to be a separate unit and play a different kind of war.
> CRAWFORD

A Class A ballot followed the final report. Before the vote, J. L. Travis, Chair of the Philosophy Department, predicted 107 votes for and 48 votes against, out of 236 possibilities. The final tally was much closer! On March 30, 1971, President Zorn reported the vote at 118 for and 110 against. Hotel was listed with 8 voting faculty (Acosta, Baltin, Basile, Catron, Levinson, Rudd, Phillips and Vallen). A projection four months earlier had shown hotel with 6 faculty members or 3% of the total faculty. At that point hotel had 337 students (see Exhibit 4-2) or 6% of the student body. That imbalance of faculty versus students was the historical mathematics of the college.

The Board of Regents approved the reorganization at its Elko meeting in May, 1971.

More About Titles and Degrees. All was not good news: The final vote left hotel as a college, but changed the title of its head from dean to director, back to the title that existed before the first reorganization. All other academic heads were titled dean. Title changes took place so rapidly that the catalogs never included the dean title. Hotel is listed as a program in the School of Business in the 1968–1969 catalog and as a program in the College of Business and Economics in the 1969–1970 catalog. From 1970 to 1974, the listing is College of Hotel Administration headed by a director.

> I was so happy to be independent that I made no noise about being called a director. It was the same title I carried in 1967 when I came. There was the Dean of the College of Business, the Dean of the College of Sciences, the Dean of the College of Education, etc. and the Director of the College of Hotel Administration.   JERRY VALLEN

I never had any problem with the position as dean.   BAEPLER

Be that as it may, Baepler refers to "Dean" White and to "Mr." Vallen in Exhibit 4-1. Perhaps the loss of dean's title reflected the "all-but-dissertation" status of its head, but just as likely it represented the traditional view of academia toward hotel administration.

I asked Don Baepler, Why is Jerry not listed as dean? And he replied, If he finished his Ph.D., he'll become dean. [The 1975–76 catalog lists hotel's administrative head as "Dean." Vallen finished his Ph.D. in 1978.]   HARDBECK

Certainly, the director's lack of a terminal degree bothered President Jay Zorn.

I spoke to Baepler about getting my Ph.D. after a brief leave of absence; I already had my committee. And Don said, Don't do it. He talked me out of it!   DWIGHT MARSHALL, DEAN OF CONTINUING EDUCATION

I was invited to speak at a professional meeting and furnished my vita to the program chair. Without knowing or caring, the program listed me as Dr. Vallen. Shortly thereafter Jay Zorn sent me a scathing note—not a visit, not a telephone call—about academic honesty. I returned his written message in kind.
President Zorn had another annoying habit. He edited written submissions. He would ink out a word, "in," for example, replacing it with "into." Maybe ten times on a memo and then send it back.   JERRY VALLEN

Communication between President Zorn and Vice President Baepler was not much better, neither as frequent nor as complete as one would imagine of two persons in offices adjacent to one another. Discussions with Baepler about issues raised previously with Zorn were often met with a degree of perplexity that suggested the vice president knew nothing about it. After a while, one worked directly with the vice president and ignored the president's office.

That's right, Zorn was a true academic insulator. That's why Baepler had to do for him. Don acted like the president and so he became the president.
[On the other hand], some faculty had worried that Zorn's predecessor, Don Moyer, had been too controlled by the community.   CRAWFORD

Jay [Zorn] was a competent traditional academician who never quite understood the applied aspects of any discipline. He never spoke negatively about hotel; he just wasn't comfortable with it and did not see the potential.   BAEPLER

Jay Zorn was a gentleman. He was know for using big words. The Board of Regents would always say, Jay taught us a new word today. But I don't think he saw the big picture.   HARDBECK

Jay was a sweet man, but an academic snob. I recall that Vallen's lack of degree irritated Zorn no end. He thought the world of Vallen like he thought the world of me. He'd rely on me, call me in because he knew I knew where the bones were buried. But I think he wished I wasn't from theater.   CRAWFORD

President Zorn had an annoying habit of calling to talk after the day officially ended. Invariably, he would telephone between 5:15 and 5:45 in the evening. One always suspected his motives.

I always worked late because I was more productive after everyone had gone. Since I had a reserved parking spot, I balanced the late hours by coming in about 9:00 am. That's how I was able to have breakfast with the children.   JERRY VALLEN

I too got the 5:00 o'clock treatment. It could have been intentional.   BAEPLER

The terminology of director remained until April of 1975 when President Baepler once again examined the issue and renamed the position "Dean." This time around, only one individual on the whole campus objected. It was Bob Catron, a faculty member in hotel. Catron and the college were parting company at the time. The official explanation for the unexpected change in titles: There was no provision in the faculty code for the title of "director." Well, there was, but not for an academic director. There were plenty of directors, but they belonged to a different administrative class: Director of the Library; Director of Continuing Education; Director of the Summer School; Director of Alumni Affairs and others. As their number grew, the Director of Hotel Administration became more ambiguous.

ACCREDITATION

Accreditation is akin to the work done by the Ad Hoc Committee, except it is an external review. UNLV is accredited every 10 years by the Commission on Colleges, Northwest Association of Schools and Colleges. Self-examination is supposed to be the essence of the process. But paperwork overwhelms the best intentions. Besides, the final disposition of the study is left to the same administrators who oversee the daily functions of the campus units. They should know already where strengths and weaknesses lie.

The first of these visits came in 1970, soon after the college was established. It was a first for each member of the hotel faculty and was made more confusing by the absence of anyone on the visiting committee who understood the discipline. Nevertheless, the results were sterling except for a hint that the program lacked overwhelming support from the broader campus community. Northwest's 1970 report (page 39) had this to say about hotel:

"This dynamic and rapidly developing program gives promise of becoming one of the most important in the University. The faculty is eager, hard-working, planning ahead, thinking big. . . . Hopefully as it becomes established and integrated into the total university program, both financially and academically, it will have the confidence and enthusiastic support of the faculty of the University as it presently has of the administration and business community."

An unexpected, special accreditation for hotel was championed by Vice President Arthur Gentile in 1975. It might have had its origin in a series of strong memos addressed to him from the dean about secretarial support and operating funds. It might have had its origin in the rapid growth of hotel's enrollment. Just as likely, the special accreditation might have had its origin in Gentile's complete lack of understanding about who and what the college was. Whatever the cause, a decision was made to have a special accreditation separate from that of the Northwest Association. This was the same year that an interim report (between the 1970 and 1980 visits) was due from the Northwest Association.

Despite the positive tone of the 1970 report, the college was unable to deter Gentile. A list of names was submitted for this special, hotel-only accreditation. Three were selected by Gentile: Bob Beck, Dean of the School of Hotel Administration at Cornell; Tom Powers, Professor in Charge at Penn State University; and Leo Lewis, local hotel executive whose knowledge of the program dated back to its beginnings. Paul Gaurnier, Cornell's Assistant Dean, eventually substituted for Beck. (During this visit Gaurnier urged Vallen to request readmission to Cornell to finish his dissertation. More important, Gaurnier promised to lend his and Beck's weight to the application which was nearly 10 years overdue.)

Despite repeated assurances to the contrary from Vice President Arthur Gentile, the Hotel College paid all the consulting fees and travel costs from the East. Certainly another first for a UNLV college.

This second, and equally positive—although unofficial—accreditation had no sooner been completed, then the college began preparing for the 1980 review. Bob Glennen was vice president now and Brock Dixon, a member of the first accreditation team, was acting president. The hotel college made a formal request for a specialized evaluator. Len Zendher, a hotel faculty member at Cal Poly in Pomona, California and formerly at Florida State University in Tallahassee, was assigned.

The 1980 report (page 22) referred to the positive comments of the 1970 report:

"In the 1970 . . . report . . . prophetic comments were made: '. . . it would be surprising if this hotel program were not one of the most effective in the university.' In 1980, it is clearly evident that the program is not only one of the most effective programs in the University of Nevada, Las Vegas, but also one of the 'best' in the nation."

On that same page, the 1980 accreditation report included an usual bon mot: The best back-handed compliment possible:

"There is a prevailing feeling among the students that the program 'will become the best in the country.' Surprisingly, there were no major complaints voiced by any one of the students interviewed. *One might conclude that no program is that good, and possibly it isn't."* [Italics added.]

Everyone uses accreditation visits to advance his own agenda. Top administrators even circulate memos suggesting points to be covered. Then, the accreditation report is used to justify those very actions. Recommendations that are contrary to perception are simply ignored.

Here's how certain actions are justified:

The graduate faculty was chafing at the idea of [teaching faculty] earning UNLV degrees. They put a bug in the ear of the accreditation team. So the team recommended no more cross-campus degrees. At least that's my interpretation of what happened.   MOREO

The 1980 accreditation report spoke to the issue,

"Another matter of concern . . . is the policy or practice at UNLV of allowing its teaching faculty to matriculate as doctoral degree-seeking students. . . ." [pages 3–4.]

and the follow-up progress report (1983), included Recommendation 4:

"The Regents' policy which allows . . . teaching faculty to matriculate as doctoral degree-seeking students at the University is, in the opinion of the team, not in the best interests of the institution."

The Board of Regents changed its own policy and granted veto authority to the graduate office, the very source that raised the issue with the accreditation team. Six years passed, during which one accreditation visit and one interim report were prepared, before hotel's initial request to President Baepler (in 1978) for cross-campus degrees was answered in the negative by President Maxson (in 1984). (Fast forward to the end of the millennium: Cross-campus degrees are now permitted, and faculty are surprised when they hear the old story.)

Comments from the same 1980 accreditation report highlight how other recommendations are ignored:

"University funding of hotel administration faculty positions seems to be inadequate. . . . The percentages clearly show the school is not getting a share of university positions or [of operating] dollars commensurate with its credit hour production and students."

At the time, hotel enrolled 6.3 % of student population and taught 6.6% of total credits but had only 4.7% of FTE faculty and a mere 2.9% of operating budgets despite the need to operate food labs.

Of course, the 1980 accreditation team was unaware of the special 1975 study by Gaurnier, Lewis and Powers, but it iterated what had been apparent five years earlier when Cornell's Paul Gaurnier submitted a similar comment.

"There is really not much an outside observer can say about this need [clerical support] because the facts are apparent to all."

Accreditation input notwithstanding, fiscal improvements were not forthcoming. Twenty-five faculty positions were allocated in 1983. Science with 385 majors received five positions; hotel with 371 majors received none. (Vice President Nitzschke, always a fair administrator, eventually found money to fund three positions with which to open Beam Hall in the Spring of 1984.)

> In my opinion, Nitzschke was an excellent academic vice president. We didn't always agree, but one always knew where one stood.   GEORGE HARDBECK, DEAN OF BUSINESS AND ECONOMICS

Hotel's 1985–1987 operating budget was cut from $65,646 to $42,302, approximately one-third. Cost cutting was campus wide that year, but hotel needed funds to operate the kitchen, which had opened the year before. Wages were also cut from a request of $12,500 to $4,522. This was especially onerous since hotel had to maintain the cleanliness of its own foodservice. Operations and Maintenance, entrusted with campus-wide sanitation, opted not to handle housekeeping in the Beam Hall kitchen. Again and again, actual circumstances made it hard to remember that the College of Hotel Administration had been identified more than once as a special, highlighted program.

Another accreditation agency is the Council on Hotel, Restaurant and Institutional Education (CHRIE). Vallen launched CHRIE's accreditation role during his two-year presidency of CHRIE, enlisting Frank Borsenik to draft preliminary guidelines. Nevertheless, CHRIE was never invited to UNLV for an accreditation visit. It didn't happen during Dean Vallen's tenure and not during Dean Christianson's tenure, which came next. (Christianson also served as CHRIE's national president.)

Unquestionably, the organizational battles between 1967 and 1971 and the accreditation commitments, especially those of 1970 and 1975, were time consuming and tedious. Fortunately, the faculty, staff and student body were able and committed. Progress was being made on all fronts despite the temporary distraction of critical resources.

ENDNOTES FOR CHAPTER 4

1. Gabe Vogliotti, Unpublished manuscript, p. 7-4A; from the personal collection of Bill Thompson.
2. A. D. Hopkins and K. J. Evans, ed., "Robbins Cahill." *The First 100, Portraits of the Men and Women Who Shaped Las Vegas* (Las Vegas: Huntington Press, 1999), pp. 125–127.
3. Vogliotti, Unpublished manuscript, pp. 1-5 and 1-8.
4. Robbins Cahill, "Reflections of Work in State Politics, Government, Taxation, Gaming Control, Clark County Administration and the Nevada Resort Association." *Oral History Project* (Reno: University of Nevada, Reno, Library), p. 1,364.
5. The Commission on Colleges, Northwest Association of Schools and Colleges. *Report of the Accreditation Committee*, 1970, p. 35.
6. Eugene P. Moehring, *Resort City in the Sunbelt.* (Reno and Las Vegas: University of Nevada Press, 1989), p. 227.
7. James W. Hulse, *The University of Nevada: A Centennial History* (Reno: University of Nevada Press, 1974), p. 77.
8. Memorandum from William T. White to Paul Burns, Chairman Ad Hoc Committee on the Developing University, dated October 14, 1970, p. 2.

The Structures—Financial and Physical

CHAPTER 5

The College's Financial Base

Although the accreditation committees absorbed a great amount of time and energy, the college was able to move ahead on many other fronts. Attention centered on curriculum, academic standards, admissions, student activities, internships and job placement.

The tasks were made easier because there was a flow of funds from companies, associations and individuals. Their support freed faculty members from financial restraints, allowing them to act on the amazing number of projects that helped earn the college its positive reputation.

Soliciting money can be a very uncomfortable experience. The awkwardness grows more manageable over time but knowing the donor through a different relationship makes it easier to initiate the approach. Helen Thompson, the first UNLV graduate to become a Regent, did just that. She volunteered an open-ended donation to be called up whenever the need arose.

Because most of the philanthropic agencies to which I belonged solicited from the same sources as did the hotel college, Jerry and I agreed that neither one of us would solicit for any non-university purpose.

Our other posture was: Never ask for a personal comp—which was pretty much SOP in those early days. Otherwise hotel executives would be reluctant to accept the college's telephone calls about more important matters. And we never did. FLOSSIE VALLEN

Often the most startling successes come from the mildest approaches. Then again, some of the most vigorous efforts are rejected. Identifying previous donors gives legitimacy to the new solicitation. So having the first gift from the Nevada Resort Association made subsequent appeals easier.

The college started with small grants from sympathetic, local professional organizations before shifting to less familiar donors and then to larger contributors. Solicitation skills were honed on recruiters who came to campus in search of graduating seniors. It was a *quid pro quo* approach. Give us scholarships to help develop students who are potential employees for your company. Pillsbury, the parent of Steak and Ale and Bennigan's Restaurants, responded to just such an appeal:

> "[This scholarship check] is sent in appreciation of the excellent job the school is doing. We are certainly pleased with the caliber of those individuals and their training."

So did Sheraton. A handwritten memo from a Sheraton interviewer, Mike O'Hara, who forwarded our request up Sheraton's hierarchy, attests to the trade off:

> "We have recruited some very fine young people from UNLV in the past few years, and any consideration you [headquarters] can give to the program would be gratefully received."

NEVADA RESORT ASSOCIATION GRANTS

Despite Vallen's accounting background, the college worked hard to reconcile the flow of NRA money with university records. The Resort Association used a calendar year, but the university operated from July 1 to June 30. Small matter if the university's records were accurate and timely, but they weren't. They originated in Reno and were always outdated and very difficult to read.

> Most everything was pretty well managed out of Reno. Who can forget [the irritation from] the old print-outs [monthly accounting statements that came from Reno].
>
> I'm sure hotel encountered the same problems. First, we didn't have enough money; second, we couldn't figure out how much we had. The print-outs were [screwed up]. One could not audit State of Nevada funds.   DWIGHT MARSHAL, DEAN OF CONTINUING EDUCATION

Numerous memos flowed between the hotel college and the business office and between the college and Robbins Cahill at the Resort Association. An October 27, 1972 memo, addressed to Tom Carr and Wayne Williams in the business office, deplored the inability to reconcile over three years. Nevertheless, it was necessary to assure Cahill that the university would assume budgetary responsibility as required by the original gift. That letter also repeated an earlier request for a second grant.

> I was not immediately privy to the financial arrangements between the university and the Nevada Resort Association. So during the early years I actually sent quarterly bills to Vogliotti and later to Cahill at the NRA. They accepted them in good humor.   JERRY VALLEN

The Second NRA Grant

Time was running out on the Nevada Resort Association's founding gift. Relations between the college and the Resort Association were strong. The fall of 1969, the start of the final academic year, was sensed as a good time to apply for the new grant. Joe Digles, who had been with the NRA for several years, was consulted. He coined the theme "A Margin of Excellence."

> I was just trying to point the right direction.   JOE DIGLES, NEVADA RESORT ASSOCIATION

The Margin of Excellence letter, dated November 3, 1969, requested funds for graduate new faculty, for in-service faculty development and for visiting faculty. Scholarships, including graduate assistantships, and travel money were also included. One faculty member, Bob Catron, had been the publisher of a trade magazine, so a naive request for funds to launch a UNLV publication was added. As the original grant had done, the new bid asked for incremental steps, budgeting $50,500 in 1970–1971 and culminating with $79,000 in 1973–1974, for a total of $259,000.

> "Jerry is a typical educator . . . he always asks for more than he is going to get." [Robbins Cahill.[1]]

To review the submission, President Al Benedict reconstituted the NRA's Advisory Committee. All those named were friends and supporters of the college. Walter Fitzpatrick, managing director of the Desert Inn, was the chair. J. K. Houssels, Jr., Tropicana; Harry Wald, Caesars Palace; Jim West, Flamingo and Sig Front, Sahara, were the members.

> I have no specific recall of that renewed grant, but I do know the committee was a very strong, outspoken group with a lot of enthusiasm [for the program].   SIG FRONT, VICE PRESIDENT, SAHARA HOTEL

Although the $111,000 approved was less than one-half the request, it was a handsome addition to the NRA's original $277,000. Specifically excluded was graduate faculty support. The Resort Association sent an unequivocal message that graduate programs should be postponed until the program had matured. Committee chair Walter Fitzpatrick wrote:

> "The NRA should not support a graduate program . . . the school should make every effort to excel at the undergraduate level."[2]

Scholarship, not faculty support, was the new emphasis. But the grant also provided $30,000 for two years for in-service development, administrative travel and visiting faculty. Lendal Kotschevar was the first such visitor. Kotschevar's experience was so good that the college developed and maintained a regular budget line for visitors for many years thereafter. And, after all, that is what "challenge money" is all about. Actually, the visitor's line for the first years (1970–1971 and 1971–1972) was funded from both state and NRA funds. Fiscal restraint during the early years had left a $42,500 surplus from the original grant.

> Vallen had a reputation as a bit of a tightwad. He wouldn't spend a dime.   AL IZZOLO, HOTEL
> FACULTY MEMBER

The NRA funds were carried over to supplement the state's assumption of the operating budget. That turnover came in 1970–1971. The director, who had never worried about state funding, reminded Vice President Baepler, who was not on staff at the time of the original grant, that the hotel college would need to be included in the new budget. Alas, that budget had been submitted two years earlier in keeping with state procedures.

> Sometimes the planning is three years ahead.   DON BAEPLER, UNLV PRESIDENT AND UNS
> CHANCELLOR

Hotel had to be squeezed out of the approved budget. Since budgets are usually built on previous years, the college suffered underfunding for years thereafter.

> Schools, colleges and programs like hotel that had to be absorbed into the budget process
> always started out behind the eightball. No question about it.   BAEPLER

Minority scholarships were one of the main thrusts of the renewed grant. The college submitted that idea on March 6, 1970 as part of a revised proposal.

> That was very unusual! Las Vegas was a Jim Crow town.   J. KELL HOUSSELS, JR., HOTELIER AND
> PRESIDENT OF THE NEVADA RESORT ASSOCIATION

The idea was well received because the black community had faced off several times with the Resort Association. Threatened marches and legal action resulted in NRA grants to the local community, particularly to the Las Vegas Branch of the National Association for the Advancement of Colored People (NAACP).

> " . . . Las Vegas [which] had been labeled, 'the Mississippi of the West' became one
> of the first [1960] U.S. cities to do something about discriminatory practices [after
> blacks threatened a sit-in at Strip hotels]. It would take 10 years for much of the
> rest of the country to advance so far. [*Las Vegas Sun*.[3]]

Segregation remained the norm until 1960. Prior to that even outstanding black performers had to leave the showrooms and seek housing in West Las Vegas.

> There was rampant discrimination in Vegas. Black entertainers were required to come in
> [to the Sahara Hotel] by the kitchen or the back door. No black guests were allowed. The

NAACP would come in periodically to highlight the situation. Little by little, things started to loosen up.   PHIL ARCE, SAHARA HOTEL MANAGER

For emphasis, a postscript was added to the scholarship-request letter. It asked each hotel to employ one of the minority applicants because that was "important to the intent of this aid." A second letter dated August 28, 1974, which listed the recipients of the scholarships, urged "NRA members to open avenues of employment for those minority students whom we have supported with NRA funds so they do not go to other cities." Unfortunately, the money was forthcoming, but job placement was not. Had it been, the federal lawsuit that followed might have been alleviated in part.

In an April 7, 1970 news release, the NRA's Joe Digles attributed remarks to the NRA's current president, Al Benedict:

"The minority scholarship plan launched by the resort hotels is unique in Nevada. . . . The goal is to broaden opportunities for participation by those now unable to take advantage of this quality program."

My memory [on that] is vague. There was a sense that education was ahead in those things [minority issues] and their [the NRA's] action was being taken [somewhat] *pro forma.* DIGLES

I knew the hotel [Riviera] had to do something, and that I was the one that had to do it. I was able to get a black man on as a bellman, and another as a car park. I even hired a handi-capped man with no hands.   FRANK WATTS, RIVIERA FINANCIAL OFFICER

Fitzpatrick's letter to the college confirms the details and describes the NRA's position on minority support:

" . . . a substantial portion of the funds [is to] be used for scholarships . . . to local students of all races, colors and creeds."

Accordingly, this second grant provided $7,000 for minority scholarships and $1,500 for general scholarships during the first two years. (Tuition was $222.50 per semester.) Each scholarship was renewable for four years, so the grant stretched forward by five years to complete scholarship awards made during the second year. Thus, for the second, third and fourth years, $14,000 was available for minority aid and $3,000 more for general scholarships. At the fifth and final year the figures were back to $7,000 and $1,500, the same as year one.

Awarding the grants was left to the university, specifically to the hotel college and the Office of Student Personnel Services in the person of Ed Lewis, one of the campus' first black professionals. Although the NRA stipulated a voting seat on the scholarship awards committee, it was never occupied. Instead, selections were sent by the college to the Resort Association after the fact and then only as a matter of courtesy. That was pretty much in keeping with the procedure for all campus scholarships. However, a brief bio on each scholarship winner was also sent to encourage job offers.

Preference went to Clark County residents. Other Nevada residents had priority over out-of-state students. In so providing, both the college and the association anticipated by almost a decade discrimination issues that were to confront the hotels of the Las Vegas Strip. From whence would come the Strip Scholarships as we shall see shortly.

The results were very disappointing. Everyone was dismayed at the absolute failure of the minority community to respond.

> Business [also] had trouble getting the black community to use them [scholarships] because they felt they would still be low man in the ranking order.   GEORGE HARDBECK, DEAN OF BUSINESS AND ECONOMICS

In August 1974, Vallen wrote again to the NRA urging them to hire minority scholarship winners as a means of promoting the cause. Ed Lewis went from high school to high school. He went to black churches and to Hispanic groups. Stories appeared in the newspapers. All to no avail, applications were few and far between. By the third year, the hotel college began offering the scholarships to the general population as the grant had provided. In his oral history, Cahill noted:

> "We saw the handwriting on the wall . . . as regards the minority problem. . . . Getting minority people to go into it [the industry] is a problem."[4]

Among the recipients, two local men—who found jobs on their own and pushed hard to make successful careers locally—stand out. Don Givens, class of 1977, is now Vice President and General Manager of the Excalibur Hotel, and Lonnie Wright, 1978, is a faculty member at the Clark County Community College.

The Strip Scholarships

Had the college and the Resort Association been more attuned to the situation and included women in the 1970 grant, they might have mitigated the 1975 action by the federal government. But by no means did the fault lie there alone. Almost twenty years earlier, in 1958, the City of Las Vegas actually adopted a resolution not to hire women dealers! One year later, North Las Vegas followed suit. This was the community position until 1967 when North Las Vegas repealed its resolution. Las Vegas acted in 1970 [*Las Vegas-Review Journal.*[5]]

> Reno's dealers were predominately women. Vegas' male dealers feared women would come down and take their jobs. Dealers talked about unionizing. At one time, the Resort Association actually paid a woman not to work!   ARCE

> Hard to believe today with so many female sales executives, but I was once fined a dollar by the local HSMA chapter [Hotel Sales Management Association] for just asking about bringing a woman student to a HSMA meeting!   JERRY VALLEN

In what-was-called the Relyea Case, sometimes the Telles Case or the Consent Decree, [6] the United States Equal Employment Opportunity Commission (EEOC) brought suit against the 19 hotels of the Strip and certain trade unions for discrimination in the hiring of women and Hispanics.[7]

> I think the first female dealer was at the Castaways or the Stardust. There was also a change in the type of dealers. The new ones often were college educated, which the pit bosses, who were standing over them, were not. ARCE

Interestingly, it was Frank "Lefty" Rosenthal of Chicago-mob fame who first hired women blackjack dealers. [Pileggi.[8]] Later, Rosenthal's activities would briefly touch the hotel college.

Two excerpts about the Vegas scene concur about Rosenthal's role:

> "During the '70s, the Stardust's Mr. Rosenthal, now an odds maker in Florida, had an idea that would increase business. He put six buxom young women behind his gaming tables, firing male dealers to make room for them. Gamblers wagered more than usual at the woman's tables, Mr. Rosenthal says and rivals were quick to copy his strategy. [*Wall Street Journal*.[9]]

> [Rosenthal] said something to a male dealer, who immediately walked away, obviously dismayed. Rosenthal than waved his hand . . . signaling to a crowd of people milling around the cashier's cage. A short heavyset young lady wearing a Stardust dealers uniform . . . assumed her post at the table. [Dick Odessky.[10]]

The Relyea Case never went to court; it was settled by the Consent Decree, which called for a corpus of $1,000,000 to be made available to settle claims. None of the trade unions were assessed any financial damages.

> In late 1980, I received a call from a member of the negotiating committee—I think it was Duff Taylor from the [original] MGM Grand—that the case was being settled and that the residual would come to the hotel college. We both guessed perhaps as much as $25,000–$50,000! JERRY VALLEN

> I don't know who gets the credit for that [giving the excess to the Hotel College], but it wasn't a bad idea! The case went on for years and we were all concerned and involved. HOUSSELS

Three unique sections of the settlement bear mentioning. (1) Hotels were required to establish personnel offices. The EEOC probably believed that hiring by department heads abetted discrimination. (2) Hotels were ordered to abridge their union contracts when and if the union hiring-hall process was unable to fill the quotas established by the Decree. (3) Unions were required to establish training programs, either independently or in cooperation with the Clark County Community College.

Newspaper advertisements and publicity of all kinds failed to raise many applicants. Apparently, the government felt there was more discrimination than did the women themselves. Nearly two-thirds of the money was unclaimed! The residual clause of the Consent Decree went into effect:

"Any residue shall go to the University of Nevada at Las Vegas for use in the University's financial aid program for needy students in an effort to bring about a greater sexual, racial, and ethnic diversity among the students in the University's Hotel Management Department."[11] [It was no surprise to its members that the College of Hotel Administration was misidentified once again.]

To everyone's amazement, the initial check was a whopping $527,500, supplemented by a second check of $26,950 on August 15, 1982. The initial presentation was accepted by the Board of Regents on December 11, 1981. Regent Chairman Bob Cashell appointed Regent June Whitley (an African American woman) as chair of a committee to develop criteria for the awards. Regent Lilly Fong (of Asian descent) and Dean Jerry Vallen were also named. Jim Kitchen and later John Lujan, from the campus' Affirmative Action Office, were added to the committee.

By the fall term 1981, hotel knew the funds were coming. A college committee headed by Richard Laughlin, a faculty member who had worked on similar issues when he was with Hyatt Hotels, was formed. Tentative guidelines were created. The committee pointed out what the NRA's original minority gift had already experienced: Minorities were not attracted to the study of hotel management. The committee wrote that:

" . . . minority students are not now enrolling in four-year hotel administration courses [anywhere in the USA], and a greater effort must be made . . . through comprehensive recruiting. At the outset, we feel that particular attention should be paid to . . . the recruiting brochure and [to] advertising."

The lack of minority students reflected the lack of minority candidates for the faculty.

I agreed to Pat Moreo's request for a one-year study leave provided he found his own replacement. He recommended our first African American faculty member and former student, Hank Melton, class of 1978. Melton remained on faculty even after Moreo returned.   JERRY VALLEN

Extensive efforts were made to publicize the opportunities. The results were no better than the college's earlier attempts with the NRA minority grant. With an okay from the Regents Committee, an expensive brochure featuring an African American woman on its cover was developed. Trouble was evident from the first visit of the EEOC representative, Elliott McCarty, from San Francisco. He ordered the entire batch of brochures destroyed because it featured a black woman on the cover. Despite the language of the grant, "bring about a greater sexual, racial, and ethnic diversity," McCarty insisted black employees were not specifically mentioned. Moreover, funds had to be made available to white males as well. According to the San Francisco office, no special group was to be targeted, the focus of the lawsuit to the contrary!

> This was a period when no one was sure what the rules or the objectives were. The Bakke Case [overturning minority quotas at universities] had just been settled. I'm certain the EEOC would have destroyed brochures with a white male on the cover.   JERRY VALLEN

Notices were sent far and wide. Mailings went to all the high schools in the state; to 200 junior colleges that offered hotel programs; to a variety of publications like the *Black Collegian*, the *Los Angeles Times* and *Hotel/Motel Magazine*. Help was solicited from the National Institute for the Foodservice Industry, the NAACP, the Latino community, from scholarship data bases, centers for employment training, career and college days and whomever and wherever leads might be generated. On September 17, 1971, the college reported the disappointing results to the Nevada Resort Association. It was fortunate that the initial decision by the EEOC allowed—indeed, directed—the college to help anyone, because minority applicants remained in short number.

Everyone worked together, but far too many cooks had entered the kitchen before the college was allowed to handle the awards—as was done with thousands of other scholarship dollars. Among attendees at one meeting or another were: Regents Fong, Kenny, McBride and Whitley; Affirmative Action Officers Kitchen and Lujan; Chancellors Bersi and Fox; President Goodall; faculty members Abbey, Christianson, Izzolo, Laughlin, Melton, Phillips and Vallen; administrators Daniels, Rivera and Standish; and Elliot McCarty of the EEOC. Wisely, the Resort Association stayed away.

New Rules. The flow of Strip Scholarship funds (eventually renamed The College of Hotel Administration Scholarship) substantiated what was growing more and more apparent. Deans were losing control of monies earmarked for their colleges. With nearly $600,000 in the account, the college anticipated earnings of no less than $60,000 to $70,000 the first year. (At that time, a personal $100,000 certificate of deposit was earning 14% annually!)

> Business was given inexpensive land that started growing in value until we sold it for $600,000. We set it up so that Harold Scott [in the business office] and I handled the investment. Those were the [President] Carter years when we were getting 10, 11, 12 percent interest.   HARDBECK

Later it was learned that the money was pooled with other university funds and that the Regents had limited the disbursement to 6% of earning. Less than $40,000 was available for scholarships although awards far in excess of that had already been made. On July 5, 1984, the college was notified that its request for an exception was denied, but that an appeal could be made provided it was submitted in 48 hours. Unable to comply—the purpose of that unrealistic time cap was never explained, it was decided to ask for a one-time exception in order to honor the grants that had been committed.

Earnings in excess of 6% were used to build the corpus. By 1996, the endowment, which started at $550,000 in 1982, had reached $1.3 million. This occurred during a period of unusually high interest rates. In retrospect, the Regents' policy appears less controversial than that which followed, the creation of the UNLV Foundation.

Notification of the change came from President Goodall (1984) and was reconfirmed by Vice President for Development Lyle Rivera. Thereafter, checks were to be payable to the UNLV Foundation, not to the Board of Regents. A percentage of each contribution raised by the college was taken by the foundation for its expenses. It was unclear whether that was in addition to or in place of the amount already being taken by the university's senior administration for soft money (not state funds) use. Many times, thereafter, hotel's dean had to remind appropriate authorities that so much money was due from certain funds on certain dates. Otherwise fund transfers somehow fell through the procedural cracks.

> We did quite well with the Stuart Hall Professorship until we lost it. It was taken away. Funds that Marge Barrett gave business to manage were eventually coopted by higher administration.
>
> One thing that might interest the readers is how every soft dollar we had was taken away.   GEORGE HARDBECK, DEAN OF BUSINESS AND ECONOMICS

> It was like that with hotel as well. A $140,000 gift to hotel from Tracinda "got lost" in the record shuffle and probably ended in the Tropicana Avenue fountain.   JERRY VALLEN

Difficulty in tracking funds was not limited to the hotel and business colleges. Buck Deadrich, executive director of the UNLV Foundation; Brock Dixon, then (1983) a professor of public administration; Jim Frey, chair of the intercollegiate athletic council; and Allen Mori, chairman of the academic faculty senate, explored that very issue in a serious of contentious memos.

The criteria and mechanics of The Strip Scholarship undergo continuous revisions and reinterpretations as new generations of EEOC officers and campus administrators review the materials in light of the latest definitions of discrimination. Although the settlement clearly states aid is to be disbursed "among the students in the University's Hotel Management Department," funds not committed by the college are escheated now to the university and given to non-hotel majors, rather than being held for another term. This is contrary to the intent of the original Consent Decree. Another example of reshuffled funds.

The Third, Fourth, and Fifth Requests

By Spring of 1972, the faculty portion of the second NRA grant, in contrast to the scholarship portion which had three more years to go, was coming to a close. So still another request for support was penned. Cahill answered Vallen on June 2, 1972, saying that the Nevada Resort Association has:

. . . "decided against renewing their commitment to supplement your operating budget.

They are aware of their commitment to the scholarship program and will, of course, continue it.

. . . this action in no way reflects any dissatisfaction with the results of our previous contribution to your program to attain a 'margin of excellence.'

To the contrary, the members in their discussion expressed the feeling that you had attained that goal and the responsibility for maintaining it should now be accepted by The Board of Regents."

A fourth and final effort by the college to interest the Nevada Resort Association in additional funding was made in 1977. The dean solicited a $165,000 grant, spread over four years, to launch a graduate program. This request was different than earlier bids. It contained a kicker: President Baepler pledged a matching grant of $250,000! But ten years had passed and the interests and configuration of the NRA had changed dramatically. Its unity was gone and its purpose had changed. This request and another in 1979 by Lyle Rivera, the campus' development officer, were met with disappointments, but not unexpectedly.

The college had been weaned from its birth mother and needed now to stand on its own. The original grant of $277,000 plus the $111,000 second grant plus the $554,450 Strip Scholarships totaled just under $1,000,000. But even then the Resort Association wasn't done. It continued financial support for the graduation luncheons, which featured many famous personalities and represented important public relations for the college. More of this in a later chapter. And it also funded the Campbell Scholarship.

The Campbell Gifts

Bill Campbell served as the Nevada Resort Association's labor expert for many years and took over as its executive officer when Robbins Cahill left in October 1977. He earned the respect of both the industry and the unions during his service as a labor negotiator.

> When Campbell took ill, the MGM sent its plane to the Del Coronado Hotel where Bill was vacationing.   PHIL ARCE, SAHARA HOTEL MANAGER

At Campbell's death in 1982, the Resort Association established a scholarship for graduate students. In a letter to the college, Vince Helm, the new Executive Director, reaffirmed the Association's continued involvement with the college.

> Because of the very high esteem and regard for Bill Campbell by the Nevada Resort Association, its Executive Committee has directed that $1,000 be contributed annually by the Association for a suitable memorial.   LETTER FROM VINCENT HELM, EXECUTIVE, NEVADA RESORT ASSOCIATION

As directed, a prize was awarded annually to a deserving graduate student, or alternatively used as a graduate prize for research in labor relations.

As the first such grant, the Campbell award played a special role in developing graduate studies. Most interesting was the NRA's shift in position. In rather strong language some twelve years earlier, it had declared its belief that the college should concentrate on undergraduate studies.

Yet another Campbell memorial, for the promotion of hotel labor education, was funded by an anonymous friend, an individual member of the NRA. That story continues in Chapter 7 as part of the opening of the college's building, Beam Hall.

FINANCIAL SUPPORT FROM THE BROAD COMMUNITY

The NRA's support for the college made it easier to solicit funds from other sources. Many of these other donors started with small grants that grew over the years to very substantial sums. Local, professional organizations were the first to step forward, but national, and later even international, firms were added to the list. The publicity from each invited ever broader university giving. Some quick math suggests that $923,950 was donated in 1982, the college's best year except for those special years with gifts of $1,000,000 or more.

> "It [the NRA's initial grant] marks the first major gift to NSU by private industry. We hope it attracts other gifts so direly needed by the struggling young school. [*Review-Journal.*[12]]

> I was especially disposed toward hotel because the industry was our biggest hope for private contributions to the [whole] university.   DON BAEPLER, UNLV PRESIDENT AND UNS CHANCELLOR

Non-Scholarship Endowments

Donors have different reasons for giving just as the college seeks resources from different sources. Gifts originate with the donor's desire to highlight a particular cause or to honor a particular person. Several such endowments were established with the opening of Beam Hall. They included gifts from Banfi Wines, the Beam family, the Boyd family, the Harrah family, the Tropicana Hotel, and the anonymous Bill Campbell memorial. Another example of specific purpose was the Kotschevar fund.

Margaret Scoles Kotschevar Fund. Lendal Kotschevar was the College's first visiting faculty member, a post that was initially funded with the second NRA grant. Thereafter, he joined the UNLV faculty several times for temporary assignments varying between one term and one year. In between, he and his wife, Margaret, joined faculty in Florida, Hawaii and Israel. Even though their Nevada residencies were interrupted, the Kotschevars became fast friends with several faculty members. Some they already knew. Jim Abbey, Dick Acosta, Don Bell, Frank Borsenik and John Stefanelli either had been on the Michigan State faculty or had been one of Kotschevar's students.

> Len Kotschevar was at UNLV and when I was ready to move to Nevada. I called him before I called the dean.   FRANK BORSENIK, HOTEL FACULTY MEMBER

Because of his time in Las Vegas, Lendal Kotschevar came to know other faculty and chose Leslie Cummings and Valentino Luciani to co-author revisions of two books from the many that he had written.

> The second time Lendal was here, he suggested that we write a book together. I was so surprised! It was a good experience to see how one does a book. And I said to Vallen, why doesn't everyone do a book? The answer was something like hang in there. And then I knew: It was an arduous process. Four years later the book was finally finished. LESLIE CUMMINGS, HOTEL FACULTY MEMBER

The faculty quickly came to appreciate Kotschevar's contributions. In the Spring of 1983, using letters of support from Bob Blomstrom (Michigan State), Gerry Lattin (Houston) and Tony Marshall (Florida International), UNLV named Lendal Kotschevar a Distinguished Visiting Professor, a very special category provided for in the university code.

Lendal and Margaret Kotschevar came to campus from their summer home in Montana. During one of those drives, Margaret was killed in an auto accident.

> One of the college's saddest days was when Margaret Kotschevar failed to make it back to campus. JIM ABBEY, HOTEL FACULTY MEMBER

From that tragedy came a wonderful gift, one that was conceived by Richard and Mari Basile, from whom the first check was received. Subsequent contributions came from former students, faculty, industry professionals, companies and friends, including Lew and Ruth Minor in particular. In keeping with the intent of the gift, earnings are used to support faculty improvement. Young faculty members have had help finishing their formal education and obtaining advanced degrees. More senior faculty members have been aided in research projects and publications and in attendance at professional meetings. As endowments are supposed to do, this account and those described below continue today facilitating the work of the college.

The General Endowment Fund. Economics Laboratory, Inc., a company that specializes in sanitation for the hospitality industry, was the first non-gaming company to support the college. The dean renewed acquaintanceships with Economics Lab's local field rep, Alan Stanchfield, at the September, 1969 monthly meeting of the Food Service Executive's Association (FSEA). The local chapter was already supporting the college and that presented an opportunity to ask Economics Lab to do the same. The dean also came to know the company's marketing vice president, Owen Potts. Before the year was out, 18 shares of common stock valued at more than $900 was on hand. In 1969, it was a substantial gift for a new program. Within six months, an additional 18 shares were donated.

> Owen Potts and I golfed together in Florida for many years, but he never knew I was Jerry Vallen's brother. On one occasion, about 1976, he told me what a great hotel school UNLV had. I disagreed sharply and disparaged it, especially the dean. Owen was really taken back,

but his surprise turned to laughter when he learned that we were brothers. He knew each of us separately 3,000 miles apart.   BERNARD VELENCHIK, JERRY VALLEN'S BROTHER

Along with the shares, Economics Labs loaned the food and beverage faculty educational films, equipment and guest speakers. Charlie Levinson, in particular, took advantage of these.

[Many years later] Economics Lab set us up with all the equipment for dispensing the soap and chemicals after the Beam Hall kitchen was completed.   CLAUDE LAMBERTZ, HOTEL FACULTY MEMBER

Several years later the shares were sold at a profit. Those dollars started a flow of money that had no specific designation. The university didn't permit endowing funds unless the sum reached the critical mass of $10,000. Small gifts were magnified by combining them. Lawry's Foods, Inc, for example, matched employee contributions—a benefit not encountered very often in the hospitality industry. Ron Avarbuch, class of 1971, made the first such gift and continued doing so for several years.

Into this account flowed a mix of miscellaneous monies. Included were donations from alumni. Alumni names and their graduating years were put on chairs in the classrooms, but the idea never took off as hoped. Other gifts were from friends of the college. Seminar earnings with continuing education, which partnered with Penton Publishing and was managed by Keith McNeil, were deposited. Rodeway Inns contributed on several occasions through one of its vice-presidents, who was a graduate of Vallen's junior-college teaching days. Earnings from the profitable seminars with the National Restaurant Association helped the account grow.

Some of the unspent funds from the Nevada Resort Association's second grant were also used to build the initial corpus. Since that gift had been called the "Margin of Excellence," the dean's office used that term for the account that the business office called The Hotel Endowment.

One thoughtful, but small gift came unexpectedly in the mail one day. It was added to the endowment. The written acknowledgment carried that information, which upset the donor who thought the college would use it for a specific purpose. The small gift turned into a big brouhaha.

The endowment still receives regular boosts from Tola and Marcia Chin of Chin's Restaurant. Their support has been enduring in several additional facets, as later chapters will relate.

Most gratifying to me is the overall success of the school.   TOLA CHIN, RESTAURANTEUR AND DONOR

For many years, Leo Lewis returned his salary checks to the college. Another Hilton executive, John Fitzgerald, followed the lead. They did so despite the major contribution of time in order to teach part time term after term. And so the account grew. A gift from the MGM Grand added several thousand dollars to the endowment in August, 1981. It was MGM's way of acknowledging the university's help during the great MGM fire. The gift was given to hotel, but some of that money was taken for university-wide use. (Standard protocol with hotel's money.)

Two interesting gifts ran for several years. The first originated in one of the gaming seminars offered by the college. A San Diego man, Jack McLeod, and his son attended and became acquainted with the program. Sometime later, he called to get tickets to a basketball game: an impossible feat in the winning days of the Rebels! The dean gave his two seats in the peanut gallery for that one game. The donor began sending annual checks.

The second came from Mrs. Joseph Broussard, whose son and daughter were students. Mrs. Broussard was so pleased with her children's Las Vegas experience that she made regular, unsolicited contributions to the account and later for building equipment. In fact, she moved to Las Vegas for a while. Equally exciting, she shipped crawfish from her home in Louisiana to be used on the buffet tables!

> Other parents got involved after Mrs. Broussard showed the way. Their participation was very welcome but never quite matched the crawfish of Mrs. Broussard.   LAMBERTZ

Building an endowment is a slow process, but by the closing date of this history, the account was substantial. Earnings are used at the direction of the dean for a variety of activities including college needs, faculty assistance and student chapter support.

The Cookie Fund. There was a Campus Host Fund—informally called the Cookie Fund—for hosting guests. In a typical year, hotel's allocation was $200. Each request had to be processed through the office of the academic vice-president. University regulations forbid the use of both the Cookie Fund and the general operating budget for memberships in trade associations or for meal reimbursements while attending local, professional meetings. Yet, it was from these associations that flowed thousands and thousands of dollars of gifts, scholarships, grants and jobs. It was suggested by upper levels of the university hierarchy that the college not bother joining but merely buy the associations' professional publications, which were covered by state funding. A serious misinterpretation of hotel's needs versus those of, say, the scientific faculty, for whom the publication may have been the important benefit. The growing endowment eliminated the issue once permission was granted to use the account for memberships and meals.

Out-of-state travel funds had similar restrictions, the product of miserly state budgets. The college had a travel budget of $690 or $22.03 per faculty member in 1987–1988, the same year as the $200 Cookie Fund allotment. Once again, the college turned to the endowment.

The Library

Building the library collection was an early priority. Library weakness was highlighted as early as the 1970 accreditation report. Lack of course specific texts was the major difficulty. Richard Strahlem acknowledged that issue in his 1966 report to the faculty (see Exhibit 3-1). To help remedy the situation, the dean became the acquisitions editor for the William C. Brown Company, Publishers, Dubuque Iowa, that was distributing a line of hotel books. The push was on to get authors including UNLV faculty members.

The library began work on the collection almost at once. There is an attachment to the 1968 meeting of the Hotel Advisory Committee agenda reporting acquisitions of gaming and hotel materials. Improvements were evident by the second accreditation review, 1980, which reported on page 19 that 85% of all relevant hotel books contained in bibliographical lists were held by UNLV. The library worked hard. Between 1972 and 1979, hotel's collection grew by 628 books, a 115% growth, fourth highest among 70 classifications listed in the UNLV Library Report of September 14, 1979.

The 1980 Accreditation Report applauded the cooperation between the college and the library. Hotel books were not always published through traditional outlets. So the first identification of new books often came through the trade press. The faculty, being trade-press readers, kept the library aware of new releases.

One trade-press ad screamed for attention. A menu collection was advertised for private sale. Unable to get library funding and being turned away by the Nevada Resort Association, the college dug into unspent money husbanded from the original NRA grant. Negotiations by mail and telephone produced results. The Henry J. Bohn collection contained 1,200 menus from the mid 1800's featuring special dinners and banquets by world-famous chefs who had prepared the meals for the elite and royalty of the 19th Century.

Two additional collections supplement those early holdings. Sylvia Hart donated the collection of her husband Nat Hart, who was a regular participant and a strong contributor to the college's seminars and curriculum.

Nat and Sylvia Hart were such good friends! Although perfection isn't always possible, Nat made the same comment after every culinary event staged by the school. How come the students didn't do this? or that? Then I would kid him, Let's go to your restaurants [Nat was corporate vice president for food and beverage at Caesars Palace] and see if they are 100%. People expected us to be perfect always. Well, these were students.   ALAN STUTTS, HOTEL FACULTY MEMBER

A library publication describes the Hart collection:

" . . . [It] documents the culinary industry in Las Vegas. From his initial position as maitre d' at the Flamingo . . . Nat Hart went on to establish the Bacchanal Room at Caesars. . . . [The collection] contains his personal cook books and menu collections, service manuals, design drawings and working files.[13]

Muriel Stevens, another committed supporter of and instructor at the hotel college, author, long-time media host and culinary expert, donated her memorabilia as the Maury and Muriel Stevens collection. This donation, like Hart's, was one gift in a series of contributions that included time, money and knowledge from both of these life-time friends.

The International Food Service Executives Association designated the UNLV library as its repository for cookbooks and association memorabilia from around the world. The idea to gather these long neglected archives was first discussed by the dean and his brother, Milton Vallen, IFSEA's international president 1978–1980. Cataloging was made possible by a grant from one of the associations most senior members, Kae deBrent Hodges and her estate. Equally important, Kae used her strong powers of persuasion to obtain materials from the local chapters.

The Gambarana Donation. The library collection would not be as strong today as it is were it nor for an exceptional gift from Eddie and Peggy Jean Gambarana. Given in perpetuity, the Gambarana family simultaneously funded their own account and that of the Kaltenborn library gift. The Gambarana portion is used to benefit the library collection of the College of Hotel Administration; the Kaltenborn portion is earmarked for the School of Engineering, including computer sciences. Excess funds accrue to the office and to the use of the university president.

The open language of the Gambarana gift necessitated some more definitive guidelines. A joint library/hotel college committee was formed in 1986. From it came a memorandum of suggested uses that was approved by both the college dean and the university's chief librarian, Mary Dale Palsson. In addition to the usual acquisitions, including periodicals, it was decided that funds could be expended for employees or graduate students working on the college's material including the IFSEA collection; the gaming collection, the Bohn menu collection and the meat slides collections. Support for dissertations, oral histories, and corporate and company memorabilia was also approved. The memo contained an extensive list of other ancillary purposes, including funds for cataloging and bibliographic work and for films, discs and tapes.

The Szathmary Gift. Alas, the strengthening alliance between the college and Chef Louis Szathmary came to a sad ending because of the library. Szathmary had a very valuable collection of cookbooks and cooking memorabilia, some 18,000 items, that he decided to contribute to UNLV's library as a supplement to its growing culinary collection. Two library directors, Hal Erickson and Mary Dale Palsson, as well as President Goodall worked diligently with the college to resolve the details of this multimillion dollar gift. Szathmary's appointment to faculty was just one of the issues.

> I may have been the channel through which the school found out about Louie's cookbook collection. [A Smith in-law was a protege of and a confidant to the chef.]   BOB SMITH, DEAN OF SCIENCE, MATHEMATICS AND ENGINEERING

Each piece had unusual value so small bits were to be given annually to fit the family's tax situation. Two rare, ancient texts appraised at several million dollars were among the first group, but one of them went missing within a very short time.

Louie was infuriated with the university's nonchalance and its failure to investigate what appeared to be an out-and-out theft. Neither the Szathmary family nor the college faculty were satisfied with the explanation that the book would be recovered the very first time it was offered to a legitimate collector. If so, everyone is still waiting.

> He donated the books and when he returned a year later one was missing. It was obvious that the thief was someone who knew something about rare books. He was so upset he took back the other book. His daughter, Barbara, remains the curator [on another campus].   LAMBERTZ

Despite pre-announcements, a publicity spread in *Restaurant Business* (February 1, 1982), a banquet with Friends of the Library and an open house for the new library wing, catered by the chef himself, the Szathmarys retracted their gift. It was a disastrous disappointment, but not the only memorable failure that the college experienced.

MEMORABLE FAILURES

Del E. Webb was the college's first big solicitation. The Sahara hotel, which was Webb's headquarters, was among the program's biggest boosters supported by Phil Arce, Doug Farley, Sig Front and Bud James.

> I looked at UNLV as a tremendous resource for the Sahara and the other Webb hotels.   SIG FRONT, VICE PRESIDENT, SAHARA HOTEL

A plan to give Webb an honorary degree was successfully passed through the many internal hurdles of the university. After all, Del E. Webb was a Las Vegas personage. He had built the Flamingo (for Bugsy Siegel), the Sahara and numerous public buildings including city hall. Boyce W. Phillips arranged to transport Webb from the Sahara to the Convention Center in a borrowed limousine. Phillips wore a chauffeur's cap! Somehow, he even convinced the police department to provide a siren escort to and from the graduation site. The plan failed simply because the new dean didn't know how to close the sale. He rode in the back with Del Webb and made small talk but never followed up the introduction by a solicitation visit. Yet every sales course contains a basic axiom: Ask for the sale.

One such sale was asked for but proved to be too cumbersome. The grand stairwell in Beam Hall led to the Boyd dining rooms on the second floor. A proposal was made to Joe Buckley, serving as an elected officer of Rotary International, that every Rotary chapter in the world pay for an inscribed tile that would be used to finish the concrete walls of the stairwell. Buckley was intrigued, but felt the plan was not workable. Since he was a Summa (Howard Hughes' company) executive, the idea was floated there, as was a proposal (suggested by Phil Arce) that Summa sponsor a room in the new building. No success on either score.

Direct Mail

Not every solicitation is successful; not every sales effort wins a customer. Some efforts falter on the solicitor's approach to the donor; some are poorly conceived; some are improperly timed; some are misdirected; and in retrospect many seem simply outrageous. Into the latter category fall solicitations made by mail without any previous contact or base.

Imagine receiving a letter asking for thousands of dollars from a solicitor whom one doesn't know. Nevertheless, that approach was used on several occasions. With local personages, Sam Joyner and Anthony Ciccarelli acting as go-betweens, a solicitation was made to the Kobrand Corporation. The vice chairman of the board, Charles Mueller, said they had given the request "careful consideration." Kobrand did provide smaller support for many years. Several other efforts were tried before the inanity of the approach was realized.

An earlier, but equally discreditable attempt was directed to the Statler Foundation, which was headed by Peter Crotty and housed in Buffalo, New York. The Statler Foundation was established by the estate of hotelman Ellsworth Statler and administered for many years before her death by his spouse, Alice Statler. The dean had corresponded with and met Mrs. Statler. Statler's biography explains that:

> The Foundation began to grant construction and scholarship monies to high schools, trade schools and junior colleges . . . and to universities offering Bachelor of Science Degrees in hotel administration. [*Statler . . . Extraordinary Hotelman.*[14]]

Vallen spoke at the international meeting of the Food Service Executives Association in Reno in 1982 and met there with Neil Goodman, an influential member of both the FSEA and the Statler Foundation. Goodman, who was also a friend of the dean's brother, promised to put in a good word with the Statler Board. There was a sense that the application procedure was somewhat *pro forma* and with that assumption, a letter of solicitation was drafted. Only later was it learned that the foundation was headed by a staid, traditional and penny-pinching board, of which Chairman Peter Crotty was the most representative. Of course, those inquiries should have been made first. A cool, terse and formal response foreclosed the college's future relationships with the Statler Foundation.

Imagine my surprise when six months later a call came from Crotty himself, no secretary, asking for a favor. Could I get him a room during one of Las Vegas' frequently sold-out dates.
JERRY VALLEN

Another New Yorker, Harry Helmsley of Helmsley Hotels and probably the largest real estate holder in New York City, didn't escape the solicitation net. Using the leverage of Steve Brener and Carmi Gamoran, both friends of UNLV and influential members of Harry's real estate division, Helmsley-Spear, an appeal for support was also addressed to New York City. After Mr. Helmsley became incapacitated, the college used the same two supplicants, to invite Leona Helmsely to speak to the graduating class. That was before her infamous trial. Neither solicitation was successful.

Another and what-was-to-be the final direct-mail attempt was made to Edgar Bronfman, Jr. Bronfman and his family controlled the Seagram Company. Seagram had been giving several thousand dollars annually for scholarships. In addition, one faculty member, Charles Levinson, was representing Seagram in liquor seminars in the USSR. That was an usual arrangement in 1982 before glasnost and peristroka. An appeal, which followed from a conversation that Larry Ruvo of Southern Wine and Spirits had with his friend Bronfman, was made by letter directly to Mr. Bronfman. The timing was too late by a year. The House of Seagram had already decided to limit its generous donations to one agency, National Institute for the Foodservice Industry, the educational arm of the National Restaurant Association. It was the final learning experience and taught the dean how not to make solicitations for large sums.

An alphabetical sampling illustrates some of the other disappointments that befell the college in its search for support.

Baggott's Boat

George Baggott of Crescent Metal Products, a manufacturer of quality kitchen equipments, was an unabashed booster of the college. He was an enthusiastic donor of equipment after the college's building was completed . Before that, he was a regular on campus, visiting with the faculty and students and always playing a supporting role. Although Baggott didn't know it, Jerry Vallen had pushed the quality of Crescent Metal's Cres-Cor and Crown X product lines during his several overseas assignments where he represented American manufacturers for the United States Department of Commerce. Baggott's support wasn't a *quid pro quo* because Baggot was unaware of Vallen's activities.

During the Spring, 1982 National Restaurant Show in Chicago, years before the building was constructed, the dean visited with Baggot in his booth. The outcome was a pledge of support, an exciting one. Cres-Cor would donate one of the catamarans that Baggott's brother manufactured. It was Mr. Baggott's suggestion that the college raffle it! Unresolved was how the boat would be transported to Las Vegas, but towing it behind a truck during the upcoming summer was discussed. It proved to be an unnecessary mental exercise.

Other plans had to be put in place before delivery. Where to exhibit it—in the middle of campus, perhaps; how to secure it; how to sell and account for the tickets; how to publicize it; were just a few of the tough, initial questions. The project collapsed on a little known provision of Nevada law. Raffles were illegal. Although many organizations held raffles, the university administration was concerned that so widely publicized a raffle would put the campus in a bad light.

The LVCB

One disappointment—a missed opportunity—was the college's go at the then-named Las Vegas Convention Bureau (LVCB), later the Las Vegas Convention and Visitors Authority (LVCVA). Through the Las Vegas Chapter of the Hotel Sales Management Association (HSMA), later the Hospitality Sales and Marketing Association International (HSMAI), friendships were cemented with two important LVCB persons, Jim Deitch and Barney Rawlings. Both men participated in the marketing course that the HSMA chapter taught for the college. Rawlings started teaching when he was the

Riviera's vice president of sales. He then moved to the Sands before becoming executive director for sales of the LVCB in 1970. Jim Deitch was director of advertising and promotion for the bureau. Numerous suggestions about financial cooperation were advanced to both of them, and were heard, but nothing materialized. Unquestionably, they were concerned with opening the floodgates to all kinds of educational requests. Finally, the opportunity came.

In a memo dated December 1, 1969, the college proposed to collect and disseminate what later became the LVCVA's detailed and very successful annual market survey. The proposal suggested a jointly appointed LVCB-researcher/faculty member. A $30,000 annual budget would underwrite both a faculty member and graduate student. Each would work half time for UNLV and half time for LVCB. Two other suggestions augmented the proposal. An internship would be started at the Bureau, and the UNLV library would become the depository of the archives of The Travel Research Association—later the Travel and Tourism Research Association (TTRA), which was just getting launched nationally, and to which LVCB personnel were heavily committed.

The ideas were good but their implementation was doomed by two mistakes. The faculty/researcher nominated by the college was a very poor politician. That became painfully apparent after several serious gaffs during his appearance before the LCVB's board. The second and bigger mistake was listening to the university's administration, which urged cooperation with the College of Business. Since college-to-college relationships were strained at that time, a sensitive ear was tuned to the administrative plea. Business college faculty were invited in, but there was an unexpected twist to the plot. Two individual faculty members from business working as private consultants, not for the College of Business and not for the College of Hotel Administration, walked away with the contract.

The college learned slowly, painfully slowly, for an almost identical scenario played out a second time with the airport and the two colleges. Again, hotel was body checked by individual business faculty members.

> Curt Shirer [hotel faculty member] and I submitted a visitor-survey proposal to the airport. We were asked to include the marketing department [College of Business]. Two of their faculty members, Henry Scuillo and Larry Dandurand took our proposal, but eliminated the large overhead charged by the university [On all its contracts, UNLV took overhead, compensation for office use, energy, stationery, etc.]. They bid the contact on their own and won.
> BORSENIK

There was one positive win. The LVCVA in the person of Rossi Ralenkotter helped to fund the research behind Jim Abbey's doctoral dissertation, which won an award from TTRA.

Hilton's Gift

The college and the Hilton Corporation had a supportive relationship that dated back almost to the program's beginnings. For nearly ten years, UNLV was one of a handful of programs invited by Senior Vice President Lloyd Farwell to attend the annual

Hilton Inn's Owner/Managers Meetings. Local Hilton executives Steve Michelle, Leo Lewis and Ted Nelson taught part time for the program over many years.

The relationship was as much a national one as a local one. Both Lloyd S. Farwell, senior vice president, and William (Bill) H..Edwards, vice chairman of Hilton Hotels Corp knew the program. Toni Aigner, Waldorf-Astoria's food and beverage executive, provided teaching materials. The long list of supporters included Hilton executives Vernon Herndon (Chicago) and John Fitzgerald in Atlantic City. Alumnus Jerry Inzerillo (class of 1975), executive assistant manager at Hilton's Fontainebleau in Miami Beach, had worked diligently, albeit unsuccessfully, with Porter Parris, Hilton's senior vice president, to get Hilton memorabilia for the library. Another graduate, Kenneth Free (1972) was Hilton's director of real estate administration.

With the help of the dean's office, Susan Bastianello-Salazar, Hilton's director of recruitment, established the first student liaison leader. The idea spread to other campuses. This paid student acted as a Hilton's spokesperson on campus and kept the company apprized of competing interviewers.

No wonder that President Maxson's 1986 surprise announcement that the Hilton Corporation had pledged $2,000,000 to the College of Business came as a shock! To the hotel faculty, it appeared that Maxson had wheedled the gift from Hilton by confusing the Business College and the Hotel College. The two are the same on many campuses. That suspicion was validated later during conversations with Acting Dean Clint Rappole, University of Houston. Houston was the chief beneficiary, about $40 million, of the Hilton Foundation's largess and was close to Jim Galbraith, Houston's Hilton-liaison executive. Of course, these two men were tied to the Hilton Foundation whereas the UNLV gift came from the Hilton Corporation. Alan Stutts, a former UNLV faculty member and one-time dean of the Houston program, explains what happened.

> Eric Hilton—I think it was Eric who told me—sat on the board of both the Hilton Foundation and the Hilton [operating] Corporation. They thought the grant was going to the hotel school. It was John Giovenco, President, Hilton Nevada Corporation, who directed the funds to business.   STUTTS

The Hilton surprise was one of three hotel gifts massaged by the college's dean and commandeered by President Maxson. Hilton compensated for the misunderstanding—certainly, not of its doing—with an annual gift of $10,000 for several years thereafter. Some of those dollars found their way into the endowment and some were used annually for equipment or for faculty and student support.

Barron Hilton, who spoke at the 1988 graduation luncheon, probably felt that his invitation was an acknowledgment of the company's gift.

Howard Hughes

Friendly ties with Howard Hughes' operations were established soon after the hotel program was up and running. The cloistered billionaire had moved to Vegas and settled in the Desert Inn in October, 1966.

Howard Hughes and Del Webb were very close. Originally, Hughes was supposed to stay at the Sahara. We had the whole place gutted and redone. Hughes' lieutenants came and said there wasn't enough air conditioning. So they cut a hole in the roof. Before the renovation was completed, it rained. Hughes ended up at the Desert Inn.

Whenever someone had to contact Howard Hughes, they called Del Webb. He always knew where Hughes was. Webb did all of Hughes' construction. [Webb was said to be one of a limited few who met Hughes face-to-face.]

Webb would tell me Howard Hughes stories that had me in stitches.   PHIL ARCE, SAHARA HOTEL MANAGER

From George Rhodine, human resources manager at the Landmark Hotel, came enticing bits of information about this secretive man, whom Rhodine had known personally—so he said—and who relied on Rhodine to accompany him in the train ride that brought Hughes to Las Vegas one quiet night—so he said. Vogliotti had this to say:

"In time, he [Hughes] changed gambling; that is, he gave so many Americans a new tolerance for it, a moral endorsement. . . . "Yet this man, who would command a series of comically incompetent managers, managed to change state history, for he speeded national acceptance of gambling."[15]

In an attempt to move communication to a higher level, personal invitations were addressed to Hughes at the Desert Inn for every event that the college held, and there were many. Not that any response was expected. Perhaps it was these invitations that brought an invitation to lunch from Hughes' executives, one of whom was Attorney Tom Bell, a member of the University's Board of Regents. The tone of the meeting was what did the school want. At that point in its development, the school wanted nothing major. The immediate focus was on internships and there is where the conversation centered. Thinking about the meeting years later after Hughes helped finance the medical school at Reno, one wonders whether that was a real opportunity lost!

Yes, I think you slipped up; I think you made a boo-boo.   TOM BELL, ATTORNEY TO THE HUGHES CORPORATION

The Riklis Fiasco

In response to a letter from the dean, a 1982 interview was arranged with Meshulam Riklis, who had purchased the Riviera Hotel in 1973. Riklis' holding company, Rapid America, was invested chiefly in retailing: Burger King, Cartier, Faberge and Schenley. He appeared to be a possible donor since he had agreed to the meeting.

Vallen arrived to find his interviewer waiting impatiently in tennis clothes, obviously headed to the courts. That set the tone of getting down to business with no time for preliminaries. Whereas the certainty of a small donation was likely, the idea was jettisoned in favor of what was the college's main need at that time. Hence to the inquiry, "What I can do for you?" came the blurted response, "We're soliciting

$11 million dollars for a new building!" Abruptly, the conversation ended and Riklis handed the interview off to his associate, Isidore Becker, before there was time to explain that for a small percentage of the figure Riklis could name the building.

Vallen already "knew" Becker, now president of the Riviera Hotel. They had lunched together a half-dozen years earlier in New York City as part of the college's solicitation of Schenley. As early as April, 1977, correspondence had been directed to Messrs. Riklis, Becker and Howard Feldman, president of Schenley Affiliated Brands. Those contact originated with Schenley's executive vice president, Oscar Greene, who had become a good friend and supporter of the college. So too had Johannes Lichtenstein, the company's traveling wine expert. Lichtenstein had even gone so far as promising a $10,000 wine tasting room in the new building. None of the solicitations was successful.

Rosenthal from the Stardust

The early history of the Stardust Hotel was a checkered one. For a brief period after Moe Dalitz's Desert Inn group exited its ownership of the property, the Stardust gained an aura of respectability. During the school year 1969–1970 the college approached the Stardust through the Parvin-Dohrmann Company (a national supplier of hotel furnishings), which had ties to the hotel.

A series of ownership turnovers followed. First, the Recrion Corporation became the Stardust's parent. Next, the Securities and Exchange Commission forced Recrion to sell the hotel to the Argent Corporation (1974) with Allen Glick as president. During this transition, the college's second proposal for $75,000 in scholarships was courteously received. Hopes were high although it had been many years since the first approach.

Under Glick, Frank "Lefty" Rosenthal became the de facto casino head. Soon after Rosenthal had launched his own, local television program, the college received a telephone call from the Stardust's publicist, Dick Odessky. The hotel wanted to discuss a possible scholarship of one million dollars! Arrangements were quickly made for an on-site visit. A very brief conversation took place at the Stardust with Allen Glick in his unusual office of whites and purples. Al Sachs along with several others whom Vallen didn't know were in attendance. Sachs ran the operation, and the dean knew him in that capacity. It was the first and only meeting with Glick. In just a few minutes an understanding was reached: The hotel would provide the money and the college would decide its disposition. Plenty of handshakes all around.

Shortly thereafter, a second telephone call came to the college asking if Frank Rosenthal could speak to one of the classes. Rosenthal was a nemesis of the Gaming Control Board. He did not hold a key-employee license (he wouldn't have gotten one had he applied because of his reputed ties to Chicago's organized crime) and yet he was making policy for the casino and the hotel. But outside speakers were not unusual. A great number of executives helped out with regular classes or occasional visits. So Rosenthal's talk was set for several weeks ahead.

Came still another telephone call, this time from Shannon Bybee. Bybee had been or still was a member of the Gaming Board and a friend of the college. So too was Jeff

Silver, chief counsel for the Board, and another occasional classroom visitor. Bybee asked if the rumored visit of Rosenthal was true. Assured that it was, Bybee suggested with emphasis that the school cancel the invitation. No additional explanation was offered; none had to be. Never explained was how the visit had become public knowledge.

> This was about the time that I was moving from the Board into private practice. So I may have been on the Board or I may have been in practice, which included legal counsel to Glick at the Stardust.   SHANNON BYBEE, STATE GAMING BOARD AND LATER HOTEL FACULTY MEMBER

The invitation was canceled and with it the $1,000,000 windfall. About that time, Odessky left his job. By January, 1976 so had Rosenthal. He was called for licensing in a heated exchange with Nevada Gaming Commission Chairman Harry Reid that made national headlines. Denied licensing, Rosenthal appealed unsuccessfully to the courts. He was placed in the State's Black Book in 1987 and moved to Florida after a near-death experience with a car bomb.

Elaine and Steve Wynn

One generous gift came about unexpectedly, very suddenly. It was that lack of fore-warning that torpedoed the donation. President Bob Maxson had a habit of announcing large gifts without cautioning the deans. Word would go out for all administrators to meet for an announcement. Maxson would make the announcement without inviting the appropriate administrator to even participate in the program. A good thing probably since no one knew what remarks to prepare.

This particular donation carried the secrecy one step further. At the height of the dining room's popularity, when gourmet dinners at $50–$100 were *de rigueur*, Steve and Elaine Wynn, Bob and Sylvia Maxson and Jerry and Flossie Vallen had dinner in the Boyd dining room. To the absolute surprise of the Vallens, the Wynns proposed a $1,000,000 gift to be used for developing a chef's school. Now if nothing else, the dean was very sensitive to the college's posture within the academic community. Without preparation, without the ability to offer alternative uses or to refine the proposal, and while the table waited expectantly, a decision had to be made. A non-degree, cooking program with students in kitchen whites parading around campus would tilt the college away from the core of the faculty and undermine all the previous work of integrating hotel into the academic setting.

With untold disappointment, the offer was refused. If only Bob Maxson had remembered the old adage: To be forewarned is to be forearmed. Now long afterwards, the Wynns made a donation that created a suite of offices and a non-administrative position for Maxson if and when he decided to step down as university president.

Despite the list of disappointments and errors in solicitation, there were more successes than letdowns. Individuals and companies realized how much their contributions helped and they were generous in their support. Details of which are outlined in the next two chapters.

ENDNOTES FOR CHAPTER 5

1. Robbins Cahill. "Reflections of Work in State Politics, Government, Taxation, Gaming Control, Clark County Administration and the Nevada Resort Association." *Oral History Project* (Reno: University of Nevada, Reno, Library), p. 1,365.

2. Letter from Walter Fitzpatrick, Chair of the NRA's reactivated advisory committee, to Al Benedict, then President of the Nevada Resort Association, dated 12/8/1969.

3. "Las Vegas Sun: The First 50 Years, Hank." *Las Vegas Sun*, July 2, 2000, p. 13S.

4. Cahill. *Oral History Project*, p. 1369.

5. "Gaming Chips." *Las Vegas-Review Journal*, January 7, 2001, p. F1.

6. The plaintiff was the San Francisco District Office of the Equal Employment Opportunity Commission in the persons of F. Cancino, Regional Attorney; Chester F. Relyea—hence the name Relyea Case, Supervisory Trial Attorney; and Elliott McCarty, Trial Attorney.

7. Those hotels or companies were the: Aladdin; Caesars Palace; Circus Circus; Dunes; Hacienda; Hilton (Flamingo, Las Vegas Hilton); Landmark; MGM Grand; Riviera; Sahara; Silver Bird (Thunderbird); Stardust; Summa Corporation (Castaways, Desert Inn, Frontier, Sands, Silver Slipper); Tropicana. Union defendants were: Local 226, Culinary Workers; Local 165, Bartenders and Beverage Dispensers; the Joint Executive Board of Locals 226 and 165; Local 995, Professional, Clerical and Miscellaneous Employees; Local 720 Theatrical Stage Employees.

8. Nicholas Pileggi. *Casino: Love and Honor in Las Vegas.* (New York: Simon & Shuster, 1995), p. 175.

9. Christina Binkley. "Las Vegas Dealers to Thrown In With the Unions." *Wall Street Journal*, March 6, 2001, p. A1.

10. Dick Odessky. *Fly on the Wall.* (Las Vegas: Huntington Press, 1999), p. 212.

11. Consent decree filed in U.S. District Court in San Francisco, CA, January, 1981, page 17, Article VI.

12. Editorial. *Las Vegas-Review Journal*, Monday, January 17, 1966.

13. University of Nevada, Las Vegas Libraries. *2001 Annual Report*, p. 19.

14. Floyd Miller. *Statler, America's Extraordinary Hotelman.* (New York: The Statler Foundation, 1968), pp. 232–33.

15. Gabe Vogliotti. Unpublished manuscript, pp. 6-4, 6-3; from the personal collection of Bill Thompson.

C H A P T E R   6

Scholarships

Scholarships, not operating endowments, were the thrust of the initial money-raising efforts. Hotel administration programs build reputations on good graduates more than on good publications. Good students attract good students. UNLV recruited and rewarded them with dollar scholarships based on achievement, not on nationally defined "needs" tests. Moreover, achievement was not measured in academic scores and grade point averages alone. Provided satisfactory academic progress was evident, the college faculty recognized and rewarded service as well as grades.

> I remember the all-day sessions of the college's scholarship committee. There were three criteria: academics; service; and potential. Someone strong out of high school had potential based on high-school grades and activities.   AL IZZOLO, HOTEL FACULTY MEMBER

Students gave service to the college, to the university and to the community. In turn, aid was given to club leaders; to participants in the professional organizations; to senators representing the college in student government; to undergrads working on student and alumni newsletters; and to those in wider campus and community activities, provided grade point averages were sustained.

> The students who stand out are the ones who went on to great success in spite of average academic performances.   DICK BASILE, HOTEL FACULTY MEMBER

Examples of service covered a broad gamut. Hotel students operated the beverage service in Judy Bailey Hall for the performing arts. Hotel students did maintenance projects at St. Jude's Ranch, a charitable facility for children. Hotel students served as "counselors" for parents and students shopping the campus. Hotel students participated in student government. And so the list grew.

> Remember, hotel students were heavily involved in student government. They would run for office and win. We had a lot of [student government] presidents.   FRANK BORSENIK, HOTEL FACULTY MEMBER

> I was vice president of the organization. Tom Poland ['78] was president. The HSMA junior chapter ran as part of the group, but we even had liberal arts students come to our activities. We did some catering, had picnics, went to the conventions and created a gathering place for all out-of-state students.   PAT MOREO, '69 STUDENT AND FACULTY MEMBER

In the true meaning of scholarships, students at the top of the GPA (grade point average) list were not ignored. Scholarships were awarded each semester to those with the top grade point averages whether or not there was also a service element. Fortunately, the community was generous and there were funds to support these twin goals of academics and service. Besides, they were not self-exclusive; good academic students were joiners and leaders.

> I liked the basis of the college's scholarship awards, which helped those in the middle, the ones who otherwise fell through the cracks. Poor students got financial aid; wealthy ones could afford to pay. A, B, C students with extra activities did more than just their class work. They were well rounded students.   JOAN REYNOLDS BEITZ, ADMINISTRATIVE ASSISTANT

NON-ENDOWED SCHOLARSHIPS
University-based Aid
Students with true financial needs had support from the university's financial services, so almost everyone was covered. There was a Catch 22 however! Financial support from the university carried a strange disincentive. Needy students who received "scholarship" money from the college for a job well done, be it academic or service, had to surrender a comparable sum if the university's financial aid was needs-based. The theory being that they weren't as needy. From a pragmatic standpoint, hotel awarded few such dollars, and only then in small, token amounts to acknowledge a job exceptionally well done. Explaining the reasoning to disappointed students mitigated the situation somewhat, but offsetting assured financial need from the university with scholarship grants from the college made little sense to the hotel faculty.

Tuition Waivers. In-state and out-of-state tuition waivers were awarded by the university. They were especially meaningful to the hotel program during its early years when private scholarship dollars were being solicited but were not yet in hand.

I remember asking the dean for an out-of-state waiver. He agreed if I did three things: (1) Maintained a 3.5 GPA; (2) Remained active in the hotel association; (3)Stayed out of trouble. With the waivers, my work and help from home, I graduated a with minimum amount of debt. ANN RITTAL, '81 STUDENT

Waivers benefitted the hotel program more than any other discipline. It was a matter of enrollment. In the early years, the college had the largest number of out-of-state students by far, upwards of two-thirds of the campus at times. As a scholarship committee member, Vallen proposed waiver distributions be pro rated among the colleges based on enrollment statistics with each college assured a minium allocation. Thus developed a system of swaps between hotel and departments in other colleges. Hotel would trade in-state waivers (worth less in dollars and cents) for out-of-state waivers, which the other colleges had but couldn't use. Then, hotel would award its in-state students cash stipends, which were worth more than the value of the in-state waivers that the college had traded away. That cash would otherwise have gone to the out-of-state student who had just been awarded the out-of-state tuition waiver.

For example, a student might win an FSEA scholarship of $500. But we would swap it for a tuition waiver of larger denomination if one became available. IZZOLO

The out-of-state students benefitted because the newly traded waivers had a greater dollar value than the available cash. Hotel's in-state students benefitted because the cash awards were greater then the in-state waivers that were traded away. Total scholarship funds was thus enhanced to benefit the largest number of students in all colleges. For example, hotel was able to award 24 tuition waivers during the 1969–1970 school year. Win/win for all.

Tuition waivers were a really big thing for out-of-state students. But we also had money from the American Hotel Foundation, HSMA and the National Restaurant Association. MOREO

Waiver allocations grew contentious when the athletic teams began to mature because the Regents had set aside half—yes, half—of all the allotted waivers for use by the ball teams. And, of course, out-of-state students were beginning to enroll in other disciplines. There were opportunities even then. To use their allotment, other units awarded out-of-state waivers to new students whom they didn't know and who often failed to arrive. Hotel garnered these waivers on the bounce on registration day. These waivers had a life span of only one term, but unused scholarship money was saved and carried over to another term.

If someone won a scholarship that was smaller than [or equal to] the waiver, we bumped them up into the waiver category. IZZOLO

Waiver competition diminished even though tuition kept creeping upward because the value of the waivers remained constant. They were part of the university's overall budget, which never had surpluses for scholarships. Over time, waivers became far less meaningful to hotel's scholarship arsenal, but by then a large number of gifts from a variety of sources was on hand.

The Three Professional Associations

Within weeks of his arrival, the new director was invited to three, what-proved-to-be important meetings with the local chapters of the HSMA (Hotel Sales Managers Association), the NAHMA (National Association of Hotel/Motel Accountants) and the FSEA (Foodservice Executives Association). Vallen already held memberships in two of the groups, but had never attended local meetings because there were none in the rural area of upper New York State where he had previously lived. The welcomes were sincere and very cordial, made more so by the dean's work experiences in all three areas: accounting; food and sales.

> We showed up unexpectedly to the 1967 annual Christmas party of the HSMA. Kay Good-will [accounting at the Tropicana] and her husband, John [sales at the Convention Center] took us to their table, gave us their party favors and welcomed us in.   FLOSSIE VALLEN

Each invitation carried the opportunity to speak to the monthly gatherings. That provided the opportunity to request scholarship aid. Pledges and the funds came immediately. So before the first year was out, three scholarships were in place.

With the passage of years, the amounts grew as tuition costs rose. The professional associations increased their contributions to meet ever-higher tuition costs. Even more satisfying was the special efforts each made to raise funds over and beyond their self-imposed chapter assessment.

Hotel/Motel Accountants. As recounted in earlier chapters, individual members of the accounting association were instrumental in launching the hotel program. Advocates included Leo Lewis, Frank Watts and Jim West. Everyone—members such as John Fredericks, Mary Fuchs, Clyde Horner, Frank Mooney, Sharon Petty and George Stillings—became boosters once the program was launched. After the initial invitations, the director paid dues and made a deliberate effort to attend the monthly meetings of all three associations.

> The [Educational Institute] classes that the accountants did at Las Vegas High School [before the hotel program was started] were so impressive that members came to believe in education.
> The Association felt that Vallen was part of us; they were strong for him.   LEO LEWIS, BINION'S FINANCIAL OFFICER AND PART-TIME FACULTY MEMBER

Just as their counterparts did in the other organizations, the hotel/motel accountants encouraged a junior chapter, but accounting has never been the forte of hotel students. The senior chapter invited students to its dinners without charge. It facilitated student attendance at the regional and national meetings. It provided classroom speakers, and it assessed itself for annual scholarship grants. Its members called the campus with full-time and part-time job leads, as did members of the other two organizations. In 1977, the local chapter also created a loan fund for student emergencies.

Searching for means to supplement their regular scholarship contributions, the local chapter refined its application process to the national organization. The national office had scholarships of significant value, but it took effort and dedication to handle the detailed procedures and gain a fair share of the national awards. That job was taken on initially by Jim Lang and then handed off to Allen Kaercher, who did yeoman work for many years as the local spokesman and coordinator. Scholarships were administered at the national headquarters by the Executive Vice President, Frances Tally. Kaercher made sure that the Las Vegas chapter always reaped a good share of the national prizes particularly in those years when Las Vegans held national offices.

Food Services Executive Association. The format at the FSEA was the same as that developed with the other professional associations. Students would attend the sessions, go to the regional and national meetings with support from the chapter, and win scholarship aid from the local and national organizations. There were three extra special affiliations with the FSEA. Milton Vallen, the dean's older brother, had been Philadelphia's FSEA president and sat on the national board for many years before serving terms as the national president and board chairman. Two local members, Mike Mavros and faculty member Al Izzolo, also served as international presidents and chairmen.

> I was on the local board when [Mike] Mavros [purchasing manager at the MGM Grand] was chapter president. He told me Anheuser-Busch wanted to donate and that Nevada Beverage would match whatever the FSEA raised in a special event. The goal was $5,000 with a matching $5,000. Max Daffner said he would help organize it at a place in the booneys called Jerry Berry's Berry Patch.   IZZOLO

Under the chairmanship of Max Daffner, the local chapter started the annual Jerry Berry's Steak Fry in 1979.

> The first year was a fantastic success! 750 people showed up. We ran out of food but raised more money than we had anticipated.   IZZOLO

The event continues to this writing with Max as its ongoing chairman. (Daffner was the original drummer for Bill Haley and the Comets of *Rock Round the Clock* fame.) Jerry Berry had a large, outdoor facility called the Berry Patch which he loaned to the group although he wasn't a member himself. The chapter's 1999 newsletter recounted Jerry Berry's contribution:

> "Folks came, ate, danced, sang, talked, hoorayed and had a knee-slappin' good time on Jerry Berry's land. Over $100,000 will [have] be[en] raised by the end

of this year [1999] and over twenty-years of good has come from that one single patch of land with sagebrush tables and rocking chairs."[1]

I first met Jerry Berry in 1985 when I went out to see the site before my first party. What a trip it was! I don't think the bean pot, which sat outdoors, had ever been cleaned! [That year the FSEA started cooking in the college kitchen.]   CLAUDE LAMBERTZ, HOTEL FACULTY MEMBER

Door prizes of all kinds are donated by community businesses to boost the night's gate. Some FSEA members donate food and supplies. Anderson Dairy's ice-cream and sundae station and Farmer Brothers coffee are particularly enduring. Initially the membership also did the cooking, sometimes with the support of members from the chef's organization. Later, UNLV students and faculty took on the food preparation.

One year Chef Hans [Lockature] from the Desert Inn and I were taking food wrapped in Saran to Jerry's on speed carts [food carriers]. As we made a turn, the ribs came flying off onto Tropicana Avenue and the freeway. After Hans pushed the carts back, he jumped from the truck onto the spilled barbeque sauce and went flying! It wasn't the only time we left food on the road.   LAMBERTZ

Although the college didn't participate in the chef's Rib Burn-off in Sunset Park, it benefitted from lending the kitchen to the chef's association. Unsold ribs, ribs galore, were given to the kitchen along with supplies such as paper plates and napkins.

Hotel Sales Managers Association. As did the other professional groups, HSMA adopted the student's junior chapter. As did the other professional groups, HSMA changed its name over the years to reflect an international scope, HSMA International. FSEA became International FSEA, and the NAHMA became International HMA and still later, Hospitality Financial and Technical Professionals.

As did the other professional groups, the senior chapter invited students to its dinners without charge. It facilitated student attendance at national meetings. It assessed itself for an annual scholarship grant, and assigned to the local program funds that had previously gone for national scholarships. That and the question about who was a voting member—the local had many purveyors among its membership—caused controversy between the local chapter and the national office.

HSMA was committed to UNLV students, and we invited them to participate. We did several things that added up to good opportunities. One of those was a trip to New York.   SIG FRONT, VICE PRESIDENT, SAHARA HOTEL

Sig made arrangements for us to fly the Sahara's junket [free airfare to gamblers] to New York. Of course, there were no tickets, just a letter from Sig. We [Moreo ('69) and Tom Poland ('78)] got on a plane that took us to Chicago. There the junket hostess directed us to another plane. No one knew anything when we got to La Guardia Airport to come home. We called Sig at 6:00 a.m. Five minutes later, we were bound for home. That was the characteristic of those pioneer days.   PAT MOREO, STUDENT AND FACULTY MEMBER

An unmeasurable contribution was made by chapter members during their far-flung business travels. They touted the attributes of the program to audiences and individuals in distant cities.

> When I was with Sheraton, I remember talking to parents and students about schools: Cornell, Michigan State, others. And then I told them about UNLV. Several told me [years later] that's why they choose Nevada. FRONT

During the first few years of this history, the HSMA chapter provided the faculty for the nation's very first course in hotel marketing. Chapter 8 explains.

Sometime in the early 1980s, the chapter began an annual, blind auction spearheaded by Val Moon, who was at the Frontier Hotel. Hotels, reps, travel planners, airlines, expo service companies and other HSMA members provided marvelous gifts for auction! All proceeds went to the scholarship fund. By the time this innovation was launched, the college was serving gourmet meals in the Boyd Dining Rooms and was successfully sponsoring the city-wide wine tasting, UNLVino. Tickets for both were contributed to the brown-bag auction. As dean, Christianson was able to wheedle basketball tickets and these, too, were added to the bidding pool.

> Jerry always bought wonderful things at the HSMA auction. The trip by Scenic Air over the Grand Canyon was probably the best of all. FLOSSIE VALLEN

Claude Rand, who was a HSMA member before he was a faculty member, helped to expedite the auctions. Some $9,000 was raised at the 1989 auction. Money from the early auctions was endowed in the Nevada System. Later, the university created the UNLV Foundation. So some HSMA money is with the state; the foundation holds the endowment from the renamed organization, Hospitality Sales & Marketing Association International.

Sampling the Potpourri of Givers

The final section of this chapter reviews the scholarship endowments that were contributed outright, or which the college created by saving small amounts from the annual gifts of regular donors. This was possible because a potpourri of other scholarship gifts underpinned the annual need for scholarships. Some contributors gave for many years; others came and went as were the dispositions of the persons representing the companies at any given time.

> Leo Lewis took me to see Benny Binion about getting money. Leo told me that we would meet in Benny's office. While we waited for him, we sat in the booth in the coffee shop. I asked, Shouldn't we go to his office? Leo answered, This is his office. JERRY VALLEN

(There's an interesting parallel with Meshulam Riklis who reportedly maintains an "office" in an elevated, upholstered booth in the food court of the Riviera Hotel.)

Not every scholarship has a several-paragraph story behind it. Most were solicited simply to meet the needs of a growing student body, and most were given to acknowledge the donor's affiliation with the campus. That connection grew from several bases. The majority of the early donors came to campus as recruiters first of all. Al Izzolo, an ex-recruiter himself, had the job of hosting them.

> Jerry's standing rule was pitch anyone who came around. I remember asking the recruiters. Most of them would say I don't make the decision, but I'll take it back to headquarters. And then they would send money.   AL IZZOLO, HOTEL FACULTY MEMBER

Other donors were friends with mutual professional interests. Professional associations at the national, as well as the local level, contributed. Still others were simply cheerleaders somewhat on the sidelines, but close enough to know the impact of their generosity (See Exhibit 6-1). A brief description of representative donors suggests the breadth and scope of the college's scholarship support.

American Hotel Foundation. The American Hotel & Lodging Foundation (AH&LF) is an arm of the American Hotel & Lodging Association (AH&LA). Both were identified originally with the word "Motel" instead of "Lodging," (i.e.) American Hotel & Motel Association. The AH&LF awards scholarships to hotel students across the nation; support is not limited to UNLV. Moreover, awards are made to the students, not to the programs. UNLV began participating in the fall of 1969. Coincidentally in the spring of 1969, several months earlier, Bob Cannon recruited Arthur Packard to be the speaker at the college's first annual luncheon for the graduating class. Packard's name has been affiliated with the AH&MA for many decades. After his death, a special Packard scholarship was established. Following that precedent, the AH&LF now has memorial scholarships for individuals such as Conrad Hilton and Karl Mehlmann and for companies such as American Express and Ecolab. (Ecolab, then named Economics Lab, was one of the program's first, direct contributors. The company's representative, Vince Feehan, remained a friend thereafter.)

Club Managers. The Club Managers Association offered student graduates a different view of the hospitality industry. Clubs in California and Arizona befriended the program long before their counterparts were present in Nevada. They hosted field trips for the student club, came to speak in many classes and club meetings and provided financial support.

> The Club Managers supported the students for travel to the conventions—they even had a special convention rate for students. The two chapters [Arizona and California] maintained a fund so several students had all their expenses paid.   IZZOLO

The club managers were a united group and represented a very positive influence on the student body. As a result, they appealed to graduates who might never have considered a club career.

> Teaching the club course was very enjoyable. We had to travel because there weren't clubs here in Vegas. The class would go to San Diego or San Francisco and do a city club, a country

Scholarship Donors

Stuart Alman Memorial Award

American Hotel Foundation (Direct to the student)

American Plan Investment Association

Anheuser Busch, Inc.

ARA Fellowship

Boyd Family (Graduate scholarship)

Bob Brown/Fong (Graduate scholarship)

William Campbell/Nevada Resort Association (Graduate scholarship)

Robert Cannon Memorial Award

Tola and Marcia Chin

California Restaurant Association (Direct to the student)

Club Managers Association of Arizona

Club Managers Association of California

Colorado/Wyoming Hotel & Motel Association (Direct to the student)

Denny Cyganek ('80) by Holiday Inn

Economics Laboratory

Joseph Esposito

Friendship Inns

Frozen Food Association of New England (Direct to the student)

Furr's Cafeterias, Inc.

Gold Plate Scholarships (National Restaurant Association) (Direct to the student)

John Goodwill Memorial Award

The Grey Line Tours

Michael Hammel Memorial Award

Harris, [Pannell] Kerr, Forster & Co.

Nat Hart Memorial Award

Hilton Corporation

Holiday Inn Corporation

David Hood Memorial Award

Jack Hooper Memorial Award

Hosts International (Loan Fund)

Hotelman's Loan Fund (Self-funded by the student association)

Hospitality Sales and Marketing Association International, Las Vegas Chapter

Howard Johnson

International Association of Holiday Inns, Inc.

International Association of Hotel-Motel Accountants

International Food Service Executives Association Endowment

Kandell Scholarships

Dick Kanellis (Public Relations Association of Las Vegas)

Kobrand

Las Vegas Endowed Scholarships (Strip scholarships)

Las Vegas Hotel Managers Association

Las Vegas Rotary Club

Lyons Restaurants

Marriott Corporation

Bill McFee

Steve Michel

Ruth Minor Loan Fund

Motor Hotel Management, Inc

National Institute for the Food Service Industry (NIFI) (Direct to the student)

National Tour Foundation

Nevada Beverage/Anheuser-Busch Endowed Scholarship

Nevada Hotel Association

New Mexico Restaurant Association (Direct to the student)

Ogden Food

Ohio Hotel & Motel Association (Direct to the student)

Bill Onorato

Bill Paulos ('69) (Through the alumni association)

Albert Pick Hotels

Pink's Produce

Red Lobster

EXHIBIT 6-1. Scholarship donors to the College of Hotel Administration between 1967 and 1989.

Ricardo's Restaurants	Tropicana Hotel
Riviera Employees Foundation	TWA, Trans-world Airline (Direct to the student)
Rodeway Inns of America	Utah/Nevada Hotel Association
Rotary Club Scholarships	Jerry Vallen (Funded by the student hotel association)
Sacramento (Ca.) Valley Hotel Association	Villa Banfi
Saga	Pete Wagner Memorial (Teamsters)
Saint Tropez Hotel	Walgreen Company
Seagram	Hiram Walker, Inc.
Service Travel Company of St. Louis (Jim Stoltz)	William Weinberger Endowed Scholarship
Sheraton Hotels	Aaron and Helen Weisberg Endowed Scholarships
SKAL	Western Association of Food Chains
Southern Wine & Spirits of Nevada (UNLVino)	Westin (Hard Corps)
Statler Foundation (Direct to the student)	Wine Spectrum
Stouffer	Women in Convention Sales
Summa	Shelby Williams Endowed Scholarship
Swerdlow Family	Wyatt Cafeterias

EXHIBIT 6-1 (CONTINUED).   Scholarship donors to the College of Hotel Administration between 1967 and 1989.

> club and a yacht club. Club managers like Jim Brewer from the LA Country Club were so good to us!   JIM ABBEY, HOTEL FACULTY MEMBER

The Gray Line Tours. The Gray Line Tours operated charter buses and also the profitable, public Strip bus service before the city commandeered it. Through its membership in the Hotel Sales Managers Association, Gray Line's Barry Perea saw a need and began contributing in 1985.

Harris, Kerr, Forster & Company (HKF). One of the college's earliest faculty appointments was an upcoming and very recent Cornell graduate named Bruce Baltin. Baltin and his wife, Phyllis, stayed at the Vallen's home until they could get established. This was not an unusual arrangement for young, starting faculty. Still, some who came were overlooked.

> I had no money to speak of when I first came and soon ran out altogether. Then I began sleeping in the office for a while.   ANONYMOUS FACULTY MEMBER

At about the same time, one of the college's earliest professional contacts was made with Charles Kaiser, an outstanding partner of Harris, Kerr, Forster & Company. Kaiser's office was in Los Angeles, so he came to interview for the entire firm. Later, he became managing partner of the national partnership. As a firm, HKF authored *Hotel Accounting*, the very first accounting text in the discipline. This brought the company and the college closer together because Dean Vallen was the consulting editor for the William C. Brown Company, the text's publisher. Kaiser also authored his own text sometime later.

Kaiser and the dean originally became acquainted during one of Vallen's talks to the accounting association, this one in Tahoe. HKF became one of the early non-Nevada donors. A scholarship check was in hand by September of 1969 and continued for many years. By 1974, HKF had a Las Vegas office that processed the check until that office closed. Each May the college prepared a reminder letter since the the company's grants committee met each summer.

Chuck Kaiser's interviewing schedule was important to the fledgling program's first graduates. Moreover, the college was able to solicit other interviewers and scholarship donors by using the name of so prestigious a company.

> Gosh, we had a lot of companies recruiting that first year. Chuck Kaiser came and I ended up working for HKF.   MOREO

The biggest surprise of Kaiser's job interviewing was HKF's bid to the college's newest faculty member, Bruce Baltin, currently senior vice president of the company's Los Angeles' consulting office. By stressing the unusual recruiting effort that the college had undertaken for HKF (which later became Pannell, Kerr, Forster, or just PKF), periodic increases in the dollar gift were negotiated.

PKF produced an expensive annual publication called *Trends*, multiple copies of which they provided for classroom use for many years.

Host Loan Fund. A different type of student support was funded by Hosts, a company that specialized in university and industrial foodservice. Some two decades later, Host was acquired by Marriott, eventually emerging as Host Marriott after several major reorganizations.

> I graduated in 1971 and spent six years with Sky Chefs before joining AMFAC at the Ontario [California] Airport. AMFAC was bought by Marriott, which then bought Hosts. So before I retired, I worked for 22 years for three separate companies and never left the same location.
> KEN KAUFMAN, '71 STUDENT

Developed from discussions with the dean, Host decided to make annual gifts quite different from the usual scholarship contributions that were the standard among the recruiting companies. Host provided and renewed annually for many years a corpus of money that was used for small, noninterest-bearing loans. Students could borrow on their signature for almost any emergency. Auto repairs or tire replacements, books, emergency travel costs, clothing for interviews were the usual reasons. Even a special date on a night out was funded! A simple application was completed and the loan was granted without question on Joan Reynolds' signature. It proved to be a nightmare for the business office. The check was issued almost immediately; that was no fuss. Accounting for the collection and repayment of small sums was another matter. Not one to which the business office ascribed a high priority.

The loan fund was a first for both the college and the company. Subsequently, the college solicited other loan funds from other donors.

Kentucky Fried Chicken (KFC). KFC was recruiting on campus as early as 1974. It began when several faculty members were invited to a KFC Convention in Las Vegas by the company's human resources executive, Gerry Rush, who previously had been with A&W International. That meeting established a good working relationship that led to on-campus interviews and eventually to scholarship dollars. KFC produced some of the earliest slides and printed matter about OSHA's recent application to the restaurant industry and the company loaned these to the college for Dick Basile's classroom use

Two incidents strengthened the relationship. From publicity in *Restaurant News*, contact was reestablished with several 20-years-ago graduates from Vallen's junior college program in upstate New York. One of them, Michael Fitzpatrick, had become a division director of KFC. Fitzpatrick made contact again two years later (1987) when CBS news came to campus to cover the Running Rebels charge toward the final four. The College of Hotel Administration was featured in a 2–3 minute piece on televison. Fitz arranged for increased scholarship funding for UNLV.

Lyons Restaurants. Lyons, which is headquartered in Foster City, California, has been a regular recruiter and a regular, uninterrupted donor for over twenty years beginning in 1978!

Motor Hotel Management (MHM). Texas-based Motor Hotel Management was among the nation's very earliest management companies. It was spun out from Rodeway Inns. Rodeway began to recruit and contribute scholarships after the dean made contact with one of that company's executives, Tom Fay, who was the first student ever to graduate under Vallen's two-year program. Management companies need management talent so both Doug Lane, who took over for Fay at Rodeway, and MHM's Fay recruited and contributed

National Association of Catering Executives (NACE). The first grant from this body came late in this history. It was one of the early efforts of a newly appointed (January, 1988) faculty member, Patti Shock. With the gift came the development of a catering sales class. Unlike catering classes in other programs, which teach food catering, this class was oriented toward the sales and management of catering services. NACE's initial $10,000 grant was the beginning of a series of gifts solicited by Shock, who has proven to be the faculty's best money-raiser ever. The National Tour Foundation, an affiliation of several national professional organizations, was another success from Shock's initial efforts at fund raising.

Nevada Hotel & Motel Association. Membership in the American Hotel & Motel Association requires prior membership in a state hotel association.[2] Five small states: Colorado, Idaho, Nevada, Utah and Wyoming were combined in the Rocky Mountain Hotel Association. This unwieldy conglomerate soon dissolved into the Utah/

Nevada Hotel Association. The rapid growth of Nevada's lodging industry allowed the eventual separation of even these two states. It took place on October 4, 1979 at Sam's Town. Phil Arce was president. Also active were Bob Cannon, Helen Naugle and Wally Talamus. Van Heffner assumed the executive post of the new Nevada Hotel & Motel Association and later of the Nevada Restaurant Association.

Through the good offices of Van Heffner, the Utah/Nevada Hotel Association contributed to the hotel college's scholarship fund. Working with Al Izzolo, who was a national officer of the IFSEA, Heffner even served as the executive officer of that organization during its period of consolidation and redefinition. Both Vallen and Christianson sat as members of the board of directors of the Nevada Hotel & Motel Association and the Restaurant Association.

Ricardo's Mexican Restaurants. Robert Ansara, who owns Ricardo's, was a board member of the Nevada Restaurant Association as was the college's dean. Through that relationship, Ansara and his chef, Gene Cleary, offered scholarships to the college. Bob Ansara was one of two restauranteurs, Tom Kapp at the Tillerman was the other, who always had jobs for hotel students willing to take entry posts.

Riviera Employees. Frank Watts was instrumental in getting Vallen invited to a board meeting of the Riviera Employees Foundation. Employees, not the hotel company, were contributing to a fund that was used for the betterment of the community. From that initial appearance came continuing scholarship grants. The dean wrote to and appeared before the board annually to make an appeal for an allotment. The initial grant in 1968 went to Roger Wagner ('69), who is currently president and chief operating officer of Trump's Castle in Atlantic City.

Although the composition of the board changed over the years, several firm supporters gave leadership to the Foundation's support of the college. Numbered among them were: Dick Chappell; Eunice Harris; Pat Lucas; Pat McNally; Leo Steinke; Inez Rambeau and, of course, Frank Watts.

> Did you know that two of the [scholarship] recipients were from the Riviera? And we didn't pick them, the school did. The mother of one winner was a salad girl and she appreciated it. The other's father was a pit boss. Both graduated.   FRANK WATTS, RIVIERA FINANCIAL OFFICER

Rotary Club. Faculty member Dick Basile was a Rotarian of long standing. His local chapter, Rotary Club #1401 of Las Vegas, provided the hotel college with scholarships that were then expanded to several other campus units. Hotel was designated as the administrator, accepting the funds in one lump sum and making internal campus distribution.

> I don't recall giving just to hotel.   JOE BUCKLEY, HUMAN RESOURCES DIRECTOR, HUGHES CORPORATION AND PRESIDENT OF THE ROTARY CLUB

As it had done with other such grants, the president's office removed the hotel college from its role of middleman.

Joe Buckley—a great supporter of the college as Summa's human resources representative—was the president of The Las Vegas Rotary Chapter, and served as Governor of Rotary District #530 when the college's building was nearing completion. Buckley, Basile and the dean focused on the possibility of tiling the main stairwell of the new building. Tiles would be donated by chapters around the world and then they would be installed up this grand stairwell with the chapter names.

That was in 1986. We were planning for Rotary International's meeting in Las Vegas. It was just one idea that didn't materialize.   BUCKLEY

The logistics and the price overwhelmed the idea, which never came to fruition.

The joke went around, but it wasn't a joke, it was true: Jerry priced everything in the building. The stairwell? Who remembers, $45,000?   IZZOLO

I solicited private businesses for money to upgrade the classrooms in exchange for their name on the door.   GEORGE HARDBECK, DEAN OF BUSINESS AND ECONOMICS

House of Seagram. Seagram was a generous scholarship donor with annual grants in the early 1980s of $5,000 annually. Then as Chapter 5 reported, Bill Friedman, Seagram's vice president for corporate affairs announced that all scholarship support would be made through the National Institute for the Foodservice Industry (NIFI). NIFI is the restaurant industry's counterpart to the hotel industry's American Hotel Foundation, AHF.

Schenley. Gifts from Schenley Affiliated Brands Corporation originated in a personal relationship that the college developed with Oscar Greene, the charismatic and supportive executive vice president of the company. As Chapter 5 relates, changing this annual gift into an endowment through Meshulam Riklis of the Riviera—a senior Schenley executive—did not prove successful.

Sheraton. Sheraton has provided scholarships continuously from 1973, as have so many recruiters. Their generosity increased measurably as the number and quality of the graduates met Sheraton's standards. Dollar amounts got a boost after Bud James and Sig Front left the Sahara to become respectively Sheraton's CEO and Vice President for Marketing. Sheraton's Mike O'Hara, assistant to the vice president of industrial relations, came to campus for many years and a personal friendship developed among the two Vallens and O'Hara.

SKAL. Before becoming a faculty member, Claude Rand secured scholarships from SKAL, an organization of travel professionals. Rand belonged by virtue of his career with TWA. The first $5,000 grant came November 15, 1984 during a special dinner prepared for the group in Beam Hall. Jim Germain, SKAL's treasurer and a hotel alum ('75) announced the award with Mike Adams. Recipients won $2,000 their first year and $1,000 in each of the remaining three years. Next, the grant was expanded to cover children of SKAL members anywhere in the world! The club's announcement of this unusual gift at an international SKAL meeting brought awareness about the program to travel professionals spanning the globe and accelerated the college's march on the international scene.

Statler Foundation. The Statler Foundation as well as the American Hotel Foundation and the National Restaurant Foundation issued scholarships directly to students. Statler's support had an additional twist in its very early years. It wanted the student to know local hoteliers so Statler required each applicant to have the endorsement of the state hotel association. It was a great idea because it forced the student, the school and the professional association to interact. Prior to Van Heffner's arrival in Las Vegas and the creation of the Nevada Hotel Association, there was no professional trade group. The college used the Nevada Resort Association (NRA). The first scholarship, which NRA's Joe Digles helped administer, was awarded to Robert P. Dickinson, Jr. in March of 1968. Bob Cahill recalled the procedure in his oral history.[3]

> "The Statler Foundation has set up scholarships. . . . And by the rules of the Foundation, it [the application] has to be submitted by a hotel group such as ours [the NRA].
>
> The Statler Foundation is evidently having the same trouble . . . getting good [minority] candidates."

Stouffer. The first gift from Stouffer came in 1973 from what was then Stouffer Restaurants and Inns. The company continued its contributions through the conclusion of this history in 1989. Appropriate increases were made annually as the name morphed to the Stouffer Corporation. Nestlé bought Stouffer just as it had purchased Minor Foods, and the Stouffer name disappeared as pieces of the company were sold. Three persons helped maintain a strong relationship including employment and faculty interchanges with management. There were two human resources persons, Robert Partridge and Rudy LaKosh, and one operating president, John Quagliata, who had been a student of the dean's many years earlier in New York. Stouffer's corporate president, Bill Hulett, was the most active hotelier in the country when it came to promoting his company among faculty and students.

Summa. For a number of years beginning in the early 1980's the Summa Corporation (Howard Hughes' empire) provided scholarship aid to the college. Here again, Joe Buckley, who was Summa's executive in charge of human resources, was the expediter. Summa broaden its giving to include support for business and for arts and letters. Hotel acted as intermediary accepting the gifts and making internal distribution as the hotel college had done with the Rotary grants. About the same time that the president's office took control of hotel's Anheuser-Busch and Rotary gifts it also replaced hotel as the recipient/distributor of Summa's support. It's fair to mention that Joe Buckley has no recall of this arrangement.

Teamsters: Peter Wagner. Relations with the Teamsters Union, Local #881 were good from the start and grew stronger over time. After the 1967 meeting that gave sanction to the internships (see Chapter 4), the college wrote letters of thanks and for several years thereafter provided the names of interns and the hotels where they were working. Continuing from 1969 until the close of this history, a contribution has been made in the name of Teamster Peter Wagner. The idea of such a scholarship was received positively by Richard (Dick) Thomas, the union's secretary-treasurer and has continued after his tenure.

The first award was made to Ken Plummer ('72), who was, happily, already a member of the union. Steve Winn was the second year's winner.

> President Jay Zorn called me in to ask why in the world was the college giving a scholarships to Steve Wynn [not Winn], who had just made big news with his Caesars Palace deal.[4] I clarified the identities of the parties.   JERRY VALLEN

ENDOWED SCHOLARSHIPS

There are three types of endowments funding the College of Hotel Administration. The operating endowments were reviewed in Chapter 5. Endowments in support of the building are discussed in Chapter 7. Here we examine the very special endowments that provide the financial base for scholarship awards. The reader is reminded that this story outlines the college's development through its first quarter century. Support in all three categories continues to this day, providing the means for growth in size and quality of offerings.

Stuart Alman Endowment

Stu Alman was a well known member of the food and beverage community, and a strong champion of the college's internship program.

> Alman invited my class to Caesars to tour the facility. It was a 7 p.m. class so we went there at night, and marched through the kitchen, storeroom, bakery. After the tour, he took us to the Barge for drinks. When the vocalist learned who we were, she directed the program to us. No one went home at 9 o'clock when the class was over.
>
> I recall a tour that was arranged at the Flamingo. As we assembled in the lobby, Myron Cohen [comic] came by. He asked what I was doing. When the class had gathered, he gave it a special performance . We laughed and asked questions.   LEO LEWIS, BINION'S FINANCIAL OFFICER AND PART-TIME FACULTY MEMBER

At his death in 1984, friends announced a scholarship in Alman's name. Michael Severino, Jr., who was the food and beverage director at the Frontier Hotel, worked with the college to raise enough money to endow the gift. Contributions came from all over, from friends of Alman's and friends of the college, including persons who would later have similar accounts established for them.

> I remember talking to Stu when he was at Caesars. He said with 600 rooms, we're a great hotel! When we added another 600 rooms, we became a factory.   JIM ABBEY, HOTEL FACULTY MEMBER

Brown/Fong Endowment

Robert Brown was a well known and somewhat controversial personality of Las Vegas in his role as editor/publisher of the *Valley Times Newspaper*. Upon his death in 1986, Wing and Lilly Fong, friends of both the college and of Robert Brown, established an endowed scholarship in Brown's name. In that year, they made a large gift to the overall campus designating enough to endow a permanent Brown scholarship for hotel's graduate students.

Robert O. Cannon Endowment

Bob Cannon was an early and avid patron of the college as previous chapters have recounted. By attaching his reputation to that of the college's, Cannon added credibility to the program, even as his national identification helped establish early links with the American Hotel & Motel Association. He was held in high regard throughout the community; called the "dean of hotel general managers" in his obituary.

> Bob Cannon worked for us [at the Tropicana and later the Union Plaza]. He was a close friend, who lent credibility to everything he did. He was recognized as one of the first truly professional hotel managers in town. Bob started at the Last Frontier, brought there by Bill Orr, who was the Steve Wynn of that time. He was "the" man on the Strip. In fact, he was head of the tax commission. He was also our [father and son Houssels] partner.   J. KELL HOUSSELS, JR., HOTELIER AND ELECTED PRESIDENT OF THE NEVADA RESORT ASSOCIATION

Indeed, it was Bob Cannon who arranged the first luncheon for the graduating class, which was held at the Desert Inn Hotel's club house. And that handful of attendees grew into the fantastic event discussed in Chapter 8.

After his death, his wife, Helen Cannon, who—as a member of the Clark County School Board—was a well known Vegas personality in her own right, endowed a scholarship in remembrance. A committee headed by Bob Prince ('72) coordinated the arrangements. On March 19, 1986, a formal ceremony was held in the Boyd dining rooms and a permanent photograph of Bob Cannon was hung in the college's gallery.

John Goodwill Endowment

The College of Hotel Administration came to know John Goodwill and his wife, Kay, through the professional associations. She worked for the Houssels at the Tropicana and was active in the accountants association. He was affiliated with HSMA because of his sales job with the Las Vegas Convention and Visitors Bureau. The two associations joined to honor John with a memorial fund. It was the first for the college (April, 1980) and established a procedure that several other memorial funds would follow. Individual contributions from across the city were amalgamated to create the necessary corpus. Short of the target, the account was put on hold until it was supplement by another scholarship drive, that of Nat Hart's, also under the minimum limit. Scholarship grants began to flow once the combined money was endowed.

Some time later, after Nat Hart's death, Sylvia Hart supplemented the two accounts, which then were separated with each fully funded.

Nat Hart Endowment

Nat Hart was in the front ranks of the college's long list of very strong supporters and a personal friend of the faculty and the dean.

> The family went to Caesars Palace for Sunday Brunch. Half way through the meal, Nat Hart spotted us as he made his rounds through that huge crowd. Did you pay for that, he demanded? Of course we had. Nat marched back to the cashier, retrieved our payment of an hour earlier and insisted on comping our luncheon.   FLOSSIE VALLEN

In his position of corporate food and beverage manager for Caesars, he was able to support the college and the community in numerous ways. His "cooking class" was famous among locals—and so difficult to get into. For several years running at the conclusion of these sessions "students" (local residents) thanked Nat by making contributions toward the scholarship fund. The dean would arrive for the graduation ceremonies including lunch and accept the check.

A surprise birthday party held for Hart in 1991 added contributions to the growing corpus that was to be the Hart scholarship endowment. After his death, his spouse, Sylvia, and his many friends boosted the account so the gift continues to remember one of the college's closest professionals.

David Hood Endowment

David Hood was the general manager and part owner of the Four Queens in downtown Las Vegas. At his death in 1977, his wife Jeanne, with the help of the hotel's publicist, Dick Odessky, establish this special memorial. It was among the college's very earliest endowments. Jeanne Hood also took over the management of the property and continued in that role to help the college grow and mature.

David Hood awards were made annually to the outstanding member of the junior class. That recognition was later rounded out by the Bob Cannon endowment, which went to the outstanding sophomore and by the Bill Weinberger endowment which was designated for the outstanding graduating senior.

The Hood scholarship was the only gift the college ever had that was endowed outside of the university. The endowment was administered by the Trust Division of Valley Bank of Nevada. For 20 years, between 1978 and 1989, the dean labored under the misconception that an external endowment was better than one administered by the university family. It was a shocking surprise, therefore, to learn that the annual awards plus the annual bank fees had consumed the fund. It should not have been a surprise because fees were greater than earnings in the very first year. The endowment was gone by 1989.

IFSEA Endowment

The International Food Service Executives Association created a three-pronged scholarship fund. As will be recounted two paragraphs hence, it parented the Nevada Beverage/Anheuser-Busch Endowment. As recounted earlier, the IFSEA still gives scholarships from the sale of tickets to its Jerry Berry's Steak Fry, held annually each autumn. That sum has surpassed the $100,000 mark. Early on, in consultation with the association's officers, but especially Al Izzolo of the hotel faculty, small sums were saved from each annual gift. When the total reached $10,000, a third account, the IFSEA endowment was funded. It's still there.

Ruth Minor Loan Fund Endowment

Ruth and Lew Minor were very close friends of Lendal and Margaret Kotschevar and they came to know UNLV through that relationship. The family company, Minor Foods, a maker of food flavor bases, supported the foods portion of the curriculum. That tradition continued even after the company was sold.

> The Minors made donations that Vallen wasn't even aware of. That gave us more latitude to work with students.   CLAUDE LAMBERTZ, HOTEL FACULTY MEMBER

To top off their support, Dr. Lew Minor came as one of the college's visiting lecturers, a concept initiated with Kotschevar's earlier appointment. Both men had been hotel faculty members at Michigan State.

Lew and Ruth Minor made their first contributions to the college in support of the memorial fund established for Margaret Kotschevar. In 1986, an endowed gift with periodic refunding was started in Ruth Minor's name for short term loans to deserving students.

Nevada Beverage/Anheuser-Busch Endowment

Within a few years of the program's launch, contact was made with Anheuser-Busch through Nevada Beverage, the local distributor for Anheuser-Busch. Two developments emerged from that relationship. A series of beer lectures and tastings was launched, and a series of scholarship checks began coming, routed through Nevada Beverage, specifically through the efforts of John Wasserburger, Nevada Beverage's vice president. The donations originated as matching grants with the local FSEA chapter.

Alcohol beverages were not permitted on campus at that time, so the beer tastings were held in the dean's home. One afternoon in each semester a Busch/Nevada Beverage truck would roll up and build a classroom/tasting facility in the dean's family room, a converted two-car garage. Eventually, the classes grew too large and the campus fathers lifted the restriction so the seminars moved to the campus. In the interim, the sessions were shifted from the family den to the facilities of Nevada Beverage starting in 1973.

What made the scholarship unique was its method of presentation. Once a year, at half-time during a basketball game in the Thomas and Mack arena, Anheuser-Busch made the presentation to the dean. One assumes that similar contributions were going to the basketball team to facilitate the ceremony. President Maxson, who was very astute about public relations saw a good thing after he replaced President Goodall. The contributions were shifted in 1987 from the College of Hotel Administration's scholarship fund to the general funds of the university. The ceremony with the dean on the basketball floor was replaced with the president and the flow of support came to an abrupt end.

> Anheuser-Busch pulled out after several years and Nevada Beverage several years after that. But during that time, IFSEA had raised $4,000 to $5,000 annually.   AL IZZOLO, HOTEL FACULTY MEMBER

Foresight won again, since the account was endowed with pieces of the annual monies and the scholarships assured for posterity.

UNLVino (Southern Wine & Spirits) Endowment

The story of this very significant source of scholarship funds is told in Chapter 8.

William Weinberger Endowment

When Bill Weinberger retired from Caesars Palace in 1977, the company honored him by creating the William Weinberger endowment. Funds were solicited by Caesars from friends, professionals and purveyors. Even guests sent checks. At the end, Caesars topped off the account to $30,000. The mechanics of this special stipend were developed by Jerry Gordon, Caesars' director of operations and executive host, working with the dean, and approved by higher-ups.

> I met several times with Jerry Gordon in his office behind the front desk. During one visit, an irate guest was ushered in, and I quickly made an exit. The entry was accompanied by very loud shouting and screaming. Other staff members who were in tow also exited. It was a bad scene. Within ten minutes the door opened to the two men arm-in-arm, laughing together and promising to meet with spouses for dinner. Jerry wouldn't say how he handled that unbelievable turnaround.   JERRY VALLEN

The Weinberger endowment was to be a scholarship account, but a special one—a cash award was to be made annually to the outstanding graduating senior. The first of these presentations went to Tom Scaramellino at the 1980 graduation luncheon. Earnings from that endowment continue annually honoring both Bill Weinberger and each year's outstanding graduate, but in a different ceremony now that the luncheons have ceased.

Aaron and Helen Weisberg

The Weisbergs came to Las Vegas in 1952 as partners in the Sands Hotel, which (according to their niece, Tobe Gleeman Daum) was so named because that's all anyone saw at the time, sand. Weisberg served as the Sand's treasurer and board member for many years. During this time, the couple made discreet contributions to numerous organizations. Sad to say, they were not known to the dean until the surprise gift made at the time of the second death, that of Mrs. Weisberg. Their $1,000,000 endowment has funded as many as 24 awards of $1,500 each annually. This gift is held in the University of Nevada System, not by the UNLV Foundation.

Shelby Williams Endowment

Shelby and Claudine Williams pioneered the very successful Holiday Inn Casino, which eventually became Harrah's in the center of the Strip. When Shelby died, a memorial fund was established (1977) by Claudine with Bill Morris, another UNLV booster, helping to handle the arrangements. Later, Claudine would be recognized in her own right when the Harrah grant was received and the Claudine Williams chair was established (see Chapter 7).

The community's dollar-and-cent response to the College of Hotel Administration was as heartwarming as was its support for the college's programs, its faculty and its students. That aid took three directions. Chapter 5 presented the results of the college's drive for private operating funds. This discussion has acknowledged the importance of student support. Chapter 7 concludes Unit III by telling the tale behind the building, Beam Hall. With financial and physical support in place, the history closes with the final unit, which tells what was done with the gifts that were given.

ENDNOTES FOR CHAPTER 6

1. *IFSEA Newsletter*, August 1999, pp. 3–4.
2. The now-named American Hotel & Lodging Association (AH&LA), which was founded in 1910 as the American Hotel Association (AHA), began reexamining this requirement in 2001.
3. Robbins Cahill. "Reflections of Work in State Politics, Government, Taxation, Gaming Control, Clark County Administration and the Nevada Resort Association." *Oral History Project* (Reno: University of Nevada, Reno, Library), pp. 1,369–1,370.
4. Wynn acquired a small piece of land south of Caesars Palace, between the hotel and Flamingo Road. His threat to develop the property was taken seriously by Caesars, which bought the land at a premium price.

C H A P T E R   7

The Building

Prospective students, many with parents in tow, were frequent visitors to the campus. The dean tried his utmost to accommodate each with an individual interview. Boyce Phillips did the same. This personal-touch technique was a marvelous marketing tool. At very few campuses are future students and families given a chance to meet with and talk to an academic rep—usually it is someone from an admissions office. On occasion, two or even three families were piggybacked, but no one seemed to care because it added informality to a process that could be intimidating, especially when the family's first member ever is about to attend a university.

> My dad and I had planned to visit several hotel programs. UNLV was first. The dean welcomed us at the desk. He gave us a private tour, opening classroom doors and ushering us around. I kept wondering does he think we're VIPs. We never went to the other campuses.   ANDY FEINSTEIN, '91 STUDENT AND FACULTY MEMBER

> My mom and I came to UNLV in August of 1982. We met Mr. Phillips in the hall and he invited us into his office. I was nervous because I was only 18 and would be living away from home for the first time. He kept telling us I would be fine and he would look after me. We still talk about that day and remember Mr. Phillips very fondly.   NANCY CHANIN '86 STUDENT

Admission was not an organizational function of the college. So informal conversations would focus on transcripts, transportation and on-campus autos, housing, work and the work requirement, budgets and allowances, and more. Often the interviews were held during a stroll around the campus. It was through the eyes of these visitors that the lack of physical identity, a building for the college, first became apparent. Later, it was a question of growth and space.

> There were two issues in 1977–78. One was the graduate program and Vallen wanted everyone to be careful about it, to really take time. The other was the new building. The philosophy about sticks and bricks was equally cautious. First, get a good solid foundation: curriculum, faculty and student body. But the program was getting big.   PAT MOREO, '69 STUDENT AND FACULTY MEMBER

GETTING THE BUILDING
Sidestepping the Dormitory

The dormitory was one of the administration's major headaches during the late 1970s. The situation was out of control from several aspects, but it boiled down to poor management and oversight. Property damage, such as holes in the wall and broken doors, as well as nonfunctioning plumbing, has its source in disruptive and uncontrollable students. There was simply no limitations or discipline. Some attributed the problem in part to rowdy athletes who were treated as prima donnas.

> The food fights between the football and basketball teams taught you how to duck.   DAVE PATTERSON, '81 STUDENT

Whatever the causes, the situation was not good. President Baepler approached the hotel college twice with two different overtures.

> I remember [considering] whether the hotel college could provide any services on campus. And, of course, [hotel was] limited by not having its own building.   DON BAEPLER, UNLV PRESIDENT AND UNS CHANCELLOR

Baepler's first proposal had hotel assuming the management of the dormitory. The rationale being that a dorm was like a hotel, so managing it would be a learning experience.

> I responded as I did when it was suggested earlier that the college take over the Landmark Hotel. The college would be willing to manage the dorm whenever the college of health sciences took over student medical care and the accounting department handled student records.   JERRY VALLEN

> No, what you said was, We'll do it when the art department paints the buildings.   AL IZZOLO, HOTEL FACULTY MEMBER

The situation deteriorated and the administration considered closing the dorm.

It got to the point [1976] where some remodeling was needed. I wanted to close the dorm, but I was unsuccessful. The proposal lost by one vote on the Board of Regents.   BAEPLER

Closing the university's single dorm would not be good for the hotel college. Most of its occupants were hotel majors. Las Vegas didn't present a strong image to parents in the East, where the bulk of hotel's enrollment originated. Parents viewed on-campus housing as a plus. The college was wooing mature junior-college graduates, for whom *required* on-campus residency was a minus. Hotel's dilemma was whether to support the dorm to minimize parent concerns, but not the required residency—to remain marketable to student shoppers—knowing all along that without the required residency the dorm was not economically viable.

I wanted us to be an urban university. Regardless of the number of dorms we might build, only a small percentage of the student body would use them. It wasn't worth chewing up valuable real estate. And the university was surrounded by private apartments. The private sector could provide the housing service.   BAEPLER

Neither the hotel college nor the athletic program wanted the dorm closed.

The athletic people were against it, but I had a solution. Private people—Bill [Wildcat] Morris, for one—would build a dormitory on Maryland Parkway. Participation by the private sector was happening around the country.   BAEPLER

The dilapidated dormitory was not good for the image of the campus as Hank Tester wrote:

"Looking at the hall [Tonopah dormitory] after just leaving what has been described as one of the three best basketball arenas in the nation can be a bit of a shocker. We could see inside some of the rooms. . . . There were holes in the ceiling, and low-watt lightbulb cast a dingy yellow glow over the musty cubicles."[1]

My first impression of Tonopah Hall was Yuk! My God. It wasn't a strong impression! Muriel [Dick's spouse] said, Oh! My gosh, Richard how could you do this! But my son, Gary, was excited because he was getting out of West Virginia.   RICHARD BROWN, DONOR INTERMEDIARY AND FATHER OF ALUMNUS, GARY

Living in the dorm was an eye opener, but I only stayed one semester. The noise drove many students to the library carrels, which proved to be make-out rooms rather than study rooms.
    I came in the fall of 1979, but the previous year the floors were co-ed.   DAVE PATTERSON, '81 STUDENT

I was amazed to find men and women on the same dorm floor, although we had separate suites.   ANN RITTAL, '81 STUDENT

President Baepler then proposed that hotel take over the upper floors of the building as its campus headquarters with the business college below. This too the college "regretted"—a good hotel (reservation) euphemism. Large dollar amounts would be required to create classrooms and laboratories within a building designed as a dormitory. The likelihood of the money coming was nil, and once the college was in, there would be no chance of getting out.

> Both colleges starting working on a proposal for a new building after Baepler tried to get us into the dorm. [The big pitch:] Your faculty will have their own private johns.   GEORGE HARDBECK, DEAN OF BUSINESS AND ECONOMICS

Ten Years in the Making

The College of Hotel Administration had been bounced from Grant Hall to Wright Hall to the Flora Dungan Humanities Building as its rapid growth dictated.

> When I came to interview in 1969, hotel was on the second floor of Grant. It was very tight. If one turned, three persons got bumped on the shoulders.   FRANK BORSENIK, HOTEL FACULTY MEMBER

Following its second move, the one from Wright Hall, the college was housed on the top floor of the humanities building adjacent to the university's senior administration. Two days after the hectic move-in, President Zorn telephoned Dean Vallen to find out whether he had keys to all the offices. He did. Whereupon the president and the dean went office to office while the president counted and criticized the number of file cabinets and bookcases that each faculty member had. The purpose of the inspection was never clear.

> After we moved into the Humanities Building, Zorn called me late one Friday, I'm going to do an inspection. I walked him through each office to see what furniture each faculty member had.   HARDBECK

Lacking a permanent identity, hotel was excited by a 1972 invitation from Dean Tony Saville to join the College of Education in its new facility. This interim arrangement would help crystallize hotel's identity. Alas, the decision was not Saville's. President Zorn chose mathematics and nursing as the new, permanent co-tenants.

> The dynamics of the college changed a bit when we went from being all on the 7th floor [of humanities]. Several of us including Borsenik, Martin and Stefanelli were assigned temporarily to the education building. But the change wasn't serious because Jerry maintained an open-door policy.   AL IZZOLO, HOTEL FACULTY MEMBER

For hotel, it was probably Zorn's most favorable decision. A building of its own was now more likely because the largest divisions of the campus, business and hotel, were still homeless. Hotel gave one office in the humanities building to its student club. Its location abetted student/faculty interaction, but generated unwanted activity on the staid administrative floor.

> Students entered a float for homecoming weekend. They put it together in the small lounge on the 7th floor. During breaks and lunch hours, the secretaries would go there and stuff colored napkins in the chicken wire frame.   JOAN REYNOLDS BEITZ, ADMINISTRATIVE ASSISTANT

The matter was resolved during the summer of 1976 when the dean left campus to complete his dissertation. An agitated Boyce Phillips called, wrote and telegraphed to Ithaca that the assigned room was being expropriated by the administration.

> Oh, I remember that episode very well. It was funny. I was the president from '73 to '78. We were expanding. The president and academic vice president had very limited space. There simply was no place to move assistants like [Paul] Aizley and [Brock] Dixon. That was a logical place to move in on.   DON BAEPLER, UNLV PRESIDENT AND UNS CHANCELLOR

The humanities assignment proved to be propitious. Proximity brought the hotel faculty into a closer relationship with the university's top administration.

> Because we were on the 7th floor, we'd see the presidents daily. They were approachable in those days. The Greek fraternities wanted housing and expected me as their advisor to act. I talked to Vice President Brock Dixon, who favored it, but he wasn't in office long enough to do anything.   IZZOLO

Vice President Brock Dixon, became interim president between Don Baepler and Leonard Goodall.

> Baepler was a great administrator. He had comprehension; he knew were he wanted to go; he had good foresight. He was a good vice president, president and [later] chancellor.
>
> When Baepler was academic vice-president, he was actually the president too. When Baepler became chancellor, he asked the deans what they though about a president. The answer was Dixon, he's the best of the vice-presidents.   GEORGE HARDBECK, DEAN OF BUSINESS AND ECONOMICS

Under Dixon's presidency, a new building was given priority and the structure became reality. One must assume that Dixon's familiarity with the faculty gave him a better understanding of the college than he might otherwise have had. Few administrators tried to understand the college as hard as Brock Dixon.

Jumping the Hurdles. Funding for new buildings rests in the hands of the state legislature. Even today despite a much larger population, the Nevada legislature still meets in biannual sessions, once every odd year during the winter/spring term. The college made its first and rather tentative stab at getting on the campus facilities list as early as 1975, when university planning was started for the 1977 session. Hotel's request was given short shrift. Only in rare cases would the Regents and the legislature consider a building that had failed to make the campus priority list. Still, politics being what it is, a high priority on the campus list was no assurance of the final outcome. Another, less traditional technique was needed.

In 1976, the idea of a joint business/hotel building was being discussed and by 1977 the idea was gaining momentum. Business and hotel were funding much of the credits taught at UNLV and yet both were lacking adequate housing.

> We were the cash colleges.   HARDBECK

Moreover, a combined building fit better into the master plan, which recommended larger, not smaller, buildings. Campus planning for the 1979 legislative session began in the fall of 1977, a few months after the '77 legislative session closed. In September, a college faculty committee (Richard Basile, Charles Levinson, Patrick Moreo and Terry Wynia) was appointed to draft a "Guide to Planning." In soliciting help, Chairman Basile announced that the committee wanted to develop "an introductory narrative emphasizing the need, the importance and the reputation of the College of Hotel Administration."

> Basically our responsibility was to get input from the users [the faculty], apply the formulas, give the information to the Public Works Board, and critique the results.   DICK BASILE, HOTEL FACULTY MEMBER

Owen Knorr, Director of Institutional Research and Planning, provided the data on which the guide was to be based. Included were the number of hotel students taught—taught being different from the number enrolled. Taught students rose from 798 in 1971 to 1,880 in 1977. Projections carried the number to 3,500 (1,400 majors) in 1986, ten years hence. Another eye opener was hotel's faculty-to-student ratio. Hotel had 53 majors per faculty member that year; the average for the balance of the campus was just 14 students per faculty member! University budgets were supposed to be based on a 20:1 figure.[2]

> At Don Baepler's request, I appeared before some legislators, who asked me if I could live with 20:1 or 25:1. I said I wish I had that [low a number]. Business was teaching at twice that ratio, while English classes were limited to 25 students.   HARDBECK

Using the prescribed menu of space allowances furnished by the University of Nevada System, the committee reported its findings in November, 1977. As one would suspect, no state-wide standards existed for hotel administration. Use those for home economics, the college was told. The committee's preliminary draft was structured around square footage needs and required facilities including laboratories and offices.

I remember when Dick Basile and Charlie Levinson and I sat on a committee—as much as there were committees in those days—and Dick said we're going to need these extra offices. I asked why [all those offices]? A couple of years later, we were out of space.   PAT MOREO, '69 STUDENT AND FACULTY MEMBER

Three months later (February 28, 1978) the second of many revised and more detailed plans was developed. Although the business college was concerned about the extra space that the food labs required, the actual distribution of square feet according to this revised projection was 39,328 square feet for hotel and 29,200 square feet for business. Business also had first claim to a 12,000 square-foot auditorium designated as "university-assigned facilities."

Look at the numbers, business was several times larger than hotel!   GEORGE HARDBECK, DEAN OF BUSINESS AND ECONOMICS

Although hotel had 24,538 square feet of laboratories, business had twice hotel's classroom and office allotments. An additional 35,155 square feet were shared in common. In total, better than 115,000 square feet were planned. For both colleges, many coveted facilities had to be deleted. Showers and lockers for food handlers were installed for safety and sanitation, but never used. On the other hand, storage space for the dining facilities proved far too inadequate

Four major hurdles had to be cleared before the first shovelful of earth was turned. First, the building had to make the campus priority list. It had then to survive the Regents' vetting of the joint university system. Finally, it had to compete favorably before the Public Works Board with capital requests from other state agencies. Only then was it forwarded to the legislature for the final obstacle—money.

The need was very apparent. Classrooms were in short supply across campus. So too were faculty offices. The first hurdle, campus approval with Dixon as acting president, was cleared.

Dixon never discussed the building with me. He could see we were pitched all over the campus. At one time, we were supposed to be in the new education building.   HARDBECK

On May 26, 1978, the Board of Regents adopted a capital improvement program for 1979–1983. First priority went to UNR for a $3.1 million addition to its business college building. Second on the list was UNLV's business and hotel administration building, Phase I, for $11,786,000. UNLV's next building (fine arts, phase III) was listed seventh on the Regent's system-wide list. Hurdle two had been jumped.

Almost immediately came a letter that was so bewildering, it was laughable. The state architect, Harry Wood, asked Acting President Brock Dixon why UNLV was duplicating comparable facilities that already existed at the community college. Dixon's August 1, 1978 response, which took Vallen's input verbatim, questioned the logic of such a query. The letter pointed out that there were many duplications on both campuses including classrooms, offices, bookstores, restrooms and cafeterias. Still, the better part of valor suggested that a list of reasons including distance, size, transportation issues and educational objectives be submitted. The inquiry appeared resolved and another hurdle was officially passed.

Lobbying With Letters. Legislative approval with financing was the final obstacle. The State Legislature was not a rubber stamp, nothing was assured. Everyone lobbied that political body to reorder the priorities list. It had been done before.

> All kinds of behind-the-scenes maneuvering takes place every two years when the capital budget is presented and the university system prioritizes its building list. Individual regents champion one project or another. They talk behind the scenes and out comes a list that no one is happy about. It's an art of compromise.   DON BAEPLER, UNLV PRESIDENT AND UNS CHANCELLOR

Fortunately, the college had an active alumni group, spearheaded by a handful of able and concerned graduates. Several of whom had held the presidency of the student hotel association during their undergraduate years.

> I held the post of VP in hotel's student club. The alumni association emerged from that early group since many of the graduates who started the alumni association were the same persons who started the hotel clubs.   MIKE UNGER, '71 STUDENT

The campaign began with a request from the dean published in the alumni news letter and the undergraduate bulletin. Legislators were identified by name. Among them were Don and Keith Ashworth (friends of Dick Basile), Jean Ford (an acquaintance of Dean and Flossie Vallen and their children) and Jack Vergiels (a long-term faculty member from education). A series of letters went out from the alumni. Writers were asked to use company stationery because many of the graduates held good positions in industry.

> I remember Unger's letter from Caesars Palace. It had very distinctive stationery that looked burnt along the edges. The letter spoke to how much the program had done and how important it was [to the state].   MOREO

> I recall the telephone conversation when the dean asked for help in getting money from the legislature. I wrote a letter and was invited to appear before the committee. Other alumni went with me.   UNGER

Although most letters originated within the state, many also came from outside Nevada. Among the non-Nevada letter writers during May, 1979 was Gary Brown ('73), with Hyatt Hotels at the time.

> My son, Gary, came to Las Vegas at the suggestion of Peter Heinrich. He worked for Peter in Rochester, New York. I talked to Peter who knew Vallen and that's how we came.

UNLV. turned Gary into a successful hotelier.   RICHARD BROWN, DONOR INTERMEDIARY AND FATHER OF ALUMNUS, GARY

Small world. I offered Peter the first faculty post the college had, even before I arrived in Las Vegas. He was running a hotel in the town in which I lived. Peter decided to stay in the industry.   JERRY VALLEN

Another out-of-state letter writer in May, 1979 was Gerard (Jerry) Inzerillo ('75). Jerry's efforts were not limited to the legislature. In August of 1978, he was in contact with Congressman James Santini trying to get federal money for the building. The two men knew each other slightly. Vallen also knew Santini, who was very sympathetic to the college's efforts.

At this time, we had a son going to Georgetown University in Washington. Senator Laxalt found this out somehow and invited our son to Thanksgiving dinner. Only in Nevada.   FLOSSIE VALLEN

In addition to the building campaign, Inzerillo, who had worked for Hilton, was trying to get Xavier Lividini of the New York Statler to give the library his extensive collection of the *Hotel/Motel Journal*. Las Vegas was vying with other schools and was thrilled when a letter, dated April 23, 1979, arrived announcing the shipment. Either the letter or the shipment was misaddressed because the journals ended up at Fairleigh Dickinson in New Jersey.

Inzerillo also worked on Hilton's Senior Vice President, Porter Paris, for memorabilia. Between 1978 and 1982, Inzerillo worked hard to get funding from Hilton for either an academic chair or a segment of the building.

Help was also solicited from outside the university family. Tradition had the Hotel Sales Management Association (HSMA) hold its election meeting on the campus each October. The 1978 dinner was catered in the dormitory dining hall under the direction of Pat Moreo. In the evening's program was a welcome from the dean:

> "Welcome HSMA members to our third annual university meeting! Our facilities are sparse but our desire to host you is warm and cordial. If you support the new building when it comes before the legislature this winter, our physical presentation will eventually match our enthusiasm."[3]

Legislative Testimony. Because the dean believed strongly in the principles behind the chain of command, he would not personally lobby the legislature for other than the recommendations supported by the university president. Apparently Dean Hardbeck felt the same.

I was interested in getting a Center for Business and Economic Research. But I couldn't lobby for it so Frank Scott and Zack Taylor did. It was approved.   HARDBECK

President Dixon's proclivity about the building was an unknown. It was decided, therefore, that the alumni would do some lobbying.

One agenda item was our building. For some reason Vallen didn't go, he had "us" go to Carson City. And the "us" was me, both a faculty member and an alumnus ['67], Mike Unger ['71], Kerry Kindig ['76], Dan Celeste ['76] and others.   PAT MOREO, '69 STUDENT AND FACULTY MEMBER

"The others"on the committee—although all did not travel to Carson City—were Cindi Kiser ('80), Kathleen Marie ('76), Jim Rafferty ('78), Jay Roberts ('71), Marc Sterbens ('75), Alex Sugden ('72), and Roger Wagner ('69).

I have no recall about any of it.   MARC STERBENS

Floyd Lamb, Finance Committee Chairman, was the committee's target. Everyone hoped that the letter campaign had softened the ground first.

It's hard to say that the letter campaign had any effect, but it certainly didn't hurt.   BAEPLER

The stage was set for the hearing, but it may not have been before Floyd Lamb.

The chairman of the hearing committee was a railroad man, a conductor or something. We were in the audience while Dixon, interim president, was testifying. The chair asked Dixon what projects were the most important to him. When he said all were, the chair insisted that they be prioritized. We're watching him expecting the answer to be the fine arts building, Phase III. When Dixon said business and hotel, the committee asked why private industry didn't fund it. Brock turned to us and asked if we would speak. Mike Unger, who was at Caesars Palace, re-introduced the letters and then spoke. He made the link to the industry's expenditures on real estate and gaming taxes. Next thing, they passed it!   MOREO

The twin attack of letter writing and testimony before the committee had proved effective; the 1979 legislature funded the building. Jim Rafferty ('78) reported to his compatriots that:

"Our efforts to support the Hotel College Building were well received at Carson City on Friday. . . . [to] Floyd Lamb, I expressed the need for a new facility and the continued growth and improvement of our college. I pointed out that many top graduates were working and contributing to the local industry. . . . The point was well made by our letters. . . . Senator Lamb assured me that copies of all the letters would be distributed to all members of the Committee."[4]

At that time, Nevada was the only state with legalized gambling. Therefore, the federal tax on gaming devices was rebated to the state with the proviso that it be used for education. Part of the construction money may have come from that source.

Remember that the first priorities of the slot monies were the Thomas and Mack Pavilion and the Lawlor Events Center in Reno. Slot tax monies were distributed over a lot of capital budgets. Some may well have gone into hotel's building.   BAEPLER

The news was reported to the student body with jubilation and finality in the Summer, 1979 issue of *Federation of Hoteliers UNLV* and in the September, 1979 issue of the student/alumni publication, *Coaster Mig*.

GETTING THE BUILDING OPEN

Nothing moves quickly with the state. Bids had to be solicited first for the architect and then, after the plans were approved, for the builder. Probably the most frustrating aspect of the procedure was the role that the two deans, business and hotel, had—or rather didn't have. Both the architect and the builder reported to their client, which was Public Works, not the academic units.

> That changed later as everyone came to realize how unproductive it was.   BROCK DIXON, UNLV ACTING PRESIDENT

The deans and their committees communicated with the architect and the builder through Public Works, except there were interim steps. To reach Public Works for financial issues, communication went though Herman Westfall, Vice President for Finance. To reach Public Works for design issues, communication went though Brock Dixon, Vice President for Administration. Dixon's term as interim president was over. Thus, each issue flowed from the college committees to the respective deans; from deans to joint college committees; from joint committees to Westfall or Dixon; from Westfall or Dixon to Public Works; from Public Works to the builder, TGK McCarthy of Phoenix and/or to the architects, John C. Mayer and David Wells of Architronics of Las Vegas. Obviously, the answers—who even remembered the questions—came in reverse order.

> It was a horrible mess. More than once, we were told: You're just the occupants, you cannot tell us what needs to be done. It was discouraging when you could see what needed to be done and the building inspector agreed, but couldn't get any support from his boss.   GEORGE HARDBECK, DEAN OF BUSINESS AND ECONOMICS

On March 28, 1980, Vice President Brock Dixon wrote a memorandum to the new president, Leonard (Pat) Goodall, noting that ideas for the building were to be presented to the Board of Regents at their Spring 1981 meeting, and that construction should begin about mid-1981. A publicity brochure projected the autumn of 1982 as the completion date. Dixon's memo projected occupancy for January 1983. The building was formally dedicated during the fall term of 1983–1984, some six years after the initial planning.

Consultants to Ourselves

A sense of frustration, of impotence and of a good deal of anger simmered during the years between Dixon's memo and the actual opening.

> Public Works treated us like little boys who didn't know what we were talking about. You would sit down with them, but you knew that half the time it was a useless meeting.   DICK BASILE, HOTEL FACULTY MEMBER

The architect, Nevada Architronics, was not specialized in kitchen design so they wisely subcontracted to a California firm. Unfortunately, that contract did not include the two small kitchen labs, but only the large, production kitchen. An unusual agreement was struck in the fall of 1980. With President Goodall's support, and over the signature of now-Chancellor Baepler, the college released faculty member Charles Levinson from a partial teaching load so he could work as a consultant to Architronics and design plans for the small labs.

I thought Charlie was top notch.   HARDBECK

Charlie Levinson got the only reduced load in the history of Jerry Vallen's tenure.   AL IZZOLO, HOTEL FACULTY MEMBER

We relieved Charlie of half a load and he still had more to teach than faculty have today! BASILE

Charlie was so involved in the kitchen design. He really worked hard on it!   JIM ABBEY, HOTEL FACULTY MEMBER

Charlie and I had difficulty with Public Works. They said the kitchen was big enough for the Hilton, not realizing that a training facility had 20-plus students who needed space to be their own chefs. Charlie did an amazing job. There was no negative reaction once it was opened.   BASILE

Levinson's release time was to be funded by Architronics, and with that money ($10,000) the college hired part-time faculty to fill the missing slot. If it sounded too good to be true, it was. Six years later, far after the completion of the building, the university was still waiting for payment. Despite letters from the university's general counsel, Elizabeth Nozero, from Vice President Herman Westfall, and from the dean, the final installment was negotiated away by the client, the State Public Works Board, which wasn't even a party to the Levinson contract! The amount still due to hotel was offset arbitrarily by Public Works for an amount Public Works allegedly owed to Architronics.

Payment was never made despite a letter from the general counsel for the University of Nevada System, Don Klasic. He supported the college arguing that the offset by the Works Board was a separate contract; the Board was not a party to Levinson's contract! The college was never paid the $4,000 balance, but the system was. Ironically, the offset was for designs purportedly done for a pond that was never built in front of the building. It was not the only time that the university failed to enforce a contract in hotel's name. The usual argument was that legal costs exceeded possible monetary rewards.

Issues

Although Architronics held regular meetings with the deans and their respective committees, issues were rarely resolved. The truth was, no one had authority to resolve anything except the client, whose attendance was sporadic. Errors of design or construction, which became apparent as the building progressed, languished despite repeated pleadings. Among the unresolved items were the lack of windows in the business dean's complex; the inadequacy of treatment of the folding doors in the dining room; the corridor and bar floors on the second tier (an experimental epoxy of some kind hinders cleanliness to this day); the low ceiling in the dining room; the incorrect height for the bar; the lack of kitchen wall tile. And so the list grew.

> I took the architects to Arizona State to see the tiered classrooms. I thought they understood it until (1) they couldn't figure out how to put the swivel seats in, and (2) they didn't dig down to allow entry from the back of the classroom.
>
> The building leaned on the business side. Office chairs rolled over to the far side of the room. Extra concrete was added to level the 4th and 5th floors.   HARDBECK

> I remember the great difficulty that business had trying to get the fifth floor of the building leveled   LESLIE CUMMINGS, HOTEL FACULTY MEMBER

> When I was asked to sign off on the kitchen, I recall saying that the kitchen wasn't what the blueprints showed. Specs said everything was to be stainless; it wasn't. 210 power was supposed to be available for certain equipment; it wasn't. So we [hotel college] ended up paying for extras to meet our needs.   CLAUDE LAMBERTZ, HOTEL FACULTY MEMBER

Despite all the issues and a sense of frustration, the completed building was wonderful to have and marvelous to see.

> I thought the architect, David Wells, did a good job. He interviewed faculty, staff and students. The amphitheater, the classrooms, student traffic, the central courtyard all flowed well.   FRANK BORSENIK, HOTEL FACULTY MEMBER

> We were all anxious to have the building and we were al pleased when it happened.   IZZOLO

The architects won a design award that gave special recognition for their attention to energy conservation, which was obtained from the cantilevered floors and swamp-cooled atrium into which the classroom doors opened.

> I had some input into the umbrella design of the courtyard. [The "umbrella" conserved the swamp-cooled air in the lobby.]   BROCK DIXON, UNLV ACTING PRESIDENT

The Dining Room. The biggest fiasco of all was the dining room floor. Charlie Levinson in his role of architectural consultant and building committee member was fully involved. He brought a friend, a state legislator, to tour the not-yet-opened building. Walking in the empty dining room, they noticed the floor shaking.

> Especially when it was walked on. More so when there was a buffet and the clean, stacked dishes rattled. Everyone was afraid of it, but it's still there.   LAMBERTZ

Suspension floors, and that's what the building had, tighten as the room fills with people. It was supposed to shake when empty.

> The floor is built like a bridge. It flattens out as it is loaded. And then it vibrates less. But as [Levinson and his colleague] walked across [the empty room], the floor shook! FRANK BORSENIK, HOTEL (ENGINEERING) FACULTY MEMBER

Assurances from the architects and engineers aside, the newspaper stories were so scary that a limit was placed on the number of persons using the dining room separate from the number proscribed by fire code. The hullabaloo actually worked in favor of the college's needs. Faculty did not want the dining room used for student social purposes. So dancing in the building was now foreclosed under the cover of safety.

> Remember that the dining room was suppose to have a sign, "no dancing allowed," because the floor was subject to collapse. HARDBECK

Fortunately, the college was able to forestall a second dining-room disaster. Throughout the period of construction and particularly as the building neared completion (January, 1983), a debate raged within the faculty senate about opening a faculty club in hotel's dining room. Full-time use of the facilities was the last thing that the dean and the faculty wanted or could afford. Running competition with the college's supporters, the local restaurants, was not an acceptable option. Besides, running a commercial establishment was contrary to good education. No other academic unit had to meet a "bottom line." A pro forma operating statement was prepared that showed the annual cost to each faculty member if everyone signed on, and the much larger cost if less than the optimum number enrolled. The idea died a natural death since its supporters had imagined a cost-free facility. There was no provision to cover a business loss.

> Some of the Hotel faculty were for it, but the majority was against. I thought it was a good idea back then, but not today because enrollment strains our capacity. LAMBERTZ

Sprinklers. The MGM fire, a terrible disaster for the community, added an unexpected hiccup to the building. A sprinkler system was added as an afterthought although it hadn't been budgeted for and initially wasn't required by code. More water was needed so an underground auxiliary main had to be dug and laid. All of which took funds from the building and threatened the completion of the fifth floor. A fortunate dip in construction demand occurred as the building went to bid allowing it to come in under projected cost, so everything was finished. But not before a decision was made to remove all electric outlets from the corridors and reduce to two their number in the offices. Most of the details were resolved by the time the building neared completion, although one of the check lists given to the contractor had nearly 100 kitchen items that needed attention.

Computers were in their infancy when the building was planned. The lack of wiring impacted ten years later, but who knew.   BORSENIK

Acquiring Wares. By the spring term 1983, the purchasing department (A. L. Cunningham and Joan Davis) was soliciting bids for carpeting, furniture, cabinets and the like. Earlier, when the reality of the building was certain, hotel had begun its own solicitation of heavy kitchen equipment. The initial response was very positive, but the effort fizzled immediately when it was learned that each dollar saved through donations had to be returned to state coffers. It seemed better to use savings from donations to create a fund for other uses. The law was the law, so the appeal fell on deaf ears.

When purchasing began its final bid processes, a second blow came. Dining room furniture, desks, cabinets and bookcases were all provided, but there was no money budgeted for the kitchens! Foodservice wares were excluded from the funding because those items were not capital goods. No money was available for pots and pans, for dishes or flatware; nothing for initial inventories of basics like flour and sugar let alone bar products.

Oh boy! When we first opened the doors, we had nothing. We had the major pieces of equipment, but no hand tools, nothing.   CLAUDE LAMBERTZ, HOTEL FACULTY MEMBER

Moreover, it was already apparent that all of the college's calls on the maintenance staff of buildings and grounds to handle minor repairs and the installation of donated equipment would be paid for from the already limited operating budget, not from the capital budget.

To anyone who would listen, I asked, Can you imagine the state opening a chemistry building without test tubes?   JERRY VALLEN

Lacking funds to buy ware (dishware, tableware, kitchenware), food inventories, bar products or cleaning supplies for that matter, the college turned once again to its friends. Each need had to be tackled.

The university's foodservice contractor, Saga—subsequently purchased by ARA Services and later renamed ARAMARK—had always been a good neighbor. The national office was an active recruiter and scholarship donor, and the local unit permitted the college to use the dormitory facility for catering classes before the new building was planned. Cooperation was strong; respect was mutual. Saga's national headquarters had approached the college soon after the building was announced, concerned about the competition that the food facility represented. Hotel had absolutely no interest in catering anything on campus—that's why it objected to the proposed faculty club—except that which was related to its academic mission. Moreover, the college was preparing guidelines that would sharply limit the use of its dining room.

Saga's executives went away from the meeting satisfied there would be no irreconcilable issues. It was further agreed that Saga would serve as the college's commissary at least in the interim. The local manager, Craig Ball, gave the college all of his discontinued—though some were chipped—chinaware, and acquisition number one was in place.

> We had blue-rimmed and red-rimmed plates. Nothing matched, but we had something. There was no money for anything! LAMBERTZ

Flatware was equally easy to obtain. A telephone call to Bill Morris, a staunch friend of the university and of the college, settled the matter in a few minutes. Joe Francis, senior vice-president and general manager of the Holiday Inn/Holiday Casino, controlled by Bill Morris and Claudine Williams, took the tableware from the buffet inventory and the college had knives, forks and spoons.

> The business community, especially Bill Morris, treated us well! He provided meals for honor students, their sponsors and parents. GEORGE HARDBECK, DEAN OF BUSINESS AND ECONOMICS

With dormitory chinaware and buffet flatware, the program was in business, although not at a gourmet level.

> I remember bringing some faculty wives for lunch right after we opened. There were a number of dishes, but just one serving spoon. We made do. FLOSSIE VALLEN

With no utilities to pay, no taxes, no labor costs, no insurance and no executive payrolls to meet, profits were assured. In a very short time, these initial table settings were replaced with a better grade of ware. With money earned, the dean approached Irv Mills, chief executive of the American Restaurant China Council, in September, 1982. Their acquaintanceship and subsequent friendship had developed by way of CHRIE. (The China Council presented gold commemorative plates to CHRIE's officers.) Mills worked diligently but unsuccessfully to get a major contribution. Syracuse China, in the person of Executive Vice President Charles Goodman, finally agreed to sell to the program at the same discount that it was then giving the Hilton chain. That price was cost less discount, less discount, less discount.

> We had no money for chinaware and then Syracuse came in with a great discount. Something like buy a dozen, we'll give a dozen. LAMBERTZ

Finding an outright donor had the same unimpressive results several years later when the dining room was considering another chinaware upgrade, to the "dean's setting."

Adequate Faculty. Faculty to operate the facility was still another matter. The need was raised with Academic Vice President Dale Nitzschke again and again in a number of memos beginning as early as 1982. New positions throughout the college were needed for the academic year 1984–85 if the college was to meet its charge. Even then, the requests were modest. Hotel had been slipping behind the curve for years (see Exhibit 7-1). It was time to play hard ball. Either the college would get staff to operate the kitchen and dining room or the facilities would remain closed. In light of the state's freeze on hiring, a memo explaining various options was sent by Vallen to Nitzschke on January 20, 1983:

> "2. . . . [funding for] the culinary staff is uncertain. . . . Therefore I intend not to commit the Beam money for [small] equipment.
>
> . . . we shall have a vacant facility and cancel the culinary courses scheduled for September, 1983. It will be an embarrassment and . . . [be] a misrepresentation in our student recruiting."

The need was not faculty alone. Only one classified position was assigned to the dean's office. Hardly adequate when the college had no assistant dean and no faculty members on B+ contracts; that is, no department head equivalents. The 20 faculty members shared three secretaries, but reconfiguring the offices when the move was made to Beam Hall broke up the clerical pool, where each classified position helped the other.

Faculty Needs, 1972 to 1981

Year	FTE	%Change	Faculty	Faculty/FTE	Comments
81	514	+ 8	17.5[*]	30:1	Preliminary
80	477	+27	17.5[*]	27:1	
79	376	+18	14	27:1	
78	318	− 0.5	14	23:1	Admission Requirements Increased
77	336	+15	12	28:1	
76	291	+ 11	10	29:1	
75	262	+10	9	29:1	
74	238	+18	7	34:1	
73	201	+14	7	29:1	
72	177		6	29:1	

[*]For two years, hotel shared faculty member, John Goodwin, with business.

EXHIBIT 7-1. October 16, 1981 memo to Academic Vice President Dale Nitschke summarizing faculty needs using statistics from the Office of the Registrar and the Office of Research.

Nevertheless, a chef-instructor and a kitchen steward were the first two priorities. Nevada Personnel actually had a classified position corresponding to our request for a steward, identified as Food Manager III. The chef was to join as a faculty member, with or without academic credentials.

Both searches were concentrated in the large and qualified talent pool of Las Vegas.

The response was amazingly strong including many members of the FSEA and the Fraternity of Chefs. The deal was closed and the starting date set about three months ahead with one of the city's best know executive chefs. A real coup! Soon thereafter another chef whom I had helped find a job contacted me through a third party. Pay-back time! He reported that our new hire harassed young women and that's why he was job seeking. We started the search anew and received another large batch of applications, among them Bob Barber as steward and Claude Lambertz as chef-instructor.   JERRY VALLEN

Vallen called before Christmas of 1983 and asked if I would like a present. Could I start with the new year. I was practically living at the hotel. Having taught before, I knew the appeal of civilized hours. I never thought I'd stay this long, maybe 3 to 5 years [now his 18th year has passed].   LAMBERTZ

The paucity of staff forced an academic decision that was not in the best interests of the curriculum. To minimize demand on the limited facility and staff, the food production course was scheduled in the senior year. Senior classes are smaller than sophomore classes, which otherwise would have been the preference. The position of food steward was finally approved for the 1989–90 budget, six years after the initial submission.

Despite his "over qualification in foods," which was the major concern of the dean's search committee (see Chapter 3), Vallen relied upon the capabilities of the food faculty in foreseeing and forestalling issues built around the kitchen. John Stefanelli's committee prepared helpful priority lists, including the issue of liquor licensing and service.

The Liquor License. The Regents approved liquor on campus in 1970, and by memo shortly thereafter (July 24) President Zorn officially notified the college. Wine service was approved for hotel's dinners in the Moyer Student Union. Prior to then, any event involving alcohol had been held off campus: the beer tastings initially in the dean's home; the summer wine courses in the convention center; the student parties, well, everywhere.

Use of the bar in the new dining room didn't seem to fall into the same category as alcohol on campus. Besides, no one really knew to what extent the bar would be used. In August, 1981, John Stefanelli's committee prepared a memorandum directing the dean's attention to a range of issues facing the new facility. Number one was obtaining a tavern license.

At a citywide social function soon thereafter, an informal conversation took place between the dean and a county commissioner about licensing for the bar. At his suggestion, language for an ordinance was drafted by the college in consultation with the university's legal officer, Lyle Rivera. The ordinance proposed that hotel notify the Office of the President whenever alcohol was to be used on campus. That was to be the licensing requirement.

Almost at once the proposed ordinance was placed on the commission's agenda. The college rallied the troops. Faculty, alumni and friends from the industry and the Nevada Resort Association gathered in the auditorium for a reading and public comment on the ordinance. Surprise! Surprise! The ordinance was approved without a hearing. None of the big guns ever testified. Their presence was probably enough.

GIFTS FOR THE BUILDING

In amazingly short order, a flow of gifts eased the pressure in opening and operating the building. Once again, private donations rather than university underwriting enabled the college to do the job to which it aspired. Indeed, the industry's generosity left a residual, a substantial endowment that still benefits the college.

Gifts of Money

The program was fortunate to received two types of support for the building. Cash allowed discretionary purchases with decisions made by the faculty and dean. Gifts in kind were usually in place faster because they did not involve prior acceptance by the Regents. Reporting such gifts was somewhat *pro forma* and always ex post facto. Gifts did not pass through the university's bid and purchasing procedures. Of course, unspent cash was endowed and was available, therefore, far into the future.

Descriptions of the gifts are listed next in alphabetical order.

The Banfi Gift. Richard (Dick) Brown was a champion of UNLV's College of Hotel Administration, holding it close to his own alma mater, the Cornell Hotel School. Dick's son, Gary ('73), attended UNLV, which cemented the relationship that started when Brown and Vallen were undergraduates, one year apart. By 1982, he was Assistant to the Chairman of Villa Banfi U.S.A., growers and importers of fine wines. The two stayed in contact because Dick was active in CHRIE and was concerned about hotel education in general. (Vallen was president and chairman of CHRIE between 1974 and 1977). Preliminary conversations were finalized during Christmas, 1982, when the first portion of a $50,000 gift arrived in Las Vegas. Banfi was also contributing to Cornell, the Culinary Institute and Johnson and Wales.

While in Las Vegas for a club managers' meeting (March, 1983), Brown and Banfi's Vice President for Public Relations, Carmel Tintle, reviewed and approved the plans to upgrade the tiered demonstration kitchen and to name it the Villa Banfi Room. Unused funds were to be endowed to support the room and wine education in general.

> Tintle, Vallen and I were having coffee in a restaurant across from the university when Governor Bryan came in. Jerry waved him over and introduced us [as major contributors]. It was exciting because that governor went on to the U.S. Senate.   BROWN

It wasn't all by accident. Supposedly, during his Vegas visits, the governor sometimes stayed in a sample home behind that coffee shop. [The state capital is Carson City, 400 miles north]. A story circulated that he overslept one night and found himself the object of observation by potential home buyers the next morning.   JERRY VALLEN

Work began on the improvements with help from Joe Cathcart in purchasing and Charlie Moody and Jerry Dove from campus engineering and architecture. By 1985 the final payments and final work were finished. From a stark, concrete barn-like room had come an appealing tiered and tiled seminar facility. Special to the room was a wonderful mural of the Castello (Castle) Banfi, the company's Italian estates, painted by Robert Beckmann assisted by his wife, Polly.

It was my responsibility for the recommendation, but not for the numbers [of dollars]. I got money for a room, not necessarily a demo or dining room. And then the dean showed me the room and came up with the idea of the mural. We sent photos [of the Castello] and the artist did the rest.   BROWN

Contributions from Banfi Vintners resumed in 1987, when the room was upgraded again with television capabilities. Further donations from the foundation continue.

Undoubtedly, the good working relationship that the college had established with Sam Costanza, general manager of McKesson Wines and Spirts, Banfi's local distributor, helped to facilitate the Banfi gifts. Through McKesson, Banfi made numerous contributions in kind to stock the initial bar and to provide wine for important dinners.

The Beam Gift. By a memorandum dated February 5, 1981, Vice President Brock Dixon suggested that the colleges begin soliciting donations for the building. A joint faculty committee, but primarily Deans Hardbeck and Vallen, created guidelines for giving. Special emphasis was placed on naming the building. With the help of the publications office, a 16-page brochure, entitled *The Colleges of Business, Economic & Hotel Administration*, was published. A separate list of dollar equivalents was also prepared, but not published.

Before anything had been done with overt solicitations, the gift was in hand! *Fait accompli.* Regent Lilly Fong and her spouse, Wing, both ardent UNLV boosters, came up with a donor, Tom Beam. The $1,000,000 gift was exciting although less than had been decided by the joint business/hotel pact. But a bird was in the hand. Unhappily, a third of the earnings was designated for the engineering college, to which Beam made a second, subsequent gift of a building. The immediate pressure was over.

Soon after Tom Beam's gift, I walked with him around the building which was nearing completion. At an opportune time, I mentioned how hard up we were for kitchen ware, hoping for a supplemental check. He looked at me in amazement, I just gave you a million dollars!   JERRY VALLEN

Wealth aside, Mr. Beam considered himself a regular guy. His business card from the California Club identified him merely as "Stockholder." Tom Beam's invariable response to meal invitations in the building that he helped fund was to ask who was paying for it. The second question dealt with dress. Was it necessary to wear a coat and tie?

> I enjoyed sitting next to Tom Beam at the graduation luncheons because he was the only other guest without a tie. We'd find each other and sit together.   LAMBERTZ

Tom Beam attributed his wealth to the wise real estate purchases made by his parents, for whom the building was named, Frank and Estella Beam Hall. But it was Tom Beam, himself, who developed land in one of Vegas' earliest housing tracts, the McNeill Estates. He was a laconic person with his own distinct character—"warts and all" was Brock Dixon's affectionate description, but at heart a warm and friendly man.

> When I asked Tom for his wife's name, Lee, so that we could prepare honorifics of one kind or another, he realized that he had forgotten to tell her of his $1,000,000 cash gift.   DIXON

The Boyd Gift. Bill Boyd, Chairman of the Boyd Group, had talked with the dean several times about a contribution to the hotel program. Indeed, a Boyd family member by marriage, John Kelly, had hinted at the possibility while Vallen was seated in Kelly's dentist's chair. As she had done before for the college, Regent Lilly Fong also acted as an intermediary. The issue was raised anew when the dean wrote (June 7, 1984) to Boyd, but nothing was finalized. An unexpected announcement from the Office of the President brought the matter to a resolution. Summoning the deans to gather with other university administrators to recognize a gift to the university was President Maxson's style. He made surprise announcements of each large donation, the type that he was so successful in obtaining. It was almost routine. But the tidings were not. The Boyd family, lead by Bill, had pledged a large sum to secure the stadium, hereafter to be called the Boyd Stadium.

During the festivities that followed the announcement, Bill Boyd approached and repeated his pledge. Money for support of Boyd Stadium was different than that earmarked for the College of Hotel Administration. The latter was stock in a local bank. Not long afterwards, on December 3, 1985, an Irrevocable Assignment of Stock was signed by Sam A. Boyd and Mary T. Boyd, Bill's parents. It transferred 12,695 shares to the college shortly before the Nevada State Bank was sold. One million dollars went to the College of Hotel Administration. The excess derived from the sale went to the Office of the President. Notice of the Boyd Family Gift appeared in the December, 1986 issue of *Town and Country Magazine*, which cited the nation's largest contributions for that year.

The $1,000,000 gift funded the dining rooms. Acoustics in the dining rooms had never been tested by the architect. Noise levels made impossible conversation with co-diners at the same table. Just in time came the Boyd gift. Jerry Dove, UNLV's architect, directed the capital outlay that paid for an acoustical study and the subsequent purchase of ceiling materials, draperies and other accouterments that solved a very serious problem. Additional track lighting upgraded the room and made it fit to carry the Boyd family identification. With three grandchildren available, the rooms were named Samuel J. Boyd, Marianne E. Boyd and William R. Boyd.

The balance of the gift was endowed to fund the Sam Boyd and Mary Boyd chair in gaming, and to support the work of distinguished professors and graduate students. Jim Kilby took the Boyd Chair when he joined the faculty as a gaming instructor and Don MacLaurin (MSHA, '87) was the first student winner. Undoubtedly, UNLV was the first and probably still the only university with a chair in gaming management! Bob Maxson called another gathering and made a second Boyd announcement. Held in the Boyd dining rooms, of course!

The Campbell Gift. Just as the demonstration lab and the dining rooms needed upgrading even before the building was finished, so, too, did the classrooms. This time there was no solicitation; an anonymous donor stepped forward after Bill Campbell died. The donor, the college and the Campbell family agreed that a small portion of this $50,000 endowment was to refurbish classroom #127. That's when the fun began

Repairs and maintenance was one of the contentious battles between the academic arms of the university and the section known as Building and Grounds (B&G). B&G's costs were always higher than those of outside contractors despite having its staff on university payroll. The estimate for the classroom upgrade was astronomical. Instead, the donor agreed to pay an outside contractor $8,600 for the work before making the contribution and to then reduce the endowment gift by that amount. Funds for the upgrade would not go through the campus—the donor would pay the contractor directly—and the college would not use B&G. This startling departure from standard procedure required special permissions to assure the integrity of the gift. The effort saved many dollars for the endowment.

Acknowledgment of this second Bill Campbell gift—the first had come from the Nevada Resort Association—was made public during the 1984 graduation luncheon at the Flamingo Hotel. In attendance to acknowledge the special classroom and the endowment to be used for labor education were Bill Campbell's sons, Don Campbell and Gary Logan.

Earnings from the Campbell endowment enabled the college to expand its series of labor seminars, the first of which had been held in 1973. Beginning in 1985, and continuing until today, the college has presented, without charge and with catered luncheons included, labor related issues under the rubric of the Campbell Seminars. Early participants were faculty members, Richard Basile and Vince Eade; union members Al Bramlet and Dick Thomas; and industry executives, Joe Buckley and Larry Levine.

Larry Levine was the sharpest labor relations person there was. JOE BUCKLEY, HUMAN RESOURCES DIRECTOR, HUGHES CORPORATION

These labor seminars identified the college as a support center for the community. They helped promote cohesion within an ever-growing and disparate hotel/labor community. The invitation to attend also acknowledged the special role of the participants, many of whom served as coordinators for the college/industry internship program.

> When we first started [mid-1970's], we conducted seminars using actual arbitration cases to bring together union and management people. [The first seminar was entitled, The Labor Contract.] Sessions were expanded later using the Campbell endowment.   DICK BASILE, HOTEL FACULTY MEMBER

> In the early days, one negotiation was carried out for all the employers with Campbell, the teamsters and the culinary sitting together.
>   At arbitration, Dick Thomas handled his own cases. Campbell on one side, Thomas on the other. They both knew the contract cover-to-cover, word-for-word. That's because they wrote it.   GEORGE HARDBECK, DEAN OF BUSINESS AND ECONOMICS

Chef Louis' Intercession. Louis Szathmary was one of the restaurant industry's most colorful characters. Louie, the pronunciation used by intimates, was easily remembered by his bulk, his flowing mustaches and his controversial positions on almost everything.

> Louie would do some interesting demonstrations. He was an exciting kind of guy; the stereotypical chef with his big handlebar mustache! He could have been on the cover of a magazine [and he had been]. He had several businesses on the side including mushroom cultivation.   ALAN STUTTS, HOTEL FACULTY MEMBER

His Chicago restaurant, The Bakery, was the destination of both gourmet diners and professional restauranteurs.

> I invited Louie and his family to dinner during one of his visits and mentioned this to my sister. The telephone message was misinterpreted. My sister and her husband drove like crazy from New Mexico to Las Vegas to eat a meal cooked by Chef Louie. There was some disappointment to learn that the dinner was prepared by Chef Flossie.   FLOSSIE VALLEN

Louie wasn't surprised, but he was delighted, to be invited as a visiting faculty member assigned to a special class and informal talks to the faculty. Louie reminisced about it in a letter:

> "It was a wonderful time. I learned a lot and I think I passed on some of my knowledge to the students, because they kept coming, visiting us [wife, Sada], calling on the phone; asking for advice; sending their friends."

> I interceded somewhat in getting Louie to campus. My sister was married to his protege, my brother-in-law Mike, who talked to them [Louie and Sada] about UNLV. Mike learned about it from me.

Adele and I took them out to dinner one of the times they came to campus. Talk about being cowed: Where are you going to take them for dinner? We certainly weren't going to feed him at home!   BOB SMITH, DEAN OF SCIENCE, MATHEMATICS AND ENGINEERING

The first invitation led to subsequent visits of an ever lengthening period. He lectured, helped the students and pontificated on any subject.

A number of leading food people used the [Banfi] room for demonstrations, including Chef Louis.   RICHARD BROWN, DONOR INTERMEDIARY AND FATHER OF ALUMNUS, GARY

While touring the building Szathmary learned that equipment and small wares for the test and demo kitchens had not been funded by the state. He made the first contribution and assured the dean that subsequent funds would come from all across the nation. And they did! Every item in the student's practice kitchen, from measuring spoons to pots, was purchased from funds that Szathmary solicited. Commemorative plaques still hang in the small kitchen attesting to the support of these donors (see Exhibit 7-2). Szathmary wrote:

"I think again of the wonderful times when I was writing to my fellow Travel-Holiday Award winning restaurant owners to sponsor the cooking stations for the test kitchen, and how proud I was when I first saw the little plaque with The Bakery's name among the names of the big shots in the industry."

Once the acquaintanceship had been made, Louie, Sada, and daughter, Barbara, joined in other activities with the college. The chef's letter continues:

"I remember the lovely evenings we spent in your home and when we went out together to dine. . . . All wonderful memories, and all connected with you [Vallen] and your family.

The Harrah Gift. The Harrah gift was the largest endowment ($5,000,000) ever received by the college or even by the whole campus to that time. Several events coincided to bring about this legacy.

One incident has its origin many years earlier when a young man, new to Las Vegas, came to the college's office. Steve Greathouse was looking for a job and many of his interviewers had directed him to the campus. He was not a student, but his persuasiveness made the dean break precedent this one and only time. The college posted jobs, but calling hotel executives to get jobs for individual students, let alone non-students, was just not done! In time, such unsolicited calls were certain to be unanswered. But Lennie Williams (class of 1979) had called earlier that morning looking for staff for the Holiday Inn/Holiday Casino.

It proved to be a great match. Greathouse attained top executive status with the company during the same period that Holiday Inn cemented its professional alliance

Donors to the Kitchen Work Stations

Anthony Anthanas
Anthony's Pier 4
[Boston, MA]

In Living Memory of
Samuel Cross
Philadelphia, PA

The Four Seasons
Tom Margittai Paul Kovi
[New York, NY]

Lawry's The Prime Rib
Las Vegas, NV

The Pirates House
Savannah, Georgia

Rodeways Inns
A Parkmount Hospitality
Corporation Company

Restaurant Tio Pepe
Baltimore, MD

In Living Memory of
N. Peter Canlis
Canlis Restaurant
[Seattle, WA]

Stanley Demos
Coach House Restaurant
[Lexington, KY]

Host International, Inc
Division of Marriott Corp.

Chef Warren Leruth
Leruths Gretna, LA

Rian's Inc
Portland, Oregon

Saga
Menlo Park

Louis & Sada Szathmary
The Bakery Restaurant
[Chicago, IL]

Chin's
Las Vegas, Nevada

Fairmont Hotels
Richard L. Swig, Chairman
[San Francisco, CA]

Kriendler/Berns
"21"
[New York, NY]

The Nut Tree
Robert Powers
[Vacaville, CA]

Andre Rochat
Andre's, Las Vegas

Win Schuler
[Marshall, MI]

EXHIBIT 7-2. Donors to the Beam Hall test kitchen are identified by plaques over the work stations. Most of the donors were solicited by Louis and Sada Szathmary. [Bracketed explanations do not appear on the plaques.]

with the program. He assumed the role of college advocate urging the financial support that the dean was requesting.

Holiday Inn was interviewing and making donations even before Greathouse came on to the scene. Working with Jeff Cava, corporate manager of college relations in Memphis, and with Gary Armentrout, assistant general manager of the local Holiday Inn/Holiday Casino, a $15,000 gift was arranged in 1985 to support the opening of the building's new computer lab. Thereafter, Armentrout, Greathouse and Vallen held several meetings to explore and develop other areas of cooperation for the college and the company.

Contact between UNLV and Holiday Inn dated back to the early 1970s. Unquestionably, that long association created a special bond that grew stronger as a variety of Holiday executives interacted with the campus. Among them was former UNLV Student Body President Dan Wade, who was a company vice president. Ken Hamlet, a frequent campus visitor became Holiday Inn's president and CEO. Dick Goeglein, Harrah's president, spoke at the college's 1985 graduation luncheon. And so the list grew.

Two distant events impacted heavily on the history of the gift. Bill Harrah died and Holiday Inn acquired the Harrah chain. Holiday was renamed Promus, and Harrah's was spun out. Industry ramifications were far reaching. Many old-line hoteliers resigned from Holiday rather than be affiliated with a gaming company. And then there was the settlement of the Harrah estate, which Gabe Vogliotti, the NRA's executive, saw in a much broader perspective:

"By about 1964, many [casino] owners wanted to get out, to quit the business that carried so much vilification. . . . [Everyone] want[ed] to sell, five [owners] urgently. In each case the five called on Parry [Thomas, a well know Vegas banker] to find a buyer and, if necessary, provide financing. . . .

The entities that did have money were corporations. The problem lay in Nevada law. Years earlier (1955) the legislature had passed a law prohibiting, in effect, a corporation from being licensed for gambling. Only individuals could be licensed.

It became obvious that to sell a casino meant changing the law, and writing a new one. . . . Bill Harrah fought corporate licensing tooth and nail. He would be shamefaced later when he, too, went public, to find that his net worth had zoomed from 200 to 400 million [dollars]."[5]

Bill Harrah had operatives everywhere. He had full-time agents working the legislature around the clock and around the year. He contributed to everyone even those running for minor offices. Harrah sensed it, worked at it and spent money on it.   JOE DIGLES, NEVADA RESORT ASSOCIATION

President Robert Maxson's role was the final element in the Harrah gift. Either Bob Maxson independently approached someone, or someone approached Maxson in response to the college's long-term Greathouse/Armentrout campaign. But when and by whom are not known to the authors. Secrecy and surprise made it appear as if the donation had been 100% Bob Maxson's doing. Whatever the source, the discussion now moved up the organizational ladders to Maxson and Phil Satre, Harrah's president. It took that level to consummate the deal.

Mead Dixon (no relationship to Brock Dixon), who served on the boards of both Holiday Inn and Harrah's, might have been the conduit. Dixon was instrumental in consummating the Holiday/Harrah's merger from his position "Of Counsel" to the law firm of Vargas & Bartlett. From Rollan Melton of the *Reno Gazette-Journal*:

"After Harrah died, directors elected Dixon chairman [of the Board]. . . . The horrendous . . . death taxes, his [Bill Harrah's] personal debts and obligations to his heirs left no option other than to join a public company. The $300 million merger with Holiday Inns followed in 1980.

[Mead] Dixon also reveals that Harrah twice almost sold out to billionaire Howard Hughes."[6]

I served several years as personnel manager for Bill Harrah. He started a bingo palace in '36 on the beach in California, and [then] he and his dad came to Reno to start Harrah's.

I was amazed that the hotel school was to be named for him, especially when I found out that Holiday Inn was doing it!   DWIGHT MARSHALL, DEAN OF CONTINUING EDUCATION

Two law firms, Vargas & Bartlett and Rudin and Appel, later provided funds to launch the college's Mead Dixon Lecture Series. Walter Read, chairman of the New Jersey Casino Control Commission was the inaugural speaker for the series on February 23, 1990. Panelists on the 1991 Dixon lecture were such stalwarts as Brian Greenspun, Grant Sawyer, E. Parry Thomas, Phil Satre, and Steve Wynn.

Three chairs were created with the gift that was jointly funded by Mrs. Verna Harrah, Bills' widow, and the new Harrah/Holiday Corporation. One was the William F. Harrah chair, named for the family. One was the Michael D. Rose Chair, named for chairman, president and chief executive officer of the new Holiday/Harrah's corporation. Another was named for Claudine B. Williams, chairman of the board of the Harrah Las Vegas property. Williams along with her now deceased husband had built and operated the original Holiday Inn Center Strip. Three fine choices that the college was proud to honor! Photographs of the three hang in the offices of the college.

How the chairs were to be funded and awarded was left to the deans. Deans, plural, because Jerry Vallen was retiring and Dave Christianson had been named incoming dean. Details were forwarded to and approved by President Robert Maxson. They provided for the president to name the holder of the Harrah Chair. The dean was to name distinguished visiting professors to the Rose Chair and, on a rotating basis, award the Williams Chair to outstanding faculty members.

I didn't go to many Regent's meetings, but I did attend the one in which the Harrah gift was being announced. As the presentation droned on, I was suddenly alert. Bob Maxson had named me as holder of the first Harrah Chair. Exhilarating!   JERRY VALLEN

The 23-year old program was finally named: The William F. Harrah College of Hotel Administration. A black-tie, invitation-only banquet honoring Verna Harrah and Michael Rose was held in the Boyd Dining Rooms on February 24, 1989. There was little time between the announcement of the gift and the banquet. Buildings and Grounds performed wonderfully, ordering the signage and hanging it hours before the party. Later, the college hosted a banquet for B&G personnel to express thanks for a job well executed.

Jack Hooper Lounge. With so much space in the new building, the hotel college invited other disciplines to take temporary quarters as visiting faculty in an effort to cement ties across the campus. There were no takers. The response from the placement office was another matter. Hotel was that office's largest client and a tight bond of cooperation existed with the director, Bill Dakin, who was delighted to have this new, expanded space.

> Hotel had always been close to placement. When hotel was on the 7th floor of the Flora Dungan Humanities Building, placement was on the 3rd floor. There was a bit of debate about inviting Dakin to join us. What sealed it was the rumor that the Board of Regents was thinking of establishing its offices on our vacant 5th floor. Jerry said, Wait a minute we have already committed that to recruiting.
>
>   Besides, the building was so big, we wondered why we built all that excess space. Now, we don't have enough.   AL IZZOLO, HOTEL FACULTY MEMBER

By then the 5th floor was being structured. Interview rooms for recruiters and a separate waiting lounge for students were designed. That upgraded interview lounge was furbished with a $15,000 gift from Verdi Hooper and in 1983 was named for her late husband Jack H. Hooper. Unused dollars were endowed as was money from other contributions to assure the upkeep of the facility. The Hoopers were the in-laws of Bucky Buchanan, a member of the Board of Regents, a speaker at the 1976 graduation luncheon and a continuing backer of the college.

Southern Wine & Spirits of Nevada. The following chapter recounts the very special friendship that the college maintained with Southern Wine & Spirits in the person of Larry Ruvo. As the building neared completion, shortages in the cocktail lounge grew more evident. Money was needed to complete this part of the building as it was for the other sections not adequately covered by the construction contract. Ruvo stepped forward to refurbish the room. A refrigerated wine closet was installed, and glassware as well as other bar accouterments were acquired. Southern Wine also provided some of the initial bar inventory, as did Villa Banfi and Seagram Liquor. For certain, there was no shortage of alcohol. The Beam bar opened with 32 cases of wine and 17 cases of spirits just from the James Beam distillery, which likely felt an affinity to the building's name.

The Tropicana/Ramada Gift. Many requests for support were floated. President Goodall, Foundation Officer Buck Deadrich and Dean Jerry Vallen worked in tandem on both local and out-of-state targets. Among them were Robert Mullane, Jr., president of Bally Manufacturing (Bally's casino), who had been a speaker at the 1987 graduation luncheon. Bud James, who had helped launch the program in 1967 and who was now the president of the Sheraton chain, was asked for $3.5 million. Sheraton's board of directors turned down the request.

One effort focused on Ramada, parent of the Tropicana Hotel. President Goodall worked on William Isbell, chairman of the board of Ramada, in Phoenix, soliciting a visit from him and sending information about the college. Although there was no direct response, the dean's approach to Jack Gallaway, president and general manager of the Tropicana Hotel did produce a gift. Perhaps it was the one-two punch.

Jack Gallaway, a very strong supporter of the college, was contributing personal time on campus. He was a frequent and enjoyable lecturer and cherished the value of education. Gallaway continued his campus affiliation years later at the University of Houston with Dean Alan Stutts, a former UNLV faculty member.

> Jack spend six months with us after he returned from South Africa where he worked with Jerry Inzerillo [UNLV '75]. We [Houston] were trying to develop a gaming focus. He still comes and does lectures.   STUTTS

When Gallaway left, John Chiero took over as president of the Tropicana and completed the $15,000 endowment to support a study room, named The Tropicana Reading Room. Trade periodicals and reference books were provided in a second-floor room so students could work and read during classroom breaks without hiking across to the library. The room was eventually transferred to the exclusive use of the graduate program as its needs ballooned through a huge growth.

Other Cash Gifts. As explained in Chapter 5, the university required a minimum of $10,000 to create a permanent endowment. Many thoughtful donors were unable to provide that level of support. They contributed what they could and the college used it to furnish the facility and improve the level of instruction in the building.

Several have their own stories. The dean was a member of the Las Vegas Chapter of the Hotel/Motel Accountants. One day he read that the State of Nevada was about to escheat as abandoned bank funds a sum of money under the chapter's name. Sharon Petty, the association's treasurer, retrieved the dollars, which were donated to the college.

A gift from the Las Vegas Hotel & Motel Association was a similar story. The dean had worked with Helen Naugle to found an association of small motel owners who would have a stronger voice in local and state issues than each had as a small business person. It was an uphill battle that eventually folded. Naugle saw to it that the treasury went to the college in support of the building. A plaque was hung to commemorate the gift (see Exhibit 7-3).

Mrs. Diana D. Broussard of Lafayette, Louisiana, whose two children attended UNLV, was a regular donor who upped her usual gift to help with the building (see Exhibit 7-3). She also gave funds in the name of her son, Michael Chesley, ('89).

The anonymous donor of the second Campbell gift made still another contribution to honor a second friend, Sam Cross, a Philadelphia purveyor. Small world story: The dean's father who was in the restaurant business in Philadelphia had done business with Sam Cross' meat company (see Exhibit 7-2).

Cash gifts came from alumni: Al Ginchereau ('71); John McLenahan ('81); Tom Jones ('84); and Skip Rapoport ('77). Their names were attached to the permanent

Donors to the Production Kitchen

L. J. Minor Corp.	Litton
Lincoln Food Service Products Inc.	Michael Chesley
Coffee Development Group	Foley Refrigeration Tradewinds
Westward Ho Employees	Cres-Cor Crown-X Cresent Metal Products, Inc.
Las Vegas Hotel & Motel Association	Diana D. Broussard

EXHIBIT 7-3. Donors to the Beam Hall production kitchen are identified by plaques on the west wall of the main kitchen.

seating that made up the alumni classrooms. Hugo Paulson, a local physician, made a variety of contributions over the years to the college's scholarship campaigns, to UNLVino and to the building. A most heartwarming gift came from Hal Halderson, a UNLV staff member who delivered mail to the college throughout the years.

An occasion arose when the college faculty were called in to help with an issue at the Westward Ho Hotel and Casino. This established an entree to the company from which two gifts resulted. One came from the employees of the Westward Ho, who had a care-and-share program similar to that of the Riviera employees. Their representatives were Elaine Stiglic and Ron Wielochowski, who was the personnel manager. The care-and-share program made a cash donation that was used to buy the tray stands for the dining room. The second gift came from owner Ralph Johnson who for several years paid the college's membership in the Travel and Tourism Research Association.

Other than years with single large gifts, 1982 was the college's best year: $923,950 was received in cash or kind.

Gifts in Kind
The Chin Gift. Tola and Marcia Chin, Chin's Restaurant, have been among the college's most sustained donors. It was no surprise therefore that they gave to the building. No sooner were the kitchens completed than Chin remedied what had been an oversight. There was no commercially sized wok.

> We needed something to introduce students to Chinese cuisine. Besides, we needed to acquaint the faculty with the equipment as well. There were no jet-burner, high-btu woks in town. That's what we went after.   TOLA CHIN, RESTAURANTEUR AND DONOR

At Chin's expense a consultant came from San Francisco. It was decided to remove an extra cooking station in the test kitchen area and replace it with the wok. Space was limited, so a special wok was designed and built. The cooking station was removed and utilities relocated to accommodate the new equipment. To top off the gift, Chin himself came to give wok lessons to faculty and students alike.

Periodic checks from this family continue to support the college. In addition, they hosted one of the programs most unusual events, the Chin Christmas party (see Chapter 8).

Coffee Development Group (CDG). Even before the building was completed, an acquaintanceship had developed with Mike Levin and Stuart Adelson of The Coffee Development Group. Improving coffee quality and coffee service and offsetting, thereby, the declining consumption of coffee was their unannounced aim.

> It was long before Starbucks. The Coffee Development reps did a good job because today every corner has a coffee shop. They worked themselves out of a job.   CLAUDE LAMBERTZ, HOTEL FACULTY MEMBER

An agreement was struck. The CDG would come and present coffee lectures including the history of coffee and the proper means of preparation and service. That fit hand in glove with the university's mini-term requirements. To assure the best results, the CDG rented all of the coffee gear including roaster, brewer, urn, grinder and espresso/cappuccino equipment to the college, but the $10 annual fee was waived.

A special blend of coffee, known as the UNLV blend, was formulated and made available to the public through Sweeney's Gourmet Coffee on Desert Inn and Eastern Avenues. The agreement stood until Sweeney's closed shop about ten years later and moved to the other side of Las Vegas.

> We worked with Sweeney's to create the blend. Suddenly, every boutique shop was carrying the UNLV blend at $8 per pound! It was unbelievable.   LAMBERTZ

Cres-Cor, Crescent Metal Products. George Baggott, president and owner of Cres-Cor, Crescent Metal Products, was always there to help. So, too, were his sons George and William. George senior made the first pledge of equipment before it was learned that monies saved from donations would be returned to the state. The first gift after the facility opened was a proof box. When a student unknowingly melted the plexiglass, it was replaced with dispatch. As equipment aged, replacements continued. All the china carts used to store the new china came from the Baggott family. So did a roast-and-hold oven and a rotary oven. It would be remiss to overlook the family's more recent support—beyond the date of this history—in making possible the kitchen in the Stan Fulton Building. That building was not state-funded , so contributions in kind were especially critical.

Qantel Computer Co. Executives of Qantel, an Australian-based computer company, befriended the program. The contact began when the company employed the dean's daughter, a computer major, for a summer job. Qantel's product was a medium sized 335 main frame that came out just before the introduction of the desktop PCs. Through Qantel's local distributors, Barry Wright of Wright Business Systems and John Southern of Mid West Computers, the company donated equipment estimated at a value of $100,000 to $200,000. President Leonard Goodall agreed that the university would buy a service contract after the six-months of donated service expired. Beside the CPU, Qantel's gift included a disk drive, two printers, four terminals and the software for several hotel functions. As part of the gift, it was agreed that prospective buyers of the system could visit the installation—great public relations—and that students and faculty would provide feedback on their experience.

Other Gifts. As was the case with cash contributors, all product donations did not rise to the $1,000,000 level. But it was this stream of practical and useful support that fleshed out the building. Among the contributions was an in-room safe from David Raymond of Elsafe of Nevada. The safe was used both for instruction and for the interim storage of funds collected at night from the dining room. Bob Martin, one of the college's own faculty members, donated a grand piano for the cocktail lounge. He played when occasions warranted.

Gifts in Kind that Helped to Open the Building

Donor	Gift
Aladdin Hotel	Roulette Chips
Del Foley, Foley Refrigeration	Tradewinds Frozen Cocktail-making Machine and Everpure Water Purification System
EATEC of Berkeley, Ca.	Software Program for Handling Food Inventory
Forbes Industries	Room Attendant Card
I. C. S. I.	Energy controls
Infolink Corporation	Electrowriters
InterMetro Industries Corp.	Mobile, Adjustable Shelf Linen Cart
Liberace Museum	Movie Screen
Lincoln Manufacturing, Fort Wayne	Variety of Kitchen Ware
NCR	Point-of-Sale Software System
Owen Fiberglass Corporation	Variety of Kitchen Ware
Paulson Dice & Card	Roulette Table
S & A Restaurant Suppliers	Variety of Kitchen Ware
Sam Rosenberg	Oak Desk
Richard Taggart	Slot Machine, $1 Manual, Progressive Alstate Model
Waring	Blender
Wear-ever	Impinger Oven/Convection Steamer Oven

EXHIBIT 7-4. Product donations enabled Beam Hall to open ready for instruction purposes.

Aerial view of the Southern Regional Division [of Reno] often called "Tumbleweed Tech," circa. 1959, after the initial building boom that saw Grant Hall, right, and Frazier Hall open along Maryland Parkway, foreground.

Aerial view of Nevada Southern University, renamed in 1966, the year that the hotel administration program was conceived and was housed in Grant Hall, lower right.

Before the campus buildings were opened, the "university" operated from the cloak room of Las Vegas High School. Seated on the left is Southern Regional Division Resident Director Jim Dickinson and Deputy Registrar Muriel Parks. Jewel Reynolds, deputy admissions officers is seated on the right and two student workers stand in the center.

Judy Lawry, was the college's first woman graduate (1971) and among the first interns in the joint university-hotel internship program that brought wide acclaim to the new program.

Food became part of the college curriculum, but never impacted on the sciences nor distracted from the "business" of hotelkeeping as members of the original search committee feared. From left, faculty members, Leslie Cummings, Dick Basile, Charlie Levinson and business faculty member, Ted Cummings, enjoy the aliments of the program.

Jewel Moyer, center, welcomes newly appointed director, Jerry Vallen, and his wife, Flossie, at a reception in their honor held in the home of President Don and Jewel Moyer in the Spring of 1967.

Visiting Professor Louis Szathmary, "Chef Louis," owner of Chicago's famous Bakery Restaurant and Hal Erickson, left, announce Szathmary's gift of books during the grand opening of the Dickinson Library.

The small production kitchen in Beam Hall was designed by faculty member Charlie Levinson under a unique arrangement that had Levinson acting as consultant to the building's architects, Nevada Architronics.

A formal signing ceremony in 1970 marked the Nevada Resort Association's renewal of its supporting grant. From left: Robbins Cahill, NRA executive officer; Walter Fitzpatrick, committee member from the Desert Inn; Al Benedict, NRA president; Jay Zorn, UNLV president; and Jerry Vallen, director of hotel administration.

Governor Richard Bryan, from left, meets with UNLV President Bob Maxon and donors Dick Brown (Banfi Wines), center, and Sam Costanza (McKesson Wines & Spirits of Las Vegas), during the 1984 dedication ceremonies of Beam Hall. Dean Jerry Vallen, right, hosted the reception.

Beam Hall's demonstration kitchen, The Banfi Room, was funded in part by Banfi Wines, represented by Dick Brown, father of alumnus, Gary Brown.

The Mead Dixon lectures were named after one of Harrah's board members who was instrumental in obtaining the Harrah grant for the college. Participating in the 1991 lecture were from left. Jon Ralston, newspaper reporter and radio host; Bobby Baldwin, Mirage Hotel's executive; Brian Greenspun, owner of the Las Vegas Sun; Phil Satre, CEO of Harrah's; Bob Maxson, UNLV president; and, right, an unidentified panelist.

Elaine Wynn, representing the UNLV Foundation, locks arms with Mary and Sam Boyd and their son, Bill Boyd, and President Bob Maxson after the 1985 announcement of the Boyd gift, The Boyd Dining Rooms, to the College of Hotel Administration.

Ground breaking for Beam Hall took place on July 16, 1981 with the help of Jerry Vallen, left, Regents Bucky Buchanan and Lilly Fong, and Dean of Business and Economics, George Hardbeck. Center individual is not identified.

Tom Beam, center facing, during the Masonic ceremonies (Zelzah Shrine Temple) that officially opened the college's building. Moya Lear, of Lear Jets, was the keynote speaker.

Beam Hall, center, shortly after its opening in 1984.

Ground breaking for Beam Hall brought together alumni from across the city: From left, Mike Unger, Caesars Palace; Gregg Hawkins, Caesars Palace; Dan Celeste, MGM Grand; Cynthia Vanucci, Hacienda; Patricia McFadden, MGM Grand; Neil Smythe, Jr., Sands; Cindy Kiser, Summa; Patrick Moreo, faculty member; and James Rafferty, Summa.

The College of Hotel Administration led a trip in 1977 to the People's Republic of China shortly after President Nixon's groundbreaking visit there. In Shanghai, they were hosted by the general manager, far right, of the Jinjiang Hotel.On the extreme left: Regent Lily Fong and Wing Fong; Flossie and Jerry Vallen, and faculty member, Claude Rand, who organized the trip. Vallen left his first textbook as a thank-you gesture.

Frank Birdsall, President of Treadway Inns, accepts the plaque from student president, Paul Weiner, and college dean, Jerome Vallen, after delivering his talk to the graduating class of 1974 .

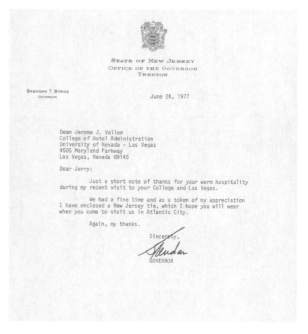

The start of gaming in Atlantic City's was previewed for Las Vegans by New Jersey's Governor Brendan Byrne at the Nevada Resort Association's 1977 Annual Luncheon for the Graduating Class

Industry executives supported the graduation lunch-eons taking their seats with students and faculty as Steve Wynn, center, has done.

No UNLVino was complete without a political representation. Jerry Vallen, left, faculty member Hank Melton, UNLV's event coordinator, and faculty member Don Bell, right, who coordinated food preparation along with faculty member Claude Lambertz, not pictured, meet with Congressman Chic Hecht.

The Boyd Dining Room set for one of its gourmet dinners, which, open to the public, were oversubscribed.

CHRIE, Council of Hotel, Restaurant and Institutional Educators, held several of its annual meetings in Las Vegas. Planning took place at the Sahara Hotel where CHRIE board member, Jerry Vallen, left, and CHRIE president, Harry Purchase, Paul Smith's College, met with Bill Dougal, Sahara Hotel President, and Leo Lewis, hotelier extraordinaire and part-time UNLV faculty member.

Nevada Senator Paul Laxalt, a hotelier in his own right, attended the Eight Annual Table Service Conference at Caesars Palace during the university's 1983 miniterm. The College of Hotel Administration partnered with the National Restaurant Association (Chicago) and was supported by Caesars' Vice President, Nat Hart, not pictured.

Jerome J. Vallen, founding dean of the College of Hotel of Administration, a great believer in the messy-desk theory, maintained an open-door policy in his new, Beam Hall office, circa 1982.

August, 1995 was the 25th anniversary of the Tokyo YMCA's summer UNLV seminar. Faculty members on the left are, back row, Curt Shirer and Dave Christianson and front row, Andy Nazarechuk and Jerry Vallen.

Dave Christianson, who was to be the college's second dean, and Alan Stutts, right, who became the dean at Houston, visit the hotel school at Anjou, France in 1991 to negotiate for the hotel college's summer abroad.

Part-time faculty members such as Phil Arce, Joe Delaney, Paul Goldman and Leo Lewis broadened the college's curriculum from its very beginnings. Another supporter was Bill Friedman, left, president of Summa's Castaways Hotel and author of the first text on casino management.

Although faculty growth never quite kept pace with student growth, this faculty meeting, circa 1988, represented the nation's best faculty and largest hotel program. Seated from left: Patty Shock; Dave Christianson; Laurie McGowan; Jerry Vallen; Skip Swerdlow; not identified, perhaps visiting faculty John Kubas of Saga Foods; Jim Kilby; and Suad Cox. Standing, from the left: Claude Rand; Gary Manago; John Goodwin; Alan Stutts; Wes Rohl; Floyd Benedict, adjunct faculty; Al Izzolo; Jerry Goll; Hank Melton; Jim Abbey; Frank Borsenik; Bob Martin; Vince Eade; Claude Lambertz; Don Bell; Charlie Levinson; Boyce Phillips, and Lyell Metcalf.

Adjunct faculty (budgeted as P-99 faculty) added untold strength to the college curriculum. Ralf Laerm, The Las Vegas Hilton, center, shows the class how to open a bottle of wine.

Hotel's staff members from left, Twyla Towns, Joan Reynolds, Sue Christianson, Joyce Jeary, Kathy Bradshaw and Annette Kanneberg surround international staffer, Pat Stahl, center, and her student intern during the 1986 staff luncheon in the Moyer Building.

Prominent national and international faculty and industry executives joined the teaching staff for periods of several weeks to one year. Rik Medlik, center, professor in charge at the University of Surrey, England, jokes with his UNLV counterpart, Jerry Vallen, left, and faculty member Charlie Levinson.

Hotel's international student body, representing several dozen nations, was large enough to warrant a special gathering. Enjoying the festivities were three of the college's major boosters, staff members Twylia Towns, left, and Joan Reynolds and honorary alumnus, Flossie Vallen.

Graduation is always a happy celebration. Congratulating the soon-to-be alumni are President Bob Maxson, Senator Dick Bryan and Dean Jerry Vallen.

The Muir Bothers, from left, Tim, Mike and Tom, were one of several families with multiple graduates. The Smythe family, father Neil was at Caesars Palace, was another. After graduation all the Muir Brothers worked for Day's Inns at one time.

Professional visitors to the campus added depth and fun to club activities and evening gatherings.

Alumni and spouses came from across the nation to celebrate Beam Hall's opening. Standing from left: Bill Hitzhusen (73); Tim Lafferty (75); Jerry Inzerillo (75); Dave Livney (82); Jerry Vallen; Charlie Collins (77); Andy Levy (81); Rusty Riley; and Dennis Haning (74). Seated are Jacqueline Inzerillo, Donna Lafferty; Jayne Siegal (79); Judi Riley (88), and Keri Haning.

Hong Kong alumni met at the Kowloon Club in 1989. From Las Vegas were Charles Levinson, front left, and Flossie and Jerry Vallen. Standing were Eddie Ho ('77), Dick Wong ('81), Vida Chow ('87), Kitty Chan ('85), David Chung ('78), Winnie Harto ('78), Alan Wong ('87), who organized the event, Henry Lai ('86), Eric Cha ('87), Danny Leung ('89) and Alywin Tai ('79).

Faculty members Bob Martin, left, Lyell Metcalf, Claude Rand and Frank Borsenik help launch the first annual (1988) faculty-student-industry golf tourney.

Festivities get underway and the band warms up for the retirement party of the colleges's first dean.

Cliff Jones, former lieutenant governor of Nevada, donated a painting, "The Siege of Bath," plus $10,000 and a variety of materials with which to open the casino classroom. Included were three unique abstracts, one of which was stolen by a maintenance worker and never recovered; nor was he prosecuted. Michele Fricke of the art department helped evaluate the loss. Clem Malone represented Cliff Jones in his working relationship with the college.

Other contributions are itemized in Exhibit 7-4.

MOVING IN

Ground breaking with golden shovels took place on July 16, 1981. Present among the university's dignitaries were distinguished alumni including Dan Celeste ('76), MGM Grand; Gregg Hawkins ('80), Caesars Palace; Cindi Kiser ('80), Summa; Pat McFadden ('80), MGM Grand; Patrick Moreo ('69), UNLV; Jim Rafferty ('78), Summa; Neil Symth, Jr. ('74), Sands; Mike Unger ('71), Caesars Palace; and Cynthia Vanucci ('79), Hacienda.

> I remember being at the ceremony in dark glasses. The mob persona was still part of marketing Las Vegas and even those who weren't mob-related would affect the same with pinky rings and sunglasses.   UNGER

The dedication ceremony took place in the autumn of 1983, a little better than two years after the groundbreaking. Claude Rand coordinated the dedication ceremony from the college's standpoint, but it was the Grand Lodge of Free and Accepted Masons, Zelzah Shrine Temple that stole the show. Their colorful march and formal dedication included a cornerstone ceremony with a time capsule in the east wall covered by a chronology plaque with the 1983 dedication date. Robert Maxson delivered the oration. The keynoter was Moya Olsen Lear, who had assumed control of LearAvia (Lear Jet) Corporation in Reno after the death of her husband. Somehow Mrs. Lear's appearance was designed to offset Reno's influence in the south of the state. It certainly had no application to the College of Hotel Administration and not much more to the College of Business and Economics.

Attendees enjoyed refreshment supplied by Villa Banfi and Southern Wine & Spirits in the rooms that carried their respective names. Music was by the Jazz Ensemble, directed by Frank Gagliardi, a good friend of the Vallens, and father of alumna Susan Gagliardi ('80).

Occupancy of the building, which predated the dedication ceremony, was almost anti-climatic. Rooms had been assigned in the spring of 1983 without controversy by Dick Basile.

> We thought the offices should be "x" square feet and Public Works thought all we needed was a cubicle. It got to the point that we always doubled whatever we needed. Still, it ended up being quite a successful building.
>
> Most of the offices were the same size so there was no need for a slide rule or tape to see who had two extra inches. Because I assigned the offices and decorated mine, it was

suggested that I had the best one. Carol Sapienza [spouse of faculty member Dunnovan Sapienza] thought I should have put in a fireplace. She still asks me, How's your fireplace?   DICK BASILE, HOTEL FACULTY MEMBER

Offices were too small for two to share, but large enough to be comfortable for one.   LESLIE CUMMINGS, HOTEL FACULTY MEMBER

The room-assignment list serves as a good reference for those who were on faculty at the time (see Exhibit 7-5).

On Staff When Beam Hall Opened

Faculty Members			
Name	**Room Assigned**	**Name**	**Room Assigned**
James Abbey	466	Richard Basile	446
Donald Bell	356	Frank Borsenik	344
Frank Brown	445	David Christianson	342A
John Goodwin	350	Al Izzolo	462
Richard Laughlin	352	Charles Levinson	452
Robert Martin	460	Lyell Metcalf	354
Patrick Moreo	464	Boyce Phillips	450
William Quain	357*	Claude Rand	363
John Stefanelli	358	Alan Stutts	359*
Jerome Vallen	442	Joseph Von Kornfeld	346
Adjunct Faculty			
Joe Delaney	365	Dale Douglas	456
Lendal Kotschevar	368	Rolf Laerm	366
Sal Munari	369		
Classified Staff			
Millie Alexander	454	Sue Christianson	342*
Joan Reynolds	449	Pat Stahl	361†
Twyla Towns	449		
Student Clubs			
Hotel Association (HA)	1st Floor		

*New hires, not previously housed on campus
†University Office of International Students

EXHIBIT 7-5. Occupants and room assignments for the new Beam Hall, July 17, 1983.

The building was occupied by the time I came. I was impressed that I had an office; that my name was already up on the board, as if I had been expected; and the office was stocked with the necessary stationery. It made a guy feel like he belonged.   JERRY GOLL, HOTEL FACULTY MEMBER

Finally in 1987, a $50,000 allocation was given to the college as part of a university wide equipment grant. Most of that budget was used for computer equipment, because the kitchen had become self-funding by then.

I recall that we were given funds to make sure that the building was wired for computers. Mike Stowers oversaw the work.   GEORGE HARDBECK, DEAN OF BUSINESS AND ECONOMICS

With money in hand and a new building that was the envy of hotel programs across the country, it was to be expected that the faculty and students would perform mightily. And they did. But the faculty and students had long before started to do their "own things," which are next described in the final unit of this history.

ENDNOTES FOR CHAPTER 7

1. Hank Tester, "A Night at the Arena." *Las Vegan Magazine*, February, 1984, p. 9.
2. Figures furnished by the Office of Institutional Research and Planning, September 9, 1977.
3. "Greetings From the Dean." *Program of the HSMA Election Dinner*, October 26, 1978.
4. Letter from Jim Rafferty to Jay Roberts, Alex Sugden, *et al*, dated February 22, 1979.
5. Gabe Vogliotti, Unpublished manuscript p. 5-10; from the personal collection of Bill Thompson.
6. Rollan Melton, "Mead Dixon Writes of Harrah Empire." Editorial in *Reno Gazette-Journal*, November 16, *1992*.

PART 4

Doing Our Thing

CHAPTER 8

The College and Its Publics

An era of exceptionally good feelings followed the program's launch and sustained it for years thereafter.

> People were extremely high on the hotel school. I never heard anyone criticize it. All of us had to live with the Sin City image, which was ludicrous, and so people were proud of UNLV.
>
> The majority of the people who worked in the industry, whether [or not] they were part of the NRA [Nevada Resort Association], felt very good about the school being there.   SIG FRONT, VICE PRESIDENT, SAHARA HOTEL

> The community was really behind it! I mean from the very beginning.   LEO LEWIS, BINION'S FINANCIAL OFFICER AND PART-TIME FACULTY MEMBER

Endorsed by the community, the college was able to cultivate a broad, global reach—Las Vegas alone was too small a market—and do so without losing local support.

> It was easy to preach the gospel about UNLV's College of Hotel Administration. It was easy because people would listen because they knew and respected it.   LARRY RUVO, SENIOR MANAGING DIRECTOR, SOUTHERN WINE & SPIRITS

Boosters were not limited to the professional community: The university was equally proud of the college's achievements.

President [Bob] Maxson had a great respect for the college. Presidents of Michigan State [where Borsenik once taught] felt the same way [about hotel studies on their campus], but it was especially true of Maxson.   FRANK BORSENIK, HOTEL FACULTY MEMBER

Regent Joan Kenney had this to say in a 1989 letter:

"Even though I am no longer a Regent, be assured that my love and admiration for the School of Hotel Administration is never going away."[1]

PUBLIC RELATIONS

The program pursued an international audience, but not at the expense of the local community. News releases were churned out on a weekly basis because the university had no public-relations office. The founding grant of the Nevada Resort Association had created an awareness that helped to sustain community interest. It was a strong tie-in. New story ideas were mailed to the community's earliest columnists: Joe Delaney, Forrest Duke, Alan Jarlson, Mary Manning, Paul Price and Hank Tester.

Mary Manning was a good friend who always had something positive to say about the university.   DON MOYER, PRESIDENT, NEVADA SOUTHERN UNIVERSITY

These entertainment and gossip columnists were not always responsive to stories about the hotel program, so many of the news releases were not used. At least, the local press knew the program existed.

Industry professionals were kept apprized through a clippings strategy. Articles from local newspapers and national trade magazines were mailed to local and national hoteliers along with appropriate notes. Busy executives often missed important printed stories, even about themselves, and were especially appreciative to receive them. Many wrote back to say so. Recruiting trips to the East and campus visits by speakers and employers contributed to the energy that was building on Maryland Parkway.

Publicity

Within a month of the college's 1967 beginnings, George Spink of *Institutions Magazine,* a trade publication, asked the hotel director for help in arranging interviews with hotel and casino executives. The initial response from the professional community was cool. National attention focused on Las Vegas, making everyone gun-shy about publicity. To gain the Nevada Resort Association's (NRA) cooperation the college vouched in writing for the magazine. Gabe Vogliotti's musings help explain the city's apprehension and the NRA's reluctance toward publicity:

"My own years with the owners were one long turbulence, the most seismic time in this country's war with gamblers. . . . Policy [against Nevada] hardened in Washington. . . . The press blasts [against the state] came to include every major newspaper and magazine. . . . They were joined by every network. The attack became leisure reading in *Gamblers Money* and *The Green Felt Jungle.*"[2]

Even I [NRA's publicist] rarely gave public announcements. Believe it or not, they [casino owners] were shy of doing things.   JOE DIGLES, NEVADA RESORT ASSOCIATION

There was a give-and-take with the Nevada Resort Association. Obviously, it was not the typical, professional hotel association. So, when it faced a rise in room taxes, it asked the hotel college to do some research. It was 1969. Lawson Odde, executive vice president of the American Hotel & Motel Association, was contacted by the college for help in fending off a flat 15-cent room tax, which was to be added to the then 3% sales tax. The tax passed.

Institutions was the first national magazine to report a story on the college. Soon came a second: a brief mention in *U. S. News and World Report*.[3] A television program about work shifts ran on a Los Angeles' TV station in November of 1979. It included interviews and information about Las Vegas' round-the-clock service based on data furnished by the college.

Joe Digles was available in the early years to provide valuable public relations guidance to the fledgling program. One suspects he might have had a hand in a very positive editorial that ran in the *Review-Journal* (see Exhibit 8-1). For certain he helped with brochures and took an active hand when requested. One such news release was prepared for the International Association of Travel Writers meeting in Las Vegas. Only 20 students were enrolled at the time, so the college per se was hardly the story. Las Vegas was and still is an appealing dateline. Several reporters and travel writers, but especially the *Los Angeles Times'* education writer, William Trombley, mentioned the college in several columns beginning with a December 1, 1967 editorial.

Efforts like these carried the program's name afar. Two national broadcasts, which originated with the basketball team, resulted in immense publicity. Despite its controversies, basketball played a positive role in the university's public image.

I remember trying to convince people that there was a university in Las Vegas. That changed dramatically when we went to the final four in Atlanta. And when they asked me what we excelled in, I always used the hotel college as a feature of the university.   DON BAEPLER, UNLV PRESIDENT AND UNS CHANCELLOR

CBS Sports covered the university during the *Running Rebels'* march toward the final four in 1987 when UNLV played Carolina in Las Vegas.

Minor foods [manufacturer of flavor basis] had come in a few days earlier to help me prepare some demonstration platters. When we learned that the culinary program, which we didn't officially have, would be featured, I used the platters for TV. Within days, we were getting calls about our culinary program.   CLAUDE LAMBERTZ, HOTEL FACULTY MEMBER

Two minutes of prime-time coverage featured the College of Hotel Administration at half-time. The response was breathtaking. Calls about the program and letters of application poured in from across the globe. The program became a believer in basketball, which Boyce Phillips had championed for years. One long-lost friend started his letter: "Imagine my surprise when my TV filled with your [Vallen's] image!"

R-J viewpoint

HOTEL-UNIVERSITY BOND STRENGTHENS

Life in Las Vegas is seldom dull. Something always seems to be going on—much of it with great fanfare. Even a supermarket opening has a way of happening on a grand scale.

That's why an event last week struck us as particularly low-keyed relative to what it marked. In a sense this was appropriate, but nevertheless it deserves a footnote.

Students in the second graduating class of the College of Hotel Administration at UNLV were honored at a luncheon hosted by Nevada Resort Association. It was a tasteful yet simple affair bringing together students, faculty and hotelmen.

But there was an underlying and important significance: the strengthening of the bond between the hotelmen and our local university, the broadening of a genuine community of interest. It began in 1965 when the Resort Association joined with the Nevada Southern University to create the Hotel College. The hotels committed themselves to fund the school in its formative years. The pledge was recently renewed, modified to meet new needs.

What's developed is a hotel administration program truly unique in America. No college can match its internship instruction program where the resort hotels literally become classrooms for the most advanced training of its kind anywhere.

The accomplishments and future prospects are a tribute to Dean Jerome J. Vallen and his faculty. Their efforts have been complemented by the cooperation of the hotels and their professional staffs.

Surely there's a message here. The university has reached out to the community and a segment of private industry has answered the call. Perhaps its what is termed "involvement" these days. At any rate, the result is of direct benefit to our young and to the future.

A university, like many of our institutions, must meet halfway with those it serves. If the end product is similar to what the Hotel College is achieving, then this community needs more of the same.

EXHIBIT 8-1. Editorial, most likely written by the Nevada Resort Association's Joe Digles, former Editor-in-Chief of the *Las Vegas Review-Journal*, applauding the annual luncheon of the College of Hotel Administration. *Review-Journal* editorial, Wednesday, May 20, 1970.

I remember well the half-time show that featured the college. It gave us a publicity boost for maybe five years. Students said that it was that broadcast that made them aware UNLV had a hotel program.   AL IZZOLO, HOTEL FACULTY MEMBER

A week later, NBC's *Saturday Night Live* spoofed the college based on the gaming and food facilities that had been featured on CBS. It wasn't complimentary, but it echoed the publicist's oldest theme—just spell our name right.

Other national coverage promoted the college more positively. *Rolling Stone* magazine published just such a story as the date of this history closes.[4] Numerous PR pieces about individual graduates taking jobs in their communities have appeared worldwide in local newspapers and in foreign lands in local languages.

The Rolling Stones issue was reprinted in Taiwan, in Chinese; one of our alumni sent it to me.
LAMBERTZ

The college's name appeared all around the globe because faculty members traveling for the
U.S. Department of Commerce were featured in local newspapers.   JERRY VALLEN

In September, 1988, CBS's *60 Minutes* featured the first country-club manager in
the People's Republic of China. It was Aylwin Y. C. Tai, a 1979 graduate who ran the
Chung Shan Hot Springs Golf Club.

Not as widely disseminated, but more important to the academic side, were the
rankings prepared initially by the University of New Orleans' Ed Nebel.

Yes, it was Ed Nebel.   FRANK BORSENIK, HOTEL FACULTY MEMBER

No, it was Tom Calnan. He was on the IFSEA board when I was. I think he was the one that
began the questionnaire.   IZZOLO

The New Orleans' survey, and one done subsequently by Donald Hansen, executive
vice president of the Texas Hotel & Motel Association (TH&MA), asked hotel program
heads to rank the nation's four-year hotel programs. Year after year UNLV ranked
second in the nation behind Cornell, despite the 30-year disparity in age.

"There are about 150 colleges in the country offering four year programs in hotel
management; by common consent, UNLV's reputation is overshadowed only by
its Ivy League archrival: Cornell's School of Hotel Administration."[5]

"I am extremely proud to note that UNLV's program is rated number two in the
nation. Personally, I think we are number one. It has often been said that reputations come too slowly and stay too long. I suspect that applies [here]. . . ."[6]

Always the spread in votes could be counted on one hand. Such was the case in
the ballot reported November 6, 1986 by the TH&MA. Just two votes separated the
programs. Michigan State and Massachusetts Amherst were ranked third and fourth
among the 26 schools considered that year. By 1988, 76 schools were participating
with UNLV holding tenaciously to that second spot! When Harrah's made its large
contribution to the college, Harrah's President and CEO, Phil Satre, cited it as "one of
the premier programs in the world."

I continue to tout UNLV's hotel school. We realize that Cornell [Brown's alma mater] is number
one, but many people, including Prof. Beck [Cornell's second dean] call UNLV number two.
RICHARD BROWN, DONOR INTERMEDIARY AND FATHER OF ALUMNUS, GARY

After Paul Gaurnier [Cornell's assistant dean] participated in our self-study he made a statement that appeared in the press: UNLV is the Cornell of the West.   BORSENIK

One candidate for dean [following Vallen's resignation] had the audacity at a faculty gathering to say, You people argue about whether you're number one or number two. Well, you're not that good and I'll come and make you better.   JERRY GOLL, HOTEL FACULTY MEMBER

We always had the number one/number two contention with Cornell. After the Mirage opened, it proved us number one! The Mirage started its management training program with half and half, Cornell and UNLV students. One and one-half years later, there were no Cornellians left, but we were still there.   LAMBERTZ

When I was G.M. in St. Louis, I had a MSU [Michigan State University] sales manager who constantly bragged about his school. When a disagreement arose at a staff meeting, this person announced that he would bring the finest book on front office. He brought the book to my office and much to his surprise, the author was the dean of UNLV's hotel school. We never heard of MSU again.   ROSS MCCLENACHAN, '75 STUDENT

Local Activities

A strong entrepreneurial spirit drove the activities of the faculty and student body. On several occasions, the local community approached the college. For example, the MGM Hotel (now Bally's) asked the college to appear at town meetings in Massachusetts, where the company lobbied for legalizing gaming. The college also testified at a Las Vegas hearing before a congressional subcommittee of the Commission on the Review of the National Policy Toward Gambling.

Students generated a good deal of positive press. For example, the *Las Vegas Sun* newspaper featured the student Hotel Association across every column of the first page of its *Sunrise Edition* of Saturday, February 25, 1978. Pictures of the student officers and the story of their annual seminar were featured. Jim Rafferty, who later lobbied the State Legislature for the college's first building (see Chapter 7), was the organization's president that year.

The local press always gave the college fair coverage. Whether it was the college's first China trip, the dedication of Beam Hall, student activities, or *UNLVino*, accurate and usually positive coverage was reported.

Campus Audiences.   The UNLV campus was another local audience that dare not be overlooked.

People [across campus] were really good: Both teaching faculty members and administrators, including Tom White [business dean while hotel was a department in business].   PAT MOREO, '69 STUDENT AND HOTEL FACULTY MEMBER

Friendships developed by hotel faculty members during key committee assignments often influenced the views held by other disciplines about an academic unit that was foreign to most of them.

I was on the executive committee of the faculty senate while representing the college. I made some good associations there. Because of the nature of my personality [tough, retired naval officer] the senate gave me some dirty jobs including getting rid of the chair of one campus committee.

I was also on the university's anti-smoking committee. Their rationale was a smoker was needed if the committee was to be objective.

We [hotel] had so few faculty that I served on the promotion and tenure committee even before I gained tenure.   GOLL

Serving on the committee to find President Goodall was very worthwhile. Goodall was good, but one had to be careful. Overenthusiastic comments put a damper on any candidate.   JIM ABBEY, HOTEL FACULTY MEMBER

I was on the budget committee for several years. I read all the material faithfully. Then each dean would come and defend the budget that each college requested. It was pointless. No one listened to the committee and there was no feedback.

Promotion and tenure committee was a mind-expanding assignment. It examined faculty promotion and tenure to assure 'comparable rigor.' Is the work of the poet the same quality as the aeronautics faculty member? It was a wonderful experience in terms of intellectual growth.   LESLIE CUMMINGS, HOTEL FACULTY MEMBER

On the one hand, the hotel program did battle with some of the other disciplines, especially business in the early years.

Business faculty claimed we were really a college of business. That we were putting hospitality in front of all the business courses [e.g. hospitality accounting]; that we didn't get paid as much; that our students were flunkies; etc., etc.   CUMMINGS

Soon after my arrival, I lobbied to drop a course in business that was comparable to our #407 [human resources] because theirs was too generalized and ours was more specific.   GOLL

Business's marketing department vetoed our request for a hotel marketing course. So the [hotel] college curriculum committee dropped business marketing from hotel's requirements. Business' marketing department lost hundreds of FTE credits when hotel students stopped taking the course. We won our request the following year.   JERRY VALLEN

I had come from industry specializing in human resources. We had to struggle to get approval for our course from the business faculty. We gave it a different name: Employee Evaluation and Appraisal. I met with Paul Loveday [business faculty member] and then we started offering the course. That opened the door for other courses that business faculty thought were theirs alone.   AL IZZOLO, HOTEL FACULTY MEMBER

Dick Strahlem used to say, There's not a bit of difference, accounting is accounting. And I felt the same way.   GEORGE HARDBECK, DEAN OF BUSINESS AND ECONOMICS

Every academic unit had a different perception of the hotel program.

> Hotel, which had a magnificent external reputation, was viewed as just another professional school—and one with a lot of money, at that—by the university research committee. They had a mind set that hotel didn't need research money. Funds should go to the arts or the sciences. It took new appointments to the chair, Cheryl Bowles [nursing], before the philosophy of that committee turned around. Studying bugs was proper but so was studying a process.   ALAN STUTTS, HOTEL FACULTY MEMBER

On the other hand, the program found and cultivated friends in many fields of study. Ralph Roske from the social sciences was one such pragmatist. Travel and tourism was just emerging as a subdiscipline, more perhaps in the social sciences than in the professional schools. A cooperative undertaking was launched to raise funds for a joint offering between the two disciplines. Roske was more experienced and better able to write grant requests, which he did with fervor during 1969–1970. He pitched many tourism-related foundations: the General American Transportation Foundation; the United Airlines Foundation; the Union Pacific Railroad Foundation; the Hancock Foundation; and the Hilton Foundation among others, as well as the Fund for Higher Education. Disappointment ran high in both colleges.

In his role as museum director, Don Baepler spent time helping hotel's research center develop grant procedures, and was happy when the first grant was landed.

Nursing and hotel weighed in for the 1988–1989 budget with a joint degree in health care management. The Priority and Program Review Committee rejected the request for a faculty member so the plan never materialized. A similar dialogue took place with Ken Hanlon, who was chair of the music department. A music/theater management program was discussed, but it too failed to materialize.

Hotel's faculty was small and it was shifted around to fill small spaces as one building after another opened. Moving from Grant Hall, which housed education and the arts; to Wright Hall, home of the social sciences; to Flora Dungan, the humanities; to Beam Hall, with business, enabled the hotel faculty to interact and establish good relationships with many senior faculty, the very persons who sat on the committees that often determined the college's fate.

> Physically we weren't far apart from business, but each unit of the university seemed to operate in its own bailiwick. Ed Goodin from business took classes with us [he actually earned a hotel degree] so we knew him on a one-to-one basis.   DICK BASILE, HOTEL FACULTY MEMBER

> Ed Goodin was the business faculty member whom I knew best. He was a hotel major who took three of my classes. He was a good speaker and I asked him to make presentations to the student, national IFSEA session. He was a riot and the students enjoyed him.   IZZOLO

Catered dinners open to both the local and campus communities were initiated by faculty member George Bussel as early as 1968. Linking that food service to the music department was Pat Moreo's idea. He reached across campus on March 17, 1978 to create the first Renaissance Festival. German Renaissance music and dance were presented by appropriately costumed performers from the music department accompanied by food of the period prepared and served by costumed students from the hotel college. Students from each college researched the appropriate products for the era. Schinken und Kase Brotchen, Rouladen, Westfalisches Blindhund, Spaetzle, and Hasel Nussecreme were featured on the first menu.

> I really wanted to do a quantity food course because we didn't do much in quantity. We had no budget so we decided to use the income to pay the bills. Later, Regent Fong asked, Pat—she knew my name—how are you handling the money? She knew the checks were made payable to me. She forestalled future problems for us because we ran the account through the business office thereafter.   MOREO

Moreo's concept cemented relations with the campus caterer, the music department and the community even as it taught students that preparation facilities are not always ideal.

> Saga [campus caterer] was amazingly cooperative allowing us to use the dorm facility after the evening meal, 7:30 at night. The marketing team sold all the tickets for the Moyer ballroom but the food was prepared in the dorm a different building. Figure the logistics: This was a six-course meal interspersed with entertainment. We were still eating at 11:00 pm that night. I think you guys [the Vallens] were helpful in making everyone laugh at the situation.   MOREO

> What do you mean? It was all Jerry's fault! He convinced you to announce guests as they entered. That cost you more than one hour to start!   FLOSSIE VALLEN

> I was amazed at the resiliency of the community. We were sold out every year and we had to hold back tickets for those who had suffered the first year.   MOREO

Campus interface wasn't limited to other academic areas. The college depended heavily on the admissions office, Dallas Norton, and the registrar's office, Muriel Parks and Jeff Halverson.

> We always got along well with the registrar's office, first Muriel Parks and then Jeff Halverson. If we had problems, they invited us over to search the files.
>   I worked mainly with secretaries in other offices. Jane Hammond in the vice president's office and Joanne Jacobs in the president's office were always helpful and always friendly.   JOAN REYNOLDS BEITZ, ADMINISTRATIVE ASSISTANT

The college looked for help to the many supporting units that make up a functioning campus, from the graduate office, Ron Smith, to buildings and grounds, to the office of international students.

> Carla Henson, director of grants and contracts, was the best! Getting a car out of the United States to the Dominican Republic was one tough issue facing us with USAID contract. We were told that one simply could not ship a car out of the U.S.A. But Carla was someone who would dig until she found a legal way to meet the contract provisions. I remember her well!   ALAN STUTTS, HOTEL FACULTY MEMBER

> I had Mike Stowers [in charge of audio-visual and technical/computer support] over to dinner to thank him for all the good things he did for me. That included arranging the set-up for my distant education course.   LESLIE CUMMINGS, HOTEL FACULTY MEMBER

Conservation was one of the least known contributions that hotel made to the university. After the oil crises of 1975, campus power costs rose 25–33% annually. Frank Borsenik was one of two faculty members (John Tryon was the other) assigned to reduce power costs and save a serious budget imbalance. Herman Westfall, vice president for business, served as committee chair and Charles Moody, director of physical plant, rounded out the committee. Simple moves proved very worthwhile. Summer thermostats were hiked; winters settings reduced. Light bulbs were changed or eliminated altogether. Buildings were closed on weekends and one month during the summer.

> Frank Brown [hotel faculty member] worked weekends on his dissertation in the non-air conditioned building. So he would lock the door and strip down to his underclothes. He forgot at times and opened the door when I knocked. His left desk drawer was filled with candy bars, so there was a trail from his desk to the door.   AL IZZOLO, HOTEL FACULTY MEMBER

Hot water temperatures were reduced. Many of UNLV's successful procedures were copied by other state agencies. Beam Hall's lobby swamp cooler likely would not have come about except for the energy emergency that was facing the nation.

> With Nevada Power, we ran energy seminars in Reno and Las Vegas for the Department of Energy. We needed a keynote speaker who would attract industry people. While I was in his office the dean called Governor Mike O'Callaghan. Just like that. The governor answered the telephone and we finalized arrangements. That was amazing! [Borsenik had come from a large state, Michigan.]   FRANK BORSENIK, HOTEL FACULTY MEMBER

Graduation Luncheons. The graduation luncheons started out almost by accident and grew to be one of the most startling public relations messages that the college delivered.

> They were very fine public relations affairs. I felt that it was a way to demonstrate to the industry what was being done. But I also distinctly remember that the industry had a sense of pride in the program.   DON BAEPLER, UNLV PRESIDENT AND UNS CHANCELLOR

In February of 1969, a letter was addressed to Gabe Vogliotti asking whether the Resort Association would underwrite a luncheon for "about a dozen men." (The language was telling: as there were only two women among the first 115 graduates.) Two months later the budget estimated that 80 persons might come from among the 100 invitations. About 30 persons, including the faculty; the speaker, Arthur Packard; and Bob Cannon, who convinced Packard to come, actually sat down to lunch at the Desert Inn Country Club. Packard was an important member of the American Hotel & Motel Association. It was a fortuitous association for the fledgling school. That luncheon was the beginning of a decades-long tradition that brought immeasurable attention to the college locally and from afar.

> Vogliotti [Nevada Resort Association executive] liked to have parties, but Cahill [Vogliotti's successor] understood it was a form of recognition. I believe it was at one of the early luncheons when Ike [Houssels, NRA president] said, Finally that's it. Meaning we had a long way to go, but the school had passed the first hurdle.   JOE DIGLES, NEVADA RESORT ASSOCIATION

Sig Front was the speaker in May of the second year when the setting was the Dunes Country Club. Several local supporters (Robbins Cahill, George Rhodine, Lewis Kurtz, and Paul Eddington) were honored that year. In 1972, Frank Watts was recognized a second time for his instrumental role in founding the college. Gordon Sutherland ('72) was the presiding student officer.

> I told them it wasn't right for me to receive a second award. It was double jeopardy!
> WATTS

The first outstanding student award, which went to Mark Moreno, was initiated the very first year. Money to accompany the award would wait for 10 years until the Weinberger endowment was created.

> The lifetime award that I received at a graduation luncheon was a highlight for me!   TOLA CHIN, RESTAURANTEUR AND DONOR

> One luncheon was on the top floor of Bally's. I was invited to attend, but I couldn't make it. Right after that Elaine Wynn, who was helpful in the school's development, called and said she had to see me for lunch. It was strange but she too was meeting on Bally's roof. It was a set-up. The school honored me with a special recognition that day.   LARRY RUVO, SENIOR MANAGING DIRECTOR, SOUTHERN WINE & SPIRITS

Graduation luncheons made good press and Joe Digles helped the college take advantage of it. A powerful commentary on the 1970 luncheon ran on KLAV-radio. It was delivered by Alan Jarlson but was penned largely by Digles. The 225 students that were then enrolled stood in marked contrast to the 20 students mentioned in the Travel Writer's release just a few years earlier.

Barron Hilton was first invited to speak in 1974 but was unable to schedule in until the second invitation in 1988. Perhaps he waited to see who else accepted. And the list was impressive: friends, governors, presidents of the industry's best known hotel companies (see Exhibit 8-2). Frank Sain, who came to head up the Las Vegas Convention and Visitor's Bureau gave his first public presentation as the luncheon speaker. Getting Governor Brendan Byrne of New Jersey shortly after that state had agreed to legalize gaming in Atlantic City was a coup. (Resorts International was the first Atlantic City casino, opening on the boardwalk in 1978.) Huge numbers turned out for that luncheon because Nevada was looking carefully at what was likely to happen in Atlantic City. Nevada's Governor Mike O'Callaghan started the day (March 11, 1977) by introducing his counterpart.

> Atlantic City was built with people from Las Vegas and many of those people were students from UNLV.   JOE DELANEY, COLUMNIST AND PART-TIME FACULTY MEMBER

The college funded air fare for the governor and his state-trooper companion, and the MGM [Bally's today] hosted their accommodations. Byrne was greeted from all over the casino by New Jersey residents as he passed in and out of the hotel.

> We housed Governor Byrne at the MGM. Hotel executives including MGM's top brass gathered to welcome him. He must have been asked a thousand times what could be done to make him comfortable. The answer: Nothing. No sooner had those with the power-of-the-pen left, then he asked to see the theater show. I couldn't find anyone to arrange comps for his party! Finally, I found one of our students at the front desk. He had no authority to comp and said so! Tell them [the showroom] that Mr. Al Benedict [MGM's president] said it was ok and I shall clear it with him in the morning. He agreed reluctantly. Neither of us heard about it again and he certainly didn't lose his job. I always wondered, had Byrne, himself, paid?   JERRY VALLEN

Larger graduating classes and a larger professional community pushed attendance into the hundreds. The college invited graduating seniors, friends, intern coordinators, labor reps, hotel executives and selected names from the *Very Important Persons* publication that the Las Vegas Chamber of Commerce first sold for $0.50.

> I always, always attended the luncheons!   WATTS

> The graduation luncheons were most delightful affairs.   JERRY GOLL, HOTEL FACULTY MEMBER

> The luncheons were a good way for the industry to see the students. Tables were always mixed: faculty, students and industry people.   ALAN STUTTS, HOTEL FACULTY MEMBER

The NRA's supporting grants didn't keep pace. In 1981 it was $1,700; $2,500 in 1983; $2,250 in 1985; $2,000 in 1987; $2,800 in 1989. During this period the executive office of the NRA rotated from Bill Campbell to Vincent Helm to John Schreiber. Both Vogliotti and Cahill were long gone. The rising costs were offset by the hotels that hosted the affairs. Fortunately, the college was in good standing with the catering managers and

Year	Hotel	Speaker	Comment
1969	Desert Inn Country Club	Arthur Packard	AH&MA
1970	Dunes	Sig Front	V.P. Sales, Sahara
1971	Sahara	Barney Rawlings	LVCVA
1972	Flamingo	Burt Cohen	President & GM, Flamingo
1973	Caesars Palace	Mike O'Callahan	Governor of Nevada
1974	Frontier	Frank Birdsall	President Treadway Inns
1975	Sahara	Tom Powers	Faculty Member Penn State
1976	Tropicana	Bucky Buchanan	Member Board of Regents
1977	Las Vegas Hilton	Brendan Byrne	Governor of New Jersey
1978	Desert Inn Country Club	William Weinberger	President Caesars Palace
1979	No record	No record	
1980	No luncheon	No speaker	Labor Strife
1981	Frontier	Frank Sain	Executive Director, LVCVA
1982	Sands	Ed Pratt	Pratt Hotels, Sands Owner
1983	Union Plaza	Richard Bryan	Governor of Nevada
1984	Flamingo	Dan Reichartz	President Caesars Palace
1985	Holiday Inn & Casino	Richard Goeglein	President/COO Holiday Inns
1986	Golden Nugget	Steve Wynn	Chairman Mirage Hotels
1987	Bally's	Robert Mullane	Chairman Bally's
1988	Las Vegas Hilton	Barron Hilton	Chairman Hilton Corp
1989	Holiday Inn & Casino	Mike Rose	Chairman, President & CEO Holiday Corporation
1990	California Hotel	Bill Boyd	Chairman, Boyd Group
1991	Mirage Hotel	Elaine Wynn	Chair of UNLV's Foundation
1992	Gold Coast	Jerry Vallen	Retired; 25th Anniversary
1993	Excalibur	Bill Paulos ('69)	V.P. Circus Circus; Alumnus
1994	Harrah's	Steve Greathouse	President Harrah's Casino Division

EXHIBIT 8-2. A record of the graduating luncheons schedule by the College of Hotel Administration and supported by the Nevada Resort Association and its individual member hotels.

the food and beverage executives who absorbed an ever-increasing portion of the total cost. Towards the end, the hosting properties were chosen according to the speaker's affiliation. Hard for an F&B manager to refuse to contribute to his own boss' speech. Among the most memorable luncheons was one arranged through Paul Houdayer, Las Vegas Hilton, for Barron Hilton's presentation.

At the head table sat the speaker, the university president, the college dean, the current president of the NRA and sometimes its executive officer. Both the current and incoming presidents of the student club were there because one was the master of ceremonies and the other would be so the following year. Rather than a long head table, the platform party of six to eight persons was seated across from one another. Head-table conversation flowed more easily from this greater sense of intimacy.

The First Sales Class. The curriculum originated with Dick Strahlem and his Phil Arce/Leo Lewis committee. It was well balanced and included what was probably the nation's first course in hotel marketing. But who was to teach it? That question was posed several times to the local chapter of the Hotel Sales Management Association (HSMA) in the 60 days between the director's arrival (July 1, 1967) and the start of the 1967–68 school year. HSMA President Bob Schmuck announced that the Hilton's Ted Nelson, who held a master's degree in engineering, was volunteered by the local chapter. Nelson and Vallen prepared a course outline. Members of the local chapter were invited to teach their specialities, around which the course had been built.

> Ted Nelson asked me to do some lectures. That was the first time that I was on the campus.
> Ted did a great job tying together HSMA and the college.   SIG FRONT, VICE PRESIDENT, SAHARA HOTEL

Both instructors attended each session, and the expertise of the faculty produced an exceptional course. It also bonded the program to the city's sales professionals.

> There was a closeness in both Las Vegas and HSMA. We always made sure that the city never lost business. That camaraderie was very useful when we started the chapter. Not merely working to get business but in supporting the college. HSMA was committed to UNLV students. Doug Farley [Sahara Hotel Sales] especially so; he loved the students.   FRONT

What had started as an academic venture proved to be a serendipitous public relations tactic as well.

> The HSMA people were so good to us! People like Sig Front and Doug Farley from the Sahara. During my second semester [Spring '74], I took students to the HSMA convention in Denver. The Las Vegas members took all of us to dinner. It was a real special experience. The whole industry was so supportive!   JIM ABBEY, HOTEL FACULTY MEMBER

Nelson missed but a few nights despite a heavy travel schedule and no reimbursement. His firm, personal commitment was a reflection of the professional community's attitude. After two years of listening, taking notes and creating examinations, Vallen took over the class. He adopted the "speakers bureau," which was not limited now to hoteliers. Representatives from airlines, convention service companies, auto-rental agencies, advertising agencies, tour companies and more broadened the students' understanding of the breadth of hotel marketing. Las Vegas is everyone's destination so the original "faculty" would direct interesting, out-of-state visitors to participate in the class. Many of them were invited back—and came from distant cities just to participate (see Exhibit 8-3).

> Having students fall asleep in class is difficult to foresee or forestall. One of our most distinguished local guests refused to come again after he experienced that affront.   JERRY VALLEN

From this supportive relationship came jobs and friendships. Sig Front had students to small, informal Sunday-afternoon sessions at his home on Roseberry Lane. Toni Front hosted them and visiting executives rapped with them.

> I wanted students in their final years to meet and talk with top people so they would have an idea of their chances in the industry. I think our first guest was the president of Sheraton Hotels.   FRONT

October meetings were election time for HSMA and they were always held on campus where Pat Moreo's (pre-Beam Hall) and Claude Lambertz's (post-Beam Hall) classes prepared the meals. Faculty member Claude Rand helped Sergeant-at-Arms Joe Lomanto count ballots. A welcoming program/menu was always prepared:

> "Your presence here assures a continuing close bond between the professional and the student. It is because of this association, stretching over a dozen years, that more and more of our alumni are here voting tonight as members."[7]

As a result of the association's support, sales blitzes (see Chapter 11) were developed locally and elsewhere, and faculty member Jim Abbey became a regular on the national HSMA's speakers circuit.

> I did a lot of seminars for HSMA, working with Dave Dorf and Buck Hoyle [HSMA Executives]. It was great publicity for the college but it took immense prep time because it was a professional audience with different expectations than the students. I prepared like crazy. ABBEY

Two Airline Seminars. HSMA was a close group. Its 1967 membership list included only 29 regular members and 38 allied members. Their mostly social meetings sometimes started with an educational session. But in late 1969, Sig Front conceived and implemented a most unusual educational program: *The Airline Seminar: Travel's Giant Leap into the '70s.* This national seminar was scheduled during the city's slow period, December 8 and 9.

Speaker	Association	Speaker	Association
Al Adams	Delta Airlines	Ed Allen	Allen Photography
Denny Ball	Dazey Travel Service	Gary Ballinger	Grey Line Tours
Clem Bernier	Hacienda Hotel	Tom Brown	Landmark Hotel
Wally Budge	Lucerne Motor Hotel	Lloyd Carswell	Sheraton Corp
Adele Castle	Golden Nugget	Hal Chandler	Frontier
Bob Coyner	Hotel Muehlebach	Ray Culley	TWA
Jim Deitch	LVCVAuthority	Frank Denton	Nevajet Tours
Harvey Diederich	MGM Grand	Art Eastman	LV Convention Svcs.
Doug Farley	Sahara	Lee Fisher	Dunes
Dick Fitzpatrick	Caesars	Sig Front	Sahara
Howard Goodwin	Imperial Palace	Scott Griffith	Holiday Models
Don Holladay	Mint Hotel	Len Hornsby	LVCVAuthority
Paul Howell	Sheraton Corp.	Wes Howery	Thunderbird Hotel
Jesse James	Air West	Al Jugo	GIANTS
Bill Kellog	Western Airlines	Hank Kovell	Kovell Advertising
Jack Ladelle	Creative Enterprises	Jim Lake	Dunes
Bob Laurion	Circus Circus	Morgan Lawrence	Singapore Promo Bd.
Marcel LeBon	Charm Unlimited	Bill Marsh	Nat't Tire Dealers
Herb McDonald	Sahara	Charlie Monahan	Caesars Palace
Nick Naff	Las Vegas Hilton	Ted Nelson	Las Vegas Hilton
Howard Ness	LV Convention Service Co.	Bill Novak	Frontier Air
Ken O'Connell	LV Chamber of Commerce	Bob Paluzzi	Caesars Palace
Barry Perea	Graylines Motor Tours	Barney Rawlings	Sands
Jack Robertson	National Airlines	Bob Schmuck	LVCVAuthority
Tom Schoch	Frontier	Marc Swain	Stardust
Bob Stein	Gardner, Stein & Frank	Fred Swartz	Aladdin
Jule Thomas	American Supply Assn	Jim Villers	Bonanza Hotel
Len Yelinek	Escape Travel	Charlie Wyre	TWA

EXHIBIT 8-3. Professional "faculty members" who participated in the initial years of the hotel marketing course, HA 280, when it was sponsored and supported by the local HSMA chapter.

The Boeing 747 was due to start flying soon. At that time I was vice president of HSMA International. So I got the idea to hold a seminar on the plane's impact on the hotel and travel industry. And whether the industry was ready for it. You know, it wasn't ready! When the demo plane landed in Las Vegas, it blew out all the lights on the runway.

Bud James had just left the Sahara to take over at Sheraton. So we had Bud and Barron Hilton and the presidents of several airlines including TWA and Western as well as reps from Boeing. [Also on the program was Majeeb Hallaby, Pan Am's president.]

National HSMA [headquarters] didn't provide the support that I had expected, but Bud Grice [national HSMA's elected president] came from Marriott to act as Master of Ceremonies.   FRONT

The president of TWA, F.C. (Bud) Wiser, Jr., appeared on the program with Howard (Bud) James. I introduced them saying that I was the thorn between two Buds. It got a laugh.   JERRY VALLEN

The most exciting aspect of this highly publicized event was the inclusion of the College of Hotel Administration as a partner with HSMA, a marriage that was advertised in the brochures and announcements. Forecasts were for 200 attendees, but some 600 registered. An encore was scheduled the following year. The second year (1970) the title was *1971: Travel's Giant Recovery*. Working with the local chapter, the college helped to secure novelist Arthur Hailey (author of *Hotel* and *Airport*) as one of 1970's speakers. Sessions were held the first year at the Sahara and at the Frontier the next. Again the program was filled with awesome names including Hailey, Robert Mitchell, the vice-president of Lockheed, and Bill Williams, a veteran of three plane hijackings.

Several local members made particularly meaningful contributions toward the success of the seminars. One such person was Jim Lake of the Dunes, who remained a strong supporter thereafter. Another was TWA's Claude Rand who took responsibility for organizing and coordinating from behind-the-scenes. Vallen was on Rand's Airline Seminar committee and from that came Rand's eventual employment as a faculty member.

Claude had an expense account and would take me to lunch occasionally at the Riviera where TWA had offices. When we started talking UNLV employment, I took Claude to lunch at McDonald's to make clear UNLV's limitations on expense-account spending.   JERRY VALLEN

Naming Circus Circus' Second Property. Excalibur was Circus Circus Enterprises' (now Mandalay Resorts) first expansion beyond their initial "tent" property. As part of the pre-opening hype, Excalibur launched a contest to name the facility. Free accommodations were the least of the many gifts offered as prizes. The company's publicity department suddenly realized what that meant in terms of mail: thousands and thousands of entries! They turned to the hotel college.

Beam Hall had recently opened and the college was housed there. Space was plentiful so a deal was negotiated. Hotel would provide the space (the three dining rooms)

and the staff (student labor) and be responsible for handling the mail. It proved to be a 24-hour a day project that ran for many weeks and depended on the close cooperation of the U.S. postal service. A student manager was hired, who then hired three shift managers. The shift managers then hired sorters, runners, tabulators and recorders and established individual work schedules. By coordinating with the hotel company, a process and a record of frequency of certain names were developed. Circus Circus paid all the salaries and a rental fee to the college for the space.

Letters and post cards with recommended names streamed in from all over the world. Duplications ran into the hundreds: One of the more popular names was "Circus Circus II." The results were turned over in a timely manner and the Excalibur name was selected although everyone was hard pressed to recall that being a nomination!

Use of the Kitchen. A policy had been promulgated even before the building was opened. It closed the use of the kitchens to the myriad social groups and individuals that would otherwise have overrun the facilities. Several rules were particularly effective. No one could bring in food that was purchased or prepared externally; no one could use the facility unless a faculty member was in attendance; all functions had to be learning oriented; charges had to be competitive with local restaurants; and the facility was not to be used as a fundraiser for nonhotel college groups.

> I always thought that some of the rules were directed toward the local charities and groups to which I belonged so as to make it easier for me.   FLOSSIE VALLEN

> We still adhere to the rules, especially having a faculty member on premises.   CLAUDE LAMBERTZ, HOTEL FACULTY MEMBER

Rules notwithstanding, the college made the kitchen available on limited occasions, renting or lending the space under special conditions to outside groups. The Minor Company (food bases and sauces) was one of the kitchen's very best friends!

> They did so much for the students because students could do much more with the Minor products. I loved that Dr. Minor.   LAMBERTZ

The relationships continued with the family but was less personal after Lew Minor retired and the company was sold to Nestlé. The Minor company used the kitchen whenever it needed the facility. Through Lew Minor and his son, Michael, top chefs came to Vegas for food testing and tasting. They held company training sessions and cooking contests in the Beam kitchens. Visitors—professionals all—saw the facilities and carried away another positive story about the value of hotel education at UNLV.

Another annual user of the kitchen was the *Las Vegas Review-Journal.* For many years the newspaper held a recipe contest to boost readership. Hundreds of recipes had to be sorted and three in each category selected for the final stage, which was a cook-off in the Beam Hall kitchens.

> I did it every year and loved it because I met so many people from the town such as Muriel Stevens, [food columnist] chefs Ed Kane [chef instructor], Chris Johns [Sands] and Andre Rochat [Andre's]. We would review the submissions at the *RJ* and make selections just by reading the recipes. A recipe for orange meatballs sounded incredible. It was chosen for the cook-off, but was just God-awful tasting. The contestant said he made it up and was amazed to be chosen as a finalist. Another time, someone did a goat dish with kidneys, but they were raw. The judges just couldn't eat them.   LAMBERTZ

The college waived charges for the facilities because of the good publicity that resulted, including a closer relationship with Albertson's, the grocery chain that was the chief sponsor. Not all kitchen users were comped. The space was rented whenever possible, usually on weekends, to a variety of caterers. Some came to do parties for *Comdex*, the big computer show, and some to cater meals for film companies, a growing source of state revenue. (City-wide facilities were limited; the city's megahotels were not yet lining the Strip.)

> One group catered a party on the roof of the gym [now the Barrick Museum of Natural History]. Benefits to the college included leftovers as well as a cash rental. We sometimes got 30–40 racks of lamb all wrapped up in the freezer.   LAMBERTZ

Some Less Successful Public Relations

Positive public relations were great, but not everything the college attempted succeeded. Student leaders often used college stationery to invite and then thank visiting speakers and those who arranged hotel tours. The college secretaries were authorized to provide the paper and even do the tying. Poor control allowed one student to obtain college letterhead. He wrote a scathing complaint letter about some personal issue using the stationery. The letter's recipient contacted university authorities much to the dismay of the dean.

City-wide Statistics. Among the earliest projects was one that foresaw the need for local information, data about business activity in Las Vegas. Hotel statistics were gathered and distributed in just about every other major hotel city. Once Bob Moore, a certified public accountant with an economic bent, was on faculty, the college planned to provide that service to help pay back those who had helped the college. Moore was to gather confidential statistics, combine them and produce macro data for the city. Bruce Baltin, a former faculty member but now with the hotel accounting firm of Harris, Kerr, Foster agreed to help. To start, Baltin submitted a form for the hotels to complete on a monthly basis.

A presentation outlining the value of the information and the method of collection was made during a meeting of the hotel accountants. Anonymity was promised. In retrospect, the college should have realized that it was too aggressive a start. Recognizing the sensitivity of what was being asked (the initial data collection was to include room statistics, food sales and covers, operating ratios and two casino figures) and recalling the casino's penchant for secrecy, it was no surprise that the idea faltered at the starting gate. Frank Watts of the Riviera Hotel, the college's long-time friend and mentor, was the only one to agree to participate. It took the advent of the public corporations, which required public disclosure, and the power of the convention authority to complete the idea.

> There were certain owners who didn't want to share. They didn't give up anything to anybody. They were all very independent and close with their information. In fact, no one was even for starting the accountants group.   WATTS

> Remember that Vegas was going through a transitional period. Each casino was an entity unto itself. One didn't share information. One dare not! No information on occupancy; none on hold [a casino's measure of gross profit]; none of nothing.   PHIL ARCE, SAHARA HOTEL MANAGER

Alcohol Awareness Courses. Heightened awareness about the impact of drunk driving came home to the nation in the late 1980s. Draconian dram-shop laws, which heaped liability on the retail establishments that sold drinks to drunk drivers, were enacted by many states.

> Liability was extended even to home cocktail parties.   VAN HEFFNER, EXECUTIVE, NEVADA HOTEL & MOTEL ASSOCIATION

Nevada did not follow this trend despite heavy lobbying from anti-drinking groups. The citizenry did acknowledge the problem, however. Alcohol Awareness Courses were mandated at the city and county levels for servers and bartenders, for everyone who handled alcoholic beverages. At the suggestion of Van Heffner, executive officer of both the Nevada Hotel & Motel Association and the Nevada Restaurant Association,[8] the college began offering alcohol awareness courses. Heffner had developed and taught just such a course, *Serving Alcohol With Care*, for the Educational Institute of the American Hotel & Motel Association.

> The course was launched at the New York Hotel Show and eventually sold several hundred thousand copies nationwide.   HEFFNER

> For a short period Van was also the national executive of the IFSEA and so I was helping him in his educational programs and took the course from him. Then the college put a program together with Alan Stutts, who was head of the college's outreach center, and who saw some potential there.   AL IZZOLO, HOTEL FACULTY MEMBER

> John Stefanelli was one of the regulars teaching *Serving Alcohol With Care*. It was a program that the State of Nevada mandated, and we became a distributor of that program.   STUTTS

A modest $25 per person fee was charged, but that was reduced to $10 per student if a group contracted for the class. It paid for the course material and provided small discretionary income for both the faculty and the college. Faculty members from law and food and beverage taught the course, but only after being certified themselves.

> One person couldn't teach all of it so Don Bell [hotel faculty member] did a historical view with the pathological consequences. Larry Strate [college of business] taught the law. Then I would cover techniques of preventing customer drunkenness.   IZZOLO

What started as a community service became a hullabaloo—the course was a profit-making endeavor for some 17 private businesses. After Las Vegas Metropolitan Police (John Moran was sheriff then) decertified graduates from one such school and referred them to the college, the pace of the college's participation accelerated.

> Everyone had to be certified within one year. In one month we did some 300–400 students. We'd have several groups of 50–60 at the MGM alone. After the deadline passed and most people were certified, Don [Bell] and Larry [Strate] and I pulled out   IZZOLO

One company, which used a brewery's material for its course, objected to the college's involvement and retained an attorney to make the protest. The complaint was founded on the fact that the complainer—a registered lobbyist—had taken an active role in convincing authorities to implement the regulation. As if this had somehow assigned him exclusive rights to the community. The second issue was the college's fee, which was about one-half that charged by the complainant. Working with Walt Elliott of the Bartenders Union, the college had even offered the course without charge to bartender apprentices.

The argument advanced to the campus' attorney, Liz Nozero, was fallacious. Taken to the extreme it meant that the college could not do what other community agencies did: no wine tastings; no cooking classes; no consulting. The complainant also implied that the UNLV course would award college credit. Of course, there was no such inference. Indeed, there wasn't even continuing education credits because the college ran the courses through its research center not through the university's division of continuing education

To keep peace, hotel agreed to two compromises. No sessions would be offered off campus unless specifically requested by a hotel and there would be no advertising by brochures. Thereafter, responses to off-campus inquiries were answered by telephone or letter. Support from John Unrue, the academic vice president, brought closure to the issue because the complainer's attorney realized that the university would bend no further.

> I did one session at a bar on Tropicana Avenue for 10 employees. Everything I said was answered with, You're right, that's true. It was like an amen choir. The air conditioning wasn't working so when we took a break the audience ended up in the walk-in cooler. It was half as big as the restaurant. We finished the last half of the program in the cooler sitting on wooden crates!   IZZOLO

Alcoholic Awareness Courses were but one of the services offered by an expanding Hospitality Research and Development Center. Chapter 9 enlarges on its services.

Shopping Audits.   Prior to and even after the establishment of the Hospitality Research Center, some consulting work was done by a private company, University Associates Incorporated (UAI), founded in 1970 by faculty members Basile and Vallen.

> During the time that Vallen was dean, all consulting business was given to the Center [after it was founded], but after his retirement UAI began operating again so I had to remind him what the college's philosophy was. There wasn't too much conflict!   STUTTS

> University Associates was a problem for Stutts because some faculty members preferred it over the Center.   FRANK BORSENIK, HOTEL FACULTY MEMBER

> I did a lot with University Associates. Basile and I did a job for Phil Arce at the Frontier. Phil was very forward looking. We did a session for Dennis Gomes. I was so young; these people were way above me. I was glad Dick [Basile] was there during the half-dozen sessions.
>   We also did a housekeeping video for Caesars. We took hundreds of slides of staff completing certain jobs. I wrote the script and we combined script and slides into a training video.
>   [John] Stefanelli and I did work for Chris Karamanos [University of Nevada Regent and entrepreneur]. I did a marketing plan for the Union Plaza and a shopping session at Caesars.   JIM ABBEY, HOTEL FACULTY MEMBER

Local hotel-casino companies growing sensitive to customer relations began to use University Associates for labor arbitration . . .

> University affiliation made me neutral in the arbitration cases. I'd bill the standard rate and then reduce it by 50% as my community contribution.   BASILE

. . . and for shopping audits—reports on employee knowledge, courtesy, dress and attitude as well as the cleanliness, safety and appearance of the property itself. In turn, UAI hired the faculty.

> I remember trying to break the toilet during one of our inspection trips at the Tropicana. The engineer came and looked at us like you idiot: All you need do is put this on this. But we were just trying to get the engineer to come to the room. We also shopped a lot of restaurants both fast food and full service.   LESLIE CUMMINGS, HOTEL FACULTY MEMBER

These assignments in the early 1970s gradually expanded to include tests of honesty and income control. Suspicion that a bartender wasn't ringing all cash transactions, or that a food server was kiting guest checks, or that a housekeeper was taking guest valuables replaced shopping audits as UAI's major service.

One interesting case involved a showroom. It was impossible to get seated in a sold-out show when a special, very popular entertainer played there. Or was it? Management had concerns. UAI was given a blank check to uncover the person providing seats to these "sold-out" shows. Flashing $50 and $100 tips, big money in the '70s, shoppers progressed up the organization from the showroom's maitre d' who referred them to a bellman, who referred them to the bell captain, who referred them to a food and beverage executive, who referred them to a top senior management person. Each level accepted the proffered gratuity. For a handsome toke, seats were found for four in the sold-out showroom. The disclosure was very embarrassing to the executive who funded the expedition since the culprit was a high-ranking member of the executive staff and kin to a top executive.

A surprise letter came one day from the state's attorney general, Dick Bryan. It followed a telephone called from someone wanting to hire the service and asking for details. The letter pointed out that what UAI was doing required licencing as private investigators. Normal corporate licensing was not enough. Thus closed that phase of the company's business.

HOW WINE PLAYED A ROLE IN THE COLLEGE'S HISTORY

The Wine Class

Soon after the program was started, a decision was made to offer classes in specialized areas that other hotel programs were overlooking. The marketing class was one such. Gaming would develop into another. Wine was a third.

The question of wine faculty arose early on as it did with the other specialties. Who would teach? Searching through his limited wine library the dean unexpectedly identified an author who was working right down the street, as a sommelier at the Dunes. Arrangements were concluded and the class was to begin when a family emergency called the new instructor back to the British Isles. Don't worry I'll get you someone good. And he did: Rolf Laerm. Laerm was at the Las Vegas Hilton, which had just opened, 1969, as the world's largest hotel, 1,512 rooms.

Laerm was knowledgeable, personable and known within the wine community. His affiliation with the college helped his reputation grow even as he contributed 15 years of enthusiasm, hard work and loyalty.

Where to get the wine was the next issue. Telephone calls, letters and personal visits were made to the wine distributors of the city. Among the early donors were Best Brands (later Southern Wine & Spirits, which invented *UNLVino*); Costello; Deluca; Sam and Skip (father and son) Hecht; McKesson Wines and Spirts (which later played a role in the Banfi gift); and Nevada Beverage (which later established the Nevada Beverage/Anheuser Busch scholarships).

To validate the college's participation, the dean accompanied Laerm during the first two years. After the relationships were well established, Laerm would merely call and "place an order." There was no place on campus to store the wine, so cases were stacked in the dean's family room, the same place the first beer tastings had been held.

Naivety paid off. At the end of each summer—the wine course was offered summers only during the first several years—Laerm and Vallen returned the unopened bottles. That stopped after the distributors pointed out that the paperwork cost more than the wine.

The college was just being straight up and honest.   RALPH DURGIN, SOUTHERN WINE & SPIRITS

Thereafter, unused wine was carried over to the following year or used for prizes, luncheons or other important occasions.

There were 16 faculty members who were a rewarding audience for my faculty development seminars, especially when stimulated by the bottles of wine supplied by the dean.   RIK MEDLIK, VISITING FACULTY MEMBER FROM ENGLAND

Coming to UNLV was a culture shock because wine was served at the first faculty meeting I attended. On my first visit to Auburn University, the small talk had evolved around the price of milk until I noted that beer couldn't be purchased at the grocery store. The school had a religious affiliation and I was informed that the only spirt discussed was the Heavenly Father.   CUMMINGS

Where to hold the class was the final item to be resolved. Alcohol including wine was banned from campus. Special permission from President Zorn was needed just to offer the class. The college turned to its friends at the convention center. For several years running, they accommodated the class with set-ups, ice, parking, and signage without rent until others began asking for the same contribution. Only then was a moderate rental charged. The off-campus setting justified special brochures to advertise *The International Wine Seminar*. After the ban on alcohol was lifted in 1971, the class was held on campus, first in the humanities building and then in Beam Hall. Brochures were produced even then. For example, the seventh annual seminar (1974) honored one of the original wine suppliers, Sam Hecht, who had died that year.

The students were the biggest surprise of the class. Hotel undergraduates worked during the summers so enrollment, which was always oversubscribed, was chiefly local persons. Many were public school teachers looking for summer credit to augment their salaries, the very persons who advised local students on career and university choices. How serendipitous! It was to many of these "students" that letters were addressed later publicizing the minority Strip Scholarships (see Chapter 5). Word of the course spread like wild fire within the community, and wine became the in-topic around town. The college had a new audience.

The food and wine experience was in vogue in Las Vegas long before it was in the rest of the nation. Sommeliers are doing today what Rolf [Laerm] started in the '70s.   LARRY RUVO, SENIOR MANAGING DIRECTOR, SOUTHERN WINE & SPIRITS

Everyone enrolled thinking the course was easy; it wasn't. Identifying a wine while blindfolded was one item on Larem's final exam! For several years, the dean sat in to help Laerm make outlines and examinations and to keep the class on schedule. As Laerm became more confident and better able to arrange hours at his regular job at the Hilton, the class branched out with one luncheon (voluntary) per week It included the wine featured in class that day. Hamburgers with expensive French champaign was the *pièce de résistance.*

> One needs a wonderful sense of humor about wine. Not to let it become self-important; it's just grape juice!   DURGIN

Rolf turned to the distributors to find speakers for those topics that he was somewhat uncertain about. Soon he became as knowledgeable as the visitors. Shades of what happened with the hotel sales class with Ted Nelson and his apprentice, Jerry Vallen.

> I lectured in Rolf's class from time to time.   RUVO

Wine thus provided an early and positive interface with another segment of the professional community. Even more thrilling, the wine class became the jumping-off place for other wine-based adventures, *UNLVino* among them.

UNLVino

UNLVino—Las Vegas' spring icon—started small, as did the university, and grew in tandem with its namesake. Each year since 1974, the citizens of Clark County have gathered to taste wine and meet old friends.

> A survey that we did indicates about a third of the attendees [8,000 persons in 2000!] came from word-of-mouth recommendations.
>
> It's become the granddaddy of all wine tastings; probably the world's largest tasting in one room. We are moving [2001] from Bally's to Paris [Hotel] because its ballroom is much larger.   RUVO

UNLVino wasn't designed as the largest continuing scholarship source for the college—and most likely for the entire university, but it became just that. Furthermore, it is probably the most unusual endowment ever given to a university. It keeps growing from annual contributions. Indeed, *UNLVino* provides academic awareness for local residents who wouldn't otherwise know about the university or its colleges.

The wine distributors of the city became acquainted with the college through the wine class that Rolf Laerm helped to launch. Among them was Southern Wine & Spirits whose senior managing director, Larry Ruvo, was the originator of *UNLVino* and continues to be its chief proponent.

I had a complaint one summer from a wine buyer whose bottle had gone bad after she left it in the trunk of her car while she went shopping. I felt we had to improve wine education; she wouldn't have treated ice cream that way. So I called the college.

With a handshake over lunch we had an agreement. I just wanted to do it exclusively. It would help the school, the consumer, the company and, frankly I thought it was a good community service.   RUVO

Larry Ruvo always hosted great lunches!   JERRY VALLEN

There may have been a touch of competition behind Ruvo's move. Southern Wine was the smallest of the city's eight wine merchants, one of which was Costello. Costello ran the well reputed *Maitre d's and Captains Tasting*, which was held in the Sahara Hotel's large pavilion, the Space Center. Ruvo was and is a tough competitor so that might have been part of the rationale. The event has changed mightily since then.

Through the good offices of Southern Wine, suppliers come from all over the world to attend (see Exhibit 8-4). Ruvo points out that they pay their own airfare, hotel room, car rental and meals. They are away from families and businesses for at least two days. They endure eight to 10 hours of standing and talking as they give away their wines. And they keep returning because the tasting is well organized and meaningful despite the huge crowds. (They also carry away the name of the College of Hotel Administration.)

Initial attendance was small enough to be accommodated in the warehouse. And there it met for five years although case upon case of spirits had to be moved to make space for the scores, not yet hundreds let alone thousands, of visitors.

A.E. Caretta & Associates	Browne Vintners
Buckingham Wine Company	Carillion Importers
Chateau & Estate Wine Co.	Dreyfus Ashby & Company
Gold Seal	Great Western
Inglenook Winery	Joseph Heitz Cellars
Klaus Dillman	Mirassou Winery
Mumms Champaign Cellars	Park Benzinger
Paul Masson Vineyards	Peel Street Wine Merchants
Robert Modavi Winery	Sandeman Sherries & Ports
Schenley Import Wine Company	Schiefflin & Company
Shaw Ross	Sonoma Vitners
Souverain Winery	Trojan Distributing
United Vintners	W.A. Taylor & Company

EXHIBIT 8-4. Exhibitors for *UNLVino*'s second tasting, May 6, 1977, in the warehouse of Southern Wine & Spirits on Wynn Road

There is a core of warehousemen who have been with the tasting as long as I have [20 years]. So I just tell them the date and the well-oiled machine kicks in.   DURGIN

We advertised from the beginning. The day before the first tasting, a call came from the office of Sheriff John McCarthy. They had seen the ad, but noticed we had no license! Southern Wine was not licensed to sell to consumers. Come down to the office and be issued a special license, I was told. Only in small-town Vegas could that sequence have unfolded!   JERRY VALLEN

During those early years we operated on a shoestring budget. The school had a bit of cheese and bread donated. But consumers and [business] customers still came. The purveyors came as a personal favor.   RUVO

Mondavi vineyards was among the very first to sign on. Robert Mondavi, not yet a household name—the vineyard was started in 1966—came to the first and second tastings. He stood in the warehouse on a platform made of cases and with a microphone borrowed from the campus and delivered the first wine seminar. Years later speakers such as Kevin Zraly, well know author of *The Windows of the World Complete Wine Course*, continued the lecture tradition, but in better accommodations.

Along with the growth in scholarship money has come a growth and a shift in the tasting itself. Attendance figures parallel the city's burgeoning population. Several dozen attendees grew to hundreds and then to thousands, requiring corresponding shifts in venue. What started in the warehouse of Southern Wine & Spirits shifted to the college's Beam Hall; next to the campus' Thomas and Mack Arena; and then to the hotel ballrooms of Bally's and Paris. Nothing dramatizes size better than Larry Ruvo's estimate of 20,000 bottles used in 2000's tasting.

Increases in ticket prices from $3 to $50 have corresponded to the passage of time and to the demand for entrance. The annual thank-you letters from the dean and the university presidents to Ruvo and to Southern Wine's General Manager, Sid Chaplin, tracked the changing environment. One thousand persons at $3,000 was reported in 1977; $6,736 in 1980; nearly $10,000 in both 1982 (1,257 attendees) and 1983. President Goodall's 1984 letter cites 1,300 in attendance and a gate of $15,512. Increases in both numbers and price have pushed the total gift towards the $1.5 million dollar total. Indeed, one marketing strategy suggests that the higher the charge the more customers will come. *UNLVino* has proven it so.

UNLVino is a joint effort with the college faculty, staff and student body carrying its share of the load. Dozens of students work each tasting under the direction of a faculty member.

The quality of student support varies with the faculty supervisor. For the most part we have had strong faculty members such as Hank Melton, Tom Jones and Mohsen Azizsoltani, who make clear exactly what students can and cannot do.   DURGIN

The college sends creative postcard announcements to a wide mailing list.

> I remember preparing the first mailing which used a mailing list from UNLV's publicity office. We realized that we had the wrong list just as we finished attaching the labels. We started trying to tear off the labels when I realized we could paste over them with the new list.   JOAN REYNOLDS BEITZ, ADMINISTRATIVE ASSISTANT

The college publicized and handled on-campus ticket sales and it provided coverage at the door for many years.

> Joan Reynolds and I took tickets at the door at three different sites for well over a dozen years. Jerry greeted tasters at the door. There was a whole group of regulars who returned every spring for a homecoming. A community party hosted by the college.   FLOSSIE VALLEN

One of the university's best contributions was made by a class in advertising that was taught by the campus publicist, Mark Hughes. From that class came the catchy theme, "UNLVino, Take a sip for scholarship."

> Mark and I [Sari worked in campus publications] and others in our group sat down at a brainstorming session. After coming up with utterly ridiculous names, Mark said what about *UNLVino*? And that was it.
>
> "Sip for scholarship" came from the class [that Hughes was teaching].   SARI PHILLIPS AIZLEY, SPOUSE OF THE COLLEGE'S FIRST FACULTY MEMBER

Food has always been a critical component because many tasters stay for hours during the traditional dinner period. Where once the big achievement was getting several loaves of bread donated, now the program's culinary prowess contributes meaningfully toward the event's overall success. Food donations still underpin the culinary portion of the day, but a more complete preparation and service are provided through faculty and student labor.

> For *UNLVino* 1984, Don [Bell] and I had nearly 1,000 stuffed chicken breasts prepared. But we didn't have enough refrigeration. So we stored them in the dining room and turned the refrigeration down! Each *UNLVino* ticket included one dinner. [In later years, the college rented refrigerated trucks.]
>
> One year, we put up between 10,000 and 11,000 hors d'oeuvres! Then I ended up in the hospital. That was the second time. Each time I was incapacitated, a chef from industry came in and finished the job.
>
> We prep for two days cutting sausages and cheese so we can use the morning of the event to decorate. Even today, everything is donated. We ask the hotels to donate. Sometimes they even put the trays together.   CLAUDE LAMBERTZ, HOTEL FACULTY MEMBER

Food also ended the day in the early years when size was still manageable. Ruvo took the suppliers to a closing dinner (by then it was 10 pm) at the Venetian, his parents' restaurant. That warm and fuzzy dinner became another casualty of growth.

As part of the metamorphosis, wine education has been supplemented with a cork-counting contest (1981), an art show, collector's items (posters and wine glasses), tour packages (door prizes), a pre-*UNLVino* fund-raising dinner and a social gathering whose imprint on the city cannot be over exaggerated.

> It's a wonderful, wonderful afternoon; a springtime get-together that takes on an energy and identity of its own. It's a fashion scene with people buying outfits and sporting special dress.
>
> The energy level, the buzz in the room is intense between 5:30 and 6:30. But it's exhausting too. DURGIN

> We always try something fresh. First we rented glasses and then gave them away with a *UNLVino* imprint. We started with a few cardboard posters and then the artist came and sold them. We produced hundreds of bottleneckers [advertisements around the neck of the retail wine bottle] which customers take home. Next year's [2001] changes have already been decided. RUVO

A "celebrity" wine auction (45 lots that raised $32,000 in 2000), was added about a dozen years after *UNLVino* was conceived.

> I had to find a celebrity. Jerry Tarkanian [UNLV's well know basketball coach] excused himself as not an auctioneer, not a wine aficionado and not interested in having his name used. Jay Leno [now a TV host] was playing Caesars, but turn us down cold. Everyone chuckles good-naturedly, but I appear as the "celebrity" each year. DURGIN

The newspapers joined in, starting with the *Las Vegas Sun*. Now both the *Sun* and the *Review-Journal (R-J)* produce a joint advertising section immediately before the event. Trudy Patterson of the *R-J* put the section together as a good vehicle for the newspaper, but it served everyone's needs. Bob Fowler of Southern Wine now coordinates the publication from the other side. Ads from vineyards, distributors, retailers and restaurants are mixed with stories about the tasting and about wines. Sherry Miller and then Betty Ellis coordinated publicity from the campus side as part of their duties as campus publicists.

Hours have been expanded several times as a means of recapturing the educational intent of the tasting.

> The focus has changed and Larry [Ruvo] suggested that we try to redevelop the educational part. I temper that reminding him what is now the essence of the event. DURGIN

Three hours before the public is admitted, doors open to the professionals: to restauranteurs, food and beverage managers, wine retailers and the like. Suppliers break out their finest products. Nothing about the earlier opening appears in the advertising. But the word has leaked out and getting in earlier became a sign of being with the "in" crowd. Soon everyone was coming early.

It happens because there was only one ticket style. Now our salesmen [who sell to the trade] put a mark on the trade tickets. Soon we may have to print them in a different color.   DURGIN

Drinking and driving has been another concern from the start. Extra security was always brought in. Equally dangerous were the very steep stairs that guests had to navigate in the Thomas and Mack (T&M) Arena.

We were closing up one time when we [with partner Tony Goitia] noticed a young man with four cases of wine [150–180 pounds] staggering up those steep and very irregular stairs like an ant laboring under its load. It was too good to stop. But he was straining and we started to feel concerned. We politely took back our wine.   DURGIN

To avoid the steps, guests were encouraged to use the T&M elevator. For those driving personal autos, faculty members Bob Martin and Jerry Goll volunteered to be designated drivers. They might have had ulterior motives:

Bob and I drove the drunk wagon. And we would compare who had the most propositions [from drunk women]. We tied. Bob, how many propositions do you get? None. How about you Jerry? The same.   GOLL

Arrangements were less formal in the early years as one of the attendees recalls in a letter:

Although I was embarrassed at the time, I now laugh at the 1980 *UNLVino* when you [Vallen] and Tim Cloonnan ('80) took me, dragged me, home because I had had too much of the fruit of the vine.   JIM DIPIETRO, '83 STUDENT

Care and planning have held mishaps to a minimum.

We had a misadventure during the third year that *UNLVino* met in the warehouse. An elderly woman, a student on medications, drank too much and became extremely agitated. She actually beat on me. I had three male students take her home in my car, leaving hers in the parking lot. The next day, she pressed kidnaping charges. The police read us our rights. I called Judge Paul Goldman, who was teaching for us at the time. Don't worry, he said, I'll arrange something. Which he did. He called back with assurances that if the police arrested me they promised to do so quietly and without handcuffs.   JERRY VALLEN

I remember the incident [the worst that the tastings ever had] here in our building. I laughed, but Vallen didn't.   RUVO

Winemakers' dinners

Rolf Laerm's wine class brought the college into contact with the local wine distributors. They, in turn, brought the program to the attention of the winemakers. From the conjunction of winemakers and distributors, but chiefly Southern Wine & Spirits, came the Winemakers' Dinners. They began shortly after the opening of Beam Hall's dining facilities and after the teaching staff was complete.

> They approached us about the idea. We sat together developing the menu and the accompanying wines. The winery would donate the wines and one of their executives would come to discuss them. No other restaurant was doing this. Today, Lawry's and many hotels put on wine dinners.   CLAUDE LAMBERTZ, HOTEL FACULTY MEMBER

These gourmet dinners brought the college to the attention of yet another segment of Las Vegas, the dining out crowd that was willing to pay $50–$100 per plate. A diverse group of celebrities formed the nucleus of the regulars. Among them were Dennis Gomes, hotelier and one-time member of the gaming board; Harley Harmon, insurance; Forrest Mars, Mars candy bars; Bob Maxson, university president; Dan Reichartz, Caesars Palace executive; Muriel Stevens, food columnist and author; Claudine Williams, hotelier and college supporter; and Governor Mike O'Callaghan, as well as many others. Some were introduced to the facility by an invitation to the dean's table.

> Jerry knew everyone and that helped spread the word and assure the success. Once they were on the mailing list, people came back.   LAMBERTZ

Working together the winemaker and the course instructor coordinated wines with the menu. A different wine from the winemaker's vineyards was introduced with each course. The winemaker explained the wine, its origin, character and the reasons it was chosen for the food being served. Tony Goitia coordinates Southern Wine's participation in the dinners just as Ralph Durgin does for *UNLVino*.

Demand soared; tickets were hard to obtain. Although the dinner was represented as a class, a learning situation, expectations also soared. Reputation grew as expectations were met time and time again. The quality of the meals was sustainable and the general ambience—students themed the menu and the room decorations differently each time—outstanding.

> The students always came up with some great ideas for the dining room. They took the initiative. Once a golf course was the theme with sand on the floor, a bridge, a pond, trees; it was great.   LAMBERTZ

The dinner's appeal diminished as on-campus parking grew more frustrating. The clientele was an off-campus audience. When parking grew tight and it was not possible for friends to find spots, they stopped coming. Appeals to the campus parking committee for a temporary allocation of space during the six or so dinners per term (of which one was the winemakers' dinner) were rejected.

The winemaker returned to campus with the opening of the Stan Fulton Building conveniently located on Flamingo Road with ample parking. In the interim between buildings, other venues of the city began offering paired wine and meal extravaganzas.

BEYOND LAS VEGAS

Students, jobs, internships and money had their source in the program's reputation, which was built as much upon a national audience as a local one. The college's range was startling. A letter from the American Embassy in Nigeria proved that to be so. Forwarded from the system's Reno office, the inquiry asked whether an advertisement from the Nigerian Institute of Catering, Hotel and Motel Administration was legitimate? Their ad in a Nigerian newspaper claimed to be an affiliate of UNLV's College of Hotel Administration.

> In my travels I find people know about our hotel program before they know any other. Every school that I've visited in Switzerland knows the hotel college.   JOE DELANEY, COLUMNIST AND PART-TIME FACULTY MEMBER

> I had dinner with [Nevada] Governor Guinn [one night in the year 2000] and I showed him a letter from a [former] hotel student in India. We tried unsuccessfully that night to reach him by telephone.   LARRY RUVO, SENIOR MANAGING DIRECTOR, SOUTHERN WINE & SPIRITS

The E. I. And the AH&MA

An unsuccessful effort to bring the Educational Institute (EI) of the American Hotel & Motel Association (AH&MA) to the UNLV campus was one try at outreach. In 1971, a mere four years after the inception of UNLV's program, the Board of Directors of the EI decided to erect a building to permanently house the Institute, which was based at Michigan State University at that time.

> I was around when they actually built the building, 1974, with profits that I generated in the previous five years. [Borsenik came to UNLV in February 1975 after a five-year stint as consultant to and then head of the EI.]   FRANK BORSENIK, HOTEL FACULTY MEMBER

Unclear is whether the decision to throw open the location to all hotel schools was a necessary public relations ploy—the Institute sold texts to everyone—or whether the possibility of moving the Institute from Michigan State was real indeed. UNLV's newly formed College of Hotel Administration submitted a bid. Also unclear is whether Nevada's invitation was accepted on face or whether it was a *pro forma* decision by the EI board.

A visiting team including Bill Connor, whom Vallen knew, having prepared his first book for the EI, came to campus. Their mere presence gave a boost of recognition to the program. And Vernon Herndon, Hilton's big name, then became a correspondent and later a visitor to the campus. Bob Cannon, AH&MA's man in Vegas, was kept apprized.

The college itself had no building, but the university had scads of land: bleak, barren desert land. Although President Zorn granted permission to pursue the bid and half-heartedly promised to secure support if the project materialized, he was too busy to visit with the very distinguished group that came. Vice President Dale

Nitzschke was aware that they would need temporary space until the building was opened. No promises were made.

An all-terrain vehicle was obtained and the group motored to the middle of the "campus." With no master plan in place, any piece of land was available! The sales pitch included: great residential area for the staff; joint faculty-EI appointments; a dollar-a-year lease; incomes and inventories free of state taxes; housekeeping services to be contracted; and more. "More" was that the building would also house the college faculty. A letter, dated October 27, 1971 iterating the advantages of the Las Vegas location, followed the on-site visit.

The effort failed probably because both sides were playing the game. The college was holding out measures that President Zorn, certainly not the college's strongest supporter, would have to deliver through the Regents. And the Education Institute was mouthing platitudes because the decision most likely had been made already.

> They brought back pictures [of the UNLV campus], but yes [it was part of a charade].
> BORSENIK

Its title, The Educational Institute of the American Hotel & Motel Association, leaves no question that the EI is an offspring of the AH&MA. In May of 1986, the parent AH&MA came to Las Vegas for its annual meeting; it was the second time.

> I attended the 1960 Puerto Rico convention using some of the profit that we made when the AH&MA met in Vegas in 1959. [*Hotel & Motel Management* reported that to be the association's 48th Annual Convention with 1,200 attending.] Vegas' registration was only $35, because the hotels [the Stardust was the headquarters hotel] comped many meals and cocktail parties. Rooms were $6 or so. There was $3,000 left over.   FRANK WATTS, RIVIERA FINANCIAL OFFICER

The College invited the 1986 AH&MA to campus for what was a spectacular buffet dinner with specialized food units scattered throughout Beam Hall. Don Bell, who coordinated the event, reported in the alumni bulletin:

> "The reception was designed on the theme 'Regional Foods of America.' . . . Eight buffet tables . . . [featured] California, New England, Dixie, Midwest, Wild Game, Cajun . . . as well as a spectacular seafood display. In the Boyd Dining Rooms was a composite table and the dessert/coffee area. Twenty ice carvings decorated the . . . tables."

> We built mountains of ice for the seafood; we put up trees with stuffed birds in them; one section was wild game. The atrium [of Beam Hall] looked great with all the lights that we strung.   LAMBERTZ

Ten bars were available to quench the thirst of a warm spring evening. It was the first time ever that the group had met on a campus, or so the college was told.

Although some 1,500 were expected, less than half of that number came. The long evening hours and perfect weather topped off a gala affair which included the cheerleaders, the UNLV pep band and the jazz band under the direction of Frank Gagliard, a music faculty member. Hotel faculty members, Bob Barber, Don Bell, Claude Lambertz, Charlie Levinson and Hank Melton, supervised some 150 students all in costume.

Student guides ushered the group throughout the building with a running commentary. The casino lab was a popular stop for those wanting to learn how to beat the house!

> I recall Bill Friedman [casino executive and part-time faculty member] saying there *was* one way to beat the odds. Play craps betting "Don't Pass, Bar Twelve" and drink the free drinks very quickly to overcome the house's small advantage.   JERRY VALLEN

Accolades were high and, judging by the following day's comments, genuine and very well received. There was real disappointment voiced by those who opted to go elsewhere. To the college it was a smashing success considering the other options that Las Vegas offered the delegates.

> We heard the next day that all the others had wished they had come to campus, whichever functions they attended.   LAMBERTZ

CHRIE Membership

The Council on Hotel, Restaurant and Institutional Education (CHRIE) is an organization of hospitality educators from all academic levels. Hotel and restaurant companies that recruit graduates of the member schools also belong. So too are publishers of hotel texts and trade associations. From the outset the CHRIE affiliation was essential to the college. Most of UNLV's hotel faculty were members.

> Pat Moreo, Frank Brown and I were active in the regional chapter, California CHRIE, CAL CHRIE.   AL IZZOLO, HOTEL FACULTY MEMBER

Frank Borsenik, Dave Christianson and Jerry Vallen have held the post of national president. Patti Shock has served in several important positions as a member of the board of directors.

> We had three faculty members on the [national] CHRIE board at one time. All of us were supported with the hotel college's [soft] money.   BORSENIK

Three types of valuable contacts arose from the college's participation. Each had its origin in the broad visibility that membership, particularly leadership, created. CHRIE meetings brought UNLV into contact with company recruiters. CHRIE was and is a major—probably the single most important—source of faculty and students, especially so during the college's formative years.

I was working in the club industry, but I had taught previously at Lansing Community College while working on my masters. Bob Blomstrom was the head at Michigan State. When I asked him about teaching jobs, he gave me a CHRIE journal. That's how I ended up at UNLV.   JIM ABBEY, HOTEL FACULTY MEMBER

CHRIE met in Atlanta in 1988. Patti Shock organized that meeting during which time she told me of her unhappiness at Georgia State. [We knew each other because] she had given me a glowing recommendation when I finished my undergraduate degree there and applied to UNLV for a master's. During the bus tour from the hotel to Stone Mountain, I reintroduced her to Vallen. I still have a picture of the two sitting on the bus talking about the job.   KAYE CHON, GRADUATE STUDENT AND HOTEL FACULTY MEMBER

National CHRIE met in Las Vegas three times during the course of this history. The lure of the Las Vegas destination worked as well on educators as on delegates of other associations. But first, the objections of Howard Meek, who had retired as Cornell's dean and had become CHRIE's executive officer, had to be overridden. During a general meeting, Harry Purchase of Paul Smith's College insisted on a membership vote. Meek's objections were overridden by an overwhelming margin.

The first Vegas gathering was at the Flamingo Hotel during the Christmas recess of 1970. (CHRIE met during Christmas break until after Meek's death.) The Sahara had also bid for the group and had actually comped rooms for Meek and other members of the site-selection committee, including Helen Weiss of the Educational Institute and Hilda Watson Gifford, director of Project Feast in San Francisco. The Sahara hosted the whole party to the showroom. Buddy Hackett played his usual tawdry monologue, which probably cost the Sahara the booking. Meek was a rather conservative person but he soldiered through the "Hackett mouth" and the subsequent Vegas meeting. Howard Meek died the following year.

I was vice president of ARA [now called ARAMARK] when CHRIE met in Philadelphia. Meek had died and ARA stepped forward rather then see the Christmas meeting canceled. I mentioned to Jerry [Vallen] that I was thinking of going back to teaching. We knew each other from Northern York. [Basile at Paul Smiths, NY; Vallen a few hours away at Canton, NY.] In his inimitable way he said You're getting pretty old so you'd better hurry up. So I came to visit in February.   DICK BASILE, HOTEL FACULTY MEMBER

Business was very quiet at Christmas time even as late as the start of the 1970s. The Flamingo management was impressed by the table action of the membership. The hotel (Burton Cohen was the president and general manager) offered to freeze rates, pay the airfares for visiting speakers and throw in a host of goodies if only CHRIE would meet at the Flamingo during Christmas for the next several years. The CHRIE board, led by Howard Meek, demurred.

Vegas was very seasonal [in the early 1960s]. A lot of people came through Vegas because they were driving across the country. We had no business after Labor Day, small volumes at

Thanksgiving and Christmas. The New Year's period was very busy and then business would drop off again.   PHIL ARCE, SAHARA HOTEL MANAGER

During the second visit, a session was held on campus in the Moyer Student Union, which overlooked Beam Hall, which was then under construction. Horrors! a workman fell from the scaffolding in full view of the CHRIE audience.

The third visit took place at Caesars Palace. Like previous meetings, it was a big success. All the Las Vegas gatherings provided unbeatable opportunities to show the junior-college faculties where to send their graduates. Vallen was president of CHRIE at this time and also acquisitions editor for the William C. Brown Publishing Company. He convinced Brown to donate several hundred dollars for a drawing and then arranged for a showgirl to push a rounded bakery tray filled with silver dollars into the closing session. Andy Schwarz of Sullivan County Community College won the drawing. In an unforgettable gesture, Schwartz had each member come forward and take a commemorative dollar. There were very few left for Andy.

CHRIE has faced bankruptcy several times. During one of those periods, 1981, while Beam Hall was in the planning stages (with ample space), tentative negotiations were begun with Vice President Dale Nitzschke to bring CHRIE headquarters to UNLV. It was not a new idea.

We discussed the possibility of housing the state hotel and restaurant associations in the new building, but decided against it because I also had private business interests.   VAN HEFFNER, EXECUTIVE, NEVADA HOTEL & MOTEL ASSOCIATION

Vallen was the elected president (Lionel Brookins acted as unpaid executive officer for a time) so moving to a campus appeared to be the best option. Then Tom Powers agreed to assume the post of executive officer, and headquarters moved onto his campus, Penn State. At the annual CHRIE meeting preceding that move, Lendal Kotschevar entered a letter into the minutes:

"The delegates of this CHRIE Convention commend its Board, Officers and Staff for the strong leadership given Council during the last three years. This was a critical time calling for adroit administration and sound financial management. This was given and the Council emerged a stronger and more unified organization than ever before. The delegates especially commend Dean Jerome Vallen who leaves the board this year and Mr. Lionel Brookins who is resigning from the Council Staff, for the faith and courage they have displayed in the Council during this critical period of re-adjustment and re-orientation. Their contributions and hard work in directing the Council did much to rebuild CHRIE into a strong organization ready to pursue new goals."

The college as an entity and its members individually brought a strong sense of commitment as they built the professional ethos discussed in the following chapter.

ENDNOTES FOR CHAPTER 8

1. Personal letter from Joan Kenney at the time of Jerry Vallen's announced retirement, November 13, 1989.

2. Gabe Vogliotti, Unpublished manuscript, p. 1-12 from the private collection of Bill Thompson.

3. January, 1968, p. 50.

4. Neal Karlen. "Dice, Drinks and a Degree." *Rolling Stone*, October 4, 1990, pp. 144–148.

5. Ibid., pp. 144

6. Memorandum from John Unrue, Vice President for Academic Affairs and Provost, to Dean Jerry Vallen, dated May 16, 1988.

7. "Greetings From the Dean," *Program of the HSMA Election Dinner*, October 26, 1978.

8. Heffner reports that the Nevada Restaurant Association was formed under similar circumstances. New food service standards were mandated by the Boards of Health. Nevada's hotel association was not able to adequately represent all of the free-standing restaurants. Heffner gathered restaurateurs such as Bob Ansara, Tola Chin, Tom Kapp, Skip Swerdlow—all mentioned elsewhere in this history—to form the initial chapter of the state restaurant association, June 7, 1982.

CHAPTER 9

A Professional Ethos

The scope of this final unit, *Doing Our Thing*, is far broader than the public-relations focus of Chapter 8. Faculty and staff members contributed to the college individually and in concert, as we shall see now in Chapters 9 and 10, as did students and alumni individually and in groups, Chapter 11.

ADMINISTRATION OF THE COLLEGE

Organizations face the challenge of integrating their many parts so that outsiders see but one identity.

> The hotel college gained its strength from the coordination and integration of the program into everything it did with the industry and with each property.   SIG FRONT, VICE PRESIDENT, SAHARA HOTEL

> UNLV succeeded because there were good dedicated and loyal people committed to hard work. That meant a great deal to me and to many others .   LARRY RUVO, SENIOR MANAGING DIRECTOR, SOUTHERN WINE & SPIRITS

> There is one thing that I shall always remember about people in Las Vegas: If I asked for something, they'd do it! It did take a while for them to understand who this newcomer was. ALAN STUTTS, HOTEL FACULTY MEMBER

Everyone supported us. One year a columnist wrote asking what right we had to charge $75 per cover for dinner. That was even before the dinner was served! For that dinner we had planned to recreate the gourmet room in the DI. The chef at the DI was so troubled by the column that he sent his crew to help. We ended up with as many DI staff in the kitchen as we had students.

Another time we were going to do a room at the Mirage even before the hotel opened. I was hospitalized that night and Gustav Mauler [Mirage's Corporate Food and Beverage Manager] ended up taking the class.   CLAUDE LAMBERTZ, HOTEL FACULTY MEMBER

Building The Culture

Presenting a single face to the outside world requires an internal cultural to which everyone in the organization can subscribe, at least to some degree. Hotel faculty presented a common front because they internalized a common culture. It united them, strengthened the student body, and cemented their relationships with one another and with their several publics.

Closeness with the faculty made it one big family; everyone knew everyone. Charlie and Bea Levinson [faculty member and wife] would say that, You're part of our family.

The faculty played tricks on one another. They would lock Abbey out of his office, for example.   JOAN REYNOLDS BEITZ, ADMINISTRATIVE ASSISTANT

Frank Borsnik and I used a classroom in which we had installed a motion sensor that was donated during the energy crisis. Stefanelli came in and said, Al, what's going on? The lights keep going off in that classroom. I said, John, the lights will stay on if you blink your eyes.   STUTTS

The small size of the early faculty and the common backgrounds of its members created a strong sense of camaraderie.

There was only a couple of us; we were fairly close.   SARI AIZLEY PHILLIPS, SPOUSE OF THE COLLEGE'S FIRST FACULTY MEMBER

We [the early faculty] were very close. That was the nice thing about it. Nobody was envious of another. There was very little jealousy. All came from industry, which gave us a support base.

I used to pick on Charlie [Levinson], but we loved each other.   DICK BASILE, HOTEL FACULTY MEMBER

Several of the faculty wives were flea-market shopping when Flossie Vallen spotted a lamp with a stained-glass shade. The dealer wanted cash only. Mariette Basile [Dick Basile's spouse] came to the rescue. We formed a human room divider while she searched in her bra bank for a secret zippered compartment that held the money.   CAROL SAPIENZA, SPOUSE OF FACULTY MEMBER DUNNOVAN SAPIENZA

Las Vegas was frontier-like. Residents were far away from blood-relatives so they found their support in extended families.

> When my mother died, Frank Brown [faculty member] went around to get donations, not
> for flowers, but to pay for the airfare back East.   REYNOLDS BEITZ

Grandma Flossie was the first to diaper the Bussel's [second faculty member] new
daughter and then later:

> Flossie [Vallen] was a proxy grandma when my son was born. She came over with diapers in
> hand. It was amazing.   PAT MOREO, '69 STUDENT AND HOTEL FACULTY MEMBER

The cohesive climate of support and group encouragement that was created by
the initial staffers was passed on to the newcomers. Alan Stutts and Claude Lambertz
came in 1983; Jerry Goll in 1986.

> There was a good balance on the faculty between industry experience and academic cre-
> dentials. Everyone had some academic credential. I'm happy to say that I've done [here at the
> University of Houston] exactly what was done in Nevada [balancing experience and degrees].
> STUTTS

> Don Bell [hotel faculty member] was good to me with teaching tips. He taught me every-
> thing to do in the classroom, and then I added my own techniques.   LAMBERTZ

> The college was a very positive, convivial, pull-together outfit. There was a spirit about the
> college that was a team thing that I thought was marvelous.   GOLL

Goll's reference to the "team thing" was reinforced by several early traditions.
No deliberate decision was made to create traditions; they just came about. Payday
luncheons was the first. Someone (probably Basile and/or Levinson) decided that
on each payday all the faculty would have lunch at a different hotel-casino. A better
understanding of each property and of one another developed. Selective class scheduling created a long lunch hour for all faculty on the same day. Then the group waited
to meet until the first scheduled day after payday.

> I remember going to lunch with the Levinson group. It took a bit of arranging, but it gave the
> faculty a lot more camaraderie.   JIM ABBEY, HOTEL FACULTY MEMBER

By the fourth year, a larger faculty size and the difficulty of scheduling put an end
to the tradition. It hung in abeyance until Beam Hall opened with an always-on coffee pot in the kitchen. Faculty members gathered there and bonded.

> The coffee drinkers had a lot of productive discussions. We were a small group, but business
> faculty members smelled the coffee [in the shared building] and I remember many times
> when several of them were there.   BASILE

> I recall the coffeepot always being on.   GOLL

We did a lot of coffee in those days especially the terms that Leo [Lewis] taught.   AL IZZOLO, HOTEL FACULTY MEMBER

Assuring the newcomers of a warm welcome became more important as the size of the faculty grew and the old timers settled into their own comfortable habits.

Bob Martin took me to breakfast during the interview and told me he was senior to me [old navy talk; both were ex-naval officers]. I answered, Mine's a doctorate and yours is a masters. He was neat guy and that was a nice beginning because Bob was a rock of the college, a key player.

Basile was here when I came. A gentleman; a wonderful person through and through. He did everything he could to make it easier for me.   GOLL

Anne and I and the children came to Las Vegas and the Vallens had a nice party at their home on Ottawa. We met all the people and we were impressed. The decision not to come at that time was difficult.   FRANK BORSENIK, HOTEL FACULTY MEMBER

On my first visit [1978] while I was on my own, my new colleagues showed me snow skiing in the morning at Mount Charleston and water skiing in the afternoon on Lake Mead.

They were wonderful hosts to us [in 1983 with spouse, Lynda] and could not have been more helpful when we needed it most, even to Dave Christianson fumigating our rented house while we went to California.   RIK MEDLIK, VISITING FACULTY MEMBER FROM ENGLAND

Vallen's family including [daughter] Rebecca was generous with its time when we first arrived. They had us over for a swim and housing talk. The transition was easier than just being plunked down. I think that's right, and we [at Houston] assign someone to that job. STUTTS

Jerry loaned me his little car, a Valiant, I think, [a Dodge Dart] until I bought a car.   ABBEY

Years later I loaned it to Bulent Kasterlak [one-term visiting faculty member] only to have it cost him for a locksmith after I gave him a broken ignition key.   JERRY VALLEN

Informal gatherings at the dean's home developed into a tradition. When the faculty body was small, there were dinners. Later on swim parties and picnic buffets.

Jerry asked us over for dinner one night. I even remember where I sat, at one end in the corner, but I don't recall what we ate. There were several couples, quite a crowd, but I don't remember any kids. I was offered the job that very night.   LESLIE CUMMINGS, HOTEL FACULTY MEMBER

I remember how Jerry and Flossie [Vallen] accepted us, by inviting us to their home.   GEORGE HARDBECK, DEAN OF BUSINESS AND ECONMICS

For one party I made a very rich crab and lobster casserole. About an hour after the dessert, Curt Shirer [hotel faculty member] returned to the refrigerator for seconds or maybe it was his fourths!   FLOSSIE VALLEN

Home gatherings for faculty and students were not exclusive to the dean's home:

> I have a better recall of the parties at the Basile's nice home.   AIZLEY PHILLIPS

Joan Reynolds Beitz hosted some:

> Joan used to have great Christmas parties.   CUMMINGS

> I remember the parties we used to have at the homes. We had one at my house, at Levinson's house, at Basile's house. It was like family; a great time.   REYNOLDS BEITZ

> The "parties" were very important to the program. As we grew space and organization limited what could be done.   BASILE

And the Basiles, Christiansons and Sapienzas hosted some:

> One summer [Dave] Christianson [hotel faculty member and, later, dean] invited his summer graduate class, seven or eight of us, to his home for a pool party. The power went off right in the middle of the party! He called the dean and the party resumed there. I recall all of the Korean decorations that hung on their wall.   KAYE CHON, GRADUATE STUDENT AND HOTEL FACULTY MEMBER

As the faculty and staff grew still larger, the dean's dinners were split among smaller faculty groups.

> I remember going to Vallen's or Basile's house for hamburgers on the grill. When we got bigger it was harder to do, but we still managed a few get-togethers.
> Several times we went to the Sapienza's [hotel faculty member] for just a social gathering.   IZZOLO

Eventually the Thanksgiving dinner, coordinated by the staff, became the focus with a family gathering that included children.

> The plan from Twylia [Towns, Secretary] and Claude Lambertz and myself was to bring everyone together. It helped the faculty to be closer and it was fun because everyone brought something.   REYNOLDS BEITZ

Special dishes were prepared by everyone who came, and Lambertz with the help of Bob Barber did the turkey and most of the cleanup.

> Claude would do a couple of turkeys with the sauce and people would bring in special dishes.   GOLL

Tola and Marcia Chin of Chin's restaurant in the Fashion Show Mall created the most enduring and most special of all the traditions. They brought together all the faculty and staff with spouses or friends during every Christmas break. It was an ideal substitute for the home-based gatherings which had long before fallen to the growing numbers. Fifty faculty and ten staff with spouses and friends necessitated a commercial-sized accommodation, which the Chins provided and hosted.

> We tried to offer a different menu each of the 14 years that we gathered. Kotschevar [hotel faculty member] was researching Chinese cuisine. He ate jelly fish and one-thousand year eggs. TOLA CHIN, RESTAURANTEUR AND DONOR

> The Chins had us to many gatherings there. For appetizers they served dishes such as Peking duck with a special sauce and green onions. Unknowingly, many of the faculty avoided the duck skin, the best part. LAMBERTZ

> Will [Beitz] and I went to the Chin's party where Will enjoyed every bite! REYNOLDS BEITZ

The Work Culture. A full day's work was the mantra of the early faculty accustomed as they were to industry standards.

> We thought we carried a light load compared to industry. Today it's seen to be a heavy load. We thought it was pretty soft. Work loads weren't a serious thing but we always had at least four classes; on occasion I had five. Other colleges had three or sometimes two. If one didn't like it he could leave. BASILE

> It always amazes me [as dean at the University of Houston] when faculty here talk about workloads. We taught 12 credits at UNLV, published and served on committees. Someone said that business taught 9! The dean's answer, Well that's their standard; our is 12. STUTTS

> It was a full-time job. Faculty were expected to be here five days per week, and the dean was here. He didn't patrol the halls [as was rumored], but he made the schedules. I knew the philosophy and agreed with it and felt that the one faculty member who always challenged [the work load] was out of place.
>
> There must be accountability! The student pays the price when faculty are not available. GOLL

> Coming from industry, the three-class load, which proved to be four, with a few office hours and a bit of committee assignments, sounded like a 20-hour week! I wound up working closer to 60 hours. IZZOLO

> Reducing the loads to two or three days was the beginning of the downgrade. Without the accountability [for making class every day] people just wouldn't be in; not enough self-discipline. They said we're off doing some research and writing. Bull!
>
> We used to teach five days per week and we were there from 8 or 8:30 in the morning to 5 or 5:30 at night. ABBEY

I said to John Goodwin [hotel faculty member] I'm working my toosh off but your light is on every night when I leave, the door is open and your briefcase is on the desk. He answered that he leaves at 2 P.M. so the cleaning crew locks up for him. The dean always walks around to see if we're working.   STUTTS

I was shocked to learn [when hired] that the load was four classes. For 10 years I had taught only two at Michigan State. But they were big classes between 150 and 300 students. [Beam hall classes had fixed, maximum sitting for 60.] The amount of work was the same. The same number of exams, term papers and grades to compute. Contact with the student is lost in large classes.   BORSENIK

The five-day-a-week schedule is so different from now. We did a lot, but we got paid a lot.
    Everyone knew what the standards were.
    But in my whole career, we didn't teach too wide a range of courses. It was possible to specialize and that has been very good.   CUMMINGS

Specialists were available in many areas, but we also had persons like Basile and Phillips who could cut across different lines.   BORSENIK

Teaching loads were four courses. The very first semester I taught three courses with two preps. Never having taught at the college level, I didn't realize how hard it would be to prepare! When the term was done, Jerry said there had been no complaints so I must be doing something right.   IZZOLO

The dean had serious reservations about me. My first contract stated that I had to get industry experience the following summer. But that was canceled after the first year.
GOLL

Jerry Vallen: Oh, did you do such a good job that year?
Goll: No, you said I was beyond hope.

The very first summer I was at UNLV, the dean sent me to work at the Americana Hotel in L.A. He knew someone there. While there, I met Jim Brewer from the L.A. Country Club and from that developed a good working relationship for my course and student tours.
    I spent another summer at the Tropicana Hotel working in marketing research under a grant from the National Restaurant Association, NRA. I think Dave Christianson did that a few times too. [During his tenure on the board of the NRA's Educational Foundation, Vallen had helped Walter Conti, a Philadelphia restauranteur, create those grants.]
ABBEY

A single, unresolved issue—smoking—lingered for a long a time. It created the one major schism among the faculty. There was tension between the smokers, Borsenik, Goll and Phillips and the chief non-smoker, Leslie Cummings. Cummings would come into meetings with a no-smoking sign and claim a portion of the room. This gave very visible focus to the issue. Before the whole campus went "nonsmoking," Cummings moved her office because of smoke from neighboring offices.

> Five years after they banned smoking in the building, Frank [Borsenik] was still smoking! CUMMINGS

> Jerry Goll and I had the last two smoking offices in the building. Phillips would come in, put up his feet and light up. Next, we had to smoke outdoors and eventually, not even within the building.   BORSENIK

> Frank and I went to what was called the *'tween deck,'* on the second floor near the dining room. Frank puffing on his pipe and Goll with cigarettes. Phillips would come and smoke also. He had stopped buying but not bumming. We had a sign made, Borsenik's and Goll's smoking lounge. Someone tore up the sign.   GOLL

Communications. Communications among a small cadre of faculty were informal and often took place in the hallways.

> At the end of my first academic year as a graduate student, the dean stopped me in the hall to ask how I was going to maintain the family over the summer. I didn't have a stipend. He said we'll give you a project. I created a computer base of alumni names and addresses.
> Russ Anderson ('72) hired me to visit almost every bar in town to make a survey, and I didn't have the faintest idea of the difference between scotch and vodka!   CHON

There were no weekly bulletins and no Internet, but there was the grapevine. Written memos were almost unknown intra-college. Although it appeared as if decisions were made without faculty input, in fact consultations were ongoing, but only with those qualified to advise on that particular topic.

> Put in the book that I was always impressed that whenever I came to talk, Vallen would get out from behind the desk and sit across from me. It made the visit feel important. But then again I came in only when we had some issue to talk about.   ABBEY

> The dean would try to get his work done between people going in and out. If we saw his desk stacked with papers, we'd come back. There would be a stream into the office about 4:45 every evening.   PAT MOREO, '69 STUDENT AND HOTEL FACULTY MEMBER

The dean's reputation for walking the halls was misinterpreted. It usually meant he was heading toward someone's office to discuss an issue.

> I did check on one part of the schedule. Was the faculty member in his office during the posted office hours? Faculty could pick their own hours, but they had to meet that commitment.   JERRY VALLEN

Honest answers and the grapevine worked wonders with communication.

> My great respect for Vallen was that he never lied. Straight talk. People knew exactly where they stood at all times.   BORSENIK

> I've told the story many times. Jerry knew his people very well. Retired from the navy with a heavy stipend, money wasn't that important to me. He knew that. What did motivate me was an unsatisfactory grade in research. My ego got me working and soon I was tenured.   GOLL

Student communication was more difficult, so the student Hotel Association was encouraged to launch a Monday-morning newsletter which those faculty members so inclined read in class. The college's philosophy made the student the customer. Once that was articulated, faculty advising, personal counseling and student services flowed directly.

Students had absolute first priority with the dean. That produced a two-way communication flow. Personal, individual issues were settled for students, and feedback about classes, staff, faculty and college issues was obtained.

> What I liked and what I thought was important was that the dean's door was always open to students. He said, If we didn't have students, we wouldn't have a college.   REYNOLDS BEITZ

> Whenever I am tempted [as director of the Oklahoma State Hotel Program] to do some report and I see a student waiting by my office, I remember the way it was at Nevada. The kid comes first.   MOREO

Faculty meetings were another means of communication, but they were held but once a term and even then were as much a forum for announcements as a forum for faculty debate.

> Faculty meetings were quick and to the point. Good meetings, we never monkeyed around. We rarely went more than an hour and we only met once a semester. I remember that we would just meet once a semester. At one of the meetings Vallen got really mad at Levinson, who complained about the work loads and no time to write. Charlie was always a bit of an antagonist.   ABBEY

A very small faculty and the need for the college to be represented on important campus committees required changes in even the election process. Less important committees were ignored in favor of appointments to more important ones.

> The dean would go around and say Frank is running for this committee. How do you vote? Young faculty were placed on some committees to show them how things worked.   BORSENIK

Organization

The organization of the college was flat with no chain of command.

It's harder today to make centralized decisions in a university. Our structure was simple: You went in and made the case. If it worked, it worked. If the dean said I don't think so, then it didn't work. More traditional academics had problems with that.   ALAN STUTTS, HOTEL FACULTY MEMBER

Unlike other academic units, hotel had no departments. One administrative officer served alone for many years and even when the post of associate dean was created, it was not hierarchal.

It was a self-sufficient faculty, professionally qualified. There was no need for a great deal of supervision.   BASILE

Dave Christianson was assistant dean And Annette Kannenberg was his secretary. There was a little bit, not a lot, but a little bit of don't meddle with our business on our floor. So we were somewhat divided. Christianson downstairs and Stutts in his own office.   JOAN REYNOLDS BEITZ, ADMINISTRATIVE ASSISTANT

There were no departments, but there were responsibilities. The college exacted accountability from its members for a wide range of activities, whether it was the Switzerland program abroad or the management of the kitchen at home. But there were no titles and no burdensome machinery. The Hospitality Research and Development Center was the exception. It was an income-earning, self-funding project which warranted a somewhat more defined structure.

Alan Stutts and his secretary, Joyce Jeary, felt like theirs was a whole separate area that the dean's office really didn't have to worry about. They ran everything smoothly, never bothered us for anything.   REYNOLDS BEITZ

Of course I had no measuring stick so I started teaching 12 credits, writing a book, and serving on committees. Then the issue of a research center came up. It was something like: You want to be a full tenured professor? Take over the center. Charlie Levinson was the only faculty member to object [to the loads].   STUTTS

Levinson was unhappy on the basis of comparison. I don't think he believed the load was heavy. The comparison [to other colleges] made it seem heavy. It was a case of he's got a bigger lawn than I have.   BASILE

No departments meant no department heads; no bickering over resource allocations; no effort to lure students to a particular major; and as little internal jealousy as is possible. Minimal time and energy were lost to the politics so rampant in other colleges. The flat, mind-your-business structure set well with the college faculty.

So long as everyone felt there was an open-door policy—faculty members could just pop in—and we were all together, there was mutual support. Everything changed after departmentalization and it was caused by more than just increasing student numbers.   AL IZZOLO, HOTEL FACULTY MEMBER

All of the early faculty appointments (Abbey, Basile, Bussel, Catron, Izzolo, Kreck, Phillips, Rudd and Vallen) had backgrounds in both education and industry. Less in education than in industry, where no expectations of self-management existed. One accreditation evaluator saw the issue differently. He wrote,

> "[The director] has made many decisions administratively that normally would be made in consultation with faculty. Presumably as the program develops . . . customary consultative procedures will be followed."[1]

Certainly, over time, the university's culture of faculty self-management could not help but seep in. So later arrivals (Claude Lambert came in 1983) saw things differently.

> I had never heard of so much self-rule. I had to compare it to industry, where there were no questions, total dictatorship. I never noticed a dictatorship here.   LAMBERTZ

With few exceptions, Charlie Levinson chief among them, the faculty left the operation of the university to the university's head and the operation of the college to the college's head. There was an understandable *quid pro quo*: The faculty was asked neither to consider nor to resolve issues that weren't theirs to decide anyway. Chapter 2 points out that faculty governance was not widespread anywhere on campus during the 1960s and early 1970s.

> At that time there wasn't much done by committee. It was a completely different situation then; it was more of what the captain said.   RUEBEN NEUMANN, BUSINESS FACULTY MEMBER

> Coming from industry, I felt that search committees were the hardest to deal with. We were bringing someone to campus for six years [tenure] with the likelihood of a lifetime contract. [The Hotel College didn't use search committees, but hotel faculty sat on cross-campus searches.]   STUTTS

> Shared governance is one thing that's wrong with academia. We faculty get involved with issues that we have no business getting involved in. Bill Corney [business faculty member] was on the committee to design Beam Hall. He was a civil engineer so that [kind of assignment] made sense.   LESLIE CUMMINGS, HOTEL FACULTY MEMBER

This hands-off posture carried into the college's relationship with the balance of the campus both on an individual faculty member basis . . .

> I missed a couple of the library committee meetings because it was a waste of time. They sent me a letter and kicked me off! The dean said, Don't worry, I don't assign much credit to some of these committees.   ABBEY

. . . and on a campus wide one:

> My recollection is that hotel faculty by and large did their job. They didn't get involved in much of the academic bickering. There was a period with all kinds of bickering and jealousies and problems with space. The hotel college just seemed to function. It didn't get involved in internecine warfare.   DONALD BAEPLER, UNLV PRESIDENT AND UNS CHANCELLOR

> Community persons have always asked me, So what's going on there [on campus], but I couldn't answer because I wasn't privy to very much.   DICK BASILE, HOTEL FACULTY MEMBER

Baepler's perception of the college was much the same as that held by a later vice president, John Unrue. Under both administrations, hotel was allowed to do its thing because its thing rarely conflicted with the goals of the university and almost never created unsurmountable public relation difficulties.

Every administrator has a unique style of management. President Maxson worked the outside and referred every internal issue to Unrue.

> Vice President Unrue once told me that his door was always open to talk over issues, but there was no need to clear every decision with him.   JERRY VALLEN

President Zorn was on the opposite side. He not only wanted knowledge of every facet of every decision, he changed the words in every written memo or proposal.

Organizational needs and structures change over time just as individual administrators do.

> I saw the college refocus to consider new concentrations and create different tracks. The diversity and chemistry of the faculty remained during the ten years that I was with the program. I never saw any big splits.   STUTTS

Change became most evident when the founding dean gave notice of his intent to retire early in the school year 1987–1988. Before that he turned to faculty members Moreo and Christianson.

> Vallen sensed that changes were coming. Young Turks who wanted more traditional participation were joining the faculty. The dean asked me and Dave Christianson to write scenarios for the direction of the college. I suggested concentrations, not departments, to improve student advising and curriculum and take the lead on faculty recruiting. [Under this format] budgets, faculty evaluation and merit would remain with the dean.
>
> Departments pigeonhole people and being in hotel and restaurant management is pigeonhole enough.   MOREO

Moreo's idea was founded on a proposal that was floated in 1972. Although the founding dean continued to oppose departmentalization, he didn't veto the idea. On the contrary, he initiated the reorganization with a memo because that was the sense of the new administration.

Dave Christianson [who became the college's second dean] favored the traditional departmental structure.

> I don't know whether that was the right move. [for UNLV]. I do know that I would never preside over departmentalizing a hotel unit.   MOREO

On August 25, 1988, the Board of Regents approved the formation of three hotel departments with Don Bell, Bob Martin and Claude Rand the initial department heads.

> Comparing different administrations is like comparing apples and oranges. That's especially true when it includes a departmentalized organization verus none. I was one of a very few that opposed departments.   CUMMINGS

> One of the things I would say [as Dean of the Hilton College at Houston and] with 20/20 hindsight is don't departmentalize. If you do, the units become divisive over resources, over people. Who is to get this one travel dollar, this one pencil? Faculty stop talking to one another. I said it, but not loud enough [when UNLV departmentalized].   STUTTS

> As we grew, we began to separate, even before we departmentalized. Once we departmentalized, we began to lose our unity. But we had gotten so big there wasn't much of a choice.   ABBEY

The Hospitality Research and Development Center (HRDC). A new phase between the college and the local professionals began to emerge by the mid-1980's. No longer was the college seen as the industry's dependent. Just the contrary, college resources were being called upon for a variety of industry needs. How to direct and service these requests was a growing question.

> Vallen and I talked about having a vehicle, some entity that the industry could come to, rather than coming to no one. We put together an internal focus group and the center was spawned.   ALAN STUTTS, HOTEL FACULTY MEMBER AND HEAD OF THE HRDC

The Hospitality Research and Development Center, which Alan Stutts was to head, somehow appeared at just the right time. Stutts had an industry background, but came to UNLV from a brief teaching assignment in North Carolina.

> We were talking about a research and development center for the hospitality industry. Richard Laughlin, [hotel faculty member] who had come from industry, said emphasize who you are in the first word. So it got turned around. "hospitality" became the first word since that's what we wanted the corporate world to notice.   STUTTS

(Laughlin held a doctorate in English and had been in human resources at Hyatt.)

Formed in 1986, the HRDC began offering services to the community almost at once. Although the industry's immediate response to the appearance of the HRDC may have appeared dramatic, it was so only because numerous projects were backlogged waiting for official approval before beginning. On September 11, 1984, the college submitted its first request for authorization. It should have been a *pro forma* thing because business had inaugurated two centers 10 years earlier.

> The Center for Economic Education was started in 1973 and the Center for Business and Economic Research in 1975.   GEORGE HARDBECK, DEAN OF BUSINESS AND ECONMICS

> I worked with Keith Schwer who headed up the business college's research center. If a project didn't fit our niche, we would pass the inquiry to the other.   STUTTS

Interim, informal pleas for action were reinforced by a second formal request in March, 1985. This was repeated again in April with urgency in order to complete a special series of projects which Rodeway Inns had requested. UNLV's contact with Rodeway was through one of its executives, Tom Fay, who was both an interviewer and a scholarship contributor.

A second contract followed shortly thereafter from The United States Agency for International Development (USAID).

> I said you know Jerry we'll need money to start this thing. He said, how much? I don't know exactly, $50,000. I'll give you $10,000, but I want it back. The contract was just short of a $1,000,000! [actually, it was $863,000.]   STUTTS

From that point forward, the center was self-funding. As its director, Stutts was given operating authority including budget oversight. The account always showed a cash surplus. Not only did Stutts manage well, but there was never a need for the broader college to dip into the center's funds. That gave the center the flexibility to risk funds on some less certain ventures. Exhibit 9-1 illustrates the scope of expertise advertised by the center.

ACTIVITIES OF THE FACULTY AND THE CENTER

An amazing variety of projects flowed into the center as it acquired a growing reputation for delivering the goods.

> For each project, I picked faculty members who would focus on the assignment and deliver on the project, not on something they wanted to do. If they wouldn't—and sometimes they couldn't—we went to someone else. In many instances, the user would call back and say, That's good stuff!
>
> On the one hand, no one wanted to pay for the work. On the other hand, some faculty complained about the "wages." Stefanelli [hotel faculty member] was the flip side. He said I don't understand these people. I have a new swimming pool with a plaque at the bottom that says courtesy of Hospitality Research and Development.   STUTTS

The positive reputation that Stutts massaged so assiduously built upon a base of excellence that already existed. Individual and group consultancies were in

CASINO
Accounting
Layout and Design
Marketing
Racebook Operations
Slot Mix
Sportsbook

FEASIBILITY
Location Analysis
Return on Investment

FRONT OFFICE
Design
Operational Manuals/Analyses

MARKETING
Segmentation
Survey designs
Trend Analyses

EMPLOYEE
Courtesy Training
Performance Review
Productivity Audit
Quality Assurance

FOOD AND BEVERAGE
Alcohol Management
Facility Design
Inventory Control
Menu Design
Purchasing Procedures

HOUSEKEEPING
Procedure Manuals
Trends
Work Measurements

EXHIBIT 9-1. Technical and training support advertised by the Hospitality and Research Development Center after its founding in 1986.

place during the fifteen years between the program's founding and the start of the center.

> Once we were approached by the Nevada Agency for the Blind to develop management training for blind concession-stand owners, who had those sites legislated under both federal and state law.   JERRY VALLEN

> The blind concessionaire stand owners were not trained in foodservice, but they did an amazing job despite their handicaps.   DICK BASILE, HOTEL FACULTY MEMBER

> I got many clients including the Sands, the Sahara, The State of New Jersey, Binion, Paul Lowden, etc. with whom I was allowed to consult privately.   LEO LEWIS, BINION'S FINANCIAL OFFICER, BUT FULL TIME FACULTY MEMBER AT THIS TIME

> A new Marriott in Desert Springs had me over to do my thing. Half the staff showed in the morning and it was a great session. A great deal of interaction made me feel good. After lunch, I was dying. When I called a break, I learned that the GM was sitting in. When I went after him, he said he never heard such liberal stuff in his whole life. Then he let me know that he was a UNLV graduate. I said that I knew who the faculty had been and that explained his stupidity. He stalked out and my wife, Jackie, who was sitting outside heard him say, Son-of-a-bitch, and she knew he was talking about me. Later, he joined us in the lobby and we ended up as friends.   JERRY GOLL, HOTEL FACULTY MEMBER

Some Sample Projects

Several samples of pre-and post-center activities are offered next. They represent the sweep of dozens and dozens of projects undertaken either by individual faculty members, by the private corporation or by the center. In numerous instances, for example, the faculty appeared in court as expert witnesses, but—at the dean's insistence—always on the hotel's side.

Increasing The Average Check. McCarran Airport's food and beverage contractor hired many hotel students to staff his operation. Thus it followed that he approached the college for help in increasing the value of the average bar check. A series of talks was scheduled with the concessionaire's employees. Emphasized were the advantages (both to the house and to the server) of selling higher-priced "call" brands rather than "well" brands of alcohol. Teams of anonymous shoppers were sent out then to test the results. If the server who had taken the class responded to the instructions by up-selling the lower-priced well brand to a higher-priced call brand, the shopper jumped up, made a big noise with a rattle and gave the server a $20 bill! A great deal of excitement was generated among the staff as the plan took hold.

Housekeeping Audits. Two housekeeping audits, one on the Strip at the old Aladdin and one in downtown Las Vegas at the Golden Nugget, strengthened the college's reputation for thoroughness. Time-and-motion studies, including stop-watch measurements, were performed at both properties to increase the efficiency of housekeepers in preparing guest rooms. Borsenik, Wynia (who left UNLV because of low salary to build his own chain of hotels, Hospitality Associates) and Abbey were the researchers. Recommendations included better ways to do the job, revised scheduling, equipment needs, and differences between stay-over and vacated rooms. Results of the audits were used later in negotiating labor contracts.

> Frank Borsenik did all of the mathematics. I am trying to recall but I think we decided a housekeeper could do 20–21 rooms if there were no check-outs and 12–15 if there were check-outs.   ABBEY

Brand Loyalty. Bobby Baldwin from the Mirage wanted a study that would quantify the loyalty of the casino's customers by concentric circles, one mile, two miles, etc., if a competing casino [e.g., the upcoming Excalibur] were to open nearby. The center discovered that the Mirage held strong brand loyalty.

Energy Studies. During the height of the 1970s power crisis, several proprietary energy projects, in addition to public seminars, were completed. They emerged from Frank Borsenik's work with the campus energy committee (see Chapter 8) and then with the state in cooperation with the Nevada Power Company. The two biggest studies were with Holiday Inn Corporation and with Kerr-McGee, a chemical company in Henderson. It was at this time that the college sought legal advice from the campus attorney regarding the confidentiality of these proprietary studies. Energy presentations were also added to the Tableservice Conferences offered at Caesars Palace in partnership with the National Restaurant Association (see below).

Parking for Recreational Vehicles. The Hacienda Hotel piqued the faculty's interest with an unusual request. Would it make economic and marketing sense to build and operate a facility adjacent to the casino to accommodate recreational vehicles? Bill Friedman, who taught part-time before taking on the full-time management of the Castaways Hotel, took the lead position. Projections and forecasts looked excellent so the facility was built on what is today the site of the Mandalay Bay. Friedman also produced one of the earliest casino studies, the Casino Card Shuffling Report.

Gaming Math. John Giovenco, president of the Hilton Nevada Corporation, heard about a course, the Mathematics of Casino Games (HOA 436), which Borsenik taught. He contacted the center just as it had been planned: "an entity that the industry could come to, rather than coming to no one." A course of several mini units was developed by faculty members Frank Borsenik (a mathematician) and Jim Kilby (a casino consultant) for senior Hilton executives. Seated in the front row were executives Giovenco and Jimmy Newman.

Demographic Studies. Knowledge of the guest and the guest's identity grew in importance as the gaming industry matured.

> I think the Research and Development Center did something for every gaming company in Nevada. Caesars, for example, wanted to know how many persons were riding their walkways and who they were. So we clicked the numbers and ran an intercept study. The demographic characteristics of guests was something every hotel wanted to know. While the Excalibur was still in the ground, President Bill Paulos ['69] guessed their target market at incomes of $75,000–$85,000 annually.   ALAN STUTTS, HOTEL FACULTY MEMBER AND HEAD OF THE HRDC

Army Club Managers. Club managers from the U.S. Army met every summer for management development seminars. Michigan State University held a headlock on the bid and then Houston took over. Finally aware of the seminar's existence, the hotel college made its move via the Hospitality Center. The club managers shifted once again when Stutts left UNLV and solicited them away from Nevada and back to Houston.

> UNLV bid it away from Houston, and then when I came down here [Houston] we bid it back for a period of time. It was better in Nevada.   STUTTS

Office of Conferences and Institutes

Not all of the many, many public offerings—in contrast to proprietary projects like those listed above—were offered by the college under the rubric of the Hospitality Research and Development Center. Very early offerings were in association with the *Practicing Law Institute*, with the *Motel/Hotel "Insider"* and other trade publications; and even with UNR, University of Nevada Reno.

Pat Moreo and I gave a dozen or more seminars for UNR's continuing education. He did something in food and I did marketing. They were arranged before I left for my doctorate work, so I flew in from Utah several times.   JIM ABBEY, HOTEL FACULTY MEMBER

The National Restaurant Association (NRA) in the persons of Steve Miller and Dick Gavin approached the college in 1976 about holding joint conferences. Despite the NRA's very strong national programs, Miller recognized that Las Vegas was different and he felt that a Las Vegas affiliation would strengthen the NRA's draw. It did so immensely. Charlie Levinson became the college's point man and he brought in Nat Hart, vice president of corporate food and beverage at Caesars World. Without Hart, the initiative may have faltered; with him it became a decade-long blockbuster.

NRA/UNLV seminars were structured about different aspects of quality table-top service and advertised as the Tableservice Conferences. There was a 50-50 split after expenses. Hotel's endowments prospered with speakers such as Chef Louis Szathmary, Anthony (Tony) Marshall and Nat Hart himself. Even Senator Paul Laxalt, who as governor had appointed Levinson to a consumer-affairs committee, made an appearance. Sessions were usually scheduled during January, Caesars' down time and UNLV's miniterm. It became Levinson's miniterm assignment.

I taught one session where the turnout was lighter than expected. So we sat in a circle and just talked shop. By the time we were done, a member of the audience offered me a job.
CLAUDE LAMBERTZ, HOTEL FACULTY MEMBER

Most seminars were administered by the university's Office of Conferences and Institutes (OCI), headed by Dwight Marshall and managed by Keith McNeil. The

Bar Management

Casino Management and Operations

Collection of Gaming Debts

Computerized Systems for Hotels

Controlling Food Costs

Food and Beverage Management Update

Hotel Fires: Prevention and Postscript

Housekeeping and Building Maintenance

How to Create, Develop and Manage a Casino

How to Prevent Employee Theft and Inventory
  Shortages

Internal Controls for Food and Beverage

The Labor Contract

Manager's Guide to Computer-Assisted Hotel
  Management

Methods of Energy Management

Purchasing for Hospitality Industry

Seminar for Absentee Owners of Hotels and Motels

A Seminar for Travel Agents

Supervisory Skills for Hospitality Managers

EXHIBIT 9-2. Representative list of seminars offered by the College of Hotel Administration in conjunction with Office of Continuing Education.

Auditing Employee Productivity—What Can I do

Emergency Planning—Is My Staff Prepared

How to Attract and Retain the Leisure Traveler

Improving Employee Productivity Through Communication Skills

Legal Liability and the Hospitality Industry

Motivational Strategies—Teaching Old Dogs New Tricks

Preparation and Service Personnel

Serving Alcohol with Care

Training and Evaluating Food Preparation and Service Personnel;

Wrongful Termination—Avoiding a Law Suit

EXHIBIT 9-3. Sample list of programs offered by the Hospitality Research and Development Center, school year 1987–1988.

on-going relationship was a win-win for both even if it did become extremely contentious at times. McNeil disputed the "high"salaries paid to hotel faculty—often industry executives—and Vallen disputed the "small" percentage of profits paid to the college.

> There was shouting and screaming because the staff was agitated about it. Of course, I was on them about revenue all the time.   DWIGHT MARSHALL, DEAN OF CONTINUING EDUCATION

Among the non-controversial joint ventures was a seminar supported by the Clark County Fire Department: *Hotel Fires: Prevention and Postscript.* Sessions were held in 1982 at the MGM Grand Hotel, which had been rebuilt after that hotel's disastrous fire. Other examples of joint presentations are listed in Exhibit 9-2, and those independently offered in Exhibit 9-3.

Gaming Seminars. Gaming became one of the college's unique course offerings, both as part of the curriculum and as an area for entrepreneurship. The location was an obvious anchor, but so was the fact that no place else in the entire country had legalized play and no one outside of Las Vegas knew anything about it.

Local industry executives were the target of the college's first (1972) gaming seminar, *Collection of Gaming Debts,* held jointly with Keith McNeil, coordinator of the Office of Conferences and Institutes. A select group was invited to hear Franklin Navarro, an attorney from Houston, who specialized in the collection of markers. Markers, gaming IOU's, were not legal debts in any jurisdiction including Nevada. Navarro was well versed in that principle of law, which dated back to the Statute of Anne (British Monarch from 1702–1714). Navarro had taken collection lawsuits to trial in most states of the union. Even so, Nevada didn't pass legislation allowing casinos to pursue gaming debts in court until 1983. Gaming debts remained unenforceable for over 100 years. The first ruling was made by the Nevada State Supreme Court in Scott v. Courtney, 1872.

Introductory gaming seminars, *What Is The Casino Business and How Does It Work,* grew very popular after the announcement of New Jersey's Atlantic City entry into the business in 1976. At first, they were held in Las Vegas; later in Atlantic City. Leo Lewis, who served on faculty part-time and full-time for many years, became a consultant to the gaming authorities in New Jersey and helped draft its gaming regulations.

> Before Atlantic City opened, we ran gaming seminars. The first was at the Sahara. [Others were at the Tropicana.] Later [1980 and 1981] I did them in Atlantic City at the Golden Nugget. It was a two-day event. We had guest speakers, big guys from industry. I made a tremendous speech for UNLV and for Keith McNeil's continuing education. Keith was a good hustler in selling courses.   LEWIS

Among the "big guys" referenced by Lewis were such well known names as: Shannon Bybee, former member of the Nevada State Gaming Board and currently a UNLV faculty member; Steve Hyde, executive VP of Caesars Boardwalk; Dean Macomber, casino executive with Bally Park Place; Jim Ritchie, former chair of the Federal Commission on Gaming; and the inimitable Jimmy "the Greek" Snyder.

> Keith was excited about what tuition we could charge. Because of who came: Blue Chip companies; vice presidents, that's who! Anyone who knew nothing about gaming was hooked once I said, Let me tell you how a casino works.   LEWIS

International Travel. International travel proved to be the most contentious battle that the college had with the office of continuing education. Hotel organized and operated international trips for golfing outings to Scotland, cultural tours to Mexico, and miniterm cruises to the Caribbean. Hotel's long list of trips included several to the People's Republic of China (the first as early as 1977, the last during the Tienaman Square uprising);[2] one trip to the USSR just as it was breaking apart; and a golf/culinary trip to Great Britain that was handled in part by Charlie Levinson (food) and in part by Claude Rand (golf). Other trips went to Southeast Asia. The 1987 Asia tour scheduled six stops including Hong Kong and Tahiti.

> I learned not to wear slacks in China or Hong Kong because the toilets were just holes in the floors. I was the last [to gain access] and so there I was running to catch the train with my pants still rolled up. They all said, We know where you've been.
>
> I enjoyed these Asian trips although I do not enjoy Asian food. Everyone else said they did, but they all ate my plain lemon chicken.   JOAN REYNOLDS BEITZ, ADMINISTRATIVE ASSISTANT

Trips scheduled during the 1983 miniterm included Thailand, Singapore, Java, Bali, and Malaysia. During this period, hotel was also running its summer studies in Switzerland (see below).

Travel was one of the benefits of the UNLV affiliation. We took one group of international students to Mexico City to learn the culture and talk with hotel and restaurant executives. Albert, a Hong Kong student, felt at home in the awful traffic crunch. We learned that UNLV had the best hotel program but Hong Kong was unequaled for teaching how to cross traffic-jammed streets.   DUNN SAPIENZA, HOTEL FACULTY MEMBER

Initially we couldn't generate interest in two of our trips to China. Phillips was to lead one and Lewis another. I got on the telephone and filled the trips. It was sensational; one of the greatest things in my life.   LEWIS

Claude [Rand, hotel faculty member] drove me nuts at times, but if it wasn't for him, I wouldn't have gone twice to Hong Kong and done all those sales blitzes.   LESLIE CUMMINGS, HOTEL FACULTY MEMBER

I ran a course at Club Med in Mexico and a combination cruise and tour of hotels in the Bahamas.   AL IZZOLO, HOTEL FACULTY MEMBER

Rand had come from the travel industry, TWA. Because he networked with the travel community, he was appointed Director of International Programs in 1983. Rand arranged all of hotel's air and land trips, and faculty member Joe Von Kornfeld organized and promoted the cruises.

I went on two of Joe's [miniterm] cruises and in both he did a very good job. He was especially nice to me because he thought I was a pipeline to the dean. The faculty included Dave Christianson who held classes, which students had to attend.   REYNOLDS BEITZ

I think that Bill Quain [hotel faculty member] went on the very first cruise. Quain did a class on ethics and manners.   IZZOLO

Both cruise and land-operated tours competed with programs offered by the office of continuing education. Real heat was generated because profits (soft money) from these tours accrued to the agency administering them. The conflict between the two competing camps accelerated when Rand affiliated with a travel agency.

I remember the fights because Claude [Rand] started his own travel agency. My staff came in and pounded the desk.   DWIGHT MARSHALL, DEAN OF CONTINUING EDUCATION

I convinced Claude to disassociate himself, but it took time.   JERRY VALLEN

Domestic travel did not raise as many objections. Perhaps because Pat Moreo teamed up with the department of music through Isabelle Emerson. Perhaps because some of them were miniterm courses. Perhaps because continuing education got a piece of the action. Using the theme of *The Art of Music and Food*, the two colleges took students and locals to operas, plays, concerts, dinners and tours in the major cosmopolitan cities of the East and West coasts.

> Be entrepreneurial was part of our college's culture. But so was, Just don't lose money. Another theme was, Don't surprise the dean. I met Isabelle Emerson through my wife, who was a music major, and plans grew from that.   PAT MOREO,'69 STUDENT AND HOTEL FACULTY MEMBER

Conflicting jurisdictions properly end up at higher administrative levels. Continuing education's argument to centralize travel within its offices won support from one of the innumerable campus committees, the Committee on International Education, chaired by J. Kent Pinney. The committee created a travel/study policy that in effect closed hotel's travel initiatives. The college appealed, arguing that tourism/travel was the very business of the hotel college. Vice President Dale Nitzschke upheld the position promulgated by the committee; that was January, 1983. The college appealed again, this time to President Goodall. Goodall cited many differences across campus—others supported hotel's position, but for their own reasons—in reversing the policy in part. The final decision came almost one year later, December, 1983. Continuing education was given primary responsibility for travel and tour activity, but individual offices could request exceptions:

> "In the case of those College of Hotel Administration faculty who specialize in teaching travel and tourism, the approval [for the exception] is likely to be granted unless there is compelling reason not to do so."[3]

Credit courses, particularly the summer in Europe, continued under the college's jurisdiction.

As each calendar year closed, the college estimated the number of persons going overseas during the following calendar year so the business office could purchase liability insurance. Fortunately, there never was a call on the university's liability coverage. Accidental injury, medical services or emergency evacuation were personal expenses.

> There were [among the students] the usual sprains and colds. Most of them were covered by parent's insurance. Students paid their bills and submitted the medical receipts when we got back home.   IZZOLO

A WORLD VIEW

No one was really certain whether the college's international presence came from the growing number of international students or whether the international students came from the college's international presence. Whichever, the possibility of becoming an international player dawned early with the support of the Nevada Resort Association.

The Japanese YMCA

A telephone call setting up a meeting was received from Robbins Cahill, executive officer of the NRA, shortly after the college was established. Over lunch, an introduction was made to representatives from the Tokyo YMCA, which offered courses in hotel management. Would UNLV's hotel program be interested in working with and hosting the group during its annual summer visit to the United States? Western stops were made before the group headed East to its religious retreat in the Blue Ridge Mountains. Correspondence with Tokyo began. Agreements were finalized about the academic program and about the mechanical arrangements: where to live; where to eat; bus transportation; recreation; costs and payment; etc.

During the YMCA's first summer visit, we brought The NRA's Robbins Cahill and University President Jay Zorn to welcome the class. Six months later, Toshio Mohri, YMCA's executive, flew back to Las Vegas to tell me over dinner—Japanese culture did not believe something as sensitive should be put in writing—that if we had such important people welcoming their group, courtesy required them to bring a similar top delegation. That meant additional costs. No special welcoming was used thereafter.

The opening session always involved gift giving. In Japan, one never opens gifts in the presence of the giver. There was a big in-take of breath when we opened our gifts at once and invited the class to do the same. That was the format thereafter.   JERRY VALLEN

And so began a warm, three-decade relationship.

UNLV prepared special, one-week courses for us. Yesterday, the Tokyo YMCA told me that they have been coming continuously for over 25 years. Las Vegas was a dreamland for the students. After class they hurried to the casinos. It was difficult for them to stay awake the next day. On departure many said to me, May I borrow some money.   TOSHIO MOHRI, HEAD OF THE TOKYO YMCA'S HOTEL STUDIES

It was difficult to teach the group because one had to stop for the translation. Momentum was lost. The first year the students seemed to be staring at the ceiling. There was no response to my best jokes. I thought this was my worst lecture ever. Later we learned the American-born interpreter couldn't speak modern Japanese! Sessions were great after we fixed that.   IZZOLO

The Japanese seminar was a very excellent program. I still correspond with Toshio Mohri, who has retired also.   DICK BASILE, HOTEL FACULTY MEMBER

The seminar increased occupancy at the dormitory during the downtimes of the summers and brought critical revenue to the university's food service. It widened the reach of the University into the Pacific Basin, which became a major revenue source for the entire campus. Of course, it generated income for participating faculty members. On a margin note (dated December 27, 1971) granting permission to proceed, President Zorn termed the venture a boondoggle for hotel faculty to make extra money. A decision was made to take the project off campus until the incumbent president left.

[There was a brief period when] the YMCA stopped coming for a bit so we brought them back with a well timed letter. They are always a very respectful group, but we were careful to balance Strip activities with classroom work.   STUTTS

One of the disappointing years was caused by hepatitis that the group picked up in Hawaii, a previous stop. The treating physician, Elias Ghanem, ordered the group not to use a pool. So we had the barbeque at my home as usual but without the usual swim.   JERRY VALLEN

Dominican Republic

In response to President Reagan's Caribbean Basin Initiative, which followed the U.S. intervention in Grenada, the United States Agency for International Development (USAID) requested the College of Hotel Administration to bid on a project in the Dominican Republic (DR). Developing tourism in the Caribbean required a cadre of qualified managers, or so the reasoning went. The specific objective was the invigoration of the hotel program at the Catholic University (La Universidad Catolica Madre Y Maestra) in the DR. The Catholic University, but not its hotel program, was a tad older than the hotel college; it celebrated its 25th anniversary during the contact period.

It was the college's first bid for a governmental contract. Colleagues across campus explained that the format and content of the college's grant request were not standard, but then again, neither was the project. Beam Hall was new, faculty specialization was broad, and Las Vegas was attractive to the on-site visitors, both those from USAID in Washington and those from the DR. It was obvious at once that UNLV would beat out the several other significant bidders. And it did, hands down. A *Review-Journal* editorial read in part:

> "The D.R. has suffered from an image problem . . . [which] has worked against [it] in its effort to attract tourism and much-needed foreign trade.
>
> Now, UNLV has been called to the rescue.
>
> UNLV's [College of Hotel Administration] will use the money to provide training and consultation. . . .
>
> This grant is the first of its kind in State Department history. . . .
>
> All this speaks very highly of the caliber of UNLV's College of Hotel Administration."

The contract required a Spanish-speaking faculty member so the search went nationwide.

We found a Spanish-speaking, hospitality faculty member who was known to a graduate of ours. Don't hire him, I was warned on the telephone! But the field was limited and we did, much to our sorrow. It was the only time I ignored recommendations from persons I knew.   JERRY VALLEN

After several months of covering for him—the least of the problems was that he really didn't speak Spanish, the American consulate helped Alan Stutts package up this new appointment and ship him back to the States. Enter Vince Eade from the Aladdin Hotel, another industry executive opting for education. Eade completed the assignment in style with accolades from the two partners and success in accomplishing the goals. He then joined the resident faculty.

President Maxson and his wife, Sylvia, traveled with the Vallens and Alan Stutts on a long airplane ride to celebrate the on-going success of the venture. Maxson gave up several days, although the plan was originally an overnight, to attend ceremonies because the two presidents, Bob Maxson and Monsignor Nunez of the Catholic University, knew one another from previous dealings when Maxson was at the University of Houston.

> It was not an auspicious beginning. The airline bumped us, and it took a lot of talking—This is the president of the university—to get us aboard. On a different leg, they moved the Maxsons to first class. When Vallen said How come I didn't get moved up? I knew this trip was going to be . . . [trouble].   STUTTS

New equipment, especially kitchen equipment, lectures on site, course development and more went into the project. Faculty members were dispatched to the DR for on-site advice and seminars for local hoteliers. And, of course, Vince Eade was in full-time residence.

> I made the trip twice and both times did sessions on sanitation. I showed a sanitation film in Spanish. The class was talking about it and taking notes and writing. I didn't understand one word of it, and I was the instructor.   AL IZZOLO, HOTEL FACULTY MEMBER

> It was my first exposure to a third-world country. One afternoon I was showing a film when the power went off. I had been warned that it might go off. There was dead silence, everyone just sat and waited. No one complained; no one got up; no one walked around; no one left.   CLAUDE LAMBERTZ, HOTEL FACULTY MEMBER

At the insistence of the hotel college, which wanted to assure a continuity of some kind, the contract required qualified faculty to be left in place. Three outstanding Dominican students took up residence in the graduate program of the college. They were funded by the contract and returned to the Dominican Republic as new, dynamic faculty members. One member, Oscar Gomez (MS '89), married another international student, Ute Birkmeier ('88). They moved to the Dominican Republic but eventually settled in Germany, Ute's homeland. Oscar wrote on May 25, 1994: "We keep very good memories of our UNLV years. I also remember the Bar-B-Q party held at your house to which I was invited together with the other two Dominican graduate students [Niurca (Ruth) Almonte and Tony Alvarez]."

International Gaming

After gaming went nationwide across the United States there were fewer and fewer calls for introductory presentations like those in Atlantic City. The college's center shifted emphasis and began catering to management seminars for gaming executives from around the world.

> We had groups coming from Australia, Japan and Korea for gaming seminars. They invited me back there as well. Jim Henry lead the Australian club group, which came for many years. Paradise Gaming [Korea] sent 10–15 executives once every other month for 3-week sessions. STUTTS

> I taught several courses as continuing education. I recall one in marketing for the Showboat and one for the Korean casino managers. They liked the fact that I spoke Korean.   KAYE CHON, GRADUATE STUDENT AND HOTEL FACULTY MEMBER

> I taught gaming for Bernard Gehri at the Swiss school that UNLV worked with in Glion. At the time, they had a national plebiscite on the issue. I spoke to the media and the press and the industry. When it passed, they called me back to help with the research.   LEO LEWIS, BINION'S FINANCIAL OFFICER, BUT FULL-TIME FACULTY MEMBER AT THIS TIME

International Linkage

As the college became a destination for overseas students, it became desirable for the college to establish itself overseas. A decision was made to accept an invitation from EUHOFA (Association Internationale des Directeurs d'Écoles Hotelieres), the European equivalent of CHRIE. The dean represented North America on an international panel that met over three days in Montreal, Canada. It was a lively debate under the title of *European Traditions and American Technology: Are They Compatible?* Following that introduction, the college began attending EUHOFA's annual meetings, although it never became a member.

> EUHOFA's 1988 meeting was held in Holland, where the group was taken to an indoor lobster farm. We rode on a barge to the center of this very dark barn. When we attempted to step back on the dock, Jerry fell into the pond pulling me in. We were lifted out and dried off: one of us by an Israeli and the other by a Palestinian. Everyone was laughing. Others fell in and went back to the hotel. We stayed—the proprietor provided warm clothing—but we missed the English-speaking bus, so we rode back with the German delegation. Three years later, we met a German couple at the New York Hotel Show. We know you they said uncertainly. Suddenly it dawned on them, You're the couple that fell into the lobster pond!   FLOSSIE VALLEN

EUHOFA offered marvelous contacts for the hotel college as well as some uncertain ones. Privately owned schools wanted to build closer relationships with UNLV. Uncertainty about academic quality caused misgivings among faculty members. Besides, the college was preoccupied elsewhere. President Maxson had approved the concept of international linkage with UNLV's ties to La Universidad Catolica Madre y Maestra in the Dominican Republic. Building on that, new international relationships were developed. One was in Korea.

The first contacts in Korea came during the dean's assignment for the U.S. Department of Commerce. Visits were made to Korean hotels, restaurants, purveyors, trade associations and schools. Similar trips to Malta, the Caribbean, Cypress, Peru and Australia by the dean and other faculty members widened UNLV's visibility across the globe. The Korean contacts eventually led to a sister-school arrangement with Kyung Hee University in Seoul, Korea (1984).

> The college had negotiated an agreement with Kyung Hee. But nothing had happened. When I became a grad student we started a dialogue again.   CHON

> Students rioted during one of our Korean visits. It was a nonevent until the military showed up and fired tear gas. I was hit, broke my glasses, and caused untold embarrassment for our hosts.   FLOSSIE VALLEN

> It was a memorable visit. Flossie had tears from the gas. The president's office was to be occupied so we were taken to a hotel. But the students were actually laughing and smiling at us.   CHON

> A friend of Kaye Chon's loaned us his car in Seoul. We gave his chauffeur a set of silver proof coins to pass on as a way of saying thanks. In an hour, he returned with an expensive lacquer box with cups. Kaye warned us not to accelerate the gift giving because there was no end to one-up-manship in this kind of exchange.   FLOSSIE VALLEN

Similar school visits were made by Alan Stutts (1988) in setting the groundwork for a Chinese affiliation with Hangzhou University in the city of the same name. Negotiations were also begun to establish an arrangement with a university in Egypt. Don Baepler, who was by now in the Harry Reid Center/Marjorie Barrick Museum, brought the hotel college into those negotiations, but they never panned out.

Summers in Switzerland

Like so many other adventures undertaken by the college, the summer semester abroad greatly exceeded every one's expectations. The beginning was much like others—talk. Real progress came after Pat Moreo and Dave Christianson had conversations in the Spring of 1978 with the college's visiting professor from Britain, Rik Medlik. After which,

> Dave and I flew to England on our own money—well, Vallen was able to get us something. We flew Freddie Laker Air at $99 each way. Talk about England, they made our bureaucracy look like kindergarten. I told Dave he should do it himself because I could never work with them and finish my doctorate at the same time. He said, I am going to wait until you're done, and he did.   MOREO

Discussions were renewed after Moreo finished his degree. A focus group composed of UNLV students who had gone overseas with Florida State University's program (directed by Ashby Stiff) helped finalize the plans. Christianson and Moreo knew Europe because both had been there for extended periods: Christianson on a mission and Moreo with the U.S. navy.

> When CHRIE [Council of Hotel Restaurant and Institutional Education] met in Vegas, I had a drink with a Swiss educator who asked, Why go to England? Come to Switzerland, to our school in Lausanne. Next thing we know plans are taking shape to escort 20 students. Vallen said, Don't lose money and don't disgrace us. In the meantime, Frank Brown had joined the faculty and had gone to Europe to study French. He did all the prep work: found us hotels in France; visited the school; tested the itinerary. He came back and pumped up the student body. We enrolled 65 the first year!   MOREO

Frank Brown, Dave Christianson and Pat Moreo led that first year's group (in 1983) to the École Hotelier Lausanne (Hotel School at Lausanne) in a program that grew more popular with each passing year. Several non-UNLV students, primarily from New York, accompanied the first class. The interaction was so positive that UNLV students were limited thereafter to 50% of the group.

> Enrollment reached 92 in the year we had [students from] 15 other programs represented.   AL IZZOLO, HOTEL FACULTY MEMBER

A warm camaraderie grew among the schools, and UNLV's reputation got another big boost in the eyes of the nation's hotel student body.

> Students heard about the overseas summer before they even came [to UNLV]. They built it into their plans: Mom said I could go next year.   IZZOLO

More faculty were needed as enrollment grew. An informal rotation began to give everyone a chance.

> Vallen kept putting me on the list until my turn came up. I used to think it was a Mickey Mouse thing. But it was a great learning program; very worthwhile. A tremendous service that we have and one that should not be stopped. I can think of no other opportunity where I interacted more with students.   LESLIE CUMMINGS, HOTEL FACULTY MEMBER

Even non-student/local residents and adjunct faculty participated. For example, Muriel Stevens, a strong supporter and adjunct faculty member, taught the summer of 1988.

> Dave [Christianson] and Pat [Moreo] started it, but Frank [Brown, hotel faculty member] was in from the beginning. Then he left UNLV. I went over the first time in 1986. When Pat left, Dave and I were the organizers. Don Bell and I after Dave became Dean.
>   I recall we took [faculty members] Cummings, Metcalf and Stutts among others.   IZZOLO

Visiting faculty from other programs also came and taught; it was an incentive for enrolling students from their own campuses.

I remember joking that I would go if there was need for support staff. And one year there was. It was a wonderful trip. The students loved it and they learned a lot about international tourism and foreign cuisine. On weekends we went to France and Italy.   JOAN REYNOLDS BEITZ, ADMINISTRATIVE ASSISTANT

The format was developed by trial and error but settled into a program of three to four days on campus and three to four days of travel. Too much travel impacted on budgets because room and meals were provided on campus but not elsewhere. Rail passes and Switzerland's central location minimized the disruption normally caused by travel. Three days on the road required minimal luggage. France, Italy, Germany and Switzerland were easily accommodated. Trips to England and Spain required an extra few days. Learning came as much from the travel as from the classroom.

Moreo would arrange for a bus to bring the summer class to Castello Banfi in Montalcino Tuscany, where Banfi had 7,300 acres. We would arrange a tour and a dinner [at the vineyard].   RICHARD BROWN, DONOR INTERMEDIARY AND FATHER OF ALUMNUS, GARY

We took one trip to Italy to find the grave site of Moreo's family. This tombstone said, Died in this battle; another said Died in that battle. All of Moreo's family were identified as chefs; none died in battle. We were in stitches! Pat said they were all too short for military service.   CUMMINGS

Pat Moreo arranged a dinner at a restaurant that specialized in snails. When we came out the Vallens and the Abbeys lagged behind and entered the Paris subway after everyone had gone. It's this way Jerry said. No, this way I said. We ended up on opposite platforms in the Metro, but the Abbeys were on the wrong side. Colleen and I left, followed the signs and expected to join the Vallens momentarily. They waited. Yes, there they were. But we were again on the wrong side, the same side that we had just left. Plenty of laughing followed.   JIM ABBEY, HOTEL FACULTY MEMBER

Jim Abbey and I made joint travel arrangements several times. The rooms assigned to the Abbeys were always better than ours. I knew I would beat him when we held classes in Hawaii during that university's summer executive program. I knew the hotel manager and he upgraded Flossie and me. Jim took me to his and Colleen's room! It was bigger and had a better ocean-view!   JERRY VALLEN

Flights to Switzerland were scheduled round trip from New York City and then by bus and auto to the school.

When we arrived Frank Brown had flowers for Julie [Christianson] and me. We rode the bus for a while before it ran out of gas. The driver went for gas and we sat for a long time before he returned. It was very late when we finally arrived. The room was beautiful and the air smelled sweet. We heard the distant cow bells.   REYNOLDS BEITZ

> When we arrived, Moreo asked me to drive a small bus. It was a gear shift vehicle and the hills were steep. I know he had set me up for a problem. But he didn't know that I had learned to drive long before automatic transmission.   JERRY VALLEN

Money was always an issue because there was no fall-back position to a state budget. The adventure had to finance itself. Each summer's planning required special attention to the fluctuating value of the Swiss franc versus the U.S. dollar. That was learned in the very first year. The U.S. dollar grew so strong that a refund was made to each participant. Better still, the remaining surplus was used to acquire the college's first PCs.

> Soon after my appointment [1981] I became the dean's computer consultant. First we moved from electric typewriters to DeckMates [predecessor to the computer]. When the colleges were given *Ability* [a software package], we went door to door to see how many of the 14 faculty members wanted computers. There were just a few. I turned in a budget and it was funded. We also had a few Macs that the company donated. [And so the computer lab began.]   CUMMINGS

Costs were the other part of the break-even equation. During the campus-wide debate about hotel's role in overseas travel (see above), someone insisted that the college bid for the group airfare to Switzerland. Purchase orders of that magnitude were supposed to be put our for bid. Prior to that, hotel had negotiated directly with the Swiss discount carrier, which even threw in free seats for faculty spouses.

> With the discount carrier, negotiations were over the telephone. Changes in departure times and dates were made to accommodate the carrier's empty space and gain the best price. Bid formats made no such provisions. I went to Herman Westfall [vice president for business] and he helped us achieve the best price by supporting our arrangement of direct negotiations.   MOREO

UNLV was romanced by other Swiss schools. Some wanted the summer business, some wanted transfer credits for their students, and some wanted UNLV faculty. Hotel professors began one-term visits at the International Center for Hotel Management at Glion, near Montreaux in 1984. Chapter 10 tells that story.

U.S. Department of Commerce

UNLV's reputation as an international program spread quickly and broadly. Hotel's large international student body was a positive fixture on the Las Vegas campus. From a recommendation by the editor of one of the trade magazines, the college was approached by the U.S. Department of Commerce. Commerce needed informed, but independent representatives to host international catalog exhibits of U.S.-made hotel and food equipment. Under that umbrella, Vallen went to approximately 20 countries from Aruba to Yugoslavia. Once Commerce was satisfied with the single performance, other faculty members took up the task, which was to show the U.S. flag as much as it was to hawk American goods. During the school year 1983–1984, Richard Basile went to the Mediterranean.

> I went to Cypress right after the civil war between Turkish and Greek supporters. I went in a jeep under diplomatic pass between the two sides. It felt pretty good. I spoke to the Cypress Hotel Association and had lunch at their hotel school. The hotels were fabulous and the luncheon just wonderful. I sent the school boxes of texts. A friend of mine was on President Reagan's staff so the Indian ambassador to Cypress thought I was important and invited me to lunch, which I reciprocated at Rotary when he visited Las Vegas soon thereafter.   BASILE

> The Commerce Department needed someone to go to Panama and Peru. I spoke a bit of Spanish so I was chosen. Alan Garcia had just won the first free election in Peru. Soldiers and tanks were everywhere. The black market was so big that even the wipers were stolen off the diplomatic car. So when the rain came, the car was wrecked in the middle of the street at two in the morning. The only others on the street were military. I was certain I would be shot. Later, when I was getting ready for bed shouting began on the street. I open the doors of my suite and stepped onto the balcony. There was a huge crowd. I felt like Juan Peron standing on his balcony, only in my underwear.
>
> As I left the U.S. ambassador gave me a rug as a gift, which caused problems when I disembarked in Panama. A sniffer dog accompanied by an armed soldier had my suitcase in hand. They let me through when I explained I was a guest of the U.S. ambassador. Later in the hotel room I found my shoes with distinct dog bites on top of the rug, which must have had some residue from the weaver.   STUTTS

> We went to Jamaica right after their revolution. The hotel grounds were surrounded by barbed wire and patrolled by armed guards and dogs. Don't leave the enclave we were warned unless you know your guides.   FLOSSIE VALLEN

International activities such as these augmented the college's academic offerings and broaden the background of the faculty in delivering their basic assignments, which are examined further in the next chapters.

ENDNOTES FOR CHAPTER 9

1. "Chapter D, Hotel Administration," *1980 Accreditation Report*. pp. 28–29.
2. The college attempted unsuccessfully to leverage its contacts in China by proposing a consulting arrangement with Jim Hynes, vice president of Inter-Continental Hotels, which was contemplating an early foothold in the People's Republic.
3. Goodall's memorandum to John Unrue, [now] Interim Academic Vice President, *et al.*, dated December 14, 1983.

The College: Its Faculty and Staff

The hotel college's reputation for excellence was earned by a faculty and staff that were extremely capable, loyal, dedicated and innovative; and from a body of undergraduates and alumni with energy, motivation, personality and enthusiasm. What was done individually and jointly contributed immeasurably to the distinction and success of the program as well as to the benefit of the individual participants.

Since the college's philosophy made the student the customer,[1] one might assume the faculty members would be the front-line employees who delivered the services. Not exactly; the faculty were far more than that. By their work and example, faculty members became the actual product to be delivered. They were the exemplars that the students carried away. Faculty demeanor and recognition of the student as an individual person ranked high on the list of faculty requirements. Dress was part of that profile. Although there was no dress code, the dean spoke to faculty when necessary and the administrative assistant, Joan Reynolds Beitz, monitored the staff.

> The subject of dress was part of the topic of management. Students held a contest to see if I could go the entire term without wearing the same outfit twice. I won a pair of white gloves as a reward. Still, the emphasis was clear: dress for the interviews and dress for the job. Today, that has changed. And that simple fact explains why a good faculty member needs to be constantly changing class content.   DICK BASILE, HOTEL FACULTY MEMBER

Basile always looked as if he had just stepped out of a bandbox; dressed very nicely.   REYNOLDS BEITZ

REGULAR FACULTY[2]

The rich diversity of the faculty enabled the college to build a reputation for quality and specialization, but that specialization took time. Faculty members were stretched at first, often called upon to teach outside their specialties.

We taught everything back then. I taught maintenance and engineering [marketing is Abbey's specialty], the intro class, tourism, anything.

My very first semester was tough! Levinson took ill—he was sick quite a bit—and I had to take over in the middle of the semester. What a mess. I had to learn all the meat slides [meat cuts and their names] for that food course.   JIM ABBEY, HOTEL FACULTY MEMBER

Other than Levinson's bad heart, faculty members were healthy and rarely missed class. Basile never took a day off, and never took sick leave in 18 years.

I remember Levinson crawling up on the table and telling us the cuts of beef by drawing pictures on himself. It was hilarious especially when he got to the rump roast!   ANN RITTAL, '81 STUDENT

In 1987 I went to the dean and pointed out that I was mediocre in three areas: nutrition, purchasing and computers. I needed to be relieved of one. He chose computers.   LESLIE CUMMINGS, HOTEL FACULTY MEMBER

Once I had to teach human relations, which wasn't my cup of tea.   BASILE

We had light loads, *just* four courses per semester. I tried to be a good player, but when someone bailed out and I was asked to teach marketing, I said I'd rather teach foods.   PAT MOREO, '69 STUDENT AND FACULTY MEMBER

Growth in size and a judicious use of local professionals as part-time teaching staff permitted faculty members to concentrate and develop the expertise that brought the industry, as well as new students, to the door. The negatives caused by increasing class sizes were offset by the positives from increasing sizes. Faculty specialization was one of those gains. So as the student body grew so did the college's capabilities.

Size enabled us to become better teachers and researchers, but we lost the closeness that we had as a small faculty.   ABBEY

One big advantage of size is a spread of name and fame. It was necessary to play the numbers game. More student credits generated more positions. The bigger the better so long as student quality remained high.   FRANK BORSENIK, HOTEL FACULTY MEMBER

Before I left [UNLV] for Virginia Tech [to get a doctorate] there were 800 students and 20 full-time faculty. When I came back [with degree in hand], there were 1,600 students and 40 faculty.   KAYE CHON, GRADUATE STUDENT AND FACULTY MEMBER

A lot of things that were institutionalized became more complicated to manage [as size increased]. Unfortunately, some felt that the way to solve the problem was to discontinue the activity.

But size just places a greater emphasis on effective management.   JERRY GOLL, HOTEL FACULTY MEMBER

I've never been a proponent of quantity; I'd rather have quality. A state school with open admission doesn't accommodate one over the other. Quantity gets more recognition and more money.   BASILE

Early Faculty Chronology

As reported in previous chapters, George Bussel, Boyce Phillips and Jerry Vallen were on hand at the start, in 1967. Dick Strahlem, who had been temporary head of the budding program, remained in the business college.

We [the earliest students] had a little song about Bussel, "Hustle, don't tussle, here comes Bussel."   MOREO

What song did you have for Vallen? **Jerry Vallen**
I don't remember. **Moreo**
Yes you do. **Vallen**

There was no real organizational structure, but B. W. Phillips, puffing on his pipe, was the Father Confessor. I don't know how he got any work done. There was a stream of students in and out all day.   MOREO

Ten years later, Boyce Phillips moved to an A-contract (12-months) to supplement the college's only other administrator, the dean, whose span of control was stretched by a booming enrollment.

Boyce was a good PR man who got along well with people across campus.   BORSENIK

When Phillips moved to a 12-month contract, he always stayed until 5 p.m. and never left without clearing his departure. Formal vacation dates were the only times he missed.   JERRY VALLEN

Boyce was a straight shooter. That was his character. Once he said something, it was in stone.   SARI PHILLIPS AIZLEY, SPOUSE OF B. W. PHILLIPS

Phillips was Vallen's partner-in-crime. Always there to support; never there to upstage.   MOREO

In succession came Lothar Kreck, February, 1968 (hired sight unseen from an industry assignment in India); John (Jack) Rudd, 1970 (hired sight unseen from a director's assignment at the College of the Virgin Islands after 25 years of service with Statler Hotels) and Robert (Bob) Catron, 1970 (owner/publisher/editor of an industry trade journal). Each made contributions over a brief period before moving on (see Exhibit 10-1).

Faculty Member	Arrival Date	Departure Date	Comments
Abbey, Jim	1973	*	Retired 2000
Acosta, Dick	1970	1972	
Baltin, Bruce	1968	1970	
Basile, Dick	1970	1988	
Bell, Don	1981	*	
Borsenik, Frank	1975	*	Retired 1994
Brown, Frank	1980	1986	
Bussel, George	1967	1969	
Carey, Regan	1986	1987	Went to business college
Catron, Bob	1970	1973	
Christianson, Dave	1977	*	College's second dean
Cox, Suad	1987	*	Left campus 1995
Cummings, Leslie	1981 & 1983	*	Retired 2000
Douglas, Dale	1982	1983	
Eade, Vincent	1986	*	
Gaston, Jolie	1988	*	Left campus 2000
Goll, Jerry	1986	*	Retired 2000
Goodwin, John	1980	*	Retired 1993
Izzolo, Al	1976	*	
Kilby, Jim	1986	*	Returned to industry
Kreck, Lothar	1968	1970	
Lambertz, Claude	1984	*	
Laughlin, Richard	1980	1985	
Levinson, Charlie	1970	1989	Deceased 1989

*On staff in 1988, the concluding date of this history.

EXHIBIT 10-1. Alphabetical listing of faculty in the College of Hotel Administration during the period 1967 through 1988.

Faculty Member	Arrival Date	Departure Date	Comments
Manago, Gary	1988	1990	
Martin, Bob	1979	1997	Deceased 1997
McGowan, Lori	1984	1988	
Melton, Hank ('78)	1985	*	Left campus 1990
Metcalf, Lyell	1979	*	Retired 1994
Moore, Bob	1971	1977	Went to business college
Moreo, Pat ('69)	1975	1988	
Pederson, Betsy Bender	1987	*	Left campus 1991
Phillips, Boyce	1967	*	Retired 1994; Deceased
Quain, Bill	1983	1985	Spent 1 year with business
Rand, Claude	1977	*	Retired 1993
Roehl, Wes	1988	*	Left campus 1999
Rudd, Jack	1970	1974	
Sackler, Ellliot	1977	1978	
Sapienza, Dunnovan	1973	1981	
Shirer, Curt	1974	1977	Returned 1993–1995
Shock, Patty	1988	*	
Stefanelli, John	1978	*	
Stutts, Alan	1983	*	Left campus 1993
Swerdlow, Skip	1981	*	From business college
Vallen, Jerry	1967	*	Retired 1998
Von Kornfeld, Joe	1982	1987	
Wynia, Terry	1976	1978	

*On staff in 1988, the concluding date of this history.

EXHIBIT 10-1 (CONTINUED). Alphabetical listing of faculty in the College of Hotel Administration during the period 1967 through 1988.

Jack Rudd had an office next to mine. It was embarrassing that he would give whatever grade the student asked for. ABBEY

Jack Rudd was called 'Honest John.' He brought wonderful stories from his days with Statler Hotels. GARY BROWN, '73 STUDENT

The faculty doffed coats in the summer, but not ties. All except Lothar Kreck who came in buttoned up in suits that fit like a glove. The dean must have had a chat with Kreck after a student delegation, which probably was headed by Lynn Waring ('69), visited because one day he came in a sport shirt and open collar and the whole tone of the class had changed.

Lothar pushed systems and I learned that from him. He and I became friends and years later he wrote an important recommendation for me.   MOREO

The next wave of faculty brought Bruce Baltin, 1968 (a recent Cornell graduate student); Richard (Dick) Basile, 1970, (vice president of the Davries Division of ARA, now ARAMARK, in Philadelphia and a previous colleague of Kreck's at Paul Smith's College where Basile served as administrative dean); and Charles (Charlie) Levinson, 1970 (a former country club manager and faculty member at Indiana State, Indiana, Pennsylvania).

Baltin had left [for a position with Pannel, Kerr, Foster] just before I came and Kreck also [to pursue a doctoral degree at Denver]. Lothar likes to say I replaced him. Phillips hosted us to dinner, and I talked him into a show. I don't think the interview fund had budgeted a show, so I paid for it.   BASILE

The university didn't even pay your travel costs if I recall, right?   VALLEN

Marcel Ambrezewicz ('72) attended the 1984 alumni homecoming, which celebrated the opening of Beam Hall. He wrote afterwards citing three of these faculty members for their personal contributions to his well being and concluded that:

"It was also reassuring to note that today's students are still being exposed to the likes of Basile, Levinson and Phillips."

Robert (Bob) Moore (comptroller Shakey's Restaurants) replaced Bruce Baltin in 1971. He would be the first hotel faculty member to pursue a terminal degree while holding his full-time assignment. As the college did later with others, it contributed to Moore's effort by special scheduling so he could drive to class in California, by relief from committee assignments and by a lighter teaching load.

Bob Moore moved to business because he had finished his Ph.D. and was looking for a business school appointment. So I spoke to Vallen and he said, Moore is a good man; let's keep him on campus.   GEORGE HARDBECK, DEAN OF BUSINESS AND ECONOMICS

James (Jim) Abbey, a 1973 appointment, replaced Richard (Dick) Acosta (1970–72). Both were Michigan State University alumni. The faculty and the curriculum offerings were strengthened still further in 1973 by the arrival of Dunnovan (Dunn) Sapienza, a former faculty member at Florida State University and the college's first terminal-degree holder. He, too, was hired sight unseen. Both parties take risks in doing that, but the college never suffered because the reputation of the new hires preceded them. Hotel education is, after all, a small discipline.

My husband, Dunn, was finishing an assignment with the United Nation's Food Organization in Bombay. We lived on the fifth floor and the one telephone was on the first floor. Although there was an elevator, no one was brave enough to ride it. So one of the hotel's staff ran up five flights and I ran down five flights to speak with Jerry when he called. The conversation between continents was perfectly clear. The local call relaying the information to Dunn required a great deal of shouting. Soon everyone knew that we were taking the job in Las Vegas.   CAROL SAPIENZA

Two Aggies vied for the one position that opened in tourism in 1974. Both Curt Shirer and David (Dave) Christianson applied from Texas A&M. Always thinking about money, the dean decided to make one flight to Texas rather than having them make two flights to Las Vegas. Both applicants were hired, but not simultaneously. Shirer had his doctorate in hand and won the initial bid. When he left three years later, Christianson, who had completed his degree by then, filled the vacancy. Christianson would later become the college's second dean. With Shirer and Christianson came terminal degree number two.

The final leg of the trip to College Station was in a small commuter plane. I was sitting to the pilot's right. Anyone meeting you he asked? When he learned there was no one, he radioed for a cab to meet me. No wonder they both wanted out.   JERRY VALLEN

Two stalwart faculty members added strength to the faculty in 1975. Frank Borsenik came in the spring term 1975, as the calendar year began. Patrick (Pat) Moreo, a graduate of the program's first class,1969, returned in September 1975 at the start of the traditional school year, 1975–76.[3] Moreo returned with several years of valuable industry experience and a new master's degree from Cornell's hotel school. Frank Borsenik's appointment came five years after his first visit and interview (see Chapter 3). He was terminal degree number three among permanent faculty, but number four counting Dr. Lendal Kotschevar's visiting status.

I was giving a seminar [for the Educational Institute of the AH&MA] in Phoenix. We [with wife, Ann] drove over and shopped housing with the realtor that had been arranged for us. Jerry came and gave us his opinion of the two houses that we had selected.   BORSENIK

Alfred (Al) Izzolo (who brought food industry experience) and Terry Wynia (who brought hotel industry experience) joined the college for the 1976–77 school year.

I assumed that the hotel college was responsible for the campus food service. That was my experience on other campuses. [Izzolo was Western district manager, Arizona to Hawaii, of ARA.] During one of my student recruiting trips to Vegas, I said, Consider me if the food service director's spot opens. I was surprised when the offer came to teach. I had taught high school, but felt that staying three to four years at a senior college would look good on my resume. [At interview time, Izzolo's tenure had stretched to 25 years.] The job actually paid more than I was getting. Jerry didn't know that.   IZZOLO

By 1976–77, ten years after the program started, and one year before the director's title was renamed dean, the catalog listed ten full-time positions. They were Abbey, Basile, Borsenik, Kotschevar, Levinson, Moore, Phillips, Sapienza, Shirer and Vallen. Catalog identification is never completely accurate because it goes to print long before the new fall term's employment process is complete. For example, Al Izzolo and Terry Wynia were newly appointed, but not listed in the 1976–77 catalog.

Faculty Recruitment

An acute shortage of desirable applicants combined with rapid growth was exacerbated by the salary policy adopted by the dean. New hires had to fall within the present salary range of current faculty.

> It's a dilemma. It creates difficult problems if you do that [pay outside the salary norms] for one person [and not for the other].   KAYE CHON, GRADUATE STUDENT AND FACULTY MEMBER

Senior faculty were not to be displaced in the salary schedule by unknown new hires with similar qualifications. Neither were new hires ever brought in with tenure.

> I took a big cut in pay when I came and I didn't get tenure until the following year [Borsenik had been a tenured, full-professor at Michigan State].
>
> I remember when one person came to see Vallen about another job offer he had had. Jerry got up and shook hands and said, Congratulations on your new job. Never made a higher counter offer.   BORSENIK

> The initial salary was embarrassingly low. Vallen said if you are as good as you say, I'll make it up to you. I was and he did.   JERRY GOLL, HOTEL FACULTY MEMBER

> Mike Olsen offered me tenure at Virginia Tech when I finished my Ph.D. So I was an assistant professor with tenure for two months before coming to UNLV, [after Vallen retired] where I gave up the tenure but was promoted to associate professor with four years toward tenure.
>
> Two prospective candidates [to Houston's program] recently turned us down for higher salaries at UNLV [after Vallen retired]. Salary negotiations are like buying cars. They [the faculty recruit] will say a number, but you don't have to pay that number. That's the starting point.   CHON

New faculty members continued coming, strengthening the organization.

> I had taught a small bit as a favor to a friend at North Carolina State. Maybe that's how UNLV and I connected; I don't remember. But the dean was very persistent, kept calling, especially when he learned I could teach property management, saying, You ought at least to come and visit. That was 1983.   ALAN STUTTS, HOTEL FACULTY MEMBER

With so new a program, almost every hire was "the first" something. Cummings the first woman; Sapienza the first terminal degree; Moore the first hired from a nontraditional source—at least for hotel programs—*The Wall Street Journal*; Borsenik the first hired as a full professor; Moreo the first alumnus; Basile, the first previous acquaintance.

Henry (Hank) Melton was another first: the first black faculty member and the first to be recruited by a faculty member going on leave, Pat Moreo. Melton came in 1985 because Moreo wanted a leave-of-absence that year. Approval had one condition: Moreo had to find his own replacement. Melton, an alumnus of 1978, did such a good job that he stayed on in his own budget line after Moreo's return.

Claude Rand joined the hotel faculty in 1977 after a big bon-voyage party from former associates at TWA. Elliott Sackler, another Cornellian, came that same year. A bit of musical chairs took place because Sackler assumed Bob Moore's budget line when Moore transferred to the business faculty. But Sackler's stay was quite brief. He left in May of 1978 to work for Caesars Palace. Six months later, the accounting position was filled by Lyell Metcalf. Metcalf came in the winter of 1979, from a controller's position with the Travelodge chain in California.

The summer issue of *Federation Of Hoteliers UNLV* (the alumni association's quarterly publication) reported the 1979 arrival of Robert (Bob) Martin, who had been managing a motor inn in the Midwest.

> Bob Martin really surprised me. He was excellent! Always well prepared.   BORSENIK

> Bob was a navy man [Basile was another] and that made him a friend. He was a great organizer who did his job well. Many students came to see me to talk about other professors. None ever complained about Bob Martin.   BASILE

Student growth was staggering in some years. More hires were needed even as some faculty positions such as Moore and Sackler turned over. Bill Quain, who had come in the winter of 1983, left to teach in Florida, but first spent a transitory year (1985–86) with UNLV's College of Business. Regan Carey (a 1986–87 appointee) also switched to business (computers) after one year balanced later by Skip Swerdlow's switch, 1988, from business to hotel. Swerdlow was a restauranteur as well as an educator. He came to know Izzolo, Stefanelli and Vallen through their common interests, specifically Swerdlow's position as a member of the Board of Directors of the Nevada Restaurant Association.

> Vallen interviewed me over lunch in my restaurant. Coming to hotel was the best decision I made in my professional life.   SKIP SWERDLOW, HOTEL FACULTY MEMBER

Dale Douglas, a non-practicing attorney, was appointed as a casino instructor, but left within a year because of poor health. Terry Wynia returned to industry in 1978 after two successful teaching years. Joe von Kornfeld was a 1982–1983 addition; Alan Stutts came in 1983. With the arrival of Lori McGowne (1984), the college faculty numbered 23.

Through the good offices of UNLV's Michigan State "alumni chapter" (Abbey, Borsenik and Kotschevar) came John Stefanelli in 1978. Once Steff was on board, the quartet turned its attention to Donald (Don) Bell, another Michigander. He made the move in 1981. All sorts of terminal degrees were piling in.

> Stefanelli actually came from the Denver program. I was on his search committee, but I had met him earlier at a conference and I had also reviewed his textbook.   IZZOLO

Francis (Frank) Brown, who had been managing large New York City hotels and teaching part time, and John Goodwin, from the law faculty at the University of West Virginia, came aboard in 1980. Goodwin's initial appointment was jointly with the business college. When budgets allowed, he elected to switch to hotel full-time.

> Neither business nor hotel had approval to hire a full-time person, so Don Baepler said to split the appointment. Goodwin was a great find.   GEORGE HARDBECK, DEAN OF BUSINESS AND ECONOMICS

> John Goodwin sent a flier to the college about a new book of his. I think he has a dozen plus books now. I returned it with a notice of the law opening asking if he knew of anyone. He wrote back, "Me."   JERRY VALLEN

Vincent (Vince) Eade, returned from his assignment in the Dominican Republic (see Chapter 9) to become full time in 1986. Dave Britton took Eade's old position for the final year of the contract with the USAID (United States Agency for International Development). In retrospect, 1986 was a very good year. Beside Eade, there was James (Jim) Kilby (casino management—funded in part by the Boyd Chair) and Gerald (Jerry) Goll (human resources). These three top candidates all became permanent faculty.

> I was teaching in Houston where Jerry Lattin [the program's head, and Vallen's Ph.D. advisor] and I agreed to disagree. Houston interviewed Richard Laughlin from UNLV's faculty and he took my office.   GOLL

> It was actually a swap. When Lattin called me for a Laughlin reference, I learned that Goll was leaving. So Laughlin went to Houston and Goll came here, taking Laughlin's office!   JERRY VALLEN

The Leo Lewis Saga. Faculty members, especially of the quality that the college sought were very hard to find. Finding those with experience, with or without advanced degrees, meant searching everywhere. So traditional academic shopping routes weren't always followed. Many top executives were approached locally and nationally while they were between jobs. Leo Lewis' appointment was one of those very special cases. Lewis had remained an adjunct instructor from the the very founding of the school in 1966 even as he held top management positions with companies such as Hilton, Mirage and Del Webb.

While I was at the Las Vegas Hilton, Vallen asked me to approach Barron Hilton about having me serve as an "executive-in-residence." In a letter, he explained how Hilton would pay my salary but I would teach full time. The idea was received like a bomb in the mail.   LEO LEWIS, BINION'S FINANCIAL OFFICER, AND HOTEL FACULTY MEMBER BOTH PART TIME AND FULL TIME

In 1979, the State of Nevada took a very rare step that had unexpected consequences for the college. It assumed control over the Aladdin after two of the hotel's top officers were found guilty in a Detroit federal court of concealing hidden interests. The state acted to save the hundreds of jobs that closing the Aladdin would have cost.

Harry Reid was Attorney General and he said that the state would not put 2,500 people out of work.   LEWIS

Reid asked Lewis to take the position of general manager, which he did in March of 1979. It was a very public job. Every move that Lewis or the state made was headlined in the daily newspapers. What happened next lies somewhere between the two accounts.

I called Leo sometime between December, 1979 and January, 1980 and said, Leo, why put up with all the aggravation? Tell the judge—the court was in control—that you have a teaching job that begins next month and you need to be relieved.   JERRY VALLEN

In December of 1979, Ed Nigro and Johnny Carson decided to buy the Aladdin. They would take over in March of 1980, but Leo Lewis had to go. That's when Vallen called and reminded me that the Hilton offer, but in a different format, was still open.   LEWIS

Lewis stayed on faculty for 2.5 years teaching, consulting and loving the freedom of movement and self-direction that only education provides. By the fall of 1982 the college was again recruiting for a casino faculty member.

I was humming along as a visiting professor. It was really good; for me it was great.   LEWIS

Both students and seminar attendees loved Lewis. He would say, You're not hired to maintain a 75% occupancy, you're hired to increase it! Get it to 85%, you're doing a good job. Get it to 90%, I'll put you in for a pay raise.   FRANK BORSENIK, HOTEL FACULTY MEMBER

I think Leo was getting $32,000 that year. So I asked him what a salary shock he must have had. He said, Jerry and I talked over the job and Jerry said we'll pay you $32,000. Leo gasped and said, And what do I get the second semester.   AL IZZOLO, HOTEL FACULTY MEMBER

The college was fortunate to have Lewis, who knew everyone in the city, but in a short time the action of the industry's excitement lured him back to the Strip.

Leo missed the power. We became good friends and he told me to see him whenever I needed something. When my mother came to town and wanted to see a show at the D. I., I asked Leo. He made a call and was amazed to be turned down. I gave this guy a job, helped him stay out of jail and that's how much he thanks me! He was devastated to be out of the trade.   IZZOLO

I said, Leo, you're a great lecturer, why don't you come back on faculty. He said, Alan when I called up to get a line pass for a show, I couldn't get it. I lost my juice so I am out of here. ALAN STUTTS, HOTEL FACULTY MEMBER

Women Faculty. Early faculty members were all men, but so was the student body. Leslie Cummings maintains she was the college's first, and also the second, female faculty member.

Ted [Leslie Cummings' spouse] loved a line that he coined: I was the first and second woman hired by the College of Hotel Administration.   CUMMINGS

Technically, Cummings was; she was the first to stay. But despite her unusual appointments, she was certainly not the first and second woman. She even says so in her own words:

Levinson was a good mentor to colleagues. One faculty member was having problems and going from office to office in tears. She wanted to get close to me [because I was the only other woman on faculty]. Charlie advised against befriending her because she was making enemies for herself.   CUMMINGS

As the designated first, full-time, permanent, female faculty member, Cummings was also the first female faculty member on a tenure track, the first to be tenured and the first to be promoted.

"First" and "second" are used because Cummings left, and returned to stay for 17 years. Her dual appointments revolved about Dunn Sapienza's career moves. Dunn was tied into the international scene. He had come to Nevada from India and left to go to the Bahamas, both moves under contract with international agencies. Cummings completed Sapienza's 1980–81 contract by teaching the spring of 1981. Donald Bell, another terminal degree holder, was appointed 1981–82 to the budgeted line from which Sapienza had taken leave and gone to Nassau. Dunn elected not to return when his leave was up. It was another year before two new positions were authorized (bringing the total faculty to 21) and Leslie Cummings was invited back to fill one of those. Hence, the hiatus of two years between her part-time appointment as visiting assistant professor and her permanent return.

I took a one-semester appointment [1981] while Dunn Sapienza went to Nassau for a brief assignment. The title indicated it was a temporary assignment. After the one term, I went out and got a job before discovering that Dunn was in a long-term commitment there. I returned in 1983 on a tenure track. Vallen asked, Wasn't I coming back? I had no contract and hadn't consider it?

The first salary was $8,981 and Levinson complained that I was being underpaid because I was a woman. I think Jerry Vallen later told me of Levinson's comments.

When I look back on it, I am surprised. The salary progression was good; it was quite generous.   CUMMINGS

The Cummings had their feet in both camps. Leslie with hotel; Ted was with business.

I was the only faculty sharing an office in the humanities building. I was on the fourth floor with Ted. [Hotel was on the seventh floor.] That wouldn't have been done with non-marrieds. It was awful. Ted is a chatty, social person; I like to close the door with a big sign, "back tomorrow." But I was so happy to be back at UNLV, we made do.   CUMMINGS

The overwhelming male-female ratio began to balance slowly. Thereafter the college's record on hiring women improved. Faculty were still hard to find, but the selection standard remained: Hire the best. No other deliberate criteria were in place. Three woman joined the college in 1987: Suad Cox; Ruth Ann Myers and Elizabeth (Betsy) Bender Pederson. Myers was a visiting, one-year appointment, but the other two were permanent. Keeping them in the college was a different statistic. Cox, who had come from Sheraton's national sales office, stayed until 1995. Pederson's tenure was less, only four years until 1991.

I can think of eight women who left. None were let go; they were just difficult to keep. Among those leaving, but not in order, were: Lori McGowan; Ruth Ann Myers; and Betsy Bender Pederson.   CUMMINGS

Among women faculty members who left after a short tenure were Deborah Breiter, Joanne Dahl (MSHA '87), Joli Gaston ('87) and Pat Jonker-Sims.

Lori McGowan came carrying CPA credentials and industry experience from the Mirage Group. She left to raise a family. Another accountant, Susan Ivancevich, came and went with the fortunes of her husband who joined and then left the business college. Suad Cox accepted another offer, and Joli Gaston left when her husband was transferred.

Despite the comings and goings, a strong sense of continuity prevailed.

One of the remarkable things was the faculty stability in the face of comparatively low salaries, especially compared to California.   JERRY GOLL, HOTEL FACULTY MEMBER

Don't forget when determining take-home pay that there were no social security or state income tax withholdings in Nevada.   JERRY VALLEN

Reminiscing, Cummings contrasted the turnover among women and men, estimating that only eight male faculty members had left, two of whom had died. The vagaries of recall are not always supported by an examination of the records, which indicate the actual number was close to two dozen (see Exhibit 10-1). Of course, most of them predated her tenure. Charlie Levinson's sudden death in 1989 was the first among the old guard, followed a half-dozen years later by Bob Martin. Moreo moved to Penn State in 1988. Dick Basile and Joan Reynolds Beitz retired that same year. Vallen stepped down as dean in 1989. Phillips retired in 1994. A new generation was arriving.

Definition of Rank

Hotel's sensitivity to terminal degrees was evidenced as early as Sapienza's and Shirer's 1973 and 1974 appointments. Recruiting terminal-degree faculty was part of the tilt toward a more balanced staff. Terminal degrees were needed to supplement the important industry experiences that the initial appointments had brought.

> I think we all came as lecturers because lecturers didn't have to meet the structure of the fixed salary scale.   DICK BASILE, HOTEL FACULTY MEMBER

> Salary quotas were very rigid at first. The university's president was not allowed to make more than the governor. In a tight labor market, we were unable to hire people we needed. So we hired them as lecturers. A lecturer could be paid anything we wanted to pay.   GEORGE HARDBECK, DEAN OF BUSINESS AND ECONOMICS

There was now a trickle of doctoral degree candidates who also had, wonder of wonders, industry experience. Again, Michigan State University proved to be the best source. John Stefanelli had been an executive chef; Don Bell a restaurant manager. A counterpoint was Dave Christianson, who supplemented his terminal degree by taking summer work in industry.

There was no supply of Ph.D.s in hotel administration per se until the late 1980s. They simply didn't exist.

> Remember that the faculty at Cornell in 1922 were industry people; few had even baccalaureates. By the 1950s-60s, a master's degree was *de rigueur* [for most programs]. By the mid-1970s, a doctorate was desirable, except only Cornell offered such a degree.   PAT MOREO, HOTEL FACULTY MEMBER

Vallen completed the college's one and only Ph.D. in hotel administration in 1977. Abbey, Christianson and Roehl held terminal degrees in tourism and outdoor recreation; Borsenik in agricultural engineering; Moore in business management. Moreo's, Sapienza's and Stefanelli's degrees were in education. Not surprisingly, hotel education remains an eclectic discipline still.

UNLV was actually better staffed than the nation's other two independent schools. Cornell's 1982 catalog indicated 11 Ph.D.s among 36 faculty (31%); Florida International had five Ph.D.s among 24 faculty (21%). Las Vegas' 1982–84 catalog reported 10 terminal degrees (one of which was law) among 19 hotel faculty (53%).

The college's preoccupation with advanced degrees recognized that academic advancement required terminal degrees. Fortunately, each college created its own definition of "terminal degree." Hotel did that in a written memorandum to Vice President Donald Baepler on May 5, 1973. The initiative to do so lay in the 1973 rewrite of the entire UNLV Faculty Bylaws. Reference was made to that definition numerous times throughout the years. It defined a "terminal degree" as a master's degree with five years of experience for an assistant professor, 10 years for an associate appointment, and 15 years for the rank of full professor.

> I came as an instructor although there was an official document defining the requirement for terminal degrees in hotel as a master's degree and so many years of work experience, which I had. In 1981, I became an assistant professor on a tenure track.   MOREO

It required nine years, June 11, 1982, before the office of the vice president, now headed by Dale Nitzchke, focused on that definition. His approval carried several caveats. Chief among them were two provisions: (1) the agreed definition was subject to his review and change at any time; and (2) job announcements would always, in Nitzschke's words, "reflect the fact that we are seeking doctoral level applicants."

Vice President Nitzschke was positive about the hotel college but less so about its policy of faculty balance. The dean saw the three criteria set by the university (teaching, research and service) from a different perspective than that of the vice president, but not much different from the business college.

> I was trying to have the faculty earn their terminal degrees. We recruited and evaluated primarily on the whole person: teaching, consulting; research and student advising. One president told me he wouldn't give a dime for professional accreditation.   HARDBECK

The college needed good teaching, research and service, but it was unreasonable to expect all three of each faculty member. Research began, of course, with the research degree, the terminal degree. The university concurred requiring two outstanding ratings but accepting some weakness in the third. That was fine in principle except when the individual faculty member came up for promotion without a publications (research) record. Nitzschke's support, tentative at best, proved fleeting when a specific case arose.

> Changes began coming with Nitzschke. Up to then, Vallen could act to benefit the college, and university administrators backed him. The dean required top classroom teaching and strength either in research or in service.   AL IZZOLO, HOTEL FACULTY MEMBER

> We visited with Nitzschke to try to get vice-presidential approval for a faculty member's tenure. He insisted on publications; publications of some kind.   MOREO

It had taken nine years for the issue of hotel's terminal degrees to be acted upon. Even then, the decision was forced. It emerged from a debate that raged over who among the campus faculty could enroll for terminal degrees at UNLV.

In Pursuit of Knowledge. With the pool of Ph.D. faculty so limited, the college took an active role developing its own doctoral candidates. Step one was an on-campus try. Jim Adams, dean of the graduate college, was absolutely opposed to the principle. And he didn't discriminate. Everyone applying for a doctorate in education—hotel wasn't the only academic unit—was summarily refused. Academics love procedures, so denial had a procedural element. Each applicant was considered and voted on by the Graduate College Issues Committee before the graduate dean's ruling. Tension ran high, but any possibility of accommodation had been preempted two years earlier when the 1980 accreditation team had been convinced that a cross-campus degree was a very bad thing (see Chapter 4).[4] Still, hotel faculty had made earlier inroads.

Internal degrees were frowned upon. So acting president Brock Dixon asked why I was applying to the College of Education. We talked and he sent me to one of the graduate school committees where the conversation was much the same, It's frowned upon. Back to see Brock. As a citizen of the state, I saw nothing—there was certainly no law—that precluded me from doing so. [Regent's policy actually permitted it at this time, 1978.] After much discussion, I suggested in a very nice way that we might need to pursue this to get a court ruling. Dixon eventually called the president at Reno. I heard only one side of the conversation, but Dixon paraphrased for me. If Reno didn't allow its doctoral students on campus they wouldn't have anyone to teach. I guess you're in! Then Frank Brown followed.   MOREO

Frank Brown, Pat Moreo and I applied for admission. Pat was ranked as a lecturer. Frank and I were both assistant professors, which meant we were not eligible, but somehow Frank got in!   IZZOLO

Encouraging faculty took other forms too, including nonpaid academic leaves, reduced teaching loads and waivers from committee assignments, especially during dissertation preparation. The college even provided money after the Kotschevar grant was established. President Don Baepler weighed in by approving secretarial support for dissertation preparation.

I wanted faculty to finish their dissertations and I asked the secretaries to help with the drafts. They did and that helped.   GEORGE HARDBECK, DEAN OF BUSINESS AND ECONOMICS

I came to Nevada ABD [all but dissertation]. Twenty years later because of the encouragement of Paul Gaurnier [associate dean at Cornell], the support of Cornell's Dean Bob Beck, the urging of Frank Borsenik and an OK from UNLV's Don Baepler, I returned one summer to complete the paper, which Joan Reynolds typed for me with four carbons. And there were no computers in those days!   JERRY VALLEN

Cornell's tuition was high so we saved to meet the costs of returning to campus. Wow! There was no tuition. We learned that once a student had paid for 8 terms of Cornell residence, tuition was met. We had double-decker ice-cream cones every night that summer.   FLOSSIE VALLEN

Several faculty members took advantage of the college's support to work on degrees. Lothar Kreck took UNLV courses that his doctoral program at Denver agreed to transfer. Brown and Moreo pursued on-campus degrees. Bob Moore commuted to Claremont in Pomona, California and many years later Hank Melton did the same to San Diego. Teaching schedules were arranged for days off including driving time to California. All continued full time with appropriate adjustments in work loads. Jim Abbey and Leslie Cummings took unpaid leaves to complete their degrees: Abbey to Utah and Cummings to Arizona.

> I had two sabbatical leaves and several non-paid leaves of absence plus the year to work on my doctorate. Leslie Cummings said, I want to be like you; you're never here!   ABBEY

Good faculty remain good students all their lives. Pursuing formal degrees is just one aspect of this continuing education. Research, consulting, travel, reading, writing and listening are other self-improvement techniques. Pat Moreo, for example, took a one-year leave to Penn State to see how others "do it." Everything adds to the accumulated knowledge of a vibrant teacher/researcher. Hence, a variety of leaves-of-absence were authorized and supported by the college. Some leaves were negotiated with minimum paper work. Others ran through the campus machinery on a *pro forma* basis. Formal absences were approved by appropriate committees and administrators. Faculty might be gone for a few weeks, a term, during the summer session, or sometimes longer. Jim Kilby got itchy feet on several occasions and returned to the casino industry while the college held open his job line. He came back refreshed and more knowledgeable, benefitting himself and the student body.

> My first leave was in 1992. It was only for one term because Don Bell as chair wouldn't support a year's leave. About then, the university introduced development leaves and I won one of those for 1995–1996.   CUMMINGS

Most leaves, including all of those taken by the dean who was on a 12-month contract, were formally scripted. Vallen's trips for the Department of Commerce and elsewhere were always preceded by paperwork. Trips were either on college business or were charged against personal leave time. They were cleared with the academic vice president just as faculty members cleared arrangements with the dean.

> One summer after a teaching assignment at the University of Hawaii, we went to Saipan where Jerry gave classes at the junior college. Alumnus Tony Guerrero ('85) was president of a resort in Saipan. He arranged to take us by very small plane over the Pacific Ocean's deepest chasm. Half way there, the pilot opened the plane door to get some air. We flew to Tinian where we joined up with a chapter of the IFSEA. The group picnicked and toured the island. [Tinian was the base for the Enola Gay's A-bomb attack on Japan during World War II. When asked the secret location of that airbase, President Roosevelt answered "Shangrila" after the mystical place in James Hilton's 1933 book, *Lost Horizon*.]   FLOSSIE VALLEN

Levinson developed a series of bar seminars which took him all across the U.S.S.R. under the auspices of the Seagram Corporation. It was a bit scary because the Soviet Union was growing less and less stable. From Levinson's contacts with the U.S.S.R's Council of Ministers and with the support of UNS Chancellor Robert Bersi, the hotel college brought Mr. Khodorkov, who headed Moscow's Hotel/Tourism School, and his colleague for a semester visit during the 1989 spring term.

Several hotel faculty, went abroad to teach at Cornell's graduate program in France. Borsenik went three times.

UNLV was being romanced by several Swiss schools. Some wanted the occupancy and income from the college's Summer Abroad program; some wanted transfer credits for their students; and some wanted UNLV faculty. Bernard Gehri, president of the International Centre de Gilon, a hotel program near Montreaux, Switzerland, began an annual trek to Las Vegas to recruit for his school's senior semester, which was taught in English. Both campuses tested the tentative arrangement with Don Bell going first. Once President Goodall approved Bell's arrangement (December, 1982), and Bell reported back positively, a stream of faculty followed.

> I left for Switzerland before the term ended one spring so the UNLV class met extra hours to assure the minimum contact hours.
> Bernard Gehri was a strong leader like Jerry Vallen.   FRANK BORSENIK, HOTEL FACULTY MEMBER

> Gehri wouldn't take Charlie Levinson until Charlie agreed to shave his beard. And as stubborn as Charlie was, he shaved it.   JERRY VALLEN

> We [with spouse Colleen] had a wonderful experience in Switzerland and that lead to teaching in Glion three times.
> I also did three different universities in Australia.   JIM ABBEY, HOTEL FACULTY MEMBER

Leo Lewis' casino specialty was unique so he was called to many different places including the Far East. He worked on New Jersey's casino regulations.

> New Jersey paid me more than I asked with the proviso that they could telephone whenever they wanted. That they did often—at 9:30 a.m. their time and 6:30 a.m. our time! [Readers should be aware that casino executives usually work late into the night.] I'm sleeping and my wife is laughing.   LEWIS

And he journeyed to Switzerland along with the others.

> Gehri's man took us to a beautiful Swiss resort, but we arrived after the kitchen closed for lunch. I said, Let's have a sandwich. They hustled me away, no one can eat without a chef on hand. The next night we had dinner and I was asked what wine I wanted. Get any wine, I said. That was heresy to the Swiss!   LEWIS

Graduate student Kaye Chon kept the channels open to Korea.

Dave Christianson, the Vallens and I flew to Korea via Tokyo. The Tokyo to Seoul leg was heavily overbooked and we were bounced. By the time I telephoned, the Seoul delegation had already left for the airport to greet us en masse. They did the whole routine again when we arrived the next day. [Meeting the arrival and accompanying the departure in costume is a measure of courtesy and honor in Korea.]   CHON

In 1983–84, Richard Laughlin traveled to Paris as consultant; Rand to Asia for his tourism trips; and Christianson to London to deliver a paper. Coincidently, students from 24 foreign nations were enrolled in the college that year.

The Faculty At Work

Every faculty member had something going on. With a mandate to do whatever benefitted the student, the college, the individual and the university, faculty undertook a range of activities. They advised student clubs, worked with alumni, planned trips, offered seminars, built rapport with professional associations, recruited students and faculty, catered special meals, supported other units of the campus, and more.

Renewal of the dormitory foodservice contract was one assignment that I enjoyed. The campus was shopping to renew its contract with Saga, but the committee picked Marriott. There was talk about the hotel college running the foodservice, but Jerry didn't want anything to do with that.   IZZOLO

Don Bell began brewing beer and developed a new course and a new club from the effort. Frank Brown conceived a new graduation robe and mortar board because UNLV had no such tradition. Unfortunately, President Goodall was leaving just at that time (Spring, 1984). President Maxson had not yet grown comfortable enough with the office to endorse the change before Brown, himself, left.

When the alumni needed a new logo, they turned to Frank Brown who was the college's best—and only—Latin scholar. His contribution, translated: *Scientific Knowledge and Practical Experience Serves Well the World*, captured the essential change in hotel and foodservice education. The old logo had pictured a loaf of bread, a decanter of wine and a wine glass, all surrounded by a sommelier's chain.   JERRY VALLEN

John Stefanelli became a major resource for small restauranteurs, advising them on locations and operations, and saving many from the high rate of failure usually experienced by first-time restaurant investors..

The college was called in to do the training for the employees of the Mint Hotel's new grand buffet, which replaced their mezzanine bingo parlor. They had already begun construction. Someone else had been their consultants. Stefanelli looked at me, They will lose their butts. Not long thereafter, the hotel tore it all out!

  Students in that class had limited attention spans and needed to be focused. So I gave each member a toy cricket. One time I used a whistle. The Mint manager came in and when I asked the class who agreed with a particular statement, everyone clicked. The executive loved it.   IZZOLO

I learned from Izzolo and Stefanelli! Thereafter, I rewarded participants in executive training sessions with small novelties or candy bars. Even management people responded positively to the silly incentives.   JERRY VALLEN

Izzolo partnered with a variety of faculty members.

Pat Moreo and I wrote a foods column called *Under Five*. We reported for the school newspaper about good restaurants where students could eat for $5 or less.   IZZOLO

Projects were not restricted to the campus or even to the city. Lyell Metcalf developed and administered a professional certification program for the national association of hotel accountants. Faculty served on national professional boards.

Dick Basile was on the National Academy of Science Military Advisory Board for six years and I replaced him serving for four years. One job was to figure out how to feed sailors aboard ship or as they disembarked. For example, an aircraft carrier may have several thousand aboard. Later, the college got a contact from the Board, so I resigned to avoid a conflict of interest.   FRANK BORSENIK, HOTEL FACULTY MEMBER

Vallen sat on the corporate board of directors of Jay Sarno's planned, but never-built, first-ever, all-suite hotel, the Grandissimo. Moreo was a Sarno consultant. Bob Martin gained national reputation as a expert for court cases involving housekeeping and security. Faculty responded to consulting calls of all kinds.

There was plenty of consulting, both through the school and privately contracted. Some of it came from articles that I had written; some from word-of-mouth, some from my activities with CHRIE. I did a training session for the Circus' new Mississippi property. I did a lot without pay. I had two incomes and I always wanted to arrive a day or two early to examine the property. So Jackie [Goll's wife] got vacations: Presidential suite at the New Orleans' Marriott, for example.   JERRY GOLL, HOTEL FACULTY MEMBER

Claude Lambertz and Don Bell enhanced the food tradition started by Bussel and Moreo. An amazing variety of services that captured the essence of the program and built a strong following among the community were offered.

To this day faculty members of the business college say that they won [AACSB] accreditation in part because of the wonderful meal we served the accreditation team.   CLAUDE LAMBERTZ, HOTEL FACULTY MEMBER

Hotel did a luncheon for some dignitaries, including a Nobel Prize winner, during an economic conference in town.   GEORGE HARDBECK, DEAN OF BUSINESS AND ECONOMICS

One highlight of the Boyd Dining Rooms was the Vanda Master Series. Charles Vanda developed a concert and lecture series that brought the world's famous to campus. Before each presentation, hotel catered a gourmet meal to a limited number of guests invited to meet the celebrity. These were spectacular dinners funded by Vanda's budget and underwritten by Marjorie Barrick.

> I attended the meals and broke bread with the famous, the likes of Sam Donaldson, Abba Eban and Lee Iacocca.   JERRY VALLEN

Las Vegas Mayor Jan Jones asked the college to cater at her ranch for the National Governors Conference. Similarly, Siegfried and Roy had the college cater an affair on their estate.

> A national association of carnival people approached us about their final dinner [to be held during their Las Vegas convention]. Don Bell and I asked if they wanted to feature wild game. Bob Barber [kitchen steward] hung an old parachute as a tent and we built a circus theme featuring a menu of camel, eland, lion and zebra. Lion is a very dense meat that tastes like beef. We ground the Zebra and made hotcake humps.   LAMBERTZ

Innovative or public relations projects notwithstanding, it was understood that nothing preempted instruction nor justified absence from the classroom. All non-classroom activities were to supplement and improve, never to detract from, classroom responsibilities.

Teaching. Hotel recruited and developed well-rounded faculty members, but the basic requirement of classroom instruction and advising remained. Undergraduate preparation, not graduate research, was the college's strength. Although hotel and business had other differences, the two programs held similar views about teaching.

> If you look back, the colleges have changed a lot. Most of it has been an improvement, but I regret to say, and I say this with all sincerity, there is far less emphasis on [classroom] teaching. I believe that an administrator ought to teach at least one class a year. We have administrators who haven't been in a classroom for years. That's my other bias.
>
> As an administrator, I put emphasis on teaching. I emphasized teaching in our hiring and faculty evaluations. We gave teaching awards.   HARDBECK

> I have served on the [university-wide] promotion and tenure committee for seven or eight years. Standards have changed! The emphasis is now on research; there's no emphasis on teaching.   ABBEY

Good classroom teaching has many components. Among them faculty preparation, classroom order and discipline, outline and structure, and currency of material.

> Good teaching means updating and upgrading the class every term.   BORSENIK

> I like to change the class every semester, sometimes even monthly. Using textbooks restricts that somewhat. [Basile distributed materials that the class members used to create textbooks.]
> BASILE

Last week I allowed a student to drop rather than get an F. Colleagues say I'm getting too easy. Students don't think so because I still believe we are here for a purpose: get them ready for the outside. [One outside organization, the Fraternity of Chefs, voted Lambertz 1989 Chef of the Year.]   LAMBERTZ

I enjoy teaching and interacting with students. I developed respect for the undergraduates and enjoyed the graduate classes so much that I chaired, in Tom Jones' words, More graduate research projects than anyone else in the college. I taught about unethical and inappropriate behavior and then did those very things waiting for the class to call me on it.

I don't think I have been the most popular teacher, but I never had an empty seat. The students would cuss me but they would get it done and would learn, and that's what I though we were here for.   GOLL

Good teaching also has a sense-of-humor component. A good class can be a fun class.

I always go early for the first class and sit as if I were a student. As the room filled, I would ask, Is this the marketing class? Who's the teacher? When I heard Abbey, I'd say, Wow he's tough; I might drop! Sometimes there would be a but-he's-a-good-teacher response. By then I would stand and we all had a good laugh.   ABBEY

Grades are part of the classroom focus. Grade inflation was a topic for both general faculty meetings and individual faculty evaluations. The registrar produced campus-wide figures of grade distributions. Hotel's grades were always skewed toward the lower end, Cs, Ds and Fs. Consequently, the college's average grades were lower than the campus average and in some years actually the lowest among all the colleges (see Exhibit 11-1).

The grade issue leads naturally to what students will do to achieve those grades. Unfortunately, cheating is one response.

Most students say there's no purpose in cheating because the others don't know any more than I do. Sometimes I would stay in the room and be intimidating. Most times, I would leave because I had to trust; that's what I was teaching. I would pass the exams and leave. If you give trust, you get trust.   GOLL

I got rid of most of the cheating by giving open-book exams. Students can bring whatever they want into the exam.   BORSENIK

Levinson was a little terrier if he thought a student had plagiarized. He would be in the library looking for the references.   CUMMINGS

There weren't too many [students who cheated]. I did have one who was so disgusted that he threw the exam down with his cheat sheet still in it.   STUTTS

Advising. One advantage of having no departments and only one standard curriculum was that everyone, including secretaries who were kept informed of rule changes, could be advisors. New faculty met with the dean to review advising procedures. Each student folder had a worksheet that corresponded to the catalog requirements of the student's year of entry. Once the advisor posted completed classes, remaining requirements and electives were evident to both parties.

Students were assigned to specific faculty members, but anyone could see anyone.

> We did two-hour advising shots. I also did the orientation and learned a lot from that. Any questions, we would go to the dean, who did more advising then everyone put together. But it went fast because we had the students update their own files so they knew beforehand what courses were still needed. The form was well laid out. Questions on transfer were referred to Phillips.   IZZOLO

This arrangement gave all-day coverage for the working students who might otherwise not be accommodated. Phillips and Vallen took their turns at individual consultations. The biggest problem came from students who thought they were hotel majors, but were not. Chapter 11 tells the reason behind the confusion and the disappointments that arose.

Academic advising established student rapport that provided a good support structure when they had non-academic problems.

> I would get rid of the academic issues first and then ask the student about any problems he or she was having.
> I have no recall of serious problem students.   BORSENIK

> I miss the students. Few come to office hours [now] and [without faculty advising] they don't feel they have business here.   CUMMINGS

> It was seen as a joke but students would line up outside my office to see me. The door was always open. The condition of the door is irrelevant; the condition of the mind is what its all about.   GOLL

Sometimes student counseling began with the parents. Parents were concerned with the problems of their children and the college was delighted to have that support.

> My first question to concerned parents was, How much money does your child get each week? Generous parents were often the cause of student problems.   JERRY VALLEN

Technically—legally—grades were the student's property. That was difficult to enforce when caring parents called to find out what their children were doing so far from home.

> Kotschevar started doing extra classes on Saturday for students who wanted to tour facilities. Monday, Wednesday, Friday schedules didn't provide the necessary block of time. I picked up on it. One student who couldn't attend the extra offering on Saturday brought his parents to seen the dean. The dean said, It's a good thing the faculty members are doing, not a bad one.   ABBEY

A group of students failed their dinner [preparation in a quantity foods class]. One man who received an F grade had his father [who was with a major hotel company] call from his assignment in England. The father said that the company would cancel its donation if we didn't straightened out the matter. Vallen replied, They haven't given that much anyway.
LAMBERTZ

I had a father come all the way from India to plead his son's academic suspension. I said to myself if this man has come so far, I shall allow a second chance because he will certainly bear down on his son. Imagine my shock when he had the boy leave the conference and then poured a handful of diamonds on to the desk! Cultures do differ. On another occasion, a second Indian student told me how amazed he was to get in to see the dean without first tipping assistants like Phillips and Reynolds.   JERRY VALLEN

Publications. Although the broad campus family gave less credit toward promotion and tenure for text book publications than for refereed articles, the college dean believed otherwise. A text's quality was judged by the market place, the least biased of reviewers. Moreover, there were relatively few books in circulation, a condition lamented by Richard Strahlem in preparing the campus for the start of the program (see Exhibit 3-1). HRI (Hotel, Restaurant, Institutional) enrollment was snowballing. Textbooks with the author's UNLV affiliation were certain to extend the program's name far and wide. Besides, it represented a supplement to faculty income. The output from the faculty was tremendous. On September 16, 1976, the dean sent Vice President Gentile a memo with the AH&MA's Educational Institute's *Study Guide* attached. The point? UNLV hotel faculty had nearly 25% of the texts listed there!

The faculty was fortunate. We were new and the emphasis was on texts, and those have paid so well. Royalties keep rolling in and there is no investment except one's time. It's a great return.
    The first book I did with Vallen and Sapienza and then Vallen [who was text editor for Brown Publishing] hooked me up with Milt Astroff to produce our *Meetings and Conventions* book.   ABBEY

The publisher, Larry Kramer, told me that Jerry's book would put all four kids through the best universities, and it did.   FLOSSIE VALLEN

As the years passed, senior faculty members invited junior faculty members to co-author revisions of their long-standing texts. Vallen's co-author is his son, Gary ('79), a professor at Northern Arizona University. Closer to home, Kotschevar teamed up with Cummings for one book and with Luciani for another. When revision times came, Goodwin invited Gaston ('87) and Martin invited Jones ('82). More recently, Feinstein ('91) co-authored with Stefanelli. Among the early unions were Borsenik and Stutts.

I had no thought of doing books until I came to UNLV. Initially, I did two chapters in Borsenik's revised text. Then I co-authored with him and came to realize how intense the process was. Then I wrote one on travel safety just as the [first] Iraqi war broke out. [Stutts' newest book came out several weeks before this interview.]   STUTTS

I made a deal with Stutts, but he didn't know if I would carry through with it. But by the second edition he was contributing and by the third edition, he was a co-author.   BORSENIK

Periodically the legislature asked the campus to report on its activities. The report of January 28, 1985, which was addressed through Vice President Unrue, included the 1984–85 release of faculty texts. In just that year came Donald Bell's *Food and Beverage Cost Control*; John Goodwin's *Travel and Lodging Law*, 2nd ed.; Robert Martin's *Hotel Housekeeping*; John Stefanelli's *Purchasing and Procurement*, 2nd ed., and another book, *Hotel Realty*; and Jerry Vallen's *Check-in; Check-out*, 3rd ed. The range of publications speaks to the breadth of faculty expertise.

With urging from the dean, Bob Moore and I and two others met several times in Moore's home in Boulder City to do a hotel accounting book. We wrote several chapters sitting on the floor. [It was never completed.]   LEO LEWIS, BINION'S FINANCIAL OFFICER, AND HOTEL FACULTY MEMBER BOTH PART TIME AND FULL TIME

Bill Friedman worked on his first casino book, while he was an adjunct faculty member.

[An interesting aside is that] Mike Unger ['71], who had taken a casino class from Friedman, brought Bill Friedman to me with a complete plan of how to market the Castaways [a Summa property.] I took the plan to [my boss] Steve Savodelli. The traditional casino people almost stoned us to death. But Friedman was eventually hired and successfully managed the Castaways and the Silver Slipper.   JOE BUCKLEY, HUMAN RESOURCES DIRECTOR, HUGHES SUMMA CORPORATION

Output from the faculty has been prodigious. In addition to over 25 texts—Dean Christianson had them aligned in his office—there has been an outpouring of articles and publications of all types. Following a tradition started by Alan Stutts, K. S. (Kaye) Chon, director of the college's graduation program, prepared annual reports: *Publications by Hotel Faculty Members of the William F. Harrah College of Hotel Administration*. Single and doubled spaced, the December, 1993 list [subsequent to Vallen's 1989 departure] required 48 pages for the 22 faculty who had published.

The faculty started with texts but were soon producing many well received articles. Leslie Cummings was the most diversified author. Her publications included topics in waste management, computer applications to the hotel industry, nutrition, and library bibliographies for a start.

The biggest splash was being named co-winner one year in the *Cornell Quarterly* for a computer article, *Computer Confusion*. Computers, printers and periphiral equipment were on hand, but we couldn't plug one into the other.

An article that I published in a UK journal generated 60 requests for copies. That one, about waste management, was based on research carried out at the Flamingo Hotel. I was on a team with Jim Deacon [biological science faculty], who had an EPA grant of $40,000 matched by the Flamingo. I was on the waste paper segment because my dissertation was on garbage disposal. Horst Dziura [Flamingo Hotel's general manager] was very pleased. He had us in the board room week after week to talk about it. The UK publication pictured the Flamingo on the cover.   CUMMINGS

Faculty articles and texts spread the name and capabilities of the college.

I still get feedback from one of my very first articles, printed in the CHRIE journal. That was my MBV, *Management By Values*, article. It even won an ethics award. Other articles have generated calls asking me to speak or to give a seminar.   GOLL

I did a monthly labor column for a periodical. I called it *Labor Pains*. Biggest problem was the size restriction, one page. These were actual cases from my membership in the American Arbitration Association. They were complex and needed more than one page to explain.   BASILE

A different kind of publication was edited and largely written by John Goodwin. Goodwin was a prolific text writer (*Business Law; Gaming Control Law, The Nevada Model;* and *Travel and Lodging Law* were but three), but his quarterly *Hotel and Casino Law Letter* was a far better public-relations product than even his dozen-plus books.

John Goodwin cranked out the books, but he enjoyed it!   STUTTS

The *Letter*, which was launched in 1980, was distributed worldwide without charge. Who knows how much goodwill this unique publication generated for the college. There's no evidence to the fact, but it may have been a contributing factor in starting the association of casino attorneys. Among the regular contributors was James Eiler, a 1983 hotel graduate, one of several alumni who pursued a law degree at the urging of professors such as John Goodwin and Jack Lehman.

SUPPORT RESOURCES

Faculty of the College of Hotel Administration were sustained by and developed specializations through the support of a dedicated group of friends. Most were locally based, but some came from afar.

Adjunct Faculty

Unhappily, adjunct faculty are often called by a less prestigious name: "P-99 faculty." That's the university's budget line identification. These selfless persons came to campus before, during and after their regular work days. They added depth and realism to the professional courses. They allowed large enrollments without heavily impacting state funding. They made possible, unequivocally, the success of the hotel program.

The teachers who actually worked in the field were the best. I loved the stories they brought to class. They were street-smart, savvy individuals able to keep the attention of rambunctious college kids.   GARY BROWN, '73 STUDENT

The university was built by the P-99s. Guys who came out of the trenches to teach the nuts and bolts.   JOE DELANEY, COLUMNIST AND PART-TIME FACULTY MEMBER

The college was fortunate beyond explanation for the services rendered by the adjunct staff. This faculty allowed full-time staff to specialize, even as the scope of course offerings was broadened. Nevada had courses that no other hotel program was able to offer. In turn, the university paid them almost nothing, which has remained the scale for several decades. Indeed, several donated their salary back to the college.

I admired the P-99 people and their level of commitment, but [their lack of availability] deprived students of faculty access and moved UNLV toward the abuse of compensatory time [time off given to regular faculty to do their regularly assigned jobs].   GOLL

Most distressing, it was impossible for these busy people to obtain parking permits.

For gosh sakes, give the P-99s a raise and provide a place for them to park.
I figured it was because I cost so little that I was kept so long.   DELANEY

The college's call for local help and the immediate response began just a few months after the program head was in place. Phil Arce and Leo Lewis were teaching as adjuncts even before that, in 1966. Chapter 3 recounts how that came to be. Arce continued to help until he took an assignment in Hawaii; Lewis remained throughout this history.

I would tell the class about day-to-day activities and what was happening: strikes; entertainment; costs; and they were in tune to that.   PHIL ARCE, SAHARA HOTEL MANAGER

Michael Gaughan [Founder of Coast Resorts] asked how I liked to teach. I said Its wonderful, fun, rewarding. He said, I always wanted to teach. Then come and teach, I'll clear it with the dean. He sat in the back, but I kept him working making exams, grading papers until he too began lecturing. He covered when I went to Switzerland.   LEWIS

Earlier, Leo Lewis had drafted Steve Michelle as a adjunct.

When I was made general manager of the Hilton Flamingo, John Giovenco recruited Steve Michelle to my old job as assistant treasurer. I told Giovenco that I was teaching and he said, Steve will take over the class.
[Earlier in time] we held classes at the Sahara Hotel. Bill Dougal [president of the Sahara,] okayed it and even appeared as a speaker. Dennis Gomes [president of the Frontier Hotel] allowed the class to analyze reg cards before the days of computers. The survey

was designed for the Frontier, so the results were better than the Convention Authority's [broader analysis].   LEWIS

Almost as soon as the program's director was in place, a letter—dated September 26, 1967—was send to Gabe Vogliotti of the Resort Association. It asked for help in finding part-time faculty for hotel realty, hotel law, and casino operations and management. Among the early volunteers were Lew Kurtz, chief financial officer at Caesars Palace and Jerry Snyder, a member of his own law firm. The 1970–1971 catalog listed the adjuncts on the college page, but not in the official alphabetical listing in the rear. This small misrepresentation magnified a very limited faculty list. Among the 12 faculty listed that year were five adjuncts. They included Bob Fielden, a principal in his own firm, teaching architecture; Lew Kurtz, Caesars Palace, teaching accounting and real estate; Rolf Laerm, Hilton's showroom captain, teaching wine; Jack Lehman, a principal in his own firm, teaching law; and Verdes Ueckert, head of the Clark County Health Department, teaching sanitation. The regular staff included Dick Acosta, Dick Basile, Bob Catron, Charlie Levinson, Boyce Phillips, Jack Rudd, and Jerry Vallen. Jack Lehman had replaced Jerry Snyder as the P-99 law professor, and served in that post for many, many years.

> Lehman was an inspirational teacher! It wasn't an easy class, you had to be prepared because he would make you talk about the case. At the end of the term, he wrote letters to two of us telling us to consider law school. [Mark Moreno, ('69) followed Lehman's advice.]
> Later I needed some legal work, Lehman had me pay by cooking him a dinner.   PAT MOREO, 69 STUDENT AND HOTEL FACULTY MEMBER

Judge Paul Goldman took over when Jack Lehman decided to "retire." Goldman would close court for a long lunch hour and race up to campus to meet his mid-day commitment. No parking was available, even for a judge!

> Goldman had a tough-judge reputation. He came to campus for several semesters. One day the campus photographer took a picture of a car parked in a no-parking zone and ran it in the school newspaper. It was Paul Goldman's. The plate read, "Judge."   MOREO

Nikolas Mastrangelo was the final adjunct professor in law. He took over after Goldman So the quality of the part-time law faculty was maintained until the college was authorized regular law faculty: first, John Goodwin; later, Joli Gaston ('87). With two regular staffers, no adjunct attorneys were needed thereafter. As an early adjunct, Bob Fielden offered a course that would otherwise not have been taught, hotel architecture.

> I took Fielden's course and "loaned" my final paper to a basketball player. Unbeknownst to me, he copied the paper verbatim. Fielden confronted us and the truth came out. My grade was "C," the athlete's grade was "A."   GARY BROWN, '73 STUDENT

Bob Fielden surrendered the assignment after a time to another long-term supporter, Homer Rissman. Brothers Rissman and Rissman were the major architects for Hilton and had designed hotels up and down the Las Vegas Strip. Homer stayed with the extra work of the class despite a heavy professional commitment. He and Dick Basile team taught for many years.

> The architectural class was a trial-and-error start. Without a textbook there was no guide. Bob Fielden and I started team teaching and then Homer Rissman came. We were a team for most of our tenure. We developed the course about what hotel managers should tell architects. That's the responsibility of the manager and it is more important in the design than is the code.
>
> Jim Abbey and I also tried team teaching, but as the students were young, the course had to change.   BASILE

> Dick and I tried team teaching with the management class [HOA 454]. It didn't work as well as we had hoped. Chiefly because the richness of two presentations didn't compensate for the loss in continuity.   ABBEY

Joe Delaney, newspaper columnist for 34 years at the time of this writing, as well as a radio personality, entrepreneur/producer and master-of-ceremonies, was the college's longest-running adjunct appointment, 26 years.[5] The course continues today taught by some of Delaney's graduates including a '77 alumnus, Sandy Hackett.

> I was doing five hours a week of live television, and 15 hours of radio talk, plus five columns per week when I began teaching in 1973.   DELANEY

Delaney's entertainment course was unique as were other courses that the college developed. It was unique in two ways. First, that there was such a course, and second, how he used the city's special resources.

> People such as Pete Barbudi, Milton Berle, Bill Cosby, Sammy Davis, Jr., Buddy Hackett, Jerry Lewis, Liberace, Rich Little, Bob Newhart and Joan Rivers were classroom regulars.
>
> Others were people who lived here such as Jim Halsey, Bob Vincent and Terry Little.
>
> Cosby was a wonderful lecturer, but he was also stern and required students to be on time.
>
> Frank Sinatra [who received an honorary degree from UNLV] never came, but he never said no to charitable appearances.   DELANEY

> Joan Rivers came to class and Marty Burzinski ('81) asked her to marry him. We howled!   ANN RITTAL, '81 STUDENT

All of these visitors carried away the story of UNLV's College of Hotel Administration.

Although it was difficult to do, I agreed not to come to Delaney's class and use the opportunity thereby to solicit funds.   JERRY VALLEN

I can remember bringing Jerry Lewis to help teach. Some people would say, What the hell is going on, you're having comics from the Strip? I'd say, Do you think on the day that Lewis came, my class got less? Or maybe more?   JERRY CRAWFORD, DEAN OF FACULTY

Entertainment directors, music directors and performers came to class. And the hotels cooperated. I was able to put the class into three or four shows each semester. Each was different: a downtown show; one-of-a-kind show; and a production show. Often we would get a backstage tour. Today the problem is class size. Sixty comped seats is a lot of seats!   DELANEY

Delaney's class followed the Liberace show from set-up during the day to afternoon rehearsal to evening performance.   RITTAL

Bob Small, who went on to head up the hotel/restaurant program at Cal Poly in Pomona, California, teethed his teaching credentials as a UNLV adjunct. Small was running the airport food concessions so he came in the evenings after the day's work was done.

Details about these half-dozen adjuncts illustrate the support that the college had from its distinguished auxiliary staff. Exhibit 10-2 provides a broader listing although it is far from complete. Some university records are missing and the authors' memories are less than exact.

Visiting Faculty

Visiting faculty were classified differently than adjuncts. These persons came full time for a brief period, usually one semester, but occasionally less than that. Two or three industry professionals might share a term. They came to enrich the program's offerings so the classes were unique. One-time course descriptions were created because the class was a one-time enrichment not to be offered again. Finding qualified faculty who could come for a semester was as difficult a job as getting the campus budget committee and the vice president to allocate the position to begin with.

There was a secondary issue for some of these less traditional faculty. University regulations stated that funds budgeted as salaries had to be used as salaries. Yet several visitors were given leave by their companies to accommodate the college. Their university pay, such as it was, belonged to those companies to offset the costs of their staff members, who were still on salary. Major negotiations were needed to convince the individuals and the companies to participate. That was nothing compared to the fancy footwork required to reimburse the negotiated costs from the salaries account, when they were technically not salaries. Once done, the business office applied the technique thereafter without issue. Among those on company leave were Greg Denton from Hospitality Evaluation Services, John Kubas from Saga and Cas Winiewics from Holiday Inns. Cas returned several times even after he left his Holiday Inn position. Other nontraditional faculty members were sought wherever possible. Bulent Kasterlack, who was an architect and city planner specializing in historical tourism,

Adjunct Faculty	Industry Position	Taught
Arce, Phil	Hotel Manager, Sahara	Front office
Campbell, Mark	Food Service Manager, Saga	Foods
Celeste, Dan ('76)	Manager of the MGM Mall	Orientation
Delaney, Joe	Columnist, Las Vegas Sun; Attorney	Entertainment
Faiss, Robert	Attorney; Assistant to the Executive Director, U. S. Travel Service	Tourism
Fielden, Robert	Architect	Hotel design
Friedman, William	President, Castaways Hotel	Gaming
Gaughn, Michael	Owner, Coast Resorts	Gaming
Goldman, Paul	Jurist	Hotel law
Heffner, Van	Hotel Association Executive	Human resources
Kincaid, Les	Food columnist	Foods
Krick, Len ('79)	Director Planning & Control, Dunes	Financial analysis
Kurtz, Lewis	Financial Office, Caesars Palace	Accounting; real estate
McClure, Florence	Sociologist	Sociology of innkeeping
Nelson, Ted	Vice President, Marketing, Hilton	Marketing
Janise, Nicholas	Chief of Police, North Las Vegas	Security
Laerm, Rolf	Show Room Captain, Hilton	Wines
Lehman, Jack	Attorney	Hotel law
Lewis, Leo	Executive with Aladdin, Binion, Gold Coast, Hilton, Mirage & Del Webb Chains	Orientation; accounting and gaming; orientation
Mastrangelo, Nikolas	Attorney	Hotel law
Michelle, Steve	Financial officer, Hilton	Casino accounting
Mulvaney, Ann	Travel Agent	Travel agency management
Ogulnick, Sy	Owner, Children's Hotel, Hilton	Recreation and camps
Ravenholt, Otto	Department of Health, Clark County	Sanitation
Rissman, Homer	Architect	Hotel design
Small, Robert	Airport Food Manager	Foods
Snyder, Jerry	Attorney	Hotel law
Starr, Michael ('81)	Hotel Manager	Front office
Stevens, Muriel	Columnist and radio personality	Foods
Ueckert, Verdes	Department of Health, Clark County	Sanitation

EXHIBIT 10-2. Many individuals helped develop the curriculum by teaching as adjunct faculty members. This representative list has been prepared from incomplete records and less than perfect memories.

came in 1979–80. His visit was set in motion by a chance meeting in 1972 at TTRA (Travel and Tourism Research Association) in Monterey, California. Carmi Gamoran, a well known hotel realtor, investor and financial advisor long associated with Helmsely-Spear and Stephen Brenner, came for a year. That was the year Leona Helmsely, whose income-tax difficulties later brought her and the hotel company unmitigated notoriety, was invited to be the graduation speaker. She declined.

Even faculty members from other programs weren't always traditionally recruited. Rik Medlik, who had headed the hotel program at the University of Surrey, England, came twice, spring 1978 and fall 1983. Medlik's introduction came through his texts and articles, which the dean read while finishing his own dissertation. Off went a letter to England and back came a reply.

> The letter was well timed. After 20 years in British education, I needed a change. That invitation [Medlik came as a Fulbright-Hays Fellow] and the enjoyable stay influenced my lifestyle for the next 15 years.
>
> When my wife Lynda joined me [for the second visit], we rented a home three miles from campus and bicycled. Students in her English class [she was P-99] were excited to be taught by a "real" Englishwoman.   RIK MEDLIK, INTERNATIONAL VISITOR

Medlik was but one of several international visitors. Two came from Australia, Dave Stevens and Ian Priestly. The dean met them during his Australian trips for the U. S. Department of Commerce. Previously mentioned was Khodorkov, Head of Moscow's Hotel/Tourism School. Still another lecturer, Monsieur Jaussi, came from yet another country, Switzerland. He was the exchange staffer promised by Bernard Gehri in response to UNLV's faculty going to Glion. Don McLaurin from Sir Sanford Fleming College, Canada, earned one of the hotel college's earliest master's degrees and stayed to teach a short time. The Orient was represented with a brief, team teaching assignment during the miniterm by Sung Baek Hwan, from Kyung Hee University (Seoul, Korea).

> We invited our Korean guests for dinner. The lady came in her stunning traditional gown. Translation was provided by a Korean graduate student and his wife. Everyone admired our Korean *objets d'art* and then to dinner. The meal was progressing nicely when Jerry got up to bus some dishes. The lady couldn't help herself! Out came a very audible gasp. Korean men never do such a domestic thing.   FLOSSIE VALLEN

More traditional faculty were solicited from more traditional campuses. Lendal Kotschevar started the visiting arrangement and came many times. As Chapter 5 relates, he was named to a rarely used appointment by the university, Distinguished Visiting Professor. Kotschevar's appointments were part of a sharing routine: fall term at UNLV; spring term at Florida International.

> One semester Kotschevar, [Louis] Szathmary [Bakery Restaurant, Chicago] and [Lew] Minor [Minor Foods] were actually on campus at the same time. Louie started it: We sat down and

ate the food that was left after his class demo. The next day, I said I'll prepare something. It took off from there. We had seven-course meals at the end. I gained 30 pounds in three weeks! LAMBERTZ

Aha, it has taken all these years for me to understand the budget imbalance.   JERRY VALLEN

Ruth Davis came from California in 1981. Mike Evans took leave from Virginia Polytechnic Institute. Lewis Minor of Minor foods and previously on Michigan State's faculty came twice. Tom Powers, Penn State, was the spring 1975 professor. The University of Massachusetts furnished two faculty members. One was Bob Bosselman, who joined the faculty full time in 1992. The other was Peter Manning, spring 1979. Exhibit 10-3 provides a sample, but incomplete listing of visiting lecturers.

Visiting Faculty Member	Regular Career
Bob Bosselman	Faculty Member, University of Massachusetts
Greg Denton	Associate, Hospitality Evaluation Services
Mike Evans	Faculty Member, Virginia Polytechnic Institute
Carmi Gamoran	Real Estate Consultant, Helmsley-Spear
Monsieur Jaussi	Swiss Hotelier
Bulent Kasterlak	Self-employed Tourism Architect
Prof. Khodorkov	Director, School of Hotel and Tourism Management, Moscow
Lendal Kotschevar	Author; Faculty Member, Michigan State University Faculty
John Kubas	Human Resources, Saga Food
Robert Lundy	Freelance Tourism Consultant
Peter Manning	Faculty Member, University of Massachusetts
Lewis Minor	Minor Foods; Faculty Member, Michigan State University
Don McLaurin	Faculty Member, Sir Sanford Fleming College, Canada
Ruth Ann Myers	CHRIE Member
Tom Powers	Faculty Member, Pennsylvania State University
Ian Priestly	Faculty Member, Footscray Institute of Technology, Australia
Dave Stevens	Blue Mountain Regional Tourism Office, Australia
Sung Baek Hwan	Dean, Kung Hee University, Seoul, Korea
Louis Szathmary	Proprietor, Bakery Restaurant
Cas Winiewics	Human Resources, Holiday Inns

EXHIBIT 10-3. Many individuals helped broadened the curriculum by teaching as visiting faculty members. This representative list has been prepared from incomplete records and less than perfect memories.

When our last child finished college, we took the family to Europe to celebrate no more tuition! At the glacier on top of the Jung Frau Mountain we met Peter Manning. Jerry was so surprised, he almost forgot Peter's name.   FLOSSIE VALLEN

All the visitors were expected to give two or three lectures to the entire faculty. Visitors were also made available to outside agencies and groups for talks and lectures.

I liked the idea and the range of visitors, but I was not enamored by the idea of going to presentations. The visits were certainly beneficial to the students and we got exposure to the likes of Bob Bosselman [and hired him].   GOLL

Some of the visitors were great, but I made it a point to go to all of the talks because not to do so would set a bad precedent for the rest of the faculty.   BORSENIK

I enjoyed those in my field the most, Kotschevar and Chef Louie. Powers talked publishing and that wasn't my thing. Faculty thought attendance was a chore, but looking back, it made sense.   IZZOLO

Staff

How very fortunate was the college to have the support of a positive, knowledgeable secretarial corps. That critical asset was highlighted during an accreditation visit.

"Intense interviews with numerous students in hotel administration revealed a great deal of satisfaction with the program. They respected the Dean and the faculty, and thought well of the secretarial staff."

" . . . [the] close proximity of the faculty offices, the dean's office and the secretarial support staff offices has had a very positive influence, developing good personal and working relationships among the entire staff. . . . There is a consciousness that everyone is part of the team on a common mission. A feeling of genuine openness and mutual support permeates the entire organization.[6]

I think the students liked us, I really do; and we liked them too! We never had serious problems with any student.

We [the support staff] helped the students with many of their activities. It was fun. I remember the closeness we had with them. We really got to know them.   JOAN REYNOLDS BEITZ, ADMINISTRATIVE ASSISTANT

Jean Elizabeth (Poo) Pulley ('84) cited this student-staff relationship in a June 19, 1984 letter to the dean extolling the support of Joan Reynolds and Twylia Towns.

College secretaries worked hard and worked together! If one was overloaded, the others pitched in.   GEORGE HARDBECK, DEAN OF BUSINESS AND ECONOMICS

Joan [Reynolds] and Twylia [Towns] were there a long time, and they were great! More like compatriots than staff.   BASILE

All the secretaries were sweethearts. They were very customer oriented. They sat right out front and that accessibility meant people barging in all the time.   IZZOLO

Because of that accessibility, the secreterial staff was the front line in a host of issues, student advising among them. Informal training sessions plus their willingness to know and to act made them knowledgeable advisors.

It saved the faculty a lot of time. After so many years, we could answer many questions. We would like to think that students got as much help from us as from faculty members, who might not be available at that moment.

I would meet the freshman orientation classes, give them an idea of what to expect and answer questions. I loved doing that orientation.   REYNOLDS BEITZ

When Twylia Towns retired, a letter was added to her personnel file. Because of the warmth and supportive nature of the classified staff, nurtured by the good sense and empathy of Joan Reynolds' leadership, the letter's content could have applied to almost all of the classified staff.

"The College has developed among the students a reputation for caring, for solving problems and for direct action from this office. This has all occurred because of your position across the desk. You have taken the time to understand procedures and policies and campus operations. You have provided a sympathetic ear followed by an ability to . . . direct the person forward. You have taken a personal concern. You have developed a proper sense of what information to give and when to refer the problem. You have taken the initiative on many occasions to prevent a problem from materializing or from deteriorating."[7]

Chronology. The first secretary, Carol McCullough, was on staff even before the first director, but she stayed only a brief time.

The college always had such great secretaries. I remember Carol; she was so good at getting things done.   MOREO

McCullough was replaced by Lynn Hicks, whose equally positive tenure was interrupted by the sudden death of her husband.

Lynn's husband built that little plane himself and it took him with it [when it crashed].   BASILE

We were sitting with Lynn waiting for the bad news. Mari [Dick Basile's wife] got up and made lunch by combining a variety of canned soups from the closet. It was a trying time.   FLOSSIE VALLEN

I met Lynn only once, when she came back to visit. But from everything I heard, everyone loved her.   REYNOLDS BEITZ:

Each administrative assistant stayed a bit longer. Charlene Baca followed Lynn Hicks who followed Carol McCullough. Baca was already on the job when Jim Abbey came in 1973. So there were two turn-overs, three occupants of the position, between 1967 and 1973

Charlene picked me up at the airport and gave me a brief tour of the city.   ABBEY

Charlene left to marry, but not before hiring Joan Reynolds.

Pick [Reynolds] had lectured in Levinson's class on sanitation. He learned from Charlie that a nine-month job was open in the college, and I was looking for a spot that gave me the summers off.
  Charlene was younger than I and at first that made it a bit difficult to work with one another.   REYNOLDS BEITZ

Reynolds then moved up to take the post that the dean called "the college secretary."

Actually my title was Administrative Assistant. Joe von Kornfeld [faculty member] always introduced me as the Executive Assistant to the Dean, which was a good sounding title.   REYNOLDS BEITZ

The dean had a great assistant, Joan Reynolds. Joan was working in the office when I came; she was a very gracious person. She handled a lot of [sticky] things very politely by smiling and saying, No, this is the way its going to be.
  After Joan left, Annette Kannenberg came into the spot and that's whom I remember best.   STUTTS

Twylia Towns took over Joan Reynolds' position when Reynolds moved to the desk of the administrative assistant. In the support position, Towns' long association in the college almost matched that of her co-worker. Sue Christianson started working as a part-time student. Later she became full time before leaving to marry Joel Breen ('80). The students recognized what wonderful women the college had because three of the staff, Charlene Baca, Sue Christianson and Millie Alexander married students. Not quite the same, but the business college also hired several away, including Elise Hanseman.

I would like someday to see Elise again and thank her! She was a bright woman, a wonderful lady.   GEORGE HARDBECK, DEAN OF BUSINESS AND ECONOMICS

The administrative staff grew as the college was reorganized into departments during the concluding year of this history. As one would expect, there was turnover among these secretarial assistants. But for the most part each gave something of herself to better the college. Among the givers were: Millie Alexander, Nancy Barry, Kathy Bradshaw, Sue Christianson Breen, Diane Bordenave, Joyce Jeary, Pat Miller and Gloria Peterson. The group added strength to the Twylia Towns/Joan Reynolds team.

Joan Reynolds elected to leave soon after the dean announced his upcoming retirement. Annette Kannenberg, who had been with the college for some time supporting the office of the associate dean, assumed the top spot. It was evident at once that her tenure would be as positive as her predecessors. Indeed, she has provided help in pushing this manuscript toward completion. Part of that task was done even before the writing when Kannenberg organized and consolidated the records of 1967–1989.

The Beam Hall kitchen opened with the aid of Bob Barber, who was hired as steward. Steward was the industry classification assigned to Barber by the dean. He was actually a state classified staffer who maintained the facility at the highest level. Barber retired in 1994 with 10 years of service.

> Bob Barber was our first steward. An ex-military man, he scared the hell out of the students. But he maintained the sanitation: You could eat off the floor.   LAMBERTZ

Kitchen and Boyd Dining Room activity had increased substantially by 1989 as this history came to a close. As part of the departmental implementation a second position was authorized for the kitchen. Pat Stahl, who had previously worked for the office of international students took the post. The international student office had been housed in Beam Hall as a service to the college's large international student body. Faculty and staff had come to know Stahl and the lateral move was a logical one.

> Pat Stahl came to work for us as our purchasing agent.
>
> In an earlier year Pat asked me to attend the luncheon that President Maxson gave for the entire university staff. It was a not-very-good buffet. The college agreed to do the next year's luncheon for 800 persons. Gary Manago and Don Bell and I ran the affair. Remember that food was an item we paid for but [student] labor was free. So we gave a sit-down luncheon that controlled the food cost; a buffet wouldn't have. This was in the Thomas & Mack Center [across campus] plus there was a program . Still, we had everyone back to work on time.   LAMBERTZ

Indeed, doing it right and on time was how the staff always worked.

The activities of the faculty and staff and that of the students and alumni have been separated for ease of chapter construction. Fortunately, there was no such separation. The interface of the four is more evident in the concluding chapter.

ENDNOTES FOR CHAPTER 10

1. The interview that the authors had with George Hardbeck confirmed that there were more similarities than differences between the two colleges. Hardbeck: "I always felt the student should come first."

2. Stories about the appointments of the faculty can be found in issues of the hotel alumni magazine, *Federation Of Hoteliers UNLV*, available through the College of Hotel Administration library in the Stan Fulton Building.

3. Warnings about inbreeding were taken seriously. Only two alumni, Moreo and Melton, were hired full-time during the span of this history, although several alumni were used as adjunct faculty.

4. Cross-campus degrees are permitted once again as of this writing, 2001.

5. Joseph P. Delaney's contribution to the university was recognized during its Honors Convocation on April 13, 2000.

6. *The 1980 Accreditation Report*, pp. 19–20.

7. Letter to Mrs. Twylia Towns from Dean Jerome Vallen, dated May 5, 1989.

C H A P T E R   1 1

The College: Its Students and Alumni

The College of Hotel Administration at UNLV flourished as measured by its ever-increasing enrollment and reputation. Without question, both were driven by the quality and success of its graduates. This concluding chapter looks at those who came and those who graduated.

WHO WERE THE STUDENTS?

The profile of the original student body remained largely intact during the developmental period of the college.

> The culture of the campus was so different than was Auburn's [Cummings' previous affiliation], especially the students, all of whom were working; all of whom lived off campus. They were causal people. So I remember it as a refreshing cultural change.   LESLIE CUMMINGS, HOTEL FACULTY MEMBER

Three demographic shifts altered the composition of the student body some dozen years out. One for the better; the other two less so in the eyes of many.

Men and Women

One very evident switch took place in the anatomy of the student body. Women began outnumbering men even as the age of the typical student dropped dramatically. Boyce Phillips commented on this divergence in a letter after his retirement.

"Remember, in one of the earliest years when you [Vallen] and I discussed what to do [about finding jobs] for all the females entering the program?" History says that we should not have worried."

The concerns that Phillips raised disappeared with changes in the national mood. Broadening job opportunities for women especially in the hotel business coincided with the broader equal-rights movement that had swept the nation during the 1960–1970 decade. The shift was not limited to the hotel college or even to UNLV, whose female graduates outstripped their male counterparts by the mid-1980s. The female/male gap grew larger and larger each year both for the college and for the university, as it did for higher education in general.

> There were only about 300 students enrolled [in 1979] and I was only one of two women in Levinson's class.   ANN RITTAL, '81 STUDENT

Age and Maturity

A decline in the maturity of the student body was the second demographic change. In the decade between 1969 and 1979, the average age of UNLV students ranged from 23.9 years to 24.3 years.[1] During that period, the college was recruiting junior-college transfers. That was still true as the decade closed (1978) when Rik Medlik was a visiting professor from the University of Surrey.

> Some of the students were in-state and some straight from high school, but they were not the majority. There were some in their thirties and forties, including some veterans and some from overseas.   MEDLIK

> When I started teaching I was not the oldest in the classroom. Many serious-minded veterans were returning. Moreover, those with families had to work.   AL IZZOLO, HOTEL FACULTY MEMBER

The average age of UNLV students has remained largely unchanged over the years. Since student age is not obtainable college-by-college, hotel's decline in maturity is more anecdotal than statistical.

> In the early years, almost every student brought experience to the classroom. During the last years, they were young high-school graduates who didn't know more than how to spell "hotel." It made a big difference in class content. But basically, they were very good people. DICK BASILE, HOTEL FACULTY MEMBER

It's more than coincidence that the change became evident when the college began recruiting through the American College Testing Program (ACT). Using the ACT program to recruit high-school students eliminated the need for travel and visits to distant junior-college campuses but brought a dramatic decline in the ages of the students. ACT, which administered college entrance exams, began offering schools a unique means of recruiting. It sold the names of students who indicated interest in a particular major at the time they sat for the exam. For 25 cents each the agency would mail students a letter prepared by the college, but approved by the agency. It was almost an endorsement because the college's letter was mailed to the students by ACT. Geographic and other criteria allowed an exquisite choice of recipients. By means of pre-addressed postal cards supplied by ACT, the student would then write for additional information. Cards came in by the hundreds until the contract dollars were met. More could have been done if all of the costs were not incurred by hotel's budget. The college even paid for the postage. Twylia Towns prepared stacks and stacks of informational packets which she mailed out immediately. The college's rapid response, the colored brochures and the details furnished (curriculum, work experience, scholarship lists, internships, recruiters, housing, etc.) impressed the recipients and their parents. Enrollment multiplied, but at a cost.

> The students changed. When I first came they were older having been to community colleges or working. Now they come as freshman. Everything is different. Less is done today even though we have more students. We knew the individual student. Now they're basically a number. Younger students have a different attitude; they do less with professional clubs.   CLAUDE LAMBERTZ, HOTEL FACULTY MEMBER

> The Hotel Association used to be very active. I spent a great deal of time as a faculty advisor. Without faculty support, there isn't much doing today.   JIM ABBEY, HOTEL FACULTY MEMBER

Geographic Origin

From the very beginning, hotel drew students from across the nation. The original graduating class (1969) had only two native Nevadans, Tim Bagwell and Mark Moreno. The more this geographic diversity remained part of hotel's demography, the more it changed. Today's draw is from around the world whereas most of the students during the first dozen years came from the northeastern states.

> The demographics have changed dramatically over the past 10 years. Students in my classes come from Brazil, France and Ireland. About one-third are Asian.   JOE DELANEY, COLUMNIST AND PART-TIME FACULTY MEMBER

For a long stretch of time, New York accounted for more students than any other state including Nevada. (New York and California led the junior-college movement that mushroomed in the mid-1960's.) Transfers came initially from four New York junior colleges: Paul Smiths College (Basile's earlier affiliation); New York State Agricultural and Technical Institutes at Canton (Vallen's previous affiliation) and Morrisville (Phillip's previous affiliation); and New York City Community College (Moreo's first college). From a general, printed policy on transfer, the college prepared itemized course-by-course evaluations for these four junior colleges. The base was expanded with each inquiry. A file drawer filled with evaluations enabled the office to respond to transfer questions with specificity, identifying courses allowed or disallowed for dozens of junior colleges.

Student Recruiting. The value of the Eastern student market was evident to the college almost immediately; less so to the university. Travel money to recruit came from the college exclusively. No dollar support was available from the offices of the vice presidents or the office of admissions. A trip east budgeted at $3,600 would produce at least 20 new students. Each student would enroll for a minimum of five semesters. Accumulated receipts from each semester of tuition, room and meals would cost the university no more than $36 per term per student in recruiting money. Yet, none of the top administrators would supplement hotel's recruiting dollars.

> There was very little specialized recruiting in the early days. It was generalized for the university.   JERRY CRAWFORD, DEAN OF FACULTY

Two factors eventually reduced the need for travel. The ACT mailing was one. Size of the student population was the other. Students brought students; alumni brought students.

> All of us told our friends about UNLV.   PAT MOREO, '69 STUDENT AND FACULTY MEMBER

> I have recruited for the school and I am a lifetime member of the alumni association.   GARY BROWN, '73 STUDENT

> Alumni often tell me that they attended a school fair and represented UNLV with materials that admissions sent. Vivian Fairburn ('84) still recruits for us in the Chicago area. One of our grads transferred to Hawaii and said he would represent us at their school fairs.   AL IZZOLO, HOTEL FACULTY MEMBER

Word-of-mouth was an especially potent tool in recruiting overseas students whose information resources were limited. They came in vast numbers once one member had established a Las Vegas beachhead.

> After we signed articulation agreements [with Kyung Hee in January 24, 1984], Korean students came immediately. But the downside was an increasing number who were not the Korean stereotype: not hard working; not diligent; not industrious. It had a lot to do with economic status. Families could afford to send their children overseas including those who could not [academically] get into Korean schools.   KAYE CHON, GRADUATE STUDENT AND FACULTY MEMBER

As Chapter 6 related, a great deal of informal word-of-mouth recruiting was done by members of the local professional associations as they traveled and rallied for the college. Although members of the Nevada Resort Association's board were rooting for hotel's success, they didn't do any outright student recruiting.

> I doubt very much whether they would have considered that to be an association function.   JOE DIGLES, NEVADA RESORT ASSOCIATION

Trade shows have been traditional recruiting sites among the hotel schools. The dean was never comfortable spending the large sums required to maintain booths at the two major shows, the National Restaurant Show in Chicago each spring and the New York Hotel Show each autumn. The cost per student recruited was not tenable. But like general advertising, it could have produced results that were not measurable. Still, UNLV's hotel college did not participate for many years.

> Jerry was reluctant at first, but Stefanelli and I worked on him and then worked in the booths. I took a Las Vegas layout with chips to [President] Maxson and said what if we give a $100 credit off the first tuition to attendees at the show if they win on the board. He thought it was a great idea! but did not want to convey the gaming aspect of the city.   IZZOLO

> It wasn't quite the same, but I approached the president about "trade-outs," swapping tuition for ads in national magazines. I had already negotiated the deal, but the idea didn't fly with the president.   JERRY VALLEN

All recruiting wasn't off-campus. Non-majors came to know the program because the hotel clubs allowed them to join. Similarly, hotel students participated in great numbers in general university activities. Offering many sections of the introductory class (HOA 101) captured uncommitted freshman who first signed up because they couldn't find any other open classes.

> During my first term I taught HOA 101. But never after that. Some two dozen students changed majors!   JERRY GOLL, HOTEL FACULTY MEMBER

"The Law Suit." Out-of-state students ran into a strange university regulation. Once admitted as nonresidents, citizen-students could never become resident students for tuition purposes—never. The dean turned to Bob Faiss whom he had first met in Washington, D.C. when Faiss was working in the federal tourism office. After his return to Nevada and after settling in, Faiss taught tourism as an adjunct professor. His interest in tourism waned, replaced by a successful career in law. Here he provided still another service.

The dean collected $10 and $20 bills from several dozen out-of-state students. Adding a few himself, Vallen approached Faiss with this paltry sum to discuss the unfairness of the residency regulation. Once admitted as a nonresident, even home owners could never gain resident status. Faiss agreed to look into it. Papers were prepared in 1973 for the students and the dean to bring suit against the Regents. President Don Baepler agreed with the position and the rules were changed before the case was heard. The rules weren't eased much, but they became less absolute. Persons who lived in the state for six months without going to school, or who dropped out for one year after enrolling, or whose parents lived here, or whom the military assigned here, or who were public school teachers could now be classified as residents for purpose of tuition. Equally important, an appeals committee, which the dean joined, was put in place.

Academic Background

It became evident at once that the original plan to attract junior-college graduates was valid and would prove successful. Junior-college enrollment was skyrocketing across the nation and none of the other senior colleges had geared up to accommodate the good graduates who wanted to continue. The University of Massachusetts would not even take transfers from its own junior college system, which had a good hospitality program.

> Oklahoma was taking transfers but it was very home-ecy. Denver, which was a private school, was too expensive.
>
> Several of us had already been accepted to Oklahoma when Dave Hertzen, who headed the New York City Community College program, told us about the new program at NSU . [Vallen knew Hertzen from CHRIE.] He assured us that September admission would be possible even though it was almost May. Yes, we're admitted and are ecstatic until we tell our parents. Las Vegas! Holy mackerel, it was if we were off to Siberia.   PAT MOREO,'69 STUDENT AND FACULTY MEMBER

Freshman admissions solicited by the ACT mailings gradually replaced junior-college transfers. Academic motivation and career orientation slipped as freshman diluted the maturity and quality of the classes—transfer students had already survived one or two years of post high-school work. In retrospect, it was a poor decision academically, although a great one numerically because other hotel programs, Florida International particularly, were soon competing for the junior-college market.

Admissions and Grade Point. Admissions standards and requirements were always under change as befitted a growing university with an improving academic reputation. Hotel supported all upgrades, but they were slow in coming. The college took the initiative. As enrollment increased, so did the price of admission, rising to a 2.3 grade point average (GPA) in 1978. Not much, but a step up from the campus' 2.0.

> "The admission standards to the [hotel] college are somewhat higher than for the University generally, which may account for a slightly higher level of interest and motivation." [1980 Accreditation Report[2]]

Hotel's 2.3 GPA was the university's highest standard except for the College of Health Administration.

> Nursing had done something similar because it had a huge number of applicants and not sufficient faculty. So it was permissible to do.   DON BAEPLER, UNLV PRESIDENT AND UNS CHANCELLOR

Stabilizing student enrollment was part of the plan. Unfortunately, it worked for only one year. Fall, 1978 admissions, the year of the first hike (admission eventually went to 2.5), declined. Total enrollment fell to 725, but it proved to be only a small blip in hotel's growth pattern. An equally important boost in academic stringency came when the college increased the grade point average required for graduation from 2.0 to 2.3. Once admitted, no slipping back was permitted.

> I was admitted on academic probation and had to prove myself before entering full time. [Like many others] it took me five years to finish.   KEN KAUFMAN, '71 STUDENT

During one of its innumerable self-examinations, the university created an academic disaster, the "University College." This new, independent unit accepted anyone, but did so with flawed machinery. Hotel applicants who didn't qualify, were not rejected and not required to file a new application. Instead, the student was accepted by the University College, but without notice. For years, students pursued their studies as if they were hotel enrolled. In fact, they were on probation waiting to improve grades before being admitted by way of an internal transfer.

University-college students admitted with a 2.0 GPA or less had a difficult time reaching the higher GPA that hotel was now requiring! The more credits they piled on, the more difficulty in pulling up their GPA. Students earned dozens and dozens of credits, many in hotel classes because there was no way to exclude them or to determine who they were. Then having reached 100 or more credits, they applied for graduation. Even if they had finally achieved the GPA, university regulations required them to earn their final 30 credits in uninterrupted residence as a hotel major. It was a cruel joke played on students who were never advised of the pitfall, or who were wise enough to say they weren't.

Students who fell below hotel's standards were suspended from the college, but not from the university. They were merely shuttled back into the University College, where they had to declare another major.

> Hotel students were transferred elsewhere when they could not maintain hotel's standards. John Unrue, Dean of Arts and Letters, warmed my heart when he told me that arts and letters was tired of being a dumping ground for poor hotel students.   JERRY VALLEN

Hotel students achieved in face of the stiffest grading on the campus. As Exhibit 11-1 indicates, hotel faculty were parsimonious about awarding high marks.

> I was surprised how ready the students were to argue about grades. I was not used to that sort of negotiation in Britain.   RIK MEDLIK. INTERNATIONAL VISITOR

The dean talked to faculty members who consistently issued unreasonably high grades. Faculty outside of hotel's jurisdiction were untouchable, but there were internal problems as well.

> A senior-level art-history class was considered to be a slam-dunk. Most of us skipped classes to avoid the instructor's ranting and raving. At the final class, each of us wrote down the grade we "deserved." Classmate, Buzz Cohen ('73) and I conferred. Wrought with guilt, he wrote "B." Never shy, I wrote "A+." Those are the grades we received. I had to buy the beer.   GARY BROWN, '73 STUDENT

Percentage of Grades Earned During Academic Year 1979

By	A	B	C	D	F & I*
Hotel Students	17.1	33.4	32.0	8.2	9.3
Campus Total Including Hotel	29.8	29.6	24.3	7.4	8.8

*I means Incomplete

EXHIBIT 11-1. Contrast of grades issued by faculty in the College of Hotel Administration versus grades issued by the total campus, including hotel, for Fall 1979–1980, the first year this statistic was reported in *Enrollment Trends & Selected Institutional Characteristic.* University of Nevada Office of Institutional Analysis and Planning, 1979.

Four of us took Rand's marketing class. We set up a rotation schedule: One would go Monday, another Wednesday, a third on Friday. We all came on exam days. Rand didn't mind, So Ms. Rittal, you're stuck with me this beautiful spring day.

He told us the best things to do around the globe [Rand had been to more than 100 countries]. At the George V in Paris, I had a martini as he had suggested. Since it was my first martini I couldn't tell if it was [Rand's words] the world's best. Upon hearing the story, the bartender gave me George V souvenirs.   ANN RITTAL, '81 STUDENT

Hotel's faculty thought highly of their own offering as did many of the community's highest profile personages. Included in the student body were children of entertainers, of senators and governors, of hotel professionals and of campus members, including offspring of two UNLV presidents. The dean's son graduated as a hotelier as did children of faculty members Fried, Izzolo, Metcalf, Phillips and Stutts; proud parents all. Good students always bring good memories.

I taught a [campus wide] honors class. They were bright students, but no brighter than our brightest. I especially remember people like Cathy Teasdale ('94) and Nancy Chanin ('86).   LESLIE CUMMINGS, HOTEL FACULTY MEMBER

CCCC's Transfer Students. Junior-college transfer students were the life blood of the college. It was appropriate therefore that hotel accept transfers from within its own system, from Clark County Community College (CCCC). Still, there were issues. CCCC had started internships, which the hotel college felt were overloading the hotels. Upper division credit was also divisive. The college did not equate junior-college courses (freshman and sophomore years) to upper-division classes (junior and senior years) even if they had the same titles. CCCC went further: It had the exact descriptions. Moreover, UNLV required a minium number (40) of upper-division credits, regardless of the total credits earned or transferred. For two years, 1972–1974, Presidents Zorn and Baepler battled the appropriateness of community college transfers and CCCC's duplication of UNLV courses. Even Chancellor Neil Humphrey got involved.

> The problem was broader than hotel's. Pre-med students discovered that chemistry was easier at the community college. So we had problems about what would transfer. It was not hotel's problem, it was a problem for the whole university.   DON BAEPLER, UNLV PRESIDENT AND UNS CHANCELLOR

Face-to-face meetings between the dean and CCCC's hotel directors, Ray Eade (brother of faculty member Vince Eade) and his successor, Lonnie Wright ('78), addressed the issues head-on. A transfer policy was amiably resolved because the relationships between the two programs were already on a cooperative footing.

International "Transfers." International students quickly learned how to use the system. They would obtain student visas by seeking admission to UNLV. Once in residence, they would take courses at Clark Country Community College. Not only were the courses less stringent, but tuition was considerably less. Some foreign nationals overloaded total credits per term by taking 12 credits at UNLV and nine at CCCC.

> Hotel had agreed to accept CCCC's transfers so an end-run was made around higher academic standards.   JERRY VALLEN

After this had gone on for some time, the college acted by inserting a statement in the 1980–82 catalog. No international student admitted to UNLV's hotel program could take courses anywhere else and have them transfer except with permission of the dean. This information was also included in material mailed and given to international students. Grapevine news was the most effective means of spreading the rule among the international student body. The change was dramatic.

Hoping to encourage top quality international students and dissuade poorer students, the college boosted its English-speaking and reading requirements, the TOEFL (Test of English as a Foreign Language) score to 525, the highest in the university. But a new loophole appeared. The university was building its English-as-a-second-language (ESL) program appealing to foreign students with poor English skills.

> The university's ESL program encouraged the admission of students with very poor TOEFL scores, who would then study English at UNLV. Somehow, they were also able to get into hotel courses.
>
> So many weak [Korean] students walked in the back door that, I believe, older UNLV graduates in Korea did not allow newer graduates to join their alumni association.   KAYE CHON, GRADUATE STUDENT AND FACULTY MEMBER

More and more students and more and more international students changed the dynamics of the classroom both in size and composition.

What was once a 20–25 person class is consistently 60 now.   JOE DELANEY, COLUMNIST AND
PART-TIME FACULTY MEMBER

International students cannot get work cards. [So they lack the practical experience that
has been the forte of UNLV graduates.] The American student who works a 40-hour week
earns "B" and "C" grades; the international student earns "A's"and "B's."   JIM ABBEY, HOTEL
FACULTY MEMBER

The most committed, serious and hard working students come from Western Europe. Asian
students are equally committed but they have more difficulties [culturally] to overcome. Our
home-growns are at the bottom of the academic list.   JERRY GOLL, HOTEL FACULTY MEMBER

The good international student is able to quote chapter, page and verse from the text book,
but is less able to respond to non-rote questions.   JERRY VALLEN

The initial trickle of international students was referred to the U.S. Immigration
and Naturalization Service (INS) for temporary work permits. The need was legitimate since work was a requirement of the degree. The college certified the student's
status in a form letter of its own creation. As the load on the INS grew, processing
slowed and the very requests became an issue. The subject was addressed in depth in
a letter from the dean on January 12, 1977. New possibilities were explored in subsequent meetings on campus and in the INS office. A final letter of understanding was
drafted a year later, February 10, 1978. It permitted the dean to sign off for permits
and thus halted the flood of paper work between the offices. That understanding was
never breached. International students were approved for work no sooner than the
summer preceding their junior year. Final processing took place in the campus office
of International Student Services.

How Many Were There?

Although many figures have been tossed about, there were actually 13 men in the
1969 graduating class. This first class had started with 18 juniors in the fall of 1967
out of a total enrollment of 70. The next graduating class, 1970, almost doubled the
number to 22 men, still no women. Aggressive junior-college recruiting was evident
by 1971 when 72 earned tassels! Two women, Judith Lawry and Maria Valenzuela, were
among them.

One-third of hotel's 1972 population was nonresident whereas only 12% of the
entire campus, including hotel, was from out of state. Enrollment by 1984 reached
800. By the time this history concluded in 1989, undergraduates exceeded 1,100, plus
some three dozen graduate students. Growth continued far beyond this history. Dean
Christianson reported to UNLV's News Bureau that its 1994 enrollment had 45 states
and 35 countries represented in a student body of 1,700. Growth was continuing but
not exponentially any longer because the 1970 numbers had been 40 states and 26
foreign nations.[3] Post millennium enrollment passed 2,000.

Some random values highlight the growth and source of the student body. An October 15, 1976 letter, directed to the Hilton Corporation inviting it to interview, reports 650 students enrolled. Five years later, January 23, 1981, a similar letter states that number at 900. By 1987, there were 1,070 majors.[4] Extensive growth was needed to sustain these numbers in the face of ever-larger graduating classes and tighter academic standards.

> I served with Levinson and Phillips as chair of the college's academic standards committee. It took tons of time because we were very thorough and heard appeals and petitions. Students knew we had standards and they knew what they were. CUMMINGS

THE COURSE OF STUDY

Creating career opportunities is one of the stated aims of professional schools, but so too is the education of well-rounded graduates. Hotel never faulted the changes in the university's core curriculum, but it did complain about a lack of flexibility and timing. Transfer students planned ahead and were baffled when the catalog of one year was strikingly different from the requirements of the last. Vice President Nitzschke and the faculty senate allowed dispensation to hotel's transfer students if changing requirements reduced transferability and impacted on enrollment. President Goodall supported the provision. Enrollment kept increasing so there was no need to implement the rule.

The Hotel Curriculum

Changes to the curriculum were also made by the faculty as resources increased and the program's emphases changed. No successful program could remain static during a quarter century of growth. Requirements and electives were added and dropped as necessitated or as ordered by the university's curriculum committee. Nevertheless, the basic outline, which the college developed after separating from business, continued to structure the degree. This standard curriculum (see Exhibit 11-2) was acceptable to both the 1970 and 1980 accreditation teams. Page 20 of the *1980 Report* said:

> "The distribution of course credit hours appears to be well balanced. It is consistent with the student's need to perform acceptably in society, in the business community generally and in his professional career specifically."

The 128 credits were eight more than the university's graduation requirement and four more than most other degrees, a discrepancy that does not now exist. Typically, hotelees earned 130–145 credits by graduation because credits were lost in transfer and transfer students were the college's audience. In addition, hotel students had work requirements.

Two Work Experiences

No other hotel program had two work requirements. But then, no other program was located close to thousands of hotel rooms. Work requirement number one was an

Courses	Credits	Courses	Credits
Mathematics:	6	Hotel	33
Algebra; Statistics		Introduction	
Arts and Letters	21	Food I & II	
English I and II		Hotel Law	
American and Nevada History		Hotel Design	
Sociology and Psychology		Human Relations	
Public Speaking		Hotel Accounting	
Business	27	Hotel Marketing	
Accounting I & II		Hotel Operations & Management	
Business Law		Internship I & II	
Economics I & II		Work Requirement (no academic	
Finance		credit)	
Management		Physical Education	4*
Marketing		Electives (At least 12 credits within the	37
Management Information Systems		Hotel College and at least 12 credits	
		outside the College)	
		Total	**128**

*Substitute electives for prior military service, age or transfer status.

EXHIBIT 11-2. Curriculum in effect for the school year 1974–75. Soon thereafter, physical education was dropped as a university requirement. The college dropped hotel design (more accurately, kitchen design) and internship II as requirements and substituted food and beverage control and hotel accounting II.

internship managed by the college. Requirement number two put the burden on the student (see Exhibit 11-3.) Employment opportunities during the school years and job placement at graduation were spin-offs from both.

Internship. Internships in the hotels were first broached during the initial interviews in 1966. To Vallen's amazement, the concept was applauded by the hoteliers who had visualized that very thing.

> The Nevada Resort Association [NRA] pitched the internships although some were against it fearing confidential information would get out. You know, the old gamblers' attitude.   LEO LEWIS, BINION'S FINANCIAL OFFICER AND HOTEL FACULTY MEMBER, BOTH PART TIME AND FULL TIME

Bob Cahill, the NRA's executive, had this to say:

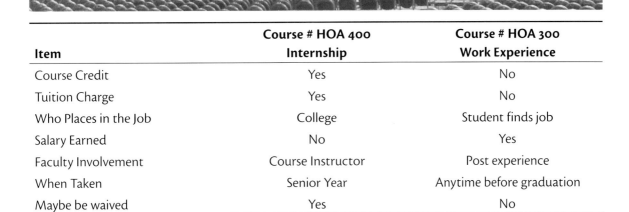

Item	Course # HOA 400 Internship	Course # HOA 300 Work Experience
Course Credit	Yes	No
Tuition Charge	Yes	No
Who Places in the Job	College	Student finds job
Salary Earned	No	Yes
Faculty Involvement	Course Instructor	Post experience
When Taken	Senior Year	Anytime before graduation
Maybe be waived	Yes	No

EXHIBIT 11-3. Comparison of the two work experiences required for graduation.

"Jerry appreciated the finest working lab in the world."[5]

It was the best internship anywhere!   TOM BELL, REGENT AND LEGAL COUNSEL FOR HUGHES NEVADA

One of the first things I remember about it [the start of hotel administration] was the apprenticeship program.   JERRY CRAWFORD, DEAN OF FACULTY

A three-credit course was scheduled during the senior year. Students rotated departments in the several hotels on a fixed schedule that the hotels met. So every intern was in engineering, or accounting, or laundry during the same week. Seminar classes built around that week's assignment were managed on a rotating basis by one of the seniors under faculty supervision. All the hotels assigned top executives as coordinators.

I always told the intern, if the department head doesn't tell you what you want to know, come and see me. The final session was always with me when we reviewed what they had done during the term.   LEWIS

What goes around, comes around:

Mark Sterbens ['75] interned at the [original] MGM. [Mavros was director of purchasing (and president of the IFSEA) and thus interacted with interns.] Many years later, Sterbens took the management of Terrible's Hotel-Casino and recommended me when a job opened within the company.   MIKE MAVROS

Internships were restricted to seniors with a GPA of 2.5 or higher. Three credits with corresponding tuition charges were earned. If space allowed, a second opportunity was permitted at a second hotel. As the program grew, interns were placed in hospitals, trade unions, restaurants, the airport, Nellis Air Base, the convention center, the tourist bureau, the school district and the state hotel and restaurant associations. Every effort was made to accommodate individual student preferences.

As enrollment increased, students were permitted to opt out of the internship if previous industry experience warranted. Some did, foolishly. Doing so was like staying away from a reputedly "hard class."

> The internship was one of the program's biggest selling points. It gave the student the hands-on experience to observe what was going on.
>
> I remember one student from the first class, Marc Marino, who came to work at the Sahara after his internship.   PHIL ARCE, HOTEL MANAGER, SAHARA HOTEL

> The internship was very successful. I would run into students in the hotels who told me, I'm an intern here. It was obvious that the hotels liked it because they did it.   JOE DELANEY, COLUMNIST AND PART-TIME FACULTY MEMBER

Gabe Vogliotti, the NRA's 1967 executive, arranged for 25 interns the first term. The program started slower than that with a half-dozen each in term three and term four. To build relationships, the dean became the first faculty coordinator. Arrangements were made by personal interviews with the top executive of every participating hotel. Caesars Palace took the first intern under the aegis of Harry Wald. History was made! Placements at the Horseshoe (Leo Lewis), the Riviera (Frank Watts) and the Sahara (Phil Arce) followed immediately.

> I interned at the Riviera under the tutleage of Frank Watts and Jim DeMaris. Frank was my mentor. I went through every department and remember especially Chef Ray McCurtin. He said, Ok lad, go down to the locker room and put on some whites. When I got back, he asked what I didn't want to do. I'm not wild about working with fish or killing anything. So he took me to a bandsaw where I cut live lobsters in half. They were doing 500–600 covers in the hour before the [dinner] show.   PAT MOREO, '69 STUDENT AND FACULTY MEMBER

> I was the Frontier Hotel's first intern. I was told to do a good job because the college wanted to be certain it was invited back. Purchasing and receiving were strong departments, and my first job was as a supply and cost controller.   KEN KAUFMAN, '71 STUDENT

> We were having record-keeping problems in the Riviera's kitchen [before Lambertz came to teach at UNLV]. If an employee took food from the production kitchen to some other kitchen, but forget to record it, we charged it to the coffee shop. The coffee shop was always in the red. We gave the problem to an intern—don't remember his name. Figure out what we should do. And he did, and it worked!   LAMBERTZ

As the program aged and the dean accessed executives by other means, the course was handed off to a variety of coordinators: Phillips, Levinson, Izzolo. Izzolo's success was so good that whenever the name of a middle manager in any hotel was needed, the college turned to Al.

> Charlie [Levinson] taught me. Drop off a card and get a card from everyone. We were always there to help with information about the school. And they would remember: Can you talk to my nephew? IZZOLO

Employment. Unlike the internship, this graduation requirement forced students to find their own jobs. To help, the college posted job openings and brought in recruiters. "Gainful employment" meant payroll stubs or federal tax statements had to be submitted as proof. Employer letters were not acceptable, and work in family businesses was discouraged. Two summers of employment, one in the front-of-the-house and one in the back-of-the-house was the original concept. Two 10-week summers at 40 hours per week equated to the 800 hours that were required. Many students worked during the school year; as much for the income as for the requirement.

> Many students took jobs while going to school. DELANEY

> The location of the school contributed to its success. Not only for training but for the opportunity to earn money. DICK BROWN, DONOR INTERMEDIARY AND FATHER OF ALUMNUS, GARY

> UNLV is not only on par with the other schools, but it offers the big advantages of internships and work in the industry while in school. SIG FRONT, VICE PRESIDENT, SAHARA HOTEL

> I received my first lessons in yield management while working at a motel. The owner taught us how to eye up the guest before quoting a rate. If they were from East Los Angeles, maybe a $28 rate; from the more prosperous suburbs, $35. If they came from Beverly Hills with shined shoes and a blazer, quote the rack rate. GARY BROWN, '73 STUDENT

> I worked the back bar at the Mint and also worked with Sizzler as a management trainee. KEN KAUFMAN, '71 STUDENT

> Really got to know Roberta Burton ('81) when we went to Bryce Canyon at the end of their season to clean rooms. ANN RITTAL, '81 STUDENT

Jobs brought meaning to classroom discussion:

> Mark Sterbens ('75), Stan Moore ('76) and John Cerali ('75) were working at the desk of Caesars. We were talking in class about overbooking. Caesars' 600 rooms were running full, but they had such good indoctrination that the students insisted Caesars never overbooked. ABBEY

> I worked at the Tropicana Golf Club [across Tropicana Avenue from the Tropicana Hotel]. Bill Hoffard, the manager, would pull the reservation cards and make the clerks sell the

rooms. I had to walk Rudy Vallee [well known singer/performer] one night because we were overbooked.   MOREO

As the program matured, the college partnered with industry to structure formal work programs during a one-term or one-year leave of absence. A pre-arranged, non-Las Vegas experience could be co-joined to meet both work experience and internship requirements.

Through his ARA contacts, Dick Basile orchestrated a 6-month work fellowship for me at Loyola University's foodservice.   GARY BROWN

I took off the first term of my senior year to return to Alaska and work.   RITTAL

Comparable off-campus programs were developed with Disney and other U.S. companies as well as assignments in China, France, Guam and Japan.

The first time we offered summer internships we had three students. Recently we had nearly 100.   IZZOLO

Why both back and front experiences? Students argued that they didn't want to do the front-of-the house (or the back-of the house) because they would never work there. Faculty knew otherwise.

My son worked for Caesars while he was going to school. Told me that never in his life would he get into food and beverage. Currently, he is assistant director of catering and convention services with Hyatt.   ALAN STUTTS, FACULTY MEMBER

Len Studley ('70) worked for Days Inns for years. One of those sworn foods guys who ended up on the hotel side.   PAT MOREO, '69 STUDENT AND FACULTY MEMBER

How to evaluate the wide range of jobs and experiences? For example, one woman sought credit for her topless show experience. Some students were managers, some supervisors, and some first-line employees. Equating them in clock hours to meet the 800-hour standard required finesse. The problem was given to Dick Basile, who created the rules, developed the guidelines and administered their application. As with every university proviso, a faculty committee stood ready to hear appeals. The burden of numbers grew until other faculty members assumed part of the load including Joe von Kornfeld and Jerry Goll.

Dick Basile did the evaluations to start, then I helped him but we used different criteria. My industry experience was from a distance. We talked in order to narrow the gap. I even rewrote some of the rules and criteria. Finally, I took it over entirely.   GOLL

Except for one explanatory orientation, there was no formal class. Consequently, there was no tuition charge and there was no academic credit. Students didn't register until the work requirement was met, which meant some seniors didn't graduate. To accommodate those who had good jobs in one industry segment or who never completed the requirement, a *Second Option* was offered. One six-month stint in industry would meet the work requirement, but the option was not available until all the academic requirements had been met. Unfortunately, this led to "alumni" who completed the academic requirements but who never graduated.

All of which raised the issue of who was to walk across the graduation stage. With so many students from distant locations, the college's position—which wasn't always the university's—was let them walk. Hotel sought the permission for international and out-of-state seniors to save them the expense of returning. Otherwise their own irresponsibility in not finishing would turn to animosity toward the university. Some parents came from the ends of the world especially when it was the first college graduate in the family. The process proved complicated to explain especially if the students had not alerted their parents. After all, they had just seen their children "graduate," when, in fact, they had not.

Job Placement. Job offers and careers were built upon the two work experiences.

> The part of the history that impresses me most is the success of the students. We put a lot of sweat and time into it, and the interns ended up as executives.   LEO LEWIS, BINION'S FINANCIAL OFFICER AND HOTEL FACULTY MEMBER, BOTH PART TIME AND FULL TIME

> Our students are not looking for someone to take care of them. They take off their coats and solve the problem. They're willing to get their hands dirty to make certain the customer is taken care of.   CLAUDE LAMBERTZ, HOTEL FACULTY MEMBER

Placing graduating students was high on the list of early priorities. Fortunately, there was almost a two-year hiatus until the first seniors hit the pavement. Even before that, came the realization that Las Vegas would not be a major source of jobs at first. Bob Cahill, executive to the NRA wrote:

"The hotels cooperated . . . in intern programs, [but] they fell short in giving . . . employment."[6]

> When we finally got [the program] started, we had difficulty selling any of the hotels on hiring the students. There were only a few that pushed it.   FRANK WATTS, RIVIERA FINANCIAL OFFICER

> The hotel's didn't hire the first graduates. They were all going out of town. I went out to the first job fair although I had no openings. I thought this was crazy, why do we have a school if we're not hiring its students? Part of the reason was the lack of college grads in the hotels. There was some apprehension. Why would they hire someone better educated than they?   PHIL ARCE, SAHARA HOTEL MANAGER

> There was trepidation with the unions and middle managers. Some kid that I trained is going to tap me on the shoulder and take my job.

I was running around trying to impress the hotel people that there wasn't going to be a stampede [of hotel graduates taking their jobs]. Many of the out-of-state kids weren't going to stay.

Personnel directors were almost unheard of [when the program was getting started]; they were a rare thing. Some guys might wear a couple of hats and one of them might say personnel director. [The federal lawsuit against the Strip Hotels, see Chapter 5, created personnel offices throughout the city.]   JOE DIGLES, NEVADA RESORT ASSOCIATION

Getting placed initially was difficult because the hoteliers were uncertain what to do with the graduates. Place them in middle management, upper management? Everyone had come up in the ranks by doing the jobs and learning them that way.   MIKE UNGER, '71 STUDENT

Grads wouldn't try to get jobs in town. The idea was get some experience and then come back. But Howie Weiner ('71) was captain in the Hilton showroom making more in a month that we were getting in a year.   MOREO

Despite such negativity, five of the first 16 graduates took jobs in the city at the Bonanza, Flamingo, Mint, Thunderbird and Sahara hotels. Exhibit 11-4 is an abbreviated list of alumni working in the Las Vegas area in 1988. One bright spot on the local scene was the special effort made by Sig Front and Doug Farley at the Sahara.

I wanted UNLV students because I needed them. I wasn't doing it out of the goodness of my heart. Doug [Farley] and I recruited for sales. We hired for six months and then brought in another. We'd get them working on the files and then move them to tour and travel. But first of all we had to convince management, beginning with Alec Shoofey [the GM] to sign on. We paid the same as comparable [non-student] positions.   SIG FRONT, VICE PRESIDENT, SAHARA HOTEL

Sig [Front] was the biggest pusher of all.   ARCE

In a way, there was a positive slant to the difficulty of breaking into the Las Vegas market:

One positive side of students not getting local jobs was the publicity those early classes gave to UNLV. They went out and publicized the school. Industry people said, The hotel school? I didn't know they had one.   ARCE

Employers outside of the city actually knew the program better and promptly came to interview. Early interviewers had to convince their bosses that Las Vegas really had a school; it wasn't to be only a fun trip. Among the earliest interviewers was Al Izzolo.

I recruited [before joining the faculty] for ARA with Don Tipton. He and I would take Levinson, Phillips and Vallen out to lunch. Then I would call and get references and the hires always seemed to work out.

Robert Abel (77)   Operations Controller, Holiday Casino/Holiday Inn
Harriet Adler (86)   Executive Housekeeper, El Rancho
Robert Appleyard (75)   Director of Purchasing, Flamingo
Gail Bardacos (73)   Casino Manager, Bally's Grand
Tim Barnett (79)   Hotel Director, Fitzgerald's
Joseph Barraza (83)   Casino Floorman, Palace Station
Floyd Benedict (73)   General Manager, Ramada Suites St. Tropez
Bruce Dozier (81)   Sales Executive, Las Vegas Convention and Visitors Authority
E. J. Fei (74)   Casino Host, Caesars Palace
William Franko (83)   Food and Beverage Controller, Bally's Grand
Jim Germain (76)   Vice President Sales and Marketing, USA Hosts
Gregory Goussak (80)   Internal Auditor, Four Queens
Marty Gross (79)   Vice President Sales, Alexis Park
Dwayne Hushaw (84)   Manager, Wherehouse Entertainment
Bruce Jackson (76)   Labor Relations Representative, Las Vegas Hilton
Al Kingham (77)   Owner, Commercial Real Estate Services
Cindi Kiser (80)   Vice President Human Resources, Sands
Margaret Kurtz (85)   Staff Writer/Public Relations Coordinator, Caesars Palace
Pat McFadden (80)   Inventory Control Supervisor, Bally's Grand
Anneliese McKenna (82)   Dealer, Bally's Grand
Christopher Moore (85)   Sales Manager, Aladdin
Andy Nazarechuk (79)   Assistant Director of Catering and Convention Services, Tropicana
Rick Padovese (83)   Assistant Controller, Riviera
Oscar Portillo (73)   Vice President Restaurant Operations, Peppermill and General Manager,
                                   Rainbow Casino
Robert Prince (72)   Vice President Hotel Operations, Union Plaza
Ronald Roark (74)   Executive Housekeeper, Caesars Palace
Richard Sabo (83)   Account Executive, Greyhound Exposition Services
Fred Simonds (82)   Senior Account Manager, Residence Inn
Neil Smyth, Jr. (74)   Assistant to the Executive Vice President, Latin American Operations,
                                   Caesars Palace.
Andy Weather (82)   Travel Consultant, Prestige Travel Centers
Brooks Whitmore (86)   Sales Manager, Imperial Palace
Joe Wilcock (86)   Games Manager, Dunes
Clayton Wright (88)   Assistant Front Office Manager, Las Vegas Club.

EXHIBIT 11-4. A representative, but incomplete listing of alumni in the Las Vegas Area, 1988. Source: *UNLV Hotel Alumni Association*, College of Hotel Administration, Summer, 1988, Vol.12, No. 2, p. 11; Vol. 13, No 1, p 15; Vol. 13, No.2, p 15

UNLV was considered a blue collar school; that is, the students had a strong work ethic. So I had heard about it even when I was still working in New York. Washington State was one of our [ARA's] prime western sources. But when I compared the work experiences, I knew why UNLV's reputation was growing.   IZZOLO

Invitations were extended by the dean's office to companies that were featured in the trade press. Many responded positively. Regular interviewers brought previous graduates back to interview friends. Charlie Brown's brought Larry Griewisch ('69), who kept moving up in that organization. Interviewers are a measure of a program's success as bread and milk deliveries measure a restaurant's success. Want to know how things are going, ask the delivery (interview) person. The alumni newsletters reported on the progress: 60 companies interviewed in 1984–85; 75 were mentioned in the dean's final column, 1989. In that year, some 2,000 interview lines were scheduled by the placement office..

UNLV's hotel college is the best place in the country to recruit top, young talent.   BILL SEARS, HUMAN RESOURCES FOR SUMMA AND LATER THE MGM GRAND

Students impressed the industry recruiters, who found their campus visits rewarding. In 1978, Sheraton made more offers to UNLV students than to any other program.   RIK MEDLIK, INTERNATIONAL VISITOR

The college responded to the two major strikes that shut down the city by emptying the classrooms. The union objected and picketed the president's office. Local employment offers increased tremendously thereafter because students had worked around the clock to staff the struck hotels.

Bill Dakin, the university's placement officer, contributed wholeheartedly to the college's success. He worked diligently to make his office the best among all universities. He held to strict rules, shaped up the students, cooperated with the college, accommodated the recruiters, and put together a complete resume on each applicant. Everyone, students, faculty and recruiters, appreciated his attention and concern.

Dakin lived the job. He was committed to having the best in the nation! Interviewers said that UNLV had the best all-around package, facilities and organization. He reviewed every student packet and personally met every recruiter.

Bill was angry if we overstayed lunch and a student was shortchanged in time. The recruiters bought lunch because I had deep pockets and a short arm. Vallen had taught me that when I was recruiting.

All were happy to comply. Several held receptions the night before interviews. I remember Four Seasons was especially pleased. Hilton would put out shrimp and food and desserts. They were amazed when 125 recruits would show up to their parties.

I recall two students vying with one another. One had 13 job offers; the other only 12.   IZZOLO

Dakin kept careful records. His 1975–76 accounting reported that of the 69 hotel students using his office, 49 had taken employment; six were still looking; one had gone home; one was in the military; and 12 failed to let him know their status. His already careful style was enhanced when he moved his office into the new Beam Hall. Chapter 7 has more of that story.

> Hotel did something that I didn't agree with. It put placement on the top floor. I said We shouldn't be giving away space that we worked so hard to get.   GEORGE HARDBECK, DEAN OF BUSINESS AND ECONOMICS

The Graduate Program

The graduate program emerged from a degree called *The Second Baccalaureate.* Responding to market demand, the college began offering a second undergraduate degree to students who already held one. Business graduates took one year; all others graduated in three semesters. The second baccalaureate included the work experience requirement, which the subsequent graduate degree did not. Graduates were older and placement was high.

Although not enthralled by the idea, the dean submitted a graduate proposal in 1979–80. One very valid argument pointed out the marketing possibilities. Cornell's master's degree, which was the only other one around, was open only to Cornell undergraduates. UNLV would open the degree to the whole nation. As with all such proposals, a series of hurdles, the graduate committee among them, had to be overcome..

> We had difficulties getting the graduate program approved primarily because Dean Hardbeck objected. We were not approved the first time. Unfortunately, I expressed my opinion at the meeting, Why does a non-accredited College of Business have the power and authority to reject a program that's considered one of the best in the United States? Christianson took over the following year. He was more political than I so we won approval then.   FRANK BORSENIK, HOTEL FACULTY MEMBER

The proposal stumbled along: The Alumni Federation's bulletin reported approval by the Board of Regents in 1981 but without any dollar commitment. Courses finally began the summer of 1983. With WICHE's (Western Interstate Commission for Higher Education) approval, residents of certain western states attended without tuition. A "summers-only" degree was featured as a means of attracting hotel teachers who needed advanced degrees. It didn't work so the offering gradually morphed into a standard graduate program with Pat Moreo the first director and Dave Christianson the second. To grow this new market, an accommodation was made for simultaneous employment by scheduling classes at 7:30 a.m. and 5:30 p.m. By the fall of 1984 there were 10 regular and 6 special students enrolled. The fall class 1986 had 28 grad students; among them were enrollees from China, Korea, the Dominican Republic, and the Netherlands.

I came in 1984 the second year of the graduate program. There were three students in the previous class; seven to eight with me. We were very close, almost like brothers and sisters. All going to class together; all drinking coffee together.

We worked very hard. The small classes required a lot of preparation. I remember talking about how extensive it was.

When I finished, I was asked to stay on, but Vallen told me if I was staying in education, I had to go for the Ph.D. So I went to Virginia Tech [and returned with degree in hand].   KAYE CHON, GRADUATE STUDENT AND FACULTY MEMBER

I had a small team of graduate students to work in the Hospitality Center and they always made us look good. I trained a few and then they trained the next generation.   ALAN STUTTS, HOTEL FACULTY MEMBER

Admission then and now requires an undergraduate GPA of 2.75 or 3.00 in the final two years; a satisfactory GMAT (Graduate Management Admissions Test) score; a 750-word essay, one year of either supervisory management or education; two letters of recommendation; and a TOEFL of 550 for international students.

STUDENT CLUBS AND ACTIVITIES

Everything was new when the program was launched. The advantage of an unchartered start was to do whatever is needed; no one can second guess. The balancing scale is that no one knew what needed to be done or how to do it. Pat Moreo's comments about his first days, which were the first days of the program, set the tableau for what most of the new students—many of whom had never been west—experienced.

"New arrivals were sent to the Topper Motel on the Strip. [I had expected to] see swirls of sand, date palms and perhaps a camel or two. Instead [it was] a glorious September morning with the Red Rock Mountains to the west. Within two days we were in the brand-new dormitory.

Bussel and his wife, Jackie, made us [the first entering class] welcome. There was no swimming pool on campus, so Bussel invited the entire student body to his apartment and everyone went swimming. Soon thereafter, the dean and his wife, Flossie, had everyone to their [Ottawa Street] home for a barbeque. It was a pattern that was to be repeated over the years. Probably more people had been in and out of the Vallen home than any residence in the world.

The reception was important because it was a signal that the faculty cared. There was a sense of both family and profession."[7]

No one knew then that the Vallen's home would also come to host graduation parties, term-end parties and alumni parties.

My second date with Karen, my wife-to-be, was at a Vallen party.   OWEN KHATOONIAN, '79 STUDENT

> We had hundreds of students and parents through the house over the years. Nothing was ever missing and nothing ever broken.   FLOSSIE VALLEN

The freshman welcoming party remained as a pool party in the dean's home until the 12th year. It was moved in 1979 to the pool of the Aladdin Hotel. At 850 students, enrollment had surpassed the capacity of a private home.

Student Activities

Hotel students were doers! Free of restrictive traditions, they created the events that built traditions. They saw needs and opportunities and carried them to completion despite personal work commitments.

> The first thing that struck me was their motivation. Many were earning a living working on the Strip, often at night. It could not have been easy to go to bed at dawn and come to lectures at 10:00 a.m, but they did.   RIK MEDLIK. INTERNATIONAL VISITOR

> I don't remember too much about the junior year except that I carried 21 credits, was busy with the hotel association, was pledge vice president of Alpha Kappa Psi, and ushered at Ham Hall. [Grades were good, she won scholarship support.] My days were planned down to laundry-times, library-times, letter-writing-times, nap-times and having fun-times.   ANN RITTAL, '81 STUDENT

The Hotel Association (HA) was the vehicle, the gathering point, the means by which ideas were put in place and consummated. Local chapters of the professional organizations, such as the FSEA (foodservice), the HSMA (sales) and the HMA (accounting), were being pressured by their nationals to create junior chapters. Chapters were formed throughout the years, some as early as 1968–69.

> Jim Rafferty ('78) came to the office and asked Why we didn't have an IFSEA chapter. I had no idea! So he said, Let's start one. It is ongoing still. In many years UNLV has had the nation's largest student chapter.   IZZOLO

The college endorsed the movement, but decided that all clubs would be under an umbrella group, the Hotel Association. One organization would minimize the competition that was evident on other campuses, including Cornell's. HA's umbrella sheltered the creation and sustenance of sub-interests. Other groups (Club Managers in 1978; Wine Tasting; Casino Management Club in 1981; AH&MA junior chapter, 1987; even a Hawaii Club) were eventually chartered as divisions of HA. After Beam Hall opened, the association was housed in a two-suite office immediately by the entrance. Its location and presence brought prestige to the group and indicated to the student body the importance that the college administration placed upon it.

> I remember our big thing was getting camel-hair blazers that had the hotel logo.   PAT MOREO, '69 STUDENT AND FACULTY MEMBER

An anonymous, "naive and grateful freshman" wrote in the *Hospitality Herald*:

"And then I saw it, a heavenly light. . . . Its letter indelibly branded on my being as
people chanted H.A., H.A. I joined everything. The club even had a special package deal: all seven clubs for one low price."

The umbrella decision proved to be a wise one. HA flourished, and its size enabled
it to rally dozens or hundreds of people to participate in campus events, build floats,
vote or just gather. By 1977 membership had reached 300; by 1982, 350!

> The Hotel Association no longer [as of 2000] serves as an umbrella group. It has been flip-
> flopped. Rather than HA as an umbrella for the various clubs, the groups umbrella the Hotel
> Association. There is no single entity representing the college. That's unfortunate.   JERRY
> GOLL, HOTEL FACULTY MEMBER

HA's reach was amazing. It elected home-coming kings and queens and took
many senior offices in student government. It maintained liaison with the professional organizations, toured the hotel properties, invited speakers, and served in
many valuable ways as an arm of the college. It was also a good citizen, participating
in a variety of community activities.

> The Hotel Association's umbrella was so strong! Cindi Kiser ('80), the first female president,
> had a great cabinet. The association did everything from speakers to donuts.   AL IZZOLO,
> HOTEL FACULTY MEMBER

Community Giving. In just one school year, 1976–77, hotel students served the community in several ways. They assumed a major maintenance and repair project for St
Jude's Ranch For Children, a favorite charity of Joe Delaney's. HA won a special com-
mendation for that work. It also provided ushers for St Jude's Nite of Stars.

> I got to meet Sinatra at the Nite of Stars. Marty Burzinski ('82) was head usher and arranged
> to take me backstage where I visited with Frank and his wife Barbara. [UNLV awarded Sinatra
> an honorary degree in 1977.]   ANN RITTAL, '81 STUDENT

The association organized a dance-a-thon that raised $10,000 for the Muscular Dys-
trophy drive. That work brought HA members to the attention of the MDA's Telethon
on Labor Day weekend, for which HA members also volunteered. Members of HA
donated the most blood during many of the annual blood drives. In cooperation with
the Hairdresser Union, it create a campus "Clip-a-Thon" that raised $2,000 for Mul-
tiple Sclerosis.

At other times and other years, HA repeated its successes and created new ones such
as the Bowl-a-thon to raise funds for the Community Food Bank, cookbook sales and a
gingerbread-man baking contest. One out-of-the-ordinary event involved W. Hodding
Carter III, former White House advisor, and then Chairman of the American Council

of Young Political Leaders. With Nevada's Attorney General, Frankie Sue Del Papa, acting as a conduit, hotel students hosted the Committee of Youth Organizations of the USSR. In Hodding's words:

"This exchange was one of the most successful in recent memory."

Campus Events. Hotel students were equally busy with campus activities. The club created the annual Oktoberfest and the Masquerade Dance and the first annual comedy night. All of which HA ran before handing them over to the student government for broader access and greater appeal. Not by coincidence, the members of HA and the officers of student government were intertwined. CSUN (Consolidated Students of the University of Nevada) presidents were hotel students in several successive years in the late 1970s.

> Marty Burzinski was president of CSUN in 1981.   RITTAL

Every political candidate, campus and community, vied for the hotel vote. During this period, the Hotel Association was the largest single organization on campus voting in a single bloc. In 1979, it elected the student president and the homecoming queen; it took first place in the campus blood drive and second place in the float contest.

> I helped [conceive] some of the floats.   FRANK BORSENIK, HOTEL FACULTY MEMBER

The club helped to move the radio station to campus and ran a radio program for some time thereafter. It aided the library during several of its fund-raiser/public-relations events.

Responding to a call from Charles Vanda, HA served as paid ushers for the opening of Artemus Ham Concert Hall and the beginning of the Master's Series.

> Marty Burzinski had become head usher, so we all ushered as a favor, but saw some great shows.   RITTAL

The club's presence led to an invitation to take over bar service and receptions during events at both the Judy Bayley Theater and Ham Hall. The hotel club assumed the responsibilities because the Las Vegas Symphonic Society was unable to staff the operation or make a profit. By 1981, HA entered into a formal agreement to operate the concessions in both facilities. They grew and prospered until the Society wanted them back. It took the intervention of President Goodall, by way of a letter (dated October 10, 1983) addressed to Managing Director Eileen Hayes, for the hotel students to retain rights to the concessions. That threw a cloud on the arrangements and the club stepped out two years later.

Newly installed officers in September 1986 decided to boost the treasury by catering on- and off-campus. Donna Leahy, that year's catering director, advertised the service. The response was unexpected. Campus catering was a no-no since hotel had agreed years earlier, when the new building was under construction, not to cater on campus in competition to Saga, UNLV's contracted foodservice provider. Technically, receptions for the performing arts were also Saga's prerogative. But they managed there no better than had the Symphonic Society and were only too happy abrogating to the hotel club.

Sports Activities. At the football games there were tailgate parties and chili nights. Football, soccer, volleyball, flag football, HA participated in all the intramural teams for men and women. HA softball teams entered the Budweiser Western Regional Softball Tournament. It fielded teams in tennis and racquetball. Golf tourneys were run in cooperation with the alumni association and separately against the faculty. HA was always present in a bloc when it came to cheering on the athletic teams.

Professional Activities. With all that the club had going on, it retained its major focus, professional growth and activities. HA ran tours of the hotels and, with space provided by the hotels, invited monthly speakers such as George Rhodine, director of community relations for Hughes Hotels, and Doug Farley, director of sales at the Sahara. A letter from Parviz Kazemzadeh recommended using Hilton's Henri Lewin as a speaker. He swept in about an hour late with an entourage, but he was as different and stimulating as every account of him reports.

The dean's office joined in to build vocabulary by posting a "word of the week," with its definition and encouraging faculty and students to use it in class or in written materials.

Senior chapters of the professional associations held campus dinner meetings once each year with students catering and organizing the event, always under the watchful eyes of chapter advisors.

The strength of the Hotel Association, the reputation of the college and the lure of Las Vegas helped HA in its bids to host the national meetings of the junior chapters of the several professional organizations. HA's strength and self-confidence assured the success of the gathering once the campus had been selected. UNLV hosted the national meeting of the junior chapters of the International Foodservice Executives Association one spring, with 200 delegates attending.

> We had been in business only a few years when we bid for the student FSEA convention. It was among the best ever because we had members such as Bernie Fried ('79), Dan Hawkins ('79), Cindi Kiser ('80), Pat McFadden ('80) and Mike Starr ('81).   AL IZZOLO, HOTEL FACULTY MEMBER

HA bid and won two HSMA student conventions. The 1987 gathering, a very, very successful event, was held in April at Hilton's Flamingo Hotel. William (Bill) H. Edwards, vice chairman of Hilton Hotels Corporation was one of the speakers. Also on the program were John Norlander, president Radisson Hotels Corp and Richard Goeglein, COO of Holiday Inns. Edwards was the only executive to attend the entire program, which included a luncheon speech by Steve Wynn.

> Wynn's speech was extremely well done. Of course, he doesn't read, so the speech seemed to be extemporaneous. How did you do that without any preparation, I asked. Who said I didn't prepare? came the reply.   JERRY VALLEN

Hilton and Wynn were battling in court over a particular issue. It was with uncertainty that the dean left the head table and approached Bill Edwards, asking him to the dais to meet Wynn. He accepted the notion that his vision was better than Wynn's and he could better navigate the stairs. Edward's wonderful courtesy was noted in a thank-you letter and he responded in kind on April 21, 1987.

> " I was extremely impressed with the image presented by the attendees and I certainly have renewed faith and confidence in the future well being of our industry having had the opportunity to associate and mix with those attending the convention."

Seminars and formal programs did not wait for national gatherings. Each year, HA organized a weekend of activities that often ended with a dinner dance. The formal dinner meeting of October 1976 had Lieutenant Governor Bob Rose as its speaker. The association used that time to lobby him for more hotel faculty and the need for a building. A dozen years later the formal event was still going strong, titled that year, *Stepping Out 1989*.

Day of the Professional was another annual event that united all the subclubs under HA's banner. Caesars Palace was the venue for the third year when some 100 students came. They were supported by the attendance of Jerry Gordon, Caesar's VP and GM. Student officers that year were Jay Cutchin ('74), treasurer; Mark Sterbens ('75), president; and Jennifer Swan ('75), secretary.

The Hotel College.   The hotel college was the chief beneficiary of the energy and activity of the hotel association. Unity among the student body and ease of interaction with the faculty played major roles in maintaining positive communications throughout. Rare was the hotel student who marched in protest. Matters of concern reached the administration through the representatives of the umbrella organization. And through them came solutions. Interactive coffee hours, *Café Hotelier*, were operated by the IFSEA chapter in the Boyd Dining Rooms. Good conversation came easily with fresh baked goods. Prior to Beam Hall, coffee hours were held in the student lounge and TGIF was a ritual at the Starboard Tack every Friday afternoon.

Student-faculty interaction took several approaches. One year, students secretly gave small gifts to favorite faculty members. At term's end came a coffee hour during which the faculty members met their "secret admirers."

> Students were active in many areas. They gave awards and plaques. Mine was for "Multiple, Multiple Choice" because my multiple-exam questions had two answers.   LESLIE CUMMINGS, HOTEL FACULTY MEMBER

In 1976, the first annual roast of student officers and faculty members began. These roasts went on for several years until the novelty turned rough.

At one of the closing student affairs, [faculty member] Frank Brown was the speaker. The faculty, staff and student body had agreed not to laugh at any of his jokes. I was sorry we did that because he didn't think it was funny even after we told him what happened.   JOAN REYNOLDS BEITZ, ADMINISTRATIVE ASSISTANT

I can't recall any specifics about the roasts, but they "got" the faculty whether you were there or not.   JIM ABBEY, HOTEL FACULTY MEMBER

Roasts got raunchy so we stopped them.   CUMMINGS

Many activities were strictly fun-times. The Big K, *Kotschevar's Kaper*—a picnic at Warm Springs Park—continued long after its sponsor, Lendal Kotschevar, had left campus. The Kaper metamorphosed into a *Road Rally*, which was a combination of scavenger hunt and picnic. It, too, was replaced, this time by *HAARD, Hotel Association's Annual River Dunk* (or *Drunk*, according to the preference). Social activities ran the gamut from Valentine parties to hay rides to beer kegs.

When I was advising HA, we would get three to four kegs, invite everyone and charge admission. Drinking on campus was allowed then.   AL IZZOLO, HOTEL FACULTY MEMBER

One Halloween, we dressed as characters from *The Wizard of Oz*. Found great buys at the Salvation Army store. We had the Good Witch and the Bad Witch and the Lion. We took first place at the campus party, and then covered the Strip hotels in costume until the MGM [now Bally's] tossed us out.   ANN RITTAL, '81 STUDENT

Richard (Dick) Storm ('73) was the first editor of *Coaster Mig*, the UNLV Student Hotel Association News Letter. Costs for the publication were underwritten in part by Saga Food and Holiday Inn and the college. Interviews and articles featured persons such as Len Hornsby, Executive Director of the Las Vegas Convention Authority and UNLV President Don Baepler. *Coaster Mig* also reported on all of HA's activities. One story covered the Sonoma and Napa Valley wine tours that the association held annually for several years. Rolf Laerm, the college's adjunct wine professor, loved those wine trips as did full-time faculty member Pat Moreo. One or both often went along to strengthen the experience and assure success.

Dan Celeste ('76) and Pat McFadden ('80) were good friends, active in alumni, and went with me on one of the wine tours.   CUMMINGS

A more serious side was evident in the intervention of HA President Al Kingham ('77). Marriott had not planned to interview that year, but then reversed the decision on very short notice. The company picked the very date of the big student-industry golf tourney. Students were between a rock and hard place. Kingham wrote a wonderful letter, inviting them to play and to interview the following day, which they did.

Sales Blitzes. Sales blitzes were joint faculty-student undertakings. They began immediately after Claude Rand's appointment. As the success of the Rand-conceived experiences grew, more faculty were drafted into service.

> I didn't go on as many blitzes as Rand and Abbey. After all, that was their forte. The blitzes were very productive affairs. Success is best measured by the frequency with which the hotels asked us back.
>
> Students made good contacts. They learned how to meet people and their shyness wore off. They gained some savior-faire.   DICK BASILE, HOTEL FACULTY MEMBER

> Claude Rand was running the blitzes, but I helped on occasion. I particularly remember the excellent one we did with the Ritz Carlton on the south side of L.A.   IZZOLO

The first blitzes were scheduled in California hotels during winter vacations and spring breaks. Later they were incorporated into the miniterm schedules. The entire state of California was eventually blitzed, from San Diego at Sheraton's sister properties, the Sheraton Harbor and the Travelodge, north to Los Angeles' not-yet-opened Americana Hotel, ending in San Francisco at the Mark Hopkins. Quickly the number and frequency burgeoned. A series of blitzes was arranged with Hilton Hotels during Hilton's annual manager's meeting in Honolulu (1982) when, as an invited guest, the dean met Nita Lloyd-Fore, Hilton's director of corporate accounts.

As time went on, the college's alumni, who had been on blitzes themselves, invited subsequent classes. In 1979 alone, Jim Mikula ('78) involved the Hyatt at Palo Alto; Russ Dazzio ('74) launched what was to become an annual invitation at the Sheraton Grande in Los Angeles; and Ron Pintello ('73) worked the group into the Sheraton Harbor.

> Russ Dazzio was a great supporter! So was his brother, Tony. Russ made sure the training was tops. He gave quizzes. He gave awards for each day's reports and prizes at week's end for those who performed best.   JIM ABBEY, HOTEL FACULTY MEMBER

Las Vegas' hotels joined in when they began to develop local business. Blitzes close to home were even held during the regular school term.

> Oh yes, students helped with the local blitzes!   SIG FRONT, VICE PRESIDENT, SAHARA HOTEL

Students preferred out-of-town soirees because the hotels put them up in wonderful accommodations and, in almost every case, granted them power-of-the-pen for meals and drinks. It was a fair trade. Participants worked hard for a full week without salaries.

> The hotels thought it was a good investment. Many students saw it as a vacation. Given the power-of-the-pen, students had caviar for breakfast and martinis for lunch!   BASILE

The format was standardized but each hotel altered it as needed. At first, the college had to teach the hotels what to do.

> I did fewer blitzes than Rand, but I think mine were more structured. We put together a strong program. I would send an operations manual in advance. It laid out everything that was important. Using a hotel-supplied list, students would send letters to the clients. So they wouldn't make cold calls, more like a warm one. Graduates in sales say it was the blitz experiences that got their careers started.   ABBEY

Students would arrive Friday evening for an introductory dinner and orientation. Saturday and Sunday were long work days. Training classes covered everything from how to get around the city to how to get around the secretary to see the boss. Role playing included what to say to the potential buyer and how to say it. Tours of the facilities were run several times because knowing the product was critical to selling it. The head of every department met with the group and discussed the issues of that department.

> There was tension between Claude Rand and the [business college's] marketing department because they didn't believe the students were getting what was needed [from his courses]. But having been on five of Rand's blitzes, I can say that I got a lot.   CUMMINGS

If not the students, then the hotels mailed introductory letters about a week before the call explaining who the "salespersons" would be and the affiliation of the hotel and the college. Very often the sales team was ushered into the potential buyer who found it hard to believe that they were doing this on their holiday and without pay. Plenty of business was booked. UNLV's hotel school became well known in California and not just within the industry. More than once, executives who were called upon, and who were also parents, directed their own children to inquire about admission.

> I went to L.A. with Claude and then again to the Mark Hopkins [San Francisco]. It was a great experience. Nothing was kept confidential from the students. The most interesting part was the student's ability to get in doors that were usually closed to sales people. The president of the company would say, Come in, what did you want to see me about?   ALAN STUTTS, HOTEL FACULTY MEMBER

On Monday the students hit the streets. Initially they were paired with each other or sometimes with a representative of the hotel. A lengthy debriefing followed each evening. Problems were discussed; techniques suggested. The day that began at about 6:30 a.m. closed after dinner about 9:00 p.m..Confidence grew and by Wednesday or Thursday many were operating solo. Usually the long lists of potential visits that the hotels had prepared were soon completed. No matter, students made cold calls. Long-term relationships were established for the hotels and short-term bookings were actually closed. Details of one operation appeared in *Coaster Mig,* (1973–74 issue, page 5) written by Paul A. Carpino ('75):

"The use of AAA sectionalized maps aided . . . in making as many personal contacts as possible. . . . Grid patterns were set up and distributed so that all students interviewed all types of businesses. . . . from Mattel Toys to Hughes Aircraft."

Friday night was the traditional party with recognition, appreciation and awards passed around. The week might end with a cocktail party at the hotel to which various potential clients had been invited by the student salespersons. Students were often allowed to stay the second weekend as guests of the house. Quoting Debra Cohen ('75) in *Coaster Mig:*

"The greatest thrill of the week took place Friday night when a banquet was held in our honor. The general manager and his staff showed their appreciation by presenting us with plaques and thanking us for a rewarding week."

Sig Front Day. With the support of the Sahara's Doug Farley and the approval of the dean, the Hotel Association created and organized Sig Front Day. Front was active in the community and very supportive of the college. Nevada Governor Mike O'Callaghan declared September 28, 1973 as *Sig Front Day.* There was no Beam Hall so the event was celebrated in the ballroom of the Moyer Student Union with hotel students doing the inviting, cooking and serving. Table and chairs were delivered from the convention center. Two hundred guests came. The *Yell,* the campus newspaper, headlined the day as the "First Truly Big Event that UNLV Has Ever Seen." The organizing committee included Mike Shubic ('76) handling parking; Marc Sterbens ('75), the bars; and Steve Smith ('76), catering. Presiding over the management and acting as master of ceremonies was HA president Tim Lafferty ('75). Among the dignitaries at the head table was UNLV President Donald Baepler.

Sig Front was one of our great supporters.   BAEPLER

Awards were made to Sig from the Chamber of Commerce, the Office of the Mayor, the Office of the Governor, national HSMA, the University of Nevada and the Hotel Association.

"Using a minimum amount of equipment and a tremendous amount of ingenuity, the Hotel Club performed an exceptionally fine job."[8]

It was the most outstanding birthday I ever had. I received the Great Seal of the State of Nevada and the governor declared Sig Front Day. HA's president [Tim Lafferty] gave me an eagle statue, which I have on my mantle still.   FRONT

THE ALUMNI

"All great schools have become greater through the influence of their alumni. The alumni owe something to their institutions. Like the proverbial pebbles in the pond, they can spread the knowledge and reputation of their College and

University so that those who come after them will find it easier to be accepted and recognized by the hospitality industry." [Medlik [9]]

I tell the students that we are tough because if one fails, the next applicant will be asked, Why should I hire you, a UNLV graduate, when I just got rid of a UNLV graduate who knew nothing?   CLAUDE LAMBERTZ, HOTEL FACULTY MEMBER

The enthusiasm of the undergraduates carried over as they became alumni. But vitality sagged under the pressure of long work hours and family commitments plus the growing number of graduates to be managed. As with every organization, enthusiasm waxed and waned with changes in leadership.

Alumni were strong when Pat Moreo (69) was director and Gus Tejeda ('89) was the office coordinator. Alumni even had an office then. Alumni operations was always an add-on [without continuing fiscal support]. Vallen's philosophy was that the alumni should fund itself.
   We had an active alumni association when Mike Unger ('71) started it.   IZZOLO

Al Izzolo took over alumni affairs in the summer of 1988, when Moreo moved to Penn State. In that year, *Federation of Hoteliers, UNLV* changed its name to *The UNLV Hotel Alumni Society* and adopted Frank Brown's redesigned logo. Although there was occasional confusion between the hotel alumni and the university alumni, relationship remained strong because Fred Albrecht, university alumni director, provided marvelous, noncompeting support.

Whether "Federation" or "Society," the alumni worked for the improvement of its members, the college and the university. Annual directories tracked the membership's many job and address changes. Alumni, paid members or not, were listed alphabetically, by year of graduation and by city of residence. Stories of interest and alumni updates were published in a semi-annual journal, *Federation of Hoteliers UNLV.* Vol. 1, No. 1 was issued during the Winter of 1977, followed by No. 2 that Spring. Alison Perry ('77) was the editor. Bally's, Holiday Inn, Saga and Summa helped to fund the publications. Days Inns of America was another sponsor, obtained through the Muir brothers. Brothers Mike ('88), Tim ('87) and Tom ('86) worked for Day's franchise division, all at the same time. Gary Paquette ('71) had his Funway Holidays Company pick up costs as well.

Job placement was another service. Alumni interested in job leads mailed the college self-addressed and stamped envelopes. Notices of open positions were mailed back periodically. Clerical time was held to a minium. A more sophisticated connection had to await the coming of the web and the college's present-day listing, http// hire.unlv.edu.

No surprise that with its concentration of graduates, Vegas was the strongest chapter.

Gary [Brown's son and UNLV alumnus] and I were impressed with how many of the students returned to live in Las Vegas.   DICK BROWN, DONOR INTERMEDIARY AND FATHER OF ALUMNUS, GARY

Much of the motivation and all of the first 10 national presidents (see Exhibit 11-5) originated in Nevada. The campus provided continuity and a base of operations.

The Clans Gather. Despite the ebb and flow of activity, chapters were founded in several other locales. Reno's Sierra Nevada Chapter started with Don Boone ('77), the first president. Bob Abel ('77), Duff Armstrong ('79), Don Helley ('78), Doug Hitt ('81), Ralph Marrone ('70) and Gary Vallen ('79) comprised the newly formed chapter. It started an annual Crab Feed with a door-prize auction in 1984. From that event came scholarships, which members supplemented by visiting high schools and assisting seniors interested in hotel studies.

A northeastern chapter emerged around greater New York under the prodding of Steve Nelson ('71); in Texas it was Jerry Inzerillo ('75); in Arizona, Allison Perry ('77). Glen Hammer ('74) worked the San Francisco area. Tom Arsulich ('81) and Tony Tamberchi ('79) were the Los Angeles drivers. Florida's chapter was formed by Bob Demichele ('71).

Responsibility rotated as career moves dictated. Jerry Inzerillo worked at the New York Statler; Mike Cooper ('77) was at the Hyatt Regency in LA; Len Williams ('79) at San Francisco's Holiday Inn. Bill Benjamin ('78) covered Chicago and Tom Poland ('78) was in Atlanta with HKF. Dave Oliver ('70), based in Ontario, coordinated the Canadian delegates.

The Northeast chapter took on the New York Hotel Show, which always produced the largest alumni gathering outside of Las Vegas. Each year Bob Hare ('78) organized receptions at his property, the Roger Smith Winthrop Hotel on Lexington Avenue. It was hosted by the hotel's owner, Fred England. Regulars attending were Emanuel Brueh ('86); Bob Hare; Jerry Inzerillo; Kirk Postmantur (84); Pat Moreo; Steve Nelson ('71); Jim Shaw ('80), and Doug Wallner ('86). Simple hors d'oeuvres were provided by Steve Nelson during the first few years. Thereafter, the group adjourned to a nearby restaurant where arrangements had been made by Kirk Postmantur. Louis Szathmary, world renowned chef and sometime faculty member, sometimes joined the dinner crowd.

Year	President		Year	President
1977–78	Mike Unger (71)		1982–83	Dan Celeste (76)*
1978–79	Pat Moreo (69)		1983–84	Owen Khatoonian (79)
1979–80	Kerry Kindig (76)		1984–85	Jim Shaw (80)
1980–81	Dan Celeste (76)		1985–86	Jeff McElroy (77)
1981–82	Leonard Williams, Jr. (79)		1986–87	Andy Nazarechuk (79)

*Over 300 grads in the Las Vegas area

EXHIBIT 11-5. First 10 presidents to lead the Hotel Alumni Association. All were working in Las Vegas at the time.

Moving the receptions to the Restaurant Shows in Chicago and California was tried but with less success. The Southern California/Los Angeles chapter focused on smaller meetings with the first in 1987 when Tony Tamberchi was elected president. His cabinet included Jim Silbar ('86) as treasurer and Larry Cech ('86) as events coordinator.

Jerry Inzerillo and Pat Moreo worked with Clint Rappole of Houston's Hilton College to develop a real Texas shindig. It brought together alumni, friends and faculty of all the nation's hotel schools to a "super evening of camaraderie, friendship and good food." UNLV sponsored year three, 1984, which Inzerillo hosted at his Four Seasons property. Attendance topped 250 persons.

The Hong Kong alumni gathered for a memorable meeting in June, 1989. Alan Wong ('87) made a special trip to the New York Hotel Show to develop the idea. Arrangements were his to make and he did so wonderfully. From Las Vegas came Charlie Levinson and Jerry and Flossie Vallen. Lunching with them at the Kowloon Club were Eric Cha ('91); Kitty Chan ('85); Vida Chow ('87); David Chung ('78); Winnie Harto ('78); Eddie Ho ('77); Henry Lai ('86); Danny Leung ('89); Alywin Tai ('79); Dick Wong ('81); and the organizer of it all, Alan Wong. Every good story has a P.S. Henry Lai returned to UNLV to work on his graduate degree and carried a Chinese-language newspaper with a story of the alumni gathering, which Eric's father had submitted.

Activities of the Vegas chapter are the easiest to chronicle. Local alumni formed an advisory group of faculty, students and alumni, The Triad Committee. Following its recommendation, courses were added in labor and human resources and eventually just such a faculty position was created, initially taken by Richard Laughlin. From the tripartite committee came the "lost sheep" program. It was to encourage those who were just short of graduation to make special arrangements to complete their requirements whether academic or work related. The college pledged to support nontraditional arrangements.

> The best support for our internships came from graduates, but then I would learn that some hadn't quite graduated. We worked out a "lost sheep" program, Vallen's terminology. The applicant had to have left campus at least three years earlier.   IZZOLO

Following the two disastrous fires at the MGM and Hilton, the Triad Committee drafted (February 11, 1981) recommendations for fire-safety programs within the city's hotels. Among its most important contributions was the Committee's intercession with Acting President Dixon on behalf of the building as related in Chapter 7.

Social activities as much as professional activities were considered part of the chapter's business. A large TV set was set up in the Boyd dining room for out-of-state games and the alumni gathered for beer and hot dogs. As always when called on to help, Greyhound Exposition Company provided the equipment to make the set-up. From the *UNLV Hotel Association* magazine, Summer issue, 1988:

> "Image a gigantic . . . television screen and complimentary food and drink including . . . beer on tap. Boyd Dining Hall was bursting with alumni and guests in anticipation of a Rebel victory."

The First Annual Hackers, Bashers & Slashers Golf Tournament was sponsored by the Alumni Association at Los Prados Country Club in 1988. Some 45 golfers braved a cold, windy day to compete for gifts donated from the Tropicana, Sahara, Caesars, Wet n'Wild, LVCVA and USA Hosts. Rumor was that Mike Unger brought a pro golfer, whom he represented to be a long-lost alumnus.

Activities included tailgate parties and Chili Nites, often in conjunction with the student chapter, and the Mt. Charleston Lodge Retreat, including bus service up and down the mountain. Each paid member received a key chain that included the college's return address. Dan Celeste recovered his lost MGM keys when someone dropped them in a mailbox. Cocktail parties were held whenever and wherever the association had members in high positions. Caesars and the MGM Grand were favorite watering places. Alumni parties were still taking place at the Vallen home but the hotels were furnishing the food.

> The alumni ran the senior swim parties at Vallen's, because he linked the students and the alumni.   UNGER

Nearly 100 alumni gathered in the fall of 1984 for alumni homecoming and their first look at the new building. Tours, seminars and a fine dinner by the students with Las-Vegas style entertainment followed.

Meeting Alumni.   The above, brief listing of the several chapters suggests the range of the college's far-flung graduates. Hotel's alumni are numerous and well placed. But that's not discernible until one begins to meet them in social and professional settings. One example: UNLV had five middle managers out of 42 attending a June, 1979 Sheraton Hotel Management Skills Seminar in Toronto. Another example from Coach Jerry Tarkanian:

> "During the past several years, I have spoken at different [basketball] clinics in places throughout the country. Perhaps at half of the hotels that I have stayed, there will be a note with a bottle of wine or fruit basket or candy. The note will be from a UNLV graduate who is in a top position in the hotel. Their comments will always be a sense of pride to me. . . . I am pleased that so many of your graduates are doing well and I think it is a very positive thing for UNLV."[10]

President Bob Maxson was a very mobile executive who would return to regale listeners with the hoteliers whom he met in the most unusable places.

> President Maxson had the greatest alumni stories. He had great respect for the program and the dean and he used to tell stories about traveling around the country and meeting UNLV hotel graduates.   FRANK BORSENIK, HOTEL FACULTY MEMBER

The stories were not limited to Maxson. All the faculty experienced them as did the college's friends and supporters.

Graduates would stop me and say, I remember you from UNLVino.

But the letters of thanks for the UNLVino scholarships were the best part of my UNLV affiliation.   LARRY RUVO, SENIOR MANAGING DIRECTOR, SOUTHERN WINE & SPIRITS

In Beijing, my party and I met a UNLV graduate who was the assistant manager of the hotel. He was a great host during our stay.

The night manager at the Hyatt Phoenix called my room and told me his name. I remembered him. He said, The practical things that you taught were those I valued most.

Patty Fitzpatrick has successful hotels in Ireland and in New York City. He feels what his sons got at UNLV has been a big factor in the growth of his chain.   JOE DELANEY, COLUMNIST AND PART-TIME FACULTY MEMBER

In one hotel I stopped, I learned that the sales manager was one of our graduates. We had dinner together, but he wasn't able to comp the check, so I picked it up.   DICK BASILE, HOTEL FACULTY MEMBER

During a visit to Korea we had dinner with the Kims, who owned the Olympia Hotel in Seoul. She had waited years to tell the story of why her child was born in the U. S. A. rather than Korea. Jerry had turned down her husband's request for 18 summer credits. The Kims had to remain for another term.   FLOSSIE VALLEN

The alumni meeting in Hong Kong [see above] was not the only exciting event there. We met Robert Piccus ('87), who was the assistant manager at the Hong Kong Regent, where we were staying. And then walking down the street, of all things, we bumped into Mr. and Mrs. Jim Mikula ('78), visiting from Taipei to celebrate their anniversary. We had drinks together.   JERRY VALLEN

The chef's convention met at the Hilton Hawaiian Village. Its open lobby was filled with chefs. Someone kept yelling, Chef! Chef! Everyone in the lobby turned around. One of our graduates waived and opened a special registration window. He assigned us to a corner room overlooking the ocean. Same thing happened at the Biltmore in Phoenix.   CLAUDE LAMBERTZ, HOTEL FACULTY MEMBER

Of course, Las Vegas offers the greatest opportunity to meet alumni.

My biggest enjoyment is to visit the F&B office of one of the hotels and find that a staffer—or even the manager—is a graduate or a recipient of one of the UNLVino scholarships.   RALPH DURGIN, SOUTHERN WINE & SPIRITS

I spoke to Dan Celeste ('76) when he first started part-time teaching. He said something to the effect, It's only the second day of class and I told them everything I know. One forgets how long it takes to learn what one knows. Stefanelli would say, Now go back and test on what you think the students know. They know nothing because you went through it at warp speed.

Bill Hornbuckle ('84) was the director of marketing at the Golden Nugget when we first met. The hospitality center did some projects for him. We delivered what he wanted and when he wanted it. So he got us linked into the opening of the Mirage writing job descriptions.   ALAN STUTTS, HOTEL FACULTY MEMBER

Many contacts grow into life-time relationships once the required distance between faculty members and students had ended.

Ms. K. . . . .still calls to talk career decisions. What should I do about this or that. Another student who came through the graduate program does the same.   STUTTS

I have great respect for Mike Unger ('71), who came as a class speaker. The students loved him.   BORSENIK

Not long ago I met Jesse Fiel in the Bellagio lobby. He insisted on taking my party into the art exhibit as his guests.   CUMMINGS

I would tell the classes and the interns, if you ever need anything call Uncle Leo. And they do to this day.   LEO LEWIS, BINION'S FINANCIAL OFFICER AND HOTEL FACULTY MEMBER, BOTH PART TIME AND FULL TIME

ENDNOTES FOR CHAPTER 11

1. *Enrollment Trends & Selected Institutional Characteristic.* University of Nevada Office of Institutional Analyses and Planning, 1979, p. 35.

2. "Chapter D, Hotel Administration," *1980 Accreditation Report,* p. 21.

3. A letter to Tom Flagg from Dave Christianson, dated January 8, 1994; and *Enrollment Trends & Selected Institutional Characteristic, 1970.*

4. *Enrollment Trends & Selected Institutional Characteristic, 1987.*

5. Robbins Cahill. "Reflections of Work in State Politics, Government, Taxation, Gaming Control, Clark County Administration and the Nevada Resort Association." *Oral History Project* (Reno: University of Nevada, Reno, Library), p. 1,360.

6. Cahill. *Ibid.* p. 1,364.

7. John R. Goodwin. "Dr. Patrick J. Moreo, His Reflections as a Hotel Student." *UNLV Hotel Alumni Association,* College of Hotel Administration, Summer, 1988, vol. 12, No. 2, p. 8.

8. UNLV *Student Hotel Association Newsletter,* 1973–74, p 1.

9. Rik Medlik, "From England to Destination America." *Federation of Hoteliers UNLV,* Spring 1978, Vol. 1, No. 2.

10. Letter from Jerry Tarkanian, Head Basketball Coach, on the occasion of Jerry Vallen's retirement from UNLV, May 17, 1989.

Postscript

The dean's intention to retire on July 1, 1989 was communicated to the faculty and administration at the start of the 1987–88 school year. No action was taken for many months. To accelerate the process, the outgoing dean made tentative moves to appoint a search committee. Vice President Unrue made it absolutely clear that was not within the province of the outgoing administrator. But it took an additional six months, March 15, 1988, before the preliminary machinery was able to begin work.

A search committee of faculty members Basile, Borsenik, Cummings, Izzolo and Stefanelli was constituted with Stutts as the chair. Dean John Wright of the College of Arts and Letters was the outside rep. Students and alumni rounded out the committee's membership.

> Interviews were structured to include the participation of industry representatives. One candidate made a very weak presentation before the faculty with Steve Wynn (Mirage) and Dan Reicharts (Caesars) in attendance. Wynn asked a question that had no correct answer. He wanted to see how the applicant would react. The guy danced around until Wynn said loud enough for those seated nearby—including the applicant's wife—The guys a bozo. ALAN STUTTS, HOTEL FACULTY MEMBER

> I remember urging Steve not to leave before hearing the man out. JERRY VALLEN

Well I remember the question to be what was one of the biggest industries in the state? The candidate answered mining!   AL IZZOLO, HOTEL FACULTY MEMBER

Dave Christianson had no such problems. He easily overcame the competition to become the college's second dean.

As the search continued, a grand banquet was catered in Beam Hall by the faculty and student body to celebrate the Harrah gift. On February 24, 1989, distinguished guests such as Mead Dixon, Robert Maxson, Michael Rose, Phil Satre and Claudine Williams joined Verna Harrah to celebrate the formal recognition that the Board of Regents had given to the name, William F. Harrah College of Hotel Administration. Thus, closed the opening phase in the life of the college.

Well, it wasn't quite closed yet.

The last and final thing was the unbelievable goodbye party that the alumni, faculty and students threw for the Vallens. Using the experience gained during the AH&MA's Beam Hall celebration (see Chapter 8) but raising that standard by several levels, friends and colleagues enabled the Vallens to close 22 years of satisfaction and service.

The party was exquisite! Our children came from across the nation. Hundreds of friends showed up. It was so exciting that none of the family ate any of the wonderful food. But we didn't realize that until we got home and realized we were all hungry.   FLOSSIE VALLEN

History is ongoing. The most that a chronicle like this can do is to tentatively close one era and allow the postscript to preface the opening of the next.

The entire town including our school has grown from three to five normal generations in just one generation. We can credit ourselves, but we must also credit the nature of Las Vegas. We should be proud that the school has produced good people.

The final line is that I am happy I made the roll.   DICK BASILE, HOTEL FACULTY MEMBER

The best move I ever made was coming to Las Vegas. It was the best [professional] thing that ever happened to me I'm glad I came!   FRANK BORSENIK, HOTEL FACULTY MEMBER

I feel a sense of pride that only intensifies over the years about my degree from UNLV and all that I learned there.   GARY BROWN, '73 STUDENT

I can say it has been wonderful; a proud affiliation. I'm glad to have been here.   LESLIE CUM-MINGS, HOTEL FACULTY MEMBER

I've enjoyed my time here and I've enjoyed the students.   JERRY GOLL, HOTEL FACULTY MEMBER

Rarely do I go out without encountering a graduate. I've changed in 20 years so the conversation always starts, Are you Al Izzolo? Almost to a person, all have positive memories of the college. They remember the professors, and the camaraderie, and the activities. And even though many have left the industry because of hours and pay they are happy they attended the hotel college and finished their degrees.   IZZOLO

My degree has been one of my greatest assets. I am so glad I attended and graduated. I never tell anyone there were only three buildings on campus because the school is so prestigious now.   KEN KAUFMAN, 71 STUDENT

I love it here; I just love it!   CLAUDE LAMBERTZ, HOTEL FACULTY MEMBER

I truly enjoyed my time at UNLV and I am glad I earned the degree.   DAVE PATTERSON, '81 STUDENT

I'll always remember my days in Las Vegas and my time at UNLV.   ANN RITTAL, '81 STUDENT

I said to someone this morning [the day of the interview], here's my good friend Jerry Vallen, who convinced me to leave industry and take a significant cut in pay. And I am pleased that I did it!   STUTTS

My years at UNLV were truly great in every way. I developed confidence, and I made some great friends. I am always proud to say I went to UNLV.   NANCY CHANIN, '86 OUTSTANDING GRADUATE

I am quite proud of the reputation that UNLV has built up worldwide. We always wanted to be a major force in the hospitality industry, which we have been for some time now.   GERARD INZERILLO, '75 STUDENT

Here! Here!   JERRY AND FLOSSIE VALLEN

Index